Captain's Diary 2006

Captain's Diary 2006

Australia's road to the battle for the Ashes

Ricky Ponting

Harper_Sports_
An imprint of HarperCollins_Publishers_

Harper*Sports*
An imprint of HarperCollins*Publishers* Australia

First published in Australia in 2006
by HarperCollins*Publishers* Australia Pty Limited
ABN 36 009 913 517
www.harpercollins.com.au

HarperCollins*Publishers*
25 Ryde Road, Pymble, Sydney, NSW 2073, Australia
31 View Road, Glenfield, Auckland 10, New Zealand
77–85 Fulham Palace Road, London, W6 8JB, United Kingdom
2 Bloor Street East, 20th floor, Toronto, Ontario M4W 1A8, Canada
10 East 53rd Street, New York NY 10022, USA

ISBN 13: 978 0 7322 8153 3
ISBN 10: 0 7322 8153 9

Cover photographs: Newspix (Ricky Ponting) and Getty Images
Cover design by Darren Holt, HarperCollins Design Studio
Internal design adapted from original by Chrisabella Designs
Typeset in 11/17 Sabon by Kirby Jones
Printed and bound in Australia by Griffin Press on 79gsm Bulky Paperback

5 4 3 2 1   06 07 08 09

This Australian team is full of men with courage, commitment and a no-surrender attitude. If we're down, it's never for long …

GEOFF ARMSTRONG

Ricky Ponting's co-author on *Captain's Diary 2006*, Geoff Armstrong, has worked — as writer, editor or publisher — on more than 70 books on sport, more than 30 of them on cricket. Between 1993 and 2005, he collaborated with Steve Waugh on each of Steve's 12 best-selling books, including all of his diaries and the former Australian captain's autobiography *Out of My Comfort Zone*. Geoff is the author of *A Century of Summers*, the centenary history of the Sheffield Shield (featuring an epilogue by Sir Donald Bradman), *ESPN's Legends of Cricket*, which profiles 25 of the game's greatest players, *The 100 Greatest Cricketers* (published in 2006), and the co-author (with Mark Gately) of *The People's Game*, a history of Australia in one-day international cricket. He has worked as co-author on books by Ian Healy, Mike Whitney, Bob Simpson and Michael Bevan, and with Ian Russell produced *Top 10s of Australian Test Cricket*, a study of Australian cricket statistics.

Geoff is also the co-author, with Peter Thompson, of *Phar Lap*, the definitive biography of the legendary racehorse, and *Melbourne Cup 1930*, the story of the most remarkable of Phar Lap's many big-race victories.

ACKNOWLEDGMENTS

We are extremely grateful to Ricky's manager Sam Halvorsen, for his constant, strong backing of the project. Thanks, too, to Peter Young, Philip Pope and Kelly Sedgeway at Cricket Australia for their support, and to everyone at HarperCollins, especially Alison Urqhuart, Belinda Yuille, Darren Holt and the legendary Graeme Jones, who were brilliant throughout. Thanks, too, to Sarah Shrubb, Stella Tarakson and Phil Jennings for their help with getting the manuscript in order.

PHOTOGRAPHS

All the photographs that appear in *Captain's Diary 2006* come from the fantastic resources of Getty Images. We are very grateful for the support of all the staff at Getty and their exceptional photographers who follow the Australian team throughout the year.

STATISTICS

The statistics, scores and averages that appear through the pages and at the end of this book were derived from a variety of sources, including three exceptional cricket websites — *Cricinfo Australia* (www.baggygreen.com.au), *Howstat.com: the cricket statisticians* (www.howstat.com.au) and *CricketArchive* (www.cricketarchive.com) — and also *Wisden*, *Wisden Australia* and the *Sydney Morning Herald*.

Contents

Introduction — No Surrender   1

Part I — Against the World   9

Part II — Caribbean Clean Sweep   43

Part III — The Chappell–Hadlee Trophy   75

Part IV — Winning the Moments that Matter   85

Part V — My Test Centenary   115

Part VI — Crash! Boom! Bang!   127

Part VII — The VB Series   133

Part VIII — Losing Our Momentum   167

Part IX — Three in Three   207

Part X — One Test After Another   247

Epilogue — No Limits   277

Scores and Averages   285

Index   363

Introduction

No Surrender

**Australia v South Africa,
Third Test, Johannesburg
April 4, 2006**

ANYONE WHO HAS PLAYED cricket with Justin Langer will tell you how much they enjoy having him in their team. Lang is a bloke with a no-surrender attitude who loves playing cricket for Australia and upholding the traditions of the game. No man fights harder, every time he walks on the field. If he gets hit, he doesn't show any pain ...

THE THIRD TEST OF our series in South Africa in March–April 2006 was Lang's 100th Test match. His family and friends had flown over especially for the occasion. On the first day of the game, during our team talk before our warm-up, I singled him out, to say how proud he should be of his achievement and that he was joining an exclusive club. I could clearly remember how excited I felt three months earlier in Sydney when I had played my 100th Test match, a game that evolved into a dream as I scored a hundred in each innings and we won the home series against the South Africans. My advice to Lang before his big game was simple: 'Enjoy it!' I knew he was going to put more pressure on himself than usual, because of the landmark he had reached, but I knew, too, that there was no point me telling him to treat it like any other game, because in your own mind it is not just like any other game.

About an hour and a half into the second day, South Africa had been bowled out in their first innings for 303, and — as he has been doing since August 2001 — out went Lang with his great mate Matthew Hayden to launch our reply. Typically, he took strike, but their best fast bowler, Makhaya Ntini, started with a short ball that Lang seemed to lose sight of and it thudded into the side of his helmet. Those around the bat quickly realised he was in serious trouble, and soon I was walking out to replace him, as he was helped from the field, retired hurt, nought. This was not the way his 100th Test was supposed to go. The prognosis was a serious concussion, with the doctors advising that he sit out the rest of the game, to forget about batting for at least three weeks.

THREE DAYS LATER, THE game came down to a thrilling conclusion. Australia, chasing 292 to complete a clean sweep in the series, were 6–248. Forty-four to win, but only *three* wickets in hand. We had been told that if Lang batted and was struck again in the head, he might die. It was that serious. Still, I knew that every competitive bone in his body would be telling him to bat. Every time he thought about the risks involved, that little voice inside his head would be imploring him not to let down his mates. One moment, I imagine, he would have been thinking about his wife and his four little daughters, the youngest just a few months old; the next, the nagging torment that came with the idea of Australia losing a Test match because *he* couldn't bat would come over him again. I pondered what I might do in the same situation ... and then I quickly started thinking about something else. I just didn't know.

Another warm-up, another team talk. This time, Lang asked to address the team, and what followed was one of the most emotional couple of minutes I have witnessed during my sporting career. He explained what the doctors had said, talked about his family, how he'd talked to his dad that morning. The poor bloke was holding back the tears ...

'I'm sorry, boys,' he said softly, but with a grim determination in his voice. 'I'm pulling the pin. I just can't do it. The doctors say I can't get out there and bat today. I hope you don't look at me and think ... I've got my kids to think about ... my family to think about ...'

We all felt for Lang so much. He was just so desperate, he wanted to go out there. But he couldn't.

THE LAST DAY STARTED well for us. Damien Martyn had been 93 not out overnight, and we all hoped that he and the other not out batsman, Brett Lee, would get us home. Bing had been involved in a famous last-wicket partnership the previous year in England, with Michael Kasprowicz, when they added 59 runs in the second Test at Edgbaston but lost by two after Kasper was caught down the legside. Marto went to his hundred with a four off Shaun Pollock, and the target was down to 34, but last ball of the same over he was lbw. The game was even money once again.

Stuart Clark, playing in his first Test series, went out at No. 9. As he did, I turned around and saw Lang sitting there in his 'civvies', trying to be chirpy. He is such a good team man, he knew that he couldn't let his disappointment spoil the vibe among the guys. We needed to be positive. Brett got two off Ntini, Stuart managed a single off Pollock, then another single. Kasper sat quietly with his pads on, last man in, no doubt thinking back to England. Part of him would have desperately hoped for the chance to get out there, to set the record straight. The other part would have been very happy to leave it to the two blokes in the middle.

Stuart had enjoyed a fantastic series: 20 wickets in the three Tests at just 15.85. Now we needed 25 runs to win, and then only 17 as he hit Ntini for two fours. But then, last ball of the over, he played a poor shot: an attempted pull that went straight up in the air. South African keeper Mark Boucher took the catch. It was up to Lee and Kasprowicz.

They were completely different out there in the middle. Big Kasper, on the outside at least, was calmness personified, the sort of bloke who'd be happy to get them one run at a time. Bing was hopping all over the place, hyperactive, emotional, but he is a good batsman who during his career in both Test and one-day cricket has played many important innings. The next over from Pollock started with three scoreless deliveries, and then, beautifully, Kasper hit straight for two, then three leg byes, then Bing played a glorious drive to the extra cover boundary. Eight to win.

I turned again, to try to see the look on Lang's face. As I did so, I was imagining he'd look back at me, and give me that wry grin of his, or maybe a wink that said it was all going to be okay. Instead, he was gone! I started looking for him, and found him with his whites on, and his pads, his arm guard, his helmet. He was running laps in the change room, trying to convince himself that he was suddenly okay.

'Mate, what are doing?' I asked. He told me he had changed his mind, that he had concluded that batting *was* worth the risk. What was worse, the matter was clearly not negotiable. I looked around for our manager, Steve Bernard. I wanted Steve to explain to Justin that Cricket Australia were adamant he wasn't going to bat. That was my 'out', my counter when Lang said, 'You'd do the same if you were in my position.' For Cricket Australia, it was a question of 'duty of care'. But our manager had been called away on another cricket matter, and there was no one else to tell Lang that he couldn't bat. I was the only one who could do anything about it.

So I told him, 'Mate, I'm not letting you do it, you can't do it.'

'No, mate,' he replied. 'We'll see how we go. If we only need a few to win, I'll be right.'

To me, he still looked wobbly on his feet. 'I'll be right,' he said again.

'You can't do it,' I argued. 'If you get hit in the head, you could die.'

'Oh, mate, what's the chance of getting hit in the head again?'

There was a huge shout from the guys on our viewing area, and a muffled roar from the crowd. We went to see for ourselves, to discover that Kasper had hit a ball from Ntini through the covers for four. Now Pollock was bowling to Bing, and there was no point reasoning with Lang. He stood at the back of the viewing area, and the television cameras picked him out with his gloves and pads on and assumed he was going to bat, if required. I had to work out what I was going to do.

I wasn't going to cause a scene by trying to physically restrain him from going out there. Anyway, he was so determined; nothing would stop him. If he was at the bowler's end, I decided, that was okay. Pollock to Lee, and a short single into the covers. Three to win. If Lang got on strike, I'd wave them in. I'd declare. Another run, a shy at the stumps, and then Pollock dropped short outside the off stump and Bing hit him over the top for four and the Test match. There was real jubilation among the lads, but for me that was tempered by the colossal wave of relief that engulfed me. Afterwards, Lang walked over and said, 'If you had declared on me, I would have declared our friendship OVER!' A little later, Mike Hussey put his hand on my shoulder and said, 'Punter, I've never ever seen you so flustered as you were today.'

I looked at the man we now know as 'Mr Cricket' and sort of laughed. It had been quite a morning. I wasn't dirty on Lang because — knowing the sort of determined bloke and team man he is — he was always going to try to bat. I just should have realised that earlier. It was my job as captain to make the decision for him, and I think in the end I would have got it right, even if I'm not sure what I would have done, if I was in Lang's shoes.

WE STILL HAD A short tour of Bangladesh to go, but in many ways that extraordinary day in Jo'burg marked the end of a long and rewarding season of cricket, which for us had become a summer of redemption. This revival had begun almost from the moment we landed back in Australia after losing the Ashes in England, when a range of commentators were lining up to criticise the team and demand changes, including a change in the captaincy. We had faced a World XI, the West Indies, New Zealand, South Africa and Sri Lanka and met every challenge.

I kept notes throughout that time. Afterwards, I sat down with Geoff Armstrong and together we sifted through those notes, piles of press clippings and talked about what went on, to come up with this story of those six months of cricket. We chose to record the events in a diary format — but not a day-by-day account, more a few days at a time — so we could focus on the major issues, remember the great performances and show how my mind was working as the story unfolded. The challenge, of course, was not to let hindsight distort the picture we were painting. For example, today, having just led Australia to 11 Test wins in 12 matches, with the other drawn, I feel totally secure as the national team captain. But that wasn't quite the case when I came back from the Ashes tour last September, when a figure as iconic as Dennis Lillee was among those calling for my sacking, when few guys in the side were truly sure of their places, when some were arguing that the Australian team's greatest days were gone. I've tried to recreate the mood of that time, how I really felt, and what we did to get the team back on track. I have also, in the season of my 100th Test, occasionally looked back on memories from earlier in my career, to give an indication of how my experiences have shaped me, as a cricketer and a captain. It's amazing to think that season 2005–06 marked my 10th anniversary as a Test batsman.

The period of time covered in this book evolved into some of the most important and rewarding months of my sporting life. We fought hard every time we walked onto the field. Justin Langer is not the only gutsy man to wear the baggy green. This Australian team is full of men with courage, commitment and a no-surrender attitude. If we're down, it's never for long. It is a great joy to be their captain.

THE AUSTRALIAN TEAMS FOR 2005–06 featured the following players:

Ricky Ponting (captain) — *Punter*

Adam Gilchrist (vice captain) — *Gilly*

Nathan Bracken — *Bracks*

Mark Cosgrove — *Cossie*

Stuart Clark — *Sarfraz*

Michael Clarke — *Pup*

Dan Cullen — *DC*

Brett Dorey — *Dores*

Jason Gillespie — *Dizzy*

Brad Haddin — *BJ*

Matthew Hayden — *Haydos*

Brad Hodge — *Hodgey*

Brad Hogg — *Hoggy*

James Hopes — *Catfish*

Michael Hussey — *Huss or Mr Cricket*

Phil Jaques — *Pro or Jaquesy*

Mitchell Johnson — *Mitch or Midge*

Michael Kasprowicz — *Kasper*

Simon Katich — *Kato*

Justin Langer — *Lang*

Brett Lee — *Bing*

Mick Lewis — *Mickey or Billy*

Stuart MacGill — *Magilla*

Glenn McGrath — *Pigeon or Pidge*

Damien Martyn — *Marto*

Andrew Symonds — *Symmo or Roy*

Shaun Tait — *Taity*

Shane Warne — *Warney*

Shane Watson — *Watto*

Cameron White — *Whitey*

Part I

Against the World

Australia v ICC World XI
October 2005

Monday, September 19

IT WAS WHILE I was in the air, coming home from the 2005 Ashes series, that the subject of my captaincy became the biggest talking point in Australian cricket. At Sydney Airport, when I met the local media on our return, the question of whether I wanted to remain in the job seemed to come just a little too rapidly. The answer was easy. I love being captain of Australia, which I consider to be one of the best jobs in world sport, but it hadn't occurred to me that my hold on the job might be weakening. The joy of the captaincy had certainly been there in England, when — though losing wasn't pleasant — I was taken by the challenge and being part of one of the all-time great series. On the flight home, I had begun thinking about what we needed to do as a group to overcome the flaws that had hindered us in England. And I set my heart on regaining the Ashes in 2006–07. What I didn't know then, but quickly learned as the journos' questions started flying, was that no less than Dennis Lillee had that very day 'called for my head' (as the reporters like to put it) in his column in the *West Australian*, a statement that had inevitably accelerated the debate about my leadership. In the great fast man's view, Shane Warne needed to be named the new Australian Test captain.

'I'm not concerned about those things,' was all I could say, after I was invited to respond to Dennis' opinion. I was told he had argued that I had been too conservative and had seemed overly willing to captain by consensus. 'As long as I am doing the right thing by everyone in the team and the coaching staff,' I continued, 'that's all I can do.'

In top-level sport, you have to get used to criticism when you lose, but as much as you say it doesn't worry you, when it comes from such an iconic figure, it does leave a mark. Still, while I certainly respected his right to comment, as I thought about my situation during the cab ride home I knew that nothing positive could come from getting angry about it, even though I also knew I'd be a mug to think that my captaincy had been perfect. 'I know I'm not going to keep everybody happy along the way,' I had continued. 'And I'm sure I've done things even before this series that other people haven't been that happy with. But as long as I am looking after the guys in my dressing-room, then I'll be happy.'

Dennis had written that it had appeared to him that Warney had been making more decisions than I had during the final Test of the Ashes series, that he was something of a 'pseudo captain'. Frankly, that was ridiculous. Sure, I talked with my team-mates out on the field, but I'd be making a mistake if I didn't, given that we are such an experienced team. I like to talk to a lot of guys out on the field and use their ideas and thoughts. People such as Adam Gilchrist, Matty Hayden, Justin Langer, Damien Martyn and Shane have been around cricket for a while, and I want to know what their thoughts on the game are. When I started as the one-day captain, Darren Lehmann was probably the first person I turned to for advice, but no one criticised me then or at any time between my international captaincy debut and the Ashes series — because we were winning. In his article, Dennis had written that Shane has 'an amazing cricket brain'. He sure does. As captain, I'd be mad to ignore it.

My main concern with the Ashes series, as I freely admitted to the reporters at the airport, was that too often during the crucial, defining moments in the Tests the ruthless edge we'd made our calling card in previous years had for some reason gone missing. We'd lost 2–1 after winning the first Test. My gut feel was that when we were challenged we'd tried *too* hard because we wanted the victory so badly, and that had stifled our natural games. England, in contrast, approached the games as if they had nothing to lose, as if all they wanted was to play the best cricket they could. The result was that they outplayed us, though in the end the margin was tight and if we'd got lucky at vital times, we might even have escaped with a draw.

In justifying his calls for a change in the captaincy, Dennis had written that 'desperate times call for desperate measures'. Among the team's leadership group and the coaching staff we didn't believe our problems were so dire, but we knew some things needed to change. I had resolved on the flight home to focus on the upcoming Super Series, due to begin early next month and set to involve most of the best cricketers in the world, but judging by the questions it seemed what really mattered to people in Australia was the next England–Australia contest. 'I rate our chances very highly of getting the Ashes back,' I said. 'I know there's a burning desire [among the team] to get those Ashes back very soon.' This wouldn't be the last time in the next few months that I'd be asked about that precious urn.

BY SEPTEMBER 16, CRICKET Australia had formed a committee that featured former captains Allan Border and Mark Taylor, as well as CA Chief Executive James Sutherland and other members of his staff, to review the tour. I had no problem with this, and I did appreciate Allan's comment about the captaincy, when he was asked what the committee would be looking at: 'The speculation over Ricky Ponting's future as captain is ridiculous.' Initially, though, I was concerned the question of team coach John Buchanan's reappointment was to be analysed as part of the review process. I love everything that Buck has done as coach, especially the fact that he has taken the Australian cricket team to a level it has never been before, largely by always challenging the players to think about how they can get more out of their cricket. Some media reports suggested his contract might not be renewed, but enquiries quickly confirmed that it was our coaching structure that was an issue, and I thought that was definitely a good thing.

When I met CA cricket operations manager Michael Brown, another member of the review committee, the subject of specialist coaches took up much of our conversation. It seemed to me that England had studied how we had built up our coaching and support staff in the previous decade, and then for the 2005 Ashes series had taken our model to a new level. Times had certainly changed since the days in the late 1980s when the Australian team would go away with a coach (Bob Simpson), a physiotherapist (Errol Alcott) and a team manager (usually a member of the Australian Cricket Board).

In recent times, we were pioneers of sorts, including not just a coach, physio and manager but also a fitness co-ordinator, masseuse, cricket analyst and at times a part-time fielding coach in our squad. But in England our opponents had more hands on deck than we did. John Buchanan had one assistant coach in Jamie Siddons. (Before the England tour, Cricket Australia had decided that Jamie and Dene Hills, the former Tasmanian Pura Cup batsman who had been Tassie's assistant coach, would share the assistant coach/performance analyst role with the Australian team, while also working with the Commonwealth Bank Centre of Excellence — the new version of the old Cricket Academy —

in Brisbane. Jamie then worked with us in England during the one-dayers and Tests, and the intention was that in the future he and Dene would alternate, one travelling with the team and the other staying at the CBCE.) England coach Duncan Fletcher had a bowling coach (the former Tasmanian paceman Troy Cooley) and a batting coach (the ex-England Test batsman Matthew Maynard), as well as physios, analysts and physiologists working with him at all times.

When I saw how some members of our team struggled at times during the Ashes tour and at the same time looked across at the resources our opponents had, I couldn't help thinking that it was a pity we didn't have a similar range of specialists on location to help our guys out.

People say you can bring a specialist in, almost on a consultancy-style basis, but often time is of the essence. With the amount of actual cricket that we are now playing, usually with many matches squeezed together, and with other commitments of a team and personal nature to be fitted in, the issue of time management is a critical one.

It is all very well to say that a coach should get as much time as he wants with his charges, but the fact is that a player has to recover from his last game before he can move on to the next; there are injuries to treat and planes to catch, sponsors to keep happy, meetings to attend, a private life, too. The coaches have to get the structure of training right, much more than they used to do in the past, in order to best work on each player's batting, bowling and fielding skills. But with time so limited, this is difficult, and though Cricket Australia responded to this by appointing an assistant coach — first Tim Nielsen, then Jamie and Dene — the success of England's model during the Ashes series demonstrated how important it is that we keep up in this area.

THE OTHER REASON WHY I believe specialist coaches are vital relates to a reality that has most likely been around in cricket since day one. The fact is that — and this will probably surprise some people — a lot of players who make it all the way to the top level do so without knowing much about their game. They can get into Test cricket because of their natural ability, but when something goes wrong they can't figure out the reasons why. So they just keep doing what they think they've always been doing, putting down their run of outs to bad luck or bad karma, unaware that it might be one little thing they need to adjust and work on.

I reckon it took me half my career before I really felt I understood my game. In this regard, I think my record speaks for itself. After the third Test of the 2001 Ashes series, my 45th Test, my Test batting average was just over 40, but I made a hundred in the first innings of the fourth Test, at Headingley (when I could have been given out, caught by Mark Ramprakash at third slip, on a decision that went to the video umpire), and things have gone pretty well since then. But when I first came into the side many things were foreign to me — for example, because I had always batted at three or four but was in the Test team as a No. 6, I didn't know how to best use my time waiting to bat. Going out to face an old flat ball was something new. The fact there were fewer bad balls to hit had me stressing out about my run-rate.

I remember Matthew Hayden, after he scored his first Test century, against the West Indies at Adelaide in 1996–97, saying afterwards that he had just learnt how to bat, that he had only begun to understand what it took to succeed at the top level. Though I'd been either in or close to the Australian team for nearly two years, I hadn't even reached the point of a cricketer's education that Matty had passed, and I didn't realise that fact.

What I needed to do was get in control of my game and my emotions, to have faith in what works for me when things are tough, and to fight the temptation to go beyond my capabilities when my game is working well.

Michael Clarke, right at the moment, is somewhere around where I was during my first 30 or 40 Tests. He is learning a lot about himself and a lot about his game as his career evolves, and I feel that I have an important mentoring role in his path to becoming an exceptional Test cricketer. Pup is aware that I know his game pretty well — and that I've struggled in the past as he is at the moment — so it is natural for him to come to me for advice. Together, we have analysed his batting though the Ashes series; tried to ascertain, for example, why he was getting trapped lbw too often. Now we have to go out to the nets and work hard on the things we believe need to change.

On a purely personal level as a batsman, all I want from my batting coach is someone who understands my technique, who can look at the way I am currently going about things and if something is out of kilter will work with me to get things right. Jamie has that understanding I need, while Dene, as a former Tasmanian team-mate, is especially adept in this area. Simply put, if there is someone round the squad who is an expert in their field and who also knows the games of the players in the squad, that has got be beneficial. As good a coach as Buck has been for us, despite all his thoroughness and his fantastic man-management skills, in my view he is not a coach with the technical knowledge to be able to tell each batsmen how to best play their shots within the framework of their individual techniques. He's certainly not able to best advise the bowlers about the ins and outs of their bowling actions. Give him the right personnel, however, and as a coaching team they'll fix things as quickly and effectively as anyone could.

MICHAEL BROWN AND I also discussed matters of programming and touched on the question of whether having partners and families travelling with the team had hurt rather than helped the side. I thought that suggestion was rubbish, a mindset from a different generation. My overall feeling was that there didn't need to be too many changes for the Super Series and beyond. I knew that a lot of guys had found out how tough sport at the highest level can be. The Ashes was the first Test series we'd lost since India in 2001; the first time we hadn't won a Test series since Steve Waugh's farewell series — the drawn Test series at home against the Indians in 2003–04. My instinct told me that if we got our attitude back on track, the team structure right and the training regime perfect, then we had the personnel to set the record straight. It was only 14 months to the start of the most eagerly anticipated Ashes series of all time. Normally, after 12 months of pretty much solid cricket, I'd have been looking for a break. Instead, knowing how important it was that our fightback began as soon as possible, I couldn't wait for the new season to start.

Thursday, September 22

THE CAPTAINCY DEBATE WAS reignited somewhat two days back when Ian Chappell launched his latest book. During the media interviews he conducted to promote the book, he suggested Cricket Australia had been 'too frightened' to pick Shane Warne when Mark Taylor retired in 1999. Instead, of course, Steve Waugh got the job. 'Warney would have been one of Test cricket's exciting captains,' Ian said, 'as well as being a very good one.' He also remarked that it was now too late for Shane, but that didn't stop a new burst of comment about whether I was the right man for the job. I was learning very quickly that only a very successful Super Series would put this matter to sleep.

Ian is someone I have always had a pretty good relationship with, going right back to my time at the Cricket Academy in the early '90s, when Rod Marsh occasionally brought him in to give us a hand, and just as I've come to grips with Dennis Lillee's comments, now I know I need to listen to what someone like Ian says. That doesn't mean I should be automatically doing as these guys order, but I can learn from what they are saying, so I am trying to sort through their remarks and see if there is anything I can take away that will make me a better captain or can improve the team. At different times, Ian has said that I have been too conservative a captain and that I might not have been using my gut instinct enough as I made the big decisions. I don't agree with him on the conservatism, but there might be some truth in the latter criticism, so this season I will aim to trust myself a little more.

Ian also claimed that I needed some 'new faces' in the Australian side, on the basis — if I interpreted him correctly — that only then would it become become *my* team, rather than one I inherited from Stephen. But I'd like to think that the team was mine from when I first became captain. After all, we did win 32 of our first 39 one-day games (with one tie and one no-result), between the 2002 series in South Africa and the 2003 World Cup, and 13 of 17 Tests (with one loss) between my first game as Test captain, in Sri Lanka in 2004, and the start of the 2005 Ashes series. Maybe, though, our selectors agreed with Ian, because they responded to the Ashes defeat by leaving Damien Martyn out of the Test side for the Super Series and Matthew Hayden out of the one-day squad. Michael Kasprowicz and Jason Gillespie, who'd lost their places in England, were also missing, with Shane Watson joining Brad Hodge and Stuart MacGill in the 13-man Test squad for the six-day match to start on October 14. Marto did keep his place in the one-day side that will play three games against the World XI from October 5 to October 9, the new faces there (from the group that played the ODIs in England) being Shaun Tait, Nathan Bracken and James Hopes. As far as one-day cricket is concerned, there is no doubt that winning the 2007 World Cup is our No. 1 long-term priority. In fact, it has been for a while. I remember when I arrived in India for our 2004 tour (I'd missed the start because of injury), I approached Buck and found him putting together a document on our preparations for the '07 Cup. Typical Buck, always a long way ahead of the game. When I talked to Trevor Hohns, the chairman of selectors, it was clear his thinking was aimed at the same thing. As he said, 'It'd be nice to win three in a row.'

As for the Test, I'm happy that Shane Watson has been picked in the squad, and am keen for him to play in Sydney, which will leave Simon Katich and Brad Hodge to fight it out for the final middle-order batting spot. There were times during the Ashes series when I was envious of England captain Michael Vaughan, with the fifth bowling option that having Andrew Flintoff batting in the top six gave him. The allrounder role is a specialist and crucial position, one that Flintoff fills perfectly for the Poms. From a batting perspective, Gilly does the job brilliantly for us, the way he bats so well with the tail so often, manipulates the strike and hits a lot of boundaries. Watto can do that, too, and also become that fifth Test-class bowler that would help us so much. He works incredibly hard on his game, he's a big, strong, fit athlete whose fast ball gets into the 140s and he has a batting technique that is as good and sound as most going around. He's a good young player.

I know that there has been plenty of comment about the age of the current Aussie team, with only Watto, Michael Clarke and Shaun Tait well short of their 30th birthdays, but to tell you the truth I don't ever think about the guys' birthdates. I just worry about whether they are the best group of players in Australia. The same questions were asked before the Ashes tour, but then we were coming off an almost unprecedented run of success — a Test series victory in India, eight Test wins out of nine in Australasia in 2004–05, 12 ODI wins from 14 games in 2004–05. If you want proof that age is not necessarily a negative, just look at Warney and the way he performed in England. Forty wickets and some very handy runs during the series, when — for all the quality of people such as Andrew Flintoff and Kevin Pietersen — he was clearly the most important player on either side, and was probably in the best form of his entire career.

While some commentators are quick to rightly praise Warney, they do seem to be in a bit of a hurry to draw a line through Marto's Test career. He might be 33, almost 34, but the fact that he's been a champion batsman and a tough bloke for a long time means that there is no reason why he can't bounce back. Same with Dizzy and Kasper; it'd be a brave man to write off such accomplished cricketers too quickly. Our two squads are as follows:

One-day squad: Ricky Ponting (captain), Adam Gilchrist (vice captain), Nathan Bracken, Michael Clarke, Brad Hogg, James Hopes, Michael Hussey, Simon Katich, Brett Lee, Glenn McGrath, Damien Martyn, Andrew Symonds, Shaun Tait, Shane Watson.

Test squad: Ricky Ponting (captain), Adam Gilchrist (vice captain), Michael Clarke, Matthew Hayden, Brad Hodge, Simon Katich, Justin Langer, Brett Lee, Stuart MacGill, Glenn McGrath, Shaun Tait, Shane Warne, Shane Watson.

Friday, September 23

ON PAPER, THE WORLD XI squads assembled by the International Cricket Council (ICC) for the Super Series are incredibly strong, to the point that when I go through their batting order, I find it hard not say to myself, 'How are we going to go against these blokes?' Not that I've done this to any great degree, because the truth is that I have been consumed with what is going on around our team, and how these matches offer us such an immediate chance to bounce back from the Ashes loss. I'm excited about the thought of playing against such talented opponents, and I'm sure the other guys in the Australian side have the same mindset.

We see the games as a challenge. It is a shame then that Sachin Tendulkar, because of his 'tennis elbow' injury, has joined South Africa's Herschelle Gibbs on the injured list. Personally, I'm very keen for us to meet and beat opposition of the highest quality. I am aware that some people see these matches as being something of a gimmick, but I like the concept and will be disappointed if it doesn't work out.

The games have been given full Test and one-day international status, which I think is a good thing. Again, a few cynics have been critical of this, but I don't see any reason why — given that the game's elite players are involved — it should not be regarded as a genuine test. Last year's 'tsunami' one-dayer, while undoubtedly for a very worthy cause, was a different matter, too much of an exhibition; though I did score a hundred then, so maybe the decision to call it a true ODI was not too bad a thing. I do know that not everyone agrees with me. Gilly, for one, has stated that he thinks Tests should be restricted to nation v nation matches, and uses the fact that World Series Cricket has never been officially recognised to support his case.

I certainly do feel strongly that — because of this status the games have been given — these games are not the appropriate forum for trialling the use of technology to 'help' umpires make their decisions. A system of referral and consultation between the on-field officials and the TV umpire will be used. 'Run outs and stumpings will be referred in the normal way to the TV umpire with the TV umpire making the final decision,' an ICC media release explained. 'But in respect of all other decisions, the on-field umpires will have the discretion to consult with the TV umpire before making the final decision.'

I can't help thinking that the system will put more pressure on the on-field umps and because of this be self-defeating. I am the first to concede that the umpiring in international cricket is not perfect, but I doubt the solution is to, in effect, give them the feeling that there is a 'big brother' looking over their shoulder. It would be fine if the video could offer clear-cut answers to all the tricky conundrums that need to be resolved, but as has been demonstrated with catches scooped up at ground level, often the doubt is accentuated rather than cleared up by the slow-motion replays. In such circumstances, I reckon the best bet is to back the umpires unreservedly, let them get on with the job, and at the same time seek to identify more good umpires who can be promoted to the international panel, so that the men who are already there don't get burnt out too quickly.

Tuesday, September 27

I MUST ADMIT TO be getting a little bit jack of all the criticism the team has been getting since we arrived home. You'd think we'd lost every game on tour, when the truth is that we're still entitled to be ranked the No. 1 team in the world. There is no doubt that England deserved to win the series, but to be 'top dog' you've got to succeed at the highest level consistently, which is something the Australian team has been doing since 1995. What I will concede is that we have to prove we still have the ability and toughness to be the best team in the world. For a number of guys, England was the first time they'd been in a losing side in a Test series, so this current summer will be a good test of character for them. The Super Series matches offer a chance to begin the 'redeeming' process, with all of us knowing that outside the squad are a number of players — a few discarded veterans and some exciting young talent — who must now feel they are only a few outstanding performances away from forcing their way into the top side.

Probably the crankiest I have got was when it was suggested that Damien Martyn had been dropped for reasons other than cricket. That was utter garbage. I certainly don't think we've seen the last of Marto. Having spoken to a few of the guys in the team, I know they share my genuine shock that he was left out and my belief that he'll fight his way back. As for the continued talk about my leadership style, I'm increasingly coming around to the view that I should be more assertive on the field. I will definitely continue to seek the advice of the senior guys in the side — that's my style, it's the way I've always done it and I'm sure it's the smart way to play. I know my thoughts and ideas aren't always going to be right and I want to hear alternative views. But I don't think 'putting my stamp on things' will hurt the side either.

What I'm most keen to do is get the guys together and rekindle the team spirit that has been our trademark. That's one thing we should have over our World XI opponents, who haven't been together and played as a group. The verve and energy that comes from being a driven and united national team can be a difficult force to overcome.

Tuesday, October 4

DURING OUR CAMP IN Brisbane leading up to the start of this new season, we sat down with the highly respected sports psychologist

Phil Jauncey, who has done a lot of work previously with the Brisbane Lions AFL club, as well as the Queensland and Australian cricket teams. Our aim was to identify the 'hand brakes' that were holding us back, and to do this we split up into small groups of three or four — one group focusing on the way we communicated our strategies and goals, another looking at time management, another on the way the team was organised. We knew, though, that it wasn't as simple as an outside consultant coming in and correcting things the way a mechanic might fix a car; the remedy had to come from the players. Through this process, with Phil as the facilitator, I think it did. We had just received a massive kick up the backside and we all want to do something about it, to change the things that are not right and revel in the things that are.

The issue of time management is a good example of how this process helped. I have written earlier of how important I see the role of specialist batting and bowling coaches, but the fact is that many times during the past couple of years, I have seen examples where team-mates have filled this role of analyst for other players' games. I've played a lot of cricket with accomplished batsmen such as Matt Hayden, Justin Langer and Damien Martyn, so I have a fair idea of how they go about things, as they do with my game. Many times, either in an informal group discussion or maybe a quiet one-on-one, we'd talk about how things were going, maybe make a suggestion, or remind each other of days when run-making looked easy. We're not going to tell each other how to play, but one of our strengths as a group has been that we do talk to each other about batting and the way we go about it. In England, however, where the schedule was so tight and for the first time in a while many guys were struggling at once, this rarely happened.

More generally, I told the guys at the camp that I wanted to be the very best player I could be, and captain of the best team in the world. All the guys, one after the other, made a similar commitment to excellence, the coaches mapped out with great care how our training would work, and by the time we left the camp, it seemed that everything we were doing was so precise. Second best was never again going to be good enough. From that camp, meetings began and ended spot on time (which didn't always happen in England), the batting and bowling in the nets was as competitive as a Test match. I asked for and got Brett Lee and Glenn McGrath charging in at me with new balls. I couldn't help but compare my excitement here with the pessimism that sometimes pervaded our outlook in England. When I spoke to Shane Warne earlier tonight, after he called to wish us the best of luck in the one-dayers, I was pretty blunt in assessing our chances. 'Mate, these blokes won't touch us,' I told him. 'They might be the best players in the world, but they won't get near us.'

THE FIRST GAME OF a new season is now less than 24 hours away. Over the past three weeks, I have been getting more and more of a feel for just how huge the Ashes series was in Australia. Judging by the number of people who've told me about their winter of cricket, there must have been a lot of weary workers staying up to 3am every morning during the Tests so they wouldn't miss a moment of the action. I was also amazed to read about how Freddie Flintoff has been received here in Melbourne — a standing ovation when he brought out the drinks for the World XI during a warm-up match last Sunday, rapturous applause at the civic reception held in the city the following day, talkback callers wishing he'd been born an Aussie. Rahul Dravid has been feeling so left out he's apparently thinking of wearing a Freddie mask to media conferences on the basis that such a move would be the best thing he could do to publicise the upcoming matches.

Despite the hype, however, from what I understand ticket sales have been slow and we won't be playing in front of a full house when the series starts tomorrow. Maybe the games are on too soon after the footy finals, or perhaps the public is a little suspicious about the World XI's commitment to the concept. I guess only time will tell. Injuries have forced a couple of changes to our one-day squad, with Brad Hogg and Shaun Tait out, replaced by Cameron White and Stuart Clark. Shaun's absence, because of a shoulder ailment which might cost him the entire Australian season, is a real setback — because of his pace and his ability to swing the ball, he is earmarked to be Brett Lee's opening partner in the years ahead, so to 'lose' a season at this stage of his career is awful luck. There is also a certain irony — given all the debate about how old the Aussie team is — that it is one of our youngest players who has broken down.

Our team for game one will look this way: Adam Gilchrist, Simon Katich, Ricky Ponting, Damien Martyn, Michael Hussey, Michael Clarke, Shane Watson, Andrew Symonds, Cameron White, Brett Lee, Nathan Bracken and Glenn McGrath. On paper, the World XI looks to be an intimidating outfit, a squad with the depth to leave Makhaya Ntini and Chris Gayle on the sidelines: Kumar Sangakkara, Virender Sehwag, Jacques Kallis, Brian Lara, Rahul Dravid, Kevin Pietersen, Andrew Flintoff, Shahid Afridi, Shaun Pollock, Daniel Vettori, Shoaib Akhtar and Muttiah Muralitharan.

AS IS CUSTOMARY FOR the day before a one-day series, a meeting was scheduled for today involving the ICC match referee, Ranjan Madugalle of Sri Lanka, the two on-field umpires, Aleem Dar (Pakistan) and Simon Taufel (Australia), the TV umpire, Rudi Koertzen (South Africa), and the two captains, Shaun Pollock and me. Inevitably, the main topic of conversation was what might happen now that on-field officials can seek a TV ump's opinion for decisions involving snicks and the line and height of the ball in lbws. They can also ask Rudi to adjudicate no-balls, if they think the bowler might have transgressed during a wicket-taking delivery. We learned that Rudi will only have the television replays to help him, and not Channel Nine's 'hawkeye' technology, and that he won't have the power to reverse a wrong decision or offer unsolicited advice. 'The umpires in the middle will continue to be supreme,' we were told.

As I pictured a game in which the officials on the field kept referring decisions 'upstairs', just to make sure, I couldn't help fearing that the actual cricket might be slowed down considerably. I could envisage a scene in which captains are called in to explain a slow over-rate and the umpires constantly making sure will be the offending team's alibi.

All three games will be played 'indoors', under the retractable roof which will stay closed throughout. 'What if someone hits the ball into the roof?' was the question. 'I doubt it will occur,' was the somewhat scornful reply. 'But if it does, it will be a dead ball.'

Monday, October 10

ICC Super Series One-Day Internationals
Game One (October 5) at Melbourne: Australia 8–255 (50 overs: AC Gilchrist 45, SM Katich 58; DL Vettori 4–33) defeated ICC World XI 162 (41.3 overs: KC Sangakkara 65; SR Watson 3–43) by 93 runs

Game Two (October 7) at Melbourne: Australia 4–328 (50 overs: AC Gilchrist 103, SM Katich 47, RT Ponting 66, DR Martyn 54) defeated ICC World XI 273 (45.3 overs: CH Gayle 54, KC Sangakkara 61, A Flintoff 42; NW Bracken 3–43) by 55 runs

Game Three (October 9) at Melbourne: Australia 5–293 (RT Ponting 68, MEK Hussey 75*, SR Watson 66*) defeated ICC World XI 137 (B Lee 4–30, SR Watson 4–39) by 156 runs

A WEEK BEFORE THE one-dayers started, I was required to go the Telstra Dome in Melbourne for a promotion and photo shoot in connection with the Super Series. While I was there I noted how cut up and slippery the playing surface was following a hard season of football, so first chance I had I told all our blokes to contact their boot suppliers and get themselves some footy boots. The field was no better on game day, so a number of us batted and bowled in normal cricket spikes but fielded in the footwear that footballers wear, and we had a massive advantage over the overseas fieldsmen — to the point that I could see them looking at our boots and the playing surface, and sense them making a mental note that they needed to catch up for game two. Sure enough, as we went through our warm-ups before the second one-dayer, many of the World XI guys were walking around in their brand spanking new footwear.

I did my warm-ups in my footy boots, but then I replaced them with my spikes before I went over to have a hit in the nets. In the next net was Rahul Dravid, who was facing up to Andrew Flintoff and Shoaib Akhtar, both of whom were tearing in. Poor Dravid was having a hell of a time, as his feet kept slipping from under him just about every ball … because he was wearing his new footy boots!

We came into this one-day series confident about our chances, but we never anticipated that we'd win quite so comfortably. The crucial factor, I believe, was that we had points to prove — to ourselves, to each other and to our critics. We built up a momentum during the first game that became irresistible towards the end, something that started with Gilly's 45 from 48 balls in the opening innings of the series and then was further boosted by a fantastic team bowling display that was spearheaded by the old pro, Glenn McGrath, who took 2–13 from seven exceptional overs. All five of our bowlers took at least one crucial wicket in this match.

I'd been desperately keen to make a statement from the jump, and began my first innings of the series in some style by smashing Freddie Flintoff for a big six forward of square leg. But soon after I was dismissed in pretty tame fashion, spooning up a simple catch after I charged Shaun Pollock. The only other negative from that game was our fielding, which was ordinary. Our batting was even better than it looked — 255 might not usually be a winning total in modern one-day international cricket, but with a sticky outfield, muggy atmosphere and slow pitch, and despite the best efforts of their spinners, Murali and Vettori, we were fairly sure it would be enough. Then Glenn reminded Virender Sehwag and Jacques Kallis just how good he is, Brian Lara drove Nathan Bracken straight to where Andrew Symonds had positioned himself at short cover, and Brett Lee induced Dravid into an ill-advised pull shot. When Shane Watson dashed in from deep backward square, picked up the ball one-handed and threw the stumps down to run out Pollock, the World XI were 8–118 and the game was as good as over.

Shaun Pollock said all the right things after that game, that their 'pride was dented' and 'the guys are hurting', but we could sense that the result mattered more to us than it did to our opponents. We were genuinely excited to be out there and to be able to express ourselves in the way we did. Although we'd only been back in the country for three weeks, we all felt as if we'd been looking forward to the game for quite a while, and that we'd worked very, very hard in the lead-up. To play the brand of cricket we know we can play is always very satisfying, especially given the circumstances we faced when we stepped out for the first game after relinquishing the Ashes.

FOR GAME TWO, THE crowd was bigger (29,371 compared with only 18,435 for the opener) and Pidge was 'rested', more as a precaution because he had experienced some tightness in his calf and hamstring muscles when bowling on the spongy Telstra Dome surface. His replacement was Stuart Clark, making his ODI debut, while Chris Gayle replaced Shahid Afridi in the World XI XII. Stuart had been called into our squad in England a couple of times, when Glenn was injured, and he had done some good things with the Australia A team on their recent tour of Pakistan. Brad Haddin and Michael Clarke, who've played a fair amount of Pura Cup cricket with him, rate Stuart highly, and we see him as being in the same mould as McGrath — steady and ultra-reliable, not that quick and not a huge swinger of the ball, but someone who hits the pitch hard, bowls a consistent line and length and can move the ball off the seam.

This was a game we took control of early, with Gilly blazing away to 103 from only 79 balls, the hundred being reached in 73 deliveries — the fastest century by an Australian in a one-day international. In England, Flintoff had enjoyed bowling to Gilly, but here he conceded 20 runs in the 10 balls he bowled to our champion keeper/batsman, while Murali was swung away for one absolutely colossal six over mid-wicket. Marto also batted really well, making a run-a-ball 54, and Symmo was explosive at the end, crashing 31 from 14 deliveries. The World team started their reply in a hurry, with Gayle, Sehwag and Sangakkara enjoying McGrath's absence in taking 125 runs from the first 16 overs — the highlight for them being a spectacular six by Gayle, hit over cover off the back foot off Brett Lee! — but our bowlers, and, critically, our fielding, responded well, and the required run-rate kept edging higher. Once Pietersen fell in the 42nd over, when they needed 10 runs per over, we knew the series was ours.

Momentum in cricket is such a big thing, and when Gilly gets going in the way he did in this game it gives us a momentum from the jump that can be impossible for the opposition to stop.

There had been a bit of talk about that perhaps he shouldn't be opening the batting in one-day cricket any more, but while he is in my side there is no way he won't be going in first, because I've seen him so clinically and savagely change games where we have previously been behind the eight-ball. I remember a classic run chase in Port Elizabeth in 2002, when we were set 327 and got them with five balls to spare. Gilly came out at the start of that innings, at a time when the South Africans were cock-a-hoop about making such a big total, and smashed 52 from 34 balls, which allowed Darren Lehmann and me to just knock the ball about, score at a run a ball, and win the game. Going in at No. 3, I get a better appreciation than most of just what sort of impact he can have on opposition attacks; the only negative is that sometimes when I go in I can feel as if the game is being dragged back on top of me, because the exceptional run-rate he established has left high expectations. The good part is that most times I can play myself in without feeling like I have to smack it all over the place from ball one (like Gilly has just done!). He is a very special player.

IF YOU'D ASKED ME after game one how I felt about our first win, I would have said 'satisfied'. I was 'excited' after our second win, mainly because of the way Gilly batted and the manner in which we found a way to get wickets when we were under pressure facing that early onslaught by the World XI's top order. And I was genuinely thrilled after game three, which we won decisively on the back of a terrific partnership between Mike Hussey and Shane Watson — featuring one spectacular blow from Hussey off Ntini which hit the Telstra Dome roof — and some excellent bowling from Watto and Brett Lee, who each took four wickets. Bing's first spell was fantastic, especially the manner in which he responded after I asked him to charge in at

Jacques Kallis, who will be one of the key men in the games against South Africa scheduled for later in the season.

Kallis was in as early as the fourth over, and Brett was at him immediately, making exactly the statement I was looking for. It took me back to the Twenty20 game we played against England at Southampton last June, when Flintoff and Steve Harmison seemed to fire up near the end of the game, when they were bowling at our fast bowlers. When Lara was caught behind for a duck, one ball after Kallis had been caught at square leg as he tried to fend off a fierce riser, the World team were 4–27 chasing 293, and Brett had 3–17 from 3.4 overs. With series against the West Indies as well as South Africa on our upcoming agenda, I couldn't help thinking that from our perspective the cricket was now going very well indeed. I was also pondering the fact that as captain it seemed that everything I was doing here under the roof was working, whereas right through the Ashes series it had seemed as if most things I tried didn't work.

The system of referring umpiring decisions 'upstairs' never became a major issue during the one-dayers, but it hardly added to the drama either. There was only one referral in the first two games, when Simon Katich was judged to be not out on a caught-behind appeal last Wednesday, but during our innings in game three the system was tested five times, resulting in only one dismissal, and that probably would have been given anyway. The weirdest moment came when Hussey was caught on the boundary by Shahid Afridi, but umpire Aleem Dar went to the video to confirm that Makhaya Ntini had bowled a no-ball. There was no doubt that in this case the referral led to the correct decision being made, at least in terms of the letter of the law, but it still didn't seem quite right. In game two, I thought I was plumb lbw but the ump didn't 'go upstairs', instead just giving me not out, while two days later Damien Martyn actually had to wait three times for the TV ump to make a ruling: first on an unlikely lbw that always looked to be going over the stumps, then an unsuccessful caught behind appeal and finally another lbw shout which proved to be his undoing.

I HAVE ALWAYS SAID that if we can focus on things *we* can do, rather than worrying about outside things that are beyond our control, we can compete with any team in the world. Our preparation as a team for this series was excellent, and there was always a feeling that everyone in the squad was heading in the same direction. It was little wonder then that I got a little dirty with the journos who after the game tonight wanted to rubbish our achievement by concentrating on the ordinary form of the World XI. The implication was that the overseas guys weren't fair dinkum. I thought it was wrong to look for negatives in this way. Similarly, I hope the fact that we have won all three games decisively doesn't hurt the future of the Super Series concept. I certainly want us to approach the Test against the World team in exactly the same way we've played here in Melbourne, but I also hope our opponents play up to their best ability. It would be a great shame if this became the one and only time a Super Series was played.

Wednesday, October 12

WITH THE ONE-DAYERS OVER, attention has moved to the six-day Test match that begins on Friday. Graeme Smith, the somewhat surprise choice as captain of the World XI Test team, arrived in Australia last Sunday, and I read with some interest the kind of questions he received during his first media conference. After he was asked about criticism of his style of leadership from Ian Chappell, it was suggested that he would enjoy leading a team with two world-class spinners. 'It's going to be a nice challenge for me,' he replied. Then someone invited him to comment on the potential difficulties of captaining such a star-studded combination. 'It would be stupid of me not to use the players around me; communication is an important part of my captaincy,' Smith said. 'It's important for me to use them but, ultimately, at the end of the day, I am leading the team and I am making the decisions.'

And then, inevitably, he was asked about sledging, with reporters referring him back to his first series against Australia, in 2001–02, when afterwards he went public with his complaints about the language we'd apparently used against him on the field. 'I am looking forward to it,' the World XI and South African captain responded. 'I love the intensity at this level. I play the game the same way. I play the game hard and I don't think there will be anything held back. I expect it to be very competitive. I am prepared for it.'

Last night, the cricket caravan was in Sydney in full force, for the annual ICC Awards function, an event that was first held in 2004. I actually spent a fair amount of time talking with Graeme, mostly general stuff about cricket and batting. It wasn't as if we were brought together or sought each other out as opposing captains; more a case of two cricketing types bumping into each other and then chatting for a while about our game. There is no doubt Graeme can be a very interesting bloke to talk to. A number of prizes were handed out during the night, with Andrew Flintoff and Jacques Kallis sharing the Sir Garfield Sobers trophy as Cricketer of the Year (based on performances between August 1, 2004 and July 31, 2005), Kallis named as Test Cricketer of the Year, Kevin Pietersen winning the ODI Player of the Year and Emerging Player of the Year awards, and Simon Taufel being named Umpire of the Year.

I was named captain of the Test team of the year, which was chosen by a selection panel chaired by Sunil Gavaskar and featuring names such as Sir Richard Hadlee, Courtney Walsh, Rodney Marsh and David Gower. It is an honour I was very proud to accept. The full team was: Virender Sehwag (India), Graeme Smith (South Africa), Ricky Ponting (Australia), Jacques Kallis (South Africa), Brian Lara (West Indies), Inzamam-ul-Haq (Pakistan), Andrew Flintoff (England), Adam Gilchrist (Australia), Shane Warne (Australia), Chaminda Vaas (Sri Lanka), Glenn McGrath (Australia); 12th man: Anil Kumble (India).

The one-day international team of the year named at the same time was: Marvan Atapattu (Captain, Sri Lanka), Adam Gilchrist (Australia), Rahul Dravid (India), Kevin Pietersen (England), Inzamam-ul-Haq (Pakistan), Andrew Flintoff (England), Andrew Symonds (Australia), Daniel Vettori (New Zealand), Brett Lee (Australia), Naved-ul-Hasan (Pakistan), Glenn McGrath (Australia); 12th man: Jacques Kallis (South Africa).

As functions go, this wasn't a bad one, and I quite liked Freddie's line when he was asked how it felt to win the night's biggest award. 'I just came here for food,' he said. 'I had no idea I would get it.'

Thursday, October 13

THE UPCOMING TEST WILL offer, among other things, a unique display of high-class spin bowling talent. Between them, Shane Warne, Stuart MacGill, Muttiah Muralitharan and Daniel Vettori have taken a total of 1553 Test wickets, and the World XI have shown what they think of the SCG wicket by leaving Shoaib Akhtar and Shaun Pollock out of their starting line-up. This means Flintoff and Harmison will get the chance to resume their battle with the Australian top-order at the earliest opportunity.

This will be Murali's first Test in Sydney. It will also be only the fourth time that Shane and Stuart will have bowled together in a Test at the SCG. The three previous games — against England in 1998–99, South Africa in 2001–02 and Pakistan in 2004–05 — have all resulted in home-town victories, with Stuey taking 27 wickets in the three games to Warney's 13. (All up, Shane has taken 54 wickets in 11 Tests at Sydney, to Stuart's 40 in eight matches.)

They might both be right-arm leg spinners, but Shane and Stuart are vastly different. Warney is more of a strategist who tries to set blokes up, whereas Stuey is always trying to bowl the perfect wicket-taking ball. Warney likes to keep things tight. Stuey believes his job is to go out and take wickets, so it doesn't matter if he goes for a few runs; he'd rather take 5–80 from 20 overs than 2–20 from 15.

Maybe when facing Stuey, you can sit back and wait for the bad balls, but if you do that you have to accept that on a turner he'll bowl you some beauties as well. If you play that waiting game against Warney, he is so good that he'll get you out eventually on just about any surface. I can only remember batting against Shane a few times; once in a Shield game in Hobart in 1997–98, when I scored 38 and 25 not out, and during the World Series Cup in 1994–95, when I was playing for Australia A. (I also played against him in a Mercantile Mutual Cup game back in 1992–93, my one-day debut for Tasmania, but I can't remember facing him in that game and looking at the scorecard — I made 22 batting four, and he took 3–31 from 5.5 overs, bowling fourth change — I doubt I did.) I recall in Adelaide in one of those Australia A games I tried to slog sweep him and was caught on the boundary after the ball came off the bottom of my bat. If I faced him now, I'd definitely try to be positive against him, because I think that's the only approach you can take. That's certainly the way Pietersen and Flintoff tried to play him in England, more so than their team-mates, and they were the ones who had the most success against him. Many batsmen around the world have tried to sweep him all the time, but Warney loves that. Jacques Kallis is one batsman who never leaves his crease against him.

To play the two leggies in the one team, I think it is almost essential that we also have a bowling allrounder, such as Shane Watson, in the side, to prevent the attack becoming too predictable if the pitch turns out to be flat. For the upcoming game, Watto will bat at seven, with Gilly moving up to No. 6 and Brad Hodge unlucky to be 12th man. Some surprise was expressed at the pre-Test media conference that Michael Clarke will be batting at No. 4, but I'm not concerned. 'He looks at home whenever he strides to the crease in both forms of the game,' I commented. 'He's got a big future and will certainly be around for some time.'

As a further fillip for us, it was confirmed publicly that John Buchanan will continue as the Australian coach, at least until the completion of the 2007 World Cup. The Cricket Australia review committee that was set up after our Ashes loss won't be releasing their conclusions until December, but they have recommended that Buck be asked to continue, which makes his reappointment a formality.

Tuesday, October 18

ICC Super Series Test Match
At Sydney (October 14–17): Australia 345 (ML Hayden 111, RT Ponting 46, AC Gilchrist 94; A Flintoff 4–59) and 199 (ML Hayden 77, RT Ponting 54) defeated ICC World XI 190 (V Sehwag 76; SCG MacGill 4–39) and 144 (SCG MacGill 5–43) by 210 runs

AS A CONTEST, I concede, this Test was something of an anti-climax. But for us, on a different level, the game was a beauty — with the fact that we performed so positively despite the lack of atmosphere throughout the game, especially on the final day when we clinched an emphatic victory, a real standout. The batting of Matt Hayden, who followed up his century in the final Ashes Test with an impressive double in this match, and Adam Gilchrist, who made an important 94 on the first day that allowed us to post the one substantial innings total of the match, was excellent, while our two great spin leg-spinners were in typically devastating Sydney form.

The World team, in contrast, were disappointing. They didn't have as much to play for as we did, and because they competed as a loose combination of men from various environments I have to concede that the playing field wasn't quite level. But still there were times when some of their star players showed their class. Right at the start, Steve Harmison tore in as if it was the first day of an Ashes Test at Lord's, and knocked over Justin Langer's off stump third ball of the game. On day two, Virender Sehwag scored a typically fearless and exhilarating 76 from 82 balls, relying on his unbelievable eye, always well balanced, never moving his feet much, while Murali was impressive in our first innings, and occasionally mesmerising in our second. This was especially evident in one magical cameo when he should have had Simon Katich stumped, beat him twice off the pitch and then had him caught and bowled off the leading edge. Not done with, he then beat Watto straightaway with a doosra, and first ball next over had Gilly caught at slip with one that spun and bounced. Superb bowling!

It was interesting — and said something about the two men concerned — to watch Hayden and Gilchrist in this match. Neither could have been happy with their batting in England;

indeed, had Hayden not scored that 138 at The Oval he might have been dropped for this game. He had batted more slowly than usual in that hundred in England, and he continued that patient game plan, looking to build his innings rather than bludgeon the bowlers as he has often done in the past. 'It's certainly the way I'd like to continue playing at Test level,' he said afterwards, in the manner of a man who had discovered something more about himself and his cricket in the previous few months. Gilly, in contrast, stuck solid to the natural run-a-ball mentality that has typified his batting since he started in Test cricket, and once again he pushed the mood of the game our way, coming in late in the middle session of day one after Kato was run out to make it 4–163 and being undefeated at stumps on 94 when the score was 6–331. He was dismissed immediately the next morning, but by then the damage had been done. Indeed, his quick 97-run partnership with Haydos, in what proved to be a fairly low-scoring game, was the key batting episode of the Test. We'd missed out on most of the key moments in England, so it was refreshing to have them going our way here.

Prior to the start of day two, Graeme Smith had said that he hoped to dismiss Australia for less than 400, so to get us for 'just' 345 must have been good for the mood in the away dressing-room. But when Lee and McGrath dismissed Smith, Dravid and Lara to reduce the World XI to 3–43, with the spinners still to bowl an over, we knew we were going to be very hard to beat. Sehwag and Kallis changed the mood for a while, but after Warney got the little Indian dynamo and Stuey had Inzamam-ul-Haq stumped for just the fourth time in the Pakistan captain's Test career, we were in control.

This was true even though, largely because of Murali and an inspired Flintoff (who was very aggressive when he charged in at Brett Lee, playing the game in the way it should be played), we lost our last nine wickets in our second innings for just 47 runs. The pitch was not easy to bat on, especially if you wanted to score quickly, and while I would have liked our batsmen to graft away to a bigger lead, I knew 355 was more than even a team made up of the best players in the world could get, especially against Warne and MacGill. I was hardly disappointed when, because of the fading light, I had Shane on to bowl the third over of the innings and though he didn't get a wicket before stumps, Stuey quickly did. It was all over before tea on day four, and the champagne flying immediately following the on-field presentation will be a cherished memory. Not for the first time, there was some comment about the exuberance of our celebration, as if it didn't fit with the way the game failed to reach any great heights. If these cynics knew how much importance we had placed on being hungry and playing to the very best of our ability, maybe they would have understood.

You can't fake that kind of joy and excitement. Back in the first one-dayer, when I'd caught Vettori to complete our victory, I threw the ball up near the roof and we ran together and embraced each other. Some outside the squad thought that reaction was over the top, but I didn't care — it captured how I felt, how the team felt. I wanted that emotion in our cricket. Between The Oval and Melbourne, Buck and I had run the meetings where we talked about how we wanted the Australian cricket team to play, but ultimately the effort and the commitment had to come from the individuals concerned. We ended up achieving what we wanted in these games, so why not be happy about it? A lot of hard work goes into winning Test matches and one-day internationals. At certain moments in every game, you are going to be challenged in some way, and there is a rare satisfaction in passing such public examinations, especially if you do so with some style.

IN THE WASH-UP TO the World XI Test, there were two issues that seemed to dominate: one, the use of technology to help the umpires with all their decisions; and two, the future of the Super Series.

There were 21 occasions during the Test when decisions were referred to the TV umpire: five times for run outs or stumpings, 11 times for catches or lbws, and five times to confirm or deny boundaries. Sometimes, watching the TV in the dressing-room, we weren't sure ourselves what the right decision was, which must have made it hard for the officials, and I came to the conclusion that the delays in the game brought on by the referrals just weren't worth it. In my view, we have to assist the umps on the field by reducing the unending pressure on them any way we can. Of course, you can't stop the media analysing the decisions, the TV producers replaying them for their TV audience, or the commentators scrutinising those replays. But administrators could stop contentious decisions being replayed at the ground, which would prevent players, fans and umpires stopping to watch the big screens and then reacting in their own ways to what they've just seen.

In our first innings here in Sydney, Michael Clarke was caught off his bat and pad, one from Vettori that popped up to Sehwag fielding close in on the offside. Rudi Koertzen, the umpire, immediately thought, 'Out.'

But then he stopped and said, 'We'll have a look at it.'

He gave the signal to Darrell Hair, the TV umpire, but unfortunately — no matter how many times it was replayed — the video couldn't conclusively make a ruling either way. Umpire Hair said he couldn't tell, and left it to Umpire Koertzen, who gave Pup out. The decision was probably right, but if it was referred, doesn't that mean there was some doubt? And if you can't tell from the replays, doesn't that also mean there was some doubt? I spoke to Rudi Koertzen after the game and he told me he hated the process as much as I did. Run outs and stumpings are fair enough — the video replays are made for those types of decisions — otherwise, I reckon leave the decision-making process as it is. We've all got to learn to take the good with the bad.

The general feeling with the Super Series appears to be that if it continues it will be played only once every four years. I don't know if my view has been clouded by the fact that we won and the positive vibe I felt in the Aussie dressing-room, but I enjoyed the games and was very proud to be leading my country in contests against all the best players in the game. Perhaps the ICC has to look closely at the people they select in the World teams, making sure they pick cricketers who take pride in performing at their best, whatever the circumstances, men who will *always* put in. My view is that the Super Series should always be played on the grounds of the No. 1 country, and I still feel the games should have Test and one-day international status. If the concept is given time to establish a tradition of its own, I'm sure it can become a worthwhile part of the cricket calendar.

Part II

Caribbean Clean Sweep

Australia v West Indies
November 2005

Monday, October 24

ING Cup 2005–06

Preliminary Game (October 22) at Brisbane: Tasmania 211 (46.5 overs: ML Di Venuto 50, DG Dawson 55; JR Hopes 4–23) lost to Queensland 8–213 (42.3 overs: JP Maher 99) by two wickets

AS I GEARED UP for my first game for Tasmania in two seasons — a one-dayer against Queensland at the Gabba — Cricket Australia began the process of rebuilding the Australian team's support staff by appointing Richard McInnes, currently a senior coach at the CBCE, as the full-time performance analyst. Previously, the job of co-ordinating the video analysis and computer software operations had been part of the job of the assistant coach, but by bringing on Richard to fill this role, at a time when the role of technology is becoming increasingly important, Jamie Siddons and Dene Hills will be free to focus on coaching. The fact that Richard is also an accredited coach means he can contribute in a number of ways, which has to be a good thing.

This appointment was announced last Friday, and 24 hours later I was bowled by Michael Kasprowicz for 19, after I won the toss and decided to bat in a game in which we fought back to almost win, after the home side reached 2–105 chasing 212. It was good to wear the Tassie colours again, though I always put a fair bit of pressure on myself to do well, so when I don't it can be frustrating. It can also be hard coming back into the Tassie side, because I play for the state so rarely and live in Sydney, so I don't mix with the guys a lot. There are a few young players I just don't know much about, except for what I've gleaned from conversations with the coach, Tim Coyle, and heard on the cricket grapevine. I can remember how shy I was when I first came into the Tassie side back in 1992 — when I shared a century stand with David Boon in my first game but hardly talked to him off the field — so I knew that with some guys the onus was on me to approach them. This was a real chance for me to learn a bit about them, and not just what they can do on the cricket field. I wanted to discover a bit about what made them tick as people, and see if there were lessons from my career that I could pass on that would make their cricket lives a little less complicated ...

I've never forgotten where I come from and how my upbringing in north Launceston, playing with the men of the Mowbray Cricket Club, shaped me as a person and a cricketer. That was where I first learnt about the game, playing organised games with adults and elsewhere at every opportunity with my younger brother and my knockabout mates from the neighbourhood. Best of all, there was a season with my dad, when he came out of retirement and topped the competition batting averages and aggregates. Always, I was wanting and hoping I could play for Tasmania and Australia. Many of the guys from whom I learned a lot about the game are still involved with the club, all of them helping out any way they can. I grew up knowing only one way to play cricket, and that came from my seasons with Mowbray, when we were always regarded as an intimidating side, a tough mob to compete with. Things were always happening in games involving the Mowbray Cricket

Club. I was a proud Tasmanian then, and today, even though I live in Sydney, I'm a proud Tasmanian still.

AROUND THIS TIME OF year, there is always a spate of cricket books released into the market, but there is a change this year in that, following England's success in the Ashes series and despite the fact that usually from September to May England is very much a football country, there are books coming out over there as well as in Australia. The latest to hit the UK bookshops is *The Coach's Story* by Duncan Fletcher, the England coach, and the reports I have read suggest that Fletcher claims that 'the Australians had been verbally abusive and physically intimidating while flouting the spirit of the game in England'. He also happily retells the story of how I 'blew my top' when he smiled at me after I was run out by England's substitute fieldsman Gary Pratt at Trent Bridge.

I am stunned that Fletcher is so strident in his commentary. I don't remember any of the umpires speaking to me or reporting us to the match officials, except for that day at Trent Bridge, when Simon Katich and I were both fined after we reacted inappropriately after we were dismissed. We tried our utmost to play in the right spirit, which I think was clear throughout the series. Indeed, many people have complimented both sides on the 'hard but fair' approach that characterised the cricket.

In my case, I lost 75 per cent of my match fee after I lost it following that run out. That same day, 24 hours before I was fined, I issued this statement:

> I was disappointed with my dismissal given that it was a crucial stage of the game and I'd worked hard to get to that position. I let myself down with my reaction and for that I apologise to those who see me as a role model. My

frustration at getting out was compounded by the fact that I was run out by a substitute fielder, an issue that has concerned us from the start of this series and one we raised before the series.

Fletcher knew that the question of how you use substitutes meant a lot to us, because we had been complaining about it consistently since the first one-day international of the tour, when we thought the Poms were giving their bowlers a rest and replacing them on the field with much superior fieldsmen. I still don't think it's right, and never will, and was frustrated that nothing was done about it. That doesn't excuse my behaviour, but neither does it give Fletcher the right to be so smug about it.

It's a pity Fletcher didn't complain directly to me about our approach while I was in England. I guess I'll have to wait until he comes out to Australia next year and maybe then we can have a chat about the controversy.

I know his team will be facing a more professional combination this time around, a team full of positive body language and that same aggressive, in-your-face aura that has, apart from the 2005 Ashes Tests, typified the Australian team when it has been challenged in recent years. If you're professional and hard-nosed off the field, your on-field performance will be like that as well. We went away from that in England, but we're not making that mistake now, and we won't be making that mistake when Duncan Fletcher is in Australia next season.

AMONG THE BOOKS PUBLISHED is my own diary of the Ashes tour, and the media have latched on to my account of the incident before our one-dayer against Bangladesh at Cardiff, when Andrew Symonds let himself down by staying out late on the night before the game. I was stuck when recalling this affair, between doing the right thing by Symmo and providing the reader with an honest account of what went on. I don't believe that it's my job in my books to offer a 'boots'n'all' insider's account, but I do want to give people — especially young cricketers and cricket fans — a taste of what it's like to be the captain of the Australian team. Maybe this time I went too far, especially as Symmo has come back from that setback in exactly the way we needed him to.

Friday, October 28

THE WEST INDIES' ONLY warm-up game before the first Test at Brisbane is a four-day game against Queensland. It appears that their early days in Australia have been awkward, with their captain Shivnarine Chanderpaul complaining that they'll be underdone going into the series, while their fast bowler Tino Best found himself banned from training by his own coach, the Australian Bennett King, over a disciplinary matter. This had come on top of a pre-tour dispute that had almost thrown the series itself into doubt. They are in some ways an unknown quantity to us, especially their pacemen, but we have always had a high regard for their batsmen — such as Brian Lara, Chanderpaul, Chris Gayle and Ramnaresh Sarwan — and not just because last time we played them they scored 7–418 to win the fourth Test of the 2003 series, at St John's, Antigua.

It's amazing how the cricket world looks differently on the West Indies these days. They still carry themselves with a sense of a swagger, but their bowlers are not feared as they once were, and over the past couple of series we have always felt we could put up some big totals against them. I'm not sure what the reason is for this decline, though I do know that when we travel through the Caribbean the sporting conversations seem to be all about soccer and American basketball. Just as significantly, the facilities over there are not the best in the cricket world. On tour there, we rarely see a decent training venue, because they simply don't exist. In a similar vein, many of the game-day wickets are so flat they dishearten and discourage the bowlers.

It is also my impression that when the West Indies were the dominant side in world cricket, no one ever took the time or the care to make sure that they had good coaching systems in place. The infrastructure around every tier of their cricket — Test, first-class, club and junior cricket — was ordinary. I think they just expected to keep producing world-class players. We are sometimes hearing in the wake of the Ashes series loss that the Australian team is about to go on a free fall similar to that suffered by the West Indies in the last decade, but the fact is Australian cricket has an effective coaching structure and youth identification programs in place. I would imagine we are the best in the world as far as this aspect of long-term cricket planning goes.

IN THE DAYS LEADING up to the announcement of the Australian squad for the first Test of 2005–06, there was something of a campaign for Stuart MacGill to play, despite the fact that the Gabba wicket has traditionally suited the quicker bowlers. I agree with Steve Waugh that Stuart has 'put up a case that you almost can't knock back', but at the same time, I'm going to reserve my judgment about what I think our best attack might be until closer to game day. The selectors will speak to me before they pick the team, to get my opinions on certain players and possible combinations, but I'm never there in the room or on the phone when the final team is chosen. They might give me a guide to how they're thinking, and ask me who I'd prefer, but in the end I'm presented with a team. There has not been a time I can remember when so many places in the final XI are up for grabs. Shane Watson is trying to lock down the allrounder's role, the fourth bowler after McGrath, Warne and Lee could be MacGill or a paceman, with a number of quicks — Jason Gillespie, Stuart Clark, Michael Kasprowicz, Nathan Bracken and Mitchell Johnson among them — competing for that spot, while the middle order is hardly settled. Michael Clarke has come out publicly saying he wants to make the No. 4 spot his own, at a time when a number of former players have said that he's not ready for the promotion. Damien Martyn, Brad Hodge, Mike Hussey and Andrew Symonds are high-class batsmen, just waiting for an opportunity.

When our 12-man Test squad was announced yesterday, MacGill and Bracken were both chosen, with Hodge the unluckiest bloke to miss out. The logic is that Bracks is better suited to the Gabba than his rival quicks, and choosing Stuey gives us more options as far as what the final make-up of our attack might be. It also pretty much assures Shane Watson's selection in the final XI, a fact that reflects just how much importance we are placing on that allrounder role.

In regard to Watto, I want to give more consideration to where he bats — before or after Adam Gilchrist. Part of me wants Gilly to stay at No. 7, but I had a long conversation with him, during which I asked him where he thought he was best suited, and he would prefer to go in at six. He'll get more opportunity there, he reckons, but my argument is that No. 7, whether in Test or one-day cricket, is a specialist spot, and he's the best there is in that role. The No. 7 has to bat with the tail all the time, which is a very difficult thing to do unless you know exactly what you are doing. It's a rare skill to know when to try to monopolise the strike and when to have faith in your partner, when to attack and when to defend, to have the patience to just the block the first four balls of an over and then contrive a quick single or go for the boundary off the last couple. It can also be hard to come in at five for not that many and still play your natural attacking game. Of course, Gilly has done that time and again, often shifting the mood and tempo of a game very much in our favour. Against that, he's a bloke who is averaging more than 50 in Test cricket, so there is absolutely no doubt he has the ability to be a top-six batsman. I sense the selectors agree with Adam, so that's most likely where we'll bat him. I can see both sides of the situation, so it's hardly the sort of issue that, as captain, I'll get adamant about.

Monday, October 31

I CAN PICTURE JUSTIN Langer, teeth clenched, refusing to touch his broken rib cage as he told a reporter, 'I'll be playing on Thursday.' He'd say the same thing to the doctors, and to me, too. Last Saturday, Lang was batting in an ING Cup game against Victoria at the Junction Oval in Melbourne when a delivery from the former Tasmanian paceman Gerard Denton thumped into his upper body, and he had to retire hurt. Scans revealed a small fracture, and afterwards he was being interviewed about his prospects of being right for the first Test, which starts in three days' time. 'Apparently, with a cracked rib the thing you have to get used to is the pain,' he explained, as if that was easy. 'I'm not trying to be a hero, but it's only pain, mate. I'm not going to miss a Test match.'

I was watching on TV, a day before Tassie's ING Cup game against New South Wales (a match that was subsequently washed out without a ball being bowled), and when I saw Lang retire hurt I suspected it was more than just a bruise. Trefor James, the

Cricket Australia doctor, was optimistic at first, and decided Justin was right to at least fly to Brisbane. But I know that the final decision will have to be taken out of Lang's hands. He is so tough, he'd most likely genuinely think he was okay even if he wasn't, and though he is a valuable member of our side — a bloke who has averaged nearly 60 with the bat over the past 12 months and who topped the Australian batting averages and aggregates during the Ashes series — if he's not fit he shouldn't start.

The 'trouble' with Lang is that when it comes to him and his recovery from injury, you just never know. He will want to leave it to the last minute, because he wants to play *that* badly, and he's shown before that he does have the ability to recover quickly and to play with pain. People are telling me that he has no chance of making it, but in the back of my mind is last year's Boxing Day Test, when he had what was described as a 'severe' back problem three days before Christmas but fought back to play, even after the medical experts said originally that he was gone.

We certainly want him to play. I've spoken with Buck about the recent changes to the team and the thing we both agree on is that we'd like to get the new side settled as quickly as we can. In the meantime, Mike Hussey has been called into the squad. Again, it was the selectors who made this decision, but I was consulted beforehand and agreed with them 100 per cent. The plan is for Lang to practise tomorrow, and if the medicos say he won't be fully able to bat or field, Huss will make his Test debut, opening the batting. It's certainly better to get the new man up here now, in case he's required, rather than wait until closer to the game, if a change has to be made.

OUR OPPONENTS HAVE CONCERNS with their own champion left-hander. Brian Lara has hardly scored a run so far during this Australian season — 0, 5 and 0 in the three Super Series one-dayers, 5 and 36 in the Super Series Test match, and 1 in the West Indians' tour game against Queensland — hardly the best preparation for a Test series where he'll be facing the likes of Glenn McGrath and Shane Warne. Of course, there are two ways of looking at this: one, he is out of form, which will work to our advantage; or two, he is due for a big one and we could be the ones to pay for his run of outs. Lara only needs to score 316 more runs to take over from Allan Border as Test cricket's leading run-getter. We will continue to target him as the No. 1 threat, and try to keep the record in Australian hands for as long as possible.

There is always a sense of expectation before the Brisbane Test, traditionally the opening international of the Australian summer. For me, this game and the cricket around Boxing Day and the New Year are the two most exciting times of the season. It's a little different this year because we've already played the Super Series, but usually you've been away from the team for a little while, you might have scored a few runs in state cricket, which has you thinking you're going to have a successful year, and everyone is in a positive mood. Even things like the once-a-year lectures from the anti-drugs and anti-corruption people add to the build-up. Much of the media talk is about the new players in the squad. It's as if we're about to go on a new adventure.

Monday, November 7

Australia v West Indies Test series
First Test (November 3–6) at Brisbane: Australia 435 (RT Ponting 149, AC Gilchrist 44, SK Warne 47, B Lee 47; CD Collymore 4–72) and 2 for 283 declared (ML Hayden 118, RT Ponting 104*) defeated West Indies 210 (DS Smith 88; SK Warne 5–48, GD McGrath 4–72) and 129 (B Lee 5–30, NW Bracken 4–48) by 379 runs

LAST YEAR, NATHAN BRACKEN took 6–27 in the Pura Cup final at the Gabba, a key factor in New South Wales' victory. Stuart MacGill has taken 11 wickets in his three Tests in Brisbane, only one of which Australia won, but 169 wickets in his 34-match Test career. Shane Watson is potentially the allrounder we crave. The choice was a tough one, with three men trying to fit into two places in the side, but in the end Stuart was the unlucky one, not least because the pitch had a bit of 'green' about it, and the atmosphere was typically humid, ideal for a good swing bowler. The Windies have a number of left-handed batsmen, which played to Bracks' advantage because he can swing the ball away from the lefties, while maybe Stuey doesn't bowl quite as well to them as he does to the right-handers. For all this, the leggie should get his chance in the second and third Tests, in Hobart and Adelaide respectively.

Also in the side was Mike Hussey, who found out about his promotion from Justin Langer, the man he replaced in the side. 'Huss, you're in,' Lang told him on Tuesday, Melbourne Cup day, after our long-time opener batted in the nets but couldn't convince either himself, the doctor or the selectors that he'd definitely be okay. Errol Alcott had told Lang that he'd need at least a week before it would be back to normal, and Lang himself had compared the injury to having barbed wire in his chest. (Not that I'm exactly sure he'd know what that feels like!) He also commented, 'After England, we promised as a group that we would increase our intensity and play like a great team. I don't think I can play like a great player over the next five days.'

I've known how good a cricketer Huss can be for a long time, having played a lot of interstate cricket against him since the time we first met at the Bellerive Oval for a Sheffield Shield game in November 1994, when we were both 19. His performances in one-day international cricket over the past nine months have been outstanding, and he is a terrific team-mate, someone who — like Lang — is very passionate about playing for Australia. When I spoke to Huss before the Test, he was so excited he was worried he'd need some sleeping tablets so he'd get some decent rest before he was presented with his first baggy green cap.

That happened in a short on-field ceremony not long before the start of play, with Australia's oldest Test cricketer Bill Brown doing the honours. Chanderpaul sent us in, and our debutant was out almost immediately, but from there we fought back to record an excellent win. The Windies bowlers really tested us on the first day, and at 4–111 and then 5–215 we could have been in trouble. Our final total of 435 was outstanding, and then McGrath and Warne went to work and I was in a position where I had to decide whether or not to enforce the follow-on. I chose not to, reasoning that facing Warney on the final day would be too much for them, and though Shane actually had no impact on the fourth innings, we still raced away to a convincing victory.

Pidge was at his very best in the first innings, during which he took his 100th Test wicket against the West Indies, quite an achievement for a bloke who grew up in the days when Malcolm Marshall and co. were ruling the cricket world. It was interesting to watch both Glenn and Shane lift when Brian Lara came out. It's no coincidence that the great bowlers are at their very best when confronted by champion batsmen, which can be unfortunate for the less accomplished player at the other end, who has to face the same high-class bowling.

I was thrilled with my own contribution. On the first day, I felt as if I got worse as the day went on, something I've rarely experienced, and which I put down to the fact that I hadn't played a long innings for a couple of months. Corey Collymore bowled really well, an awesome line and length, especially in the middle session when he dismissed Clarke and Katich in successive overs, and I felt the runs were well earned. At the media conference after play, the journos asked me how I felt about passing David Boon and Mark Taylor on the all-time Test runscoring list, and joining Greg Chappell and Viv Richards on 24 Test centuries. 'To tell you the truth, it's something I don't think about,' I answered honestly. Until they mentioned it I wasn't aware of these achievements, which to a large degree I put down to the simple fact that by being a Test cricketer for most of the past decade, it is inevitable that I'll amass some decent figures. 'If I was worried about stats I would have known that already,' I continued. 'I wouldn't know how many Tests Viv played and he'll be regarded as a better player than me. I'm just happy with the way things worked out today for us.'

This was the third Test in a row that featured a Matthew Hayden hundred, but whereas at The Oval versus England and in Sydney against the World XI he was more guarded than he has often been in the past, here he was at his domineering best, pulling and driving with great power as he and I added 187 for the second wicket. Scoring runs becomes a habit. I never thought of it being that way until about four or five years ago, when Justin Langer said it to me one day. I think I was struggling a bit, and Lang told me that when he was doing it tough, he'd go back to interstate cricket or club cricket and try to play the same way he would in a Test match — just scoring runs until it became a habit. Haydos is back in that vogue now, and so am I.

Sure, the Windies' fielding fell away, there were probably too many cheap singles about, and I might have been a bit fortunate, especially when I was caught at second slip off a no-ball. But I was thrilled by the way we showed them no mercy, and by stumps on day three we were in an unassailable position, 508 runs in front with two days left to bowl the Windies out. In the end, we only needed 49 overs, even though Pidge and Warney didn't take a wicket between them. Nathan Bracken took four wickets, and bowled very well, but for me the highlight was the way Brett Lee bowled, finishing with 5–30, his first five-wicket haul in a Test match since November 2001. The only downer was the dislocated shoulder suffered by Shane Watson as he dived to stop an on-drive from Sarwan. Indications are that Watto could be out for a couple of months; the contrast between his joy when he had Gayle caught in the fashion of an overhead AFL mark by Warney at slip and his pain later, as he realised that he'd sustained a serious injury, was stark.

One of the crazier questions I copped after the Test was the one asking if I worried about complacency affecting the team for the second Test. 'If complacency crept into this team after what a lot of the guys have been through in the last few months I'd be very disappointed,' I shot back. 'We've still got areas to work on and we've worked harder than we ever have coming in to this series.'

Also, a bit strangely given we've just dominated a Test match, there are several conundrums for the selectors to solve. Lang will definitely come back into the team if his rib is right; if not, Mike Hussey will get another cap. That one is clearcut (with it seeming likely that Lang won't be right), but Watto's injury is a real setback for the team as well as himself, because there aren't too many candidates for the allrounder role that we've identified as being so important to the team balance. The alternatives are to play Andrew Symonds, who can definitely serve as the fifth bowler, or to keep Gilly at six and have five bowlers batting from seven to 11, as we did in the Caribbean in 2003 (this is the strategy Allan Border is pushing in the papers), or to go back to what we did in England when we played a top six that didn't include a genuine fifth bowler. That third option is definitely my least favoured preference. Whatever path we take, there's a fair chance Stuart MacGill will play. The middle-order batsmen remain under pressure.

I MUST ADMIT THAT this Test was my most satisfying to date as captain, not because of the runs I scored — but because of the way Brett Lee bowled in the second innings.

Before the West Indies' first innings, Brett had watched Corey Collymore bowl beautifully — excellent line and length, good movement off the seam, four top-order wickets (Hayden, Clarke, Katich and Gilchrist). When they began their reply, I said to Brett, 'How do you want to start? What sort of field do you want?'

He told me he was going to bowl exactly the same way Collymore had. I stared at him with a bemused look on my face and thought, 'Collymore bowls at 125k, you bowl at 150. You can't bowl that way.' But Brett had seen someone else have some success with a certain style, and thought that was the way to go. Glenn McGrath was bowling as well as he always does, and that probably influenced him as well.

'I want two slips, a gully, point, cover, mid-off, no bat-pad, a mid-wicket,' he said. 'That's how I want to start.'

'Mate, you can't do that,' I replied. But he was determined. When Brian Lara came in at 2–74, Brett was wicketless, and when he came back on to bowl the great batsman handled him pretty easily. Last two balls of the third over of this new spell, Lara hit him through mid-wicket for two and then pulled him well in front of square for four, and when I went up to Bing he muttered, 'Take me off. I'm bowling rubbish. Just take me off.'

Third ball of his next over, with no addition to the score, he got Lara lbw, but it was that short exchange at the end of the previous over that revealed his mindset. It was his only wicket of the innings, and afterwards I sat down with him, just him and me, and said, 'Look, we've got to do something about this; we've got to turn your whole thought process around.'

We talked about what his strengths were as a bowler, and what things he was most concerned about. His best assets were his speed and the fact that he could swing a new ball at pace. He was worried, though, that if he bowled fast he'd go for too many runs. Throughout his career, he has been criticised for being wild and expensive, but as I pointed out, part of that was simply a by-product of being quick. The slip cordon was less likely to stop an edge that bounced in front of them, while the man at fine leg had no time to get the boundary to stop an inside edge or a fine leg-glance. With a slightly slower bowler, like Glenn McGrath, they'd be singles. With Bing, they're four.

'You tell me what field you want so you can bowl to your strengths,' I said, 'and then I want you to run in and bowl the way you know you can.'

I was quickly learning that part of his problem was a confidence thing. Too many people had been offering him too much advice, to the point that he didn't quite know who to please or how to please them. He certainly wasn't satisfying himself as a bowler, despite all the effort he was putting in, or making the impact he and the team needed. He had made his name as a *quick* bowler. I was confident that direction was what he required, and also that he needed to know that we had faith in him. He said he wanted more fielders on the offside, that he didn't need three slips, or a bat-pad; he'd rather a man at point and one at square leg, to keep the runs down. I'd probably been as guilty as anyone of wanting to have people up for catches, but now I saw where he was coming from. In one-day cricket, Bing bowls with just two slips and no bat-pad, but he is still a dangerous attacking bowler who often takes wickets in his opening spell. He really did want to bowl 'full on', and get the ball to swing, and in the Windies' second innings he went and bowled fast and fantastic with that 'defensive' field. It was as if he was a different cricketer. Afterwards, as I reflected on our conversation, I had this wonderful gut feeling that in recognising he was struggling and getting my response to his problems right, I'd done the sort of thing a good captain should do.

Tuesday, November 15

THE SELECTORS EVENTUALLY DECIDED to make two changes for the second Test, with Simon Katich being replaced by Brad Hodge and Andrew Symonds coming in for Shane Watson. Hodge promptly celebrated his selection by scoring a run-a-ball 177 against the West Indians in a tour game at the Junction Oval in Melbourne, and is an almost certain starter in Hobart, where the choice of 12th man will come down to Symonds, Bracken or MacGill. I'm pushing for Symmo to play, and unless the Bellerive Oval wicket is different from what I've come to expect, I think we should go with the two spinners. Shane has enjoyed some success here in the past, and there is no reason why Stuey shouldn't join him — except for the fact that Bracks bowled so well in Brisbane that it's almost unfair to leave him out. At least this was what we were thinking until Warney revealed today that his back is playing up. Knowing the bloke's toughness, I'm sure he'll be right to play, but the talk is that as a precaution we're going to bring in another player as cover. At this point, it hasn't been decided who that potential replacement might be.

Incredibly, if Shane and Stuart do both play, it will be only the second time they have played as a duet in the same Test, that game being in Australia but away from the Sydney Cricket Ground. The other occasion was Stuey's Test debut, against South

Africa in Adelaide in early 1998, a match that ended in a draw with Warney taking three wickets and Stuey five. This is also the first time the West Indies will play a Test match in Tasmania, and the first time I have captained Australia in Tassie.

I can only hope this game goes better than my early Tests in my home state. I started by making 4 against New Zealand in my only innings in 1997–98, and then made a pair against Pakistan two years later. In 2001–02, again versus the Black Caps, I made 157 not out, thus boosting my career Test average on the ground from 1.33 to 53.67, but more importantly convincing my mum that she wasn't a total jinx whenever she came to watch me bat! Then in 2003, in my first year as one-day captain, we earned a really good one-day result down here, against England, when Damien Martyn scored a not out hundred and Shane Watson bowled us to a seven-run victory. Two more one-day victories followed, against Zimbabwe and Pakistan, but my highest ODI score at Bellerive is still only 37.

Unfortunately, the opportunities for me to come back to Tassie from my new home in Sydney are now few and far between. As a professional cricketer, I do an enormous amount of travelling, and I'm the kind of person who — when I do get some time off — would rather stay at home and take it easy. I was at Launceston for my sister's wedding last November, but didn't return there until Cricket Australia staged a special 'club cricket weekend' a month ago, when I made a pilgrimage back to Mowbray. However, I know a lot of family and friends are making the drive down to Bellerive for the Test, which will make it a really special experience for me.

I have always found that playing for Australia in Tasmania is a different experience from that of the 'mainland' guys when they appear in a Test in their home city. They can sleep in their own bed and just drive to the ground each day. I always lived in Launceston and all the big games were in Hobart, so it was almost like every match was an 'away' game. Living in Sydney and coming back to play at Hobart is really not that much different — it's just a two-hour flight rather than a two-hour drive. Last season's Sydney Test was the first time I was able to go home after stumps each day to relax.

IN MY MIND, THE only real question about Brad Hodge's involvement in this upcoming Test is whether he will bat at four or five, and frankly I'm not sure which way to go. Pup has struggled since moving up the order after Damien Martyn was dropped, and Brad has been the regular No. 4 for Victoria for the past few years, but I'm not sure I'll be sending the right signals to Pup if I 'demote' him down the order. Putting myself in his position, I know I'd want to stay put and fight for my place from there. We initially moved him up because we saw him as a player who would hold down the spot for the next few years, and I still think he can do the job. It's my decision, but I will talk to both men and the selectors before the names are written in the scorebook.

Symmo's selection completes something of a test of character for him, given what occurred when he was suspended in England. As I reiterated when asked about it this week, at the time I did what I had to do as captain, because it was something that had to be sorted out quickly. I felt then and still feel now that he let me and the team down, but he has been fantastic since then, both as a bloke and player, and has plenty to offer. We all know from what he has done in domestic cricket and one-day internationals just how good a cricketer he can be, and one of the frustrations of that incident was that he is a bloke who always brings a positive vibe to the dressing-room, a guy with the happy knack of being able to say the right thing, raise a laugh when it's needed and bring a sense a reality to a tense or overwrought dressing-room. I'll be backing him all the way.

Australia v West Indies Test series

Second Test (November 17–21) at Hobart: West Indies 149 (CH Gayle 56; GD McGrath 4–31) and 334 (BC Lara 45, DJJ Bravo 113, D Ramdin 71; SK Warne 4–112) lost to Australia 406 (ML Hayden 110, MEK Hussey 137, BJ Hodge 60) and 1–78 (ML Hayden 46) by nine wickets

FOR THREE DAYS, THE second Test appeared to be heading for another comfortable Australian victory, but then two cricketers most Australian cricket fans could hardly have been familiar with — allrounder Dwayne Bravo and wicketkeeper Denesh Ramdin, men playing in their eighth and fourth Tests respectively — built a second-inning seventh-wicket partnership of 182 and the game went into a fifth day when few observers expected it to. Warney's effort in the second innings, bowling 39 overs and taking four wickets despite his crook back, was fantastic, while Pidge bowled 25 overs for just 29 runs, so you could never say Bravo and Ramdin did it easy even if the wicket was pretty flat. Our winning margin was decisive, but we leave Hobart feeling as if we've been involved in a contest, which is never a bad thing.

At stumps on day three, with the Windies 4–82 in the second dig and still trailing by 175 runs, it seemed that only a great innings by Brian Lara, who was 16 not out, could prevent us winning by an innings and plenty. Instead it was Bravo, who'd been left out in Brisbane, who made a real impression by batting for nearly five hours as he completed his first Test century. Ramdin had batted well in the first innings at the Gabba, and later in that game had announced that the fourth innings target of 509 was not impossible, and that sort of positive attitude, allied to the batting skill he and Bravo showed here, suggests the Windies might be moving in the right direction.

The Test had started with everyone buoyant after Australia had qualified for football's 2006 World Cup, after beating Uruguay in a penalty shootout in Sydney. Brian Lara also seemed to be in a chirpy mood following Trinidad and Tobago's defeat of Bahrain, which got them to Germany 2006 as well, though his good humour would have been tempered when he was given out, lbw to Brett Lee, for just 13. Bing bowled beautifully to him, following up his second-innings effort at the Gabba with some very quick and intelligent overs. After McGrath, Lee and MacGill shared the first-innings wickets, our reply was dominated by Matthew Hayden's 24th Test hundred (and fourth in his last four Tests) and Mike Hussey's first. It's always terrific to see a 'rookie' succeed, and we all revelled in Huss' exuberant celebrations when he reached three figures. Their 231-run partnership occupied only 56.2 overs, on a pitch on which our opponents had been dismissed for 149, and at times during the second afternoon they were scoring at better than a run a ball. Huss had been dismissed twice at the Gabba playing pull shots, and with Lang certain to return to the team for the third Test, another failure here would almost certainly have cost him his place.

The second day was interrupted by rain, with the entire opening session lost, but Huss had waited 176 first-class matches before he made his Test debut, so a couple more hours before his maiden Test ton was hardly going to worry him. Nor did the way he was dismissed in Brisbane stop him playing his hook and pull shots when the Windies' quicks tested his resolve. It was as if he was releasing a decade's worth of emotion after he leg-glanced Fidel Edwards to reach three figures. You'd have to go a long way to find a bloke more addicted to the game than Mike Hussey, whom Symmo has christened 'Mr Cricket'. Now that he's got himself a Test-match century, he might be very hard to shift.

As for Matty Hayden, he looks to be getting back to his absolute best, a mix between the more cautious approach he used at the Oval and against the World XI, and the bludgeoning buccaneer of days gone by. Personally, I like the game plan he adopted in this innings, but maybe he'd like to be more belligerent. 'I'm still swimming between the flags at this stage,' he explained to the media scrum, as if his batting resurgence is still a work in progress. The quality of our openers' batting was highlighted by what occurred during the rest of the innings, in which only Brad Hodge — who looked sensational as he crafted 60 on his Test debut — got past 20. Andrew Symonds' return to the batting crease in Test cricket lasted two minutes longer than it should have, after the TV umpire pressed the wrong button when ruling on a run-out decision. Symmo was clearly out, one of those situations where the on-field ump went to the video just to make sure, and he was already halfway to the pavilion when the green light started shining. Anger turned to bemusement and then frustration as he wandered back to the middle, only for the officials to get together and set things right.

I had been 17 not out at stumps on day two, play resumed early the next morning to make up for time lost, and straightaway I was bowled off the inside edge by Edwards. Mum and Dad had once again made the long drive south, but they were still in the queue outside the ground, unaware that we were starting early, when I was dismissed. The jinx had struck again! They had made plans to stay over between the second and third days, and we had dinner together that night, and I reckon I must have said half a dozen times that Mum is banned from all future matches. Problem is, unless I suffer an injury between now and then, the Sydney Test in the first week of January will be my 100th Test, and my family has already made plans to fly up for the occasion.

Thursday, November 24

ONE OF THE HARDEST parts of being Australian captain is when it comes to informing players that they have missed out on a game or, much worse, been dropped from the squad. There is no easy way to do it, not least because you've suffered the pain yourself in the past, so you know how much it hurts. I don't think anybody else — not even the media guys who travel with the team and see us every day — really understands what it's like to be left out of the Australian team. Suddenly, you're divorced from mates you've been spending so much time with; it's like being stopped from seeing your family, with no indication of when you might be with them again. You haven't just been dropped from a cricket team. Your whole lifestyle has been taken from you.

It was my job, after the Hobart Test, to tell Michael Clarke that he would not be in the team for the third Test. Pup and I have spent a lot of time chatting about life and cricket since he first came into the team (one-dayers in 2003, Tests the following year), and I knew he would have wanted me to be the one to tell him he was out, so I broke the news to him before the selectors explained why the decision had been made. Pup and I then had a good talk about his new situation before he left the dressing-room to fly back to Sydney. I don't mind admitting that I didn't like the idea of leaving Pup out, because I know he will play a lot more Test cricket for Australia, but with Justin Langer sure to be right for Adelaide and Michael Hussey and Brad Hodge having performed so impressively, I am also well aware that the selectors had no alternative.

I told Pup that plenty of us have been in the same situation. I was dropped from the Test team in 1996 and 1998, and I think only Adam Gilchrist of the senior players in the current team hasn't been demoted at some stage of their careers. And Gilly, of course, had to bide his time while Ian Healy was everyone's first choice as Australian keeper. We can only hope that being dropped has the same effect on Pup as it did on most of us, and that he comes back a better player as a result of the experience. The main thing I learned from my time in the 'wilderness' was that you can't go back to interstate cricket with the sole objective of immediately scoring a stack of runs so you can get back in the Test team as quickly as possible. Pup's batting doesn't need a complete overhaul, but he does need to accept that things aren't right, think about his game, listen to the right people, work hard to get his technique and mental approach to batting right, and *then* set out to score so many runs that when the next opportunity comes up, the case for his re-selection is irresistible.

In a way, this time was also difficult for Mike Hussey. He had just experienced the greatest game of his life to date — making his first Test hundred, making a major contribution to the winning of a Test match for Australia, securing the man-of-the-match award, being part of the team that won The Frank Worrell Trophy — but when I told him that he was still in the team, he suffered the mixed emotions of knowing that while he was staying in the squad, a good mate was not. It was tough for all of us, but what we have to do is remember that once the day is over we have to move on. Part of my job is to do my best to make sure the mood within the squad remains positive.

The extent of the change that's happening in the side right now is not something we've seen in recent years. Brad Hodge was the seventh man to make his Test debut since I became captain in 2004; in Steve Waugh's five years as skipper he saw seven men make their first Test appearance. So far, the evidence from this summer is that there are a number of players in Australian cricket who are good enough to come in and succeed straightaway. What I do know is that there is certainly a different feeling around the place, and right at the moment probably a bit of a different dynamic as well.

PEOPLE HAVE SUGGESTED TO me that it must be disappointing to be involved in some one-sided Test matches after all the excitement of the Ashes series. To be honest, I would much rather win games in the way we have over the past couple of weeks than suffer thrilling but painful losses! We do know that come next month we'll be facing a bigger challenge from stronger opponents in South Africa. So far this season we certainly haven't been challenged for the extended periods of time that we were in England, but the quality of our training continues to be fantastic. I'm confident we'll be as well prepared as possible when Graeme Smith and his team land in Australia.

Michael Clarke does stay in the one-day squad for our short tour of New Zealand in early December, for the Chappell–Hadlee Trophy. Brad Hodge, who is yet to play an ODI, has also been included, as has Mick Lewis, the Victorian medium-pacer, who will tour in place of Glenn McGrath, who will be rested. We also wanted to give Gilly a break before the South Africa Test series that starts in mid-December, but unfortunately Cricket Australia — who were keen that we send at least close to a full-strength side — wouldn't let that happen. Shane Watson, James Hopes and Damien Martyn are all injured, but Stuart Clark, Cameron White and Nathan Bracken retain the places they held during the Super Series one-dayers, while Brad Hogg returns having recovered from the knee injury that forced him to miss those matches.

Wednesday, November 30

Australia v West Indies Test series

Third Test (November 25–29) at Adelaide: West Indies 405 (BC Lara 226) and 204 (RR Sarwan 62, DJJ Bravo 64; SK Warne 6–80) lost to Australia 428 (JL Langer 99, ML Hayden 47, RT Ponting 56, MEK Hussey 133*; DJJ Bravo 6–84) and 3–182 (ML Hayden 87*) by seven wickets

THIS WAS A STRANGE Test match in the sense that we won by seven wickets to seal the series 3–0, yet the lead story was definitely not about us, how we played or what we'd achieved. Rather, it became Brian Lara's Test, most likely his last in Australia, because during his superb first-innings 226 he became Test cricket's leading run-getter. He entered on day one to a standing ovation from the Adelaide members, was lucky to survive a very tight lbw shout when facing Andrew Symonds' first ball (which was a little ironic given Brian had been the victim of a couple of dodgy decisions in the previous two Tests), but once he got past around 40 he was at his regal best. Even bowlers as great as McGrath and Warne didn't look like getting him out, as he played some fantastic shots that less gifted batsmen wouldn't try because they are too risky. He made them look commonplace. He started day two needing another 12 runs to pass Allan Border's old record, and he reached that landmark with an astonishing shot, stepping in front of stumps to half-glance, half-sweep Pidge to deep fine leg.

I've always said that Sachin Tendulkar is the best batsman I've played against, because when he is at his finest you just don't feel like you're going to get him out. Brian is close to him, a truly brilliant player. The difference between them, I reckon, is that the way the man from Trinidad plays, you often feel like you're a chance to dismiss him, particularly early on. But when he is at his best, he can manipulate the fields you set and seemingly hit any ball wherever he wants to. Pitch a ball in a certain spot and he'll put it through a gap; block that spot and bowl the same ball, and he'll work it through another gap somewhere else. This is especially true against the spinners, against whom he can be phenomenal.

We'd been waiting for a big innings from him. He's too great a player to miss out six innings out of six, and Adelaide — with its short boundaries square of the wicket and not too much bounce in the wicket — is a perfect ground for him. I remembered somewhat grimly his last Test there, in 2000–01, when he scratched around for his first 60 balls for maybe 15 runs, having hardly scored a run so far in the series. Then I ran past him, and had a snipe at him. 'What are you doing? Get on with it,' I asked and suggested, hoping he might go for an illogical shot and get himself out. From that moment, he hit everything in the middle of the bat, ended up with 182, and after the game he made a point of thanking me. I told him I'd never have a go at him on the field again and I never have. He explained that every time he goes out to bat, the only thing he focuses on is facing the first 60 balls of his innings. It doesn't matter how many runs he gets, that's his time for getting his eye in. My advice had come just when he was ready to go on the attack.

I've never tried to copy that game plan, but I've never forgotten it either, because it seems eminently sensible to me. This time Brian was 25 after 60 balls. His fifty came up from 91 balls, the 100 from 144, the 200 from 261. When he was dismissed for 226, he'd scored almost 60 per cent of his team's runs.

IN REPLY, WE STARTED okay, but at 8–295 we were facing a significant first-innings deficit. But then the man now known to the public as well as the team as Mr Cricket found a willing ally in Stuart MacGill. Huss was 35 when Stuey joined him in the middle, and the pair added 93 before the leggie was dismissed for 22. Huss had just hit a six and a single to go to 99, but there was a sort of surreal calm in the dressing-room as Glenn McGrath walked out to join him. Pidge has helped a number of batsmen to notable landmarks over the years, and it seemed so unlikely that he'd fail this time, especially given that Stuey was out from the last ball of an over. Sure enough, five balls later Huss swung Wavell Hinds away for the four that brought up his second Test hundred. The last-wicket stand eventually amounted to 40, and we finished with a first-innings advantage of 23.

Now, Andrew Symonds is calling Huss the 'the left-handed Bradman'. As we watched this magnificent knock, Symmo was in the viewing area mimicking Mr Cricket's style, exclaiming admirably, 'Look at that front elbow (Symmo 'follows through' with his hand) … and the head, right over the ball.' He also took us back to the Brisbane Test, when Huss was out trying to pull short balls in both innings. He did that deliberately, Symmo reckons, so the Windies bowlers would keep bouncing him, and certainly since the Gabba I don't think Mr Cricket has miscued even one pull shot. Afterwards, Huss seemed pretty embarrassed as Symmo continued to lavish accolades on him, reflecting the fact that he's a pretty shy sort of bloke, who's trying to take his new-found fame and freakish batting form in his stride.

These little exchanges are also an example of the positive vibe that Symmo brings to our dressing-room. It was one of the reasons why I wanted him in the World Cup squad back in 2003, when maybe his numbers didn't demand that he be picked but I knew that he'd play an important role (which, of course, he subsequently did, both as a cricketer and a team-mate). He's a guy who works hard on his game, and also brings a sense of fun to what we do, and he does it simply by being himself. While being a good fella will never be enough on its own to get anyone in the Australian Test team, the fact that Symmo brings these qualities means that his true value cannot be measured just by the runs he scores, the wickets he takes or the brilliance he so often displays in the field.

The other thing I admire about Symmo is that we always get the same bloke regardless of how he's going, or how the team's going. This is actually a pretty rare quality, especially in a naturally outgoing person, but it's so important when you're working in a team environment. I can think of some excellent Test cricketers of recent times who were the funniest blokes in the world when things were going great, but when the runs or wickets weren't coming they'd sit in the corner and wouldn't say a word.

Dwayne Bravo had followed up his Hobart hundred by bowling extremely well in our first innings, the highlight being a brilliant caught-and-bowled that dismissed Shane Warne. Then, after Warney and Bing reduced the Windies to 7–106, he and Denesh Ramdin were at it again, holding us up for 16 overs while they added 54. Bravo finished with 64, having done enough to suggest the Windies might have found themselves a genuine allrounder, and his effort meant we were left with a tricky 182 to get to sweep the series. We got there for the loss of three wickets, but only after a tense period of play at the start of the final day, when a couple of quick breakthroughs might have made it interesting. Most certainly, the Windies team we beat here was a much tougher side than the one we handled comfortably three weeks ago at the Gabba.

Brian Lara's final Test innings in Australia ended in stunning fashion when he was 17, out to a brilliant reflex grab by Matt Hayden at slip. Warney was bowling around the wicket, without a man at point and cover, and aiming at the bowlers' footmarks outside the great left-hander's off stump. He wanted Brian to try to square drive him through the gap, and hopefully get a catch to the keeper, slip or maybe the fieldsman at backward point. Straightaway, Brian got him though the gap for a four and a three; otherwise he just used his pad or pushed the ball away. To me, fielding close in on the offside, this strategy wasn't working, so I went up to Shane and said, 'Warney, are you sure this is right?'

'Yep, yep, it's right,' he replied. 'Leave it, leave it, leave it.'

First ball of the next over, Lara drove wide of mid-off for two runs. The next was played defensively, the third was padded away. Then, fourth ball, Lara went for the big slashing drive. I reckon Haydos was entitled to duck for cover, but instead he held his ground, thrust his left hand towards the ball and held on, one of the best catches I've ever 'seen'. I put seen in inverted commas because when Brian swung his bat I covered up and could only guess from the noise that the ball had come off the edge of the bat. It all happened so quickly; by the time I'd regained my balance Haydos had pocketed the bullet as it sped past him, and Lara was on his way. It might not have been as spectacular as a diving outfield catch that comes after a 30-metre run, but it was better. A real cricketer's catch.

Warney's bowling in the second innings was superb, right up there with his absolute best. His bad back wasn't helping him, but he spun the ball consistently and bowled for much of the day, finishing with 6–80 after he took his first five wickets on a flat deck for just 43 runs. He was now within just one of equalling Dennis Lillee's record of 85 wickets in a calendar year.

Warney's only problem came when he was reported but later cleared of a charge of dissent. Some people have started murmuring that we are appealing too much, but I don't agree with that. If you've got two quality spinners bowling a lot of overs there are going to be a lot of appeals, and in Warne and MacGill we've got two of the very best. Inevitably, the teams who are never accused of over-appealing are the ones who rely on their quick bowlers, who haven't got a decent spinner in their side.

It had been a controversial series in regard to umpiring decisions, and at the post-Test media conference I was asked the same questions about the use of technology to help the umpires that I'd been asked during the Super Series. I thought the major problem with the umps could be that they are just overworked. I know the ICC are talking about increasing the number of elite umpires, but at the moment there are only seven umps on the panel and three of them — Simon Taufel, Darrell Hair and Daryl Harper — are Australian and therefore can't stand in our matches. No wonder we see the same blokes all the time!

MEANWHILE, NEWS CAME FROM Sydney that Michael Clarke had scored 201 not out for New South Wales in a Pura Cup match against Queensland. I knew Pup wouldn't be down for long, but with Michael Hussey and Brad Hodge looking the goods, there might not be a vacancy in the Test team for a while.

The press boys were into me about Symmo's future, but as I've said many times, I love the balance he brings to the team make-up and that certain vibe he adds to the dressing-room. I also can't see why — given he can be so destructive a batsman in one-day cricket — he can't be equally effective in a Test match. Often, it can take just one innings to blast away the self-doubt. I remember how I used to fight myself when I first started, when I didn't really know how to make runs in Test cricket. Times have changed for me, and I'm hoping they will change for Andrew Symonds, too.

Part III

The Chappell–Hadlee Trophy

Australia v New Zealand
December 2005

Thursday, December 1

THE IDEA BEHIND THE Chappell–Hadlee Trophy, an annual one-day series between neighbours and traditional rivals, is a good one, the only problem being how best to fit it into an already crowded program. This year's timing, between two Test series (against the West Indies and South Africa) is hardly ideal — imagine if they schedule it for the same time in 2006–07, in the middle of the Ashes series! — but really not as big a bogey as it might have been a few years back, when as a team we struggled to adjust from Test cricket to one-day internationals, and vice versa. I remember there was a stage when we could never win the opening one-dayer of the Australian season, when it came immediately after a Test series that ended with the back-to-back Melbourne and Sydney Tests over the Christmas–New Year period.

The key is to be able to immediately switch into one-day mode in *everything* you do. Preparation has to be about repeating what you'll be doing out in the middle, so in the nets you want to be hitting over the top, maybe even charging the bowling, not letting the ball go. Our coaches need to be up to speed with what our opponents have been doing; it's not a case of waiting and learning from the first couple of games what their strengths and weakness might be. It is also a little easier to make the adjustment these days because, at least with the batting, the run-rates in Tests have increased to a point where there is not as much difference between the two forms of the game as there once was.

The timing of this year's Chappell–Hadlee matches is probably not perfect for the Black Caps either, because their leader, Stephen Fleming, will be missing from at least the first two games, as he recovers from recent facial surgery, and their best quick bowler, Shane Bond, is also unlikely to play. Daniel Vettori will be captain of a side that will also feature Chris Cairns, and there are indications that the games might have a bit of an edge to them, mainly because the locals remember the one-dayers from our tour of late last season, when Brett Lee bowled very, very quickly at different times and also caused some consternation with the occasional accidental beamer as he strove for high speed.

With the 2007 World Cup just a little more than a year away, matches such as these are important for newcomers to the Australian one-day squad such as Brad Hodge, Mick Lewis, Stuart Clark and Cameron White; for the rest of us, the matches have value simply because we are wearing the Aussie colours. It has been ingrained in us all over the past 15 or 20 years that every game matters, that we have to always do our best for ourselves, our colleagues and for Australian cricket. Last year's inaugural Chappell-Hadlee series ended square, one-all, with the third game in Brisbane washed out. Those games were played almost immediately after we'd beaten New Zealand decisively in two Test matches, and the way they came back at us underlined just how competitive the Black Caps always are in the limited-over game. But for all their tenacity, if we play up to the form we showed in the one-dayers against the World XI, I'm sure we can win this time. We'd certainly like to get our hands on that new trophy.

Sunday, December 4

Chappell–Hadlee Trophy 2005–06

Game One (December 3) at Auckland: Australia 8–252 (50 overs: SM Katich 54, RT Ponting 63, A Symonds 44) defeated New Zealand 105 (27.4 overs: B Lee 3–5, SR Clark 3–19) by 147 runs

THE DAY BEFORE THE first ODI of this short tour, we learned that the ICC had decided to increase the number of umpires on their elite panel, from seven to nine or 10. I couldn't help thinking, 'About time!' The decision came at around the same time the West Indies Cricket Board lodged an official complaint with the ICC about the quality of umpiring in the just completed series in Australia.

The danger, I guess, is that the new umps won't be up to standard, but I'm confident that across the cricket world there are at least 10 blokes who can do a good job. ICC chief executive Malcolm Speed was quoted as saying that 'cricket is the hardest game to umpire', so slightly reducing the workload of the blokes currently on the panel can't be a bad thing.

The first game here was free of major umpiring controversies, but as has become typical of one-day games in New Zealand there was some crowd trouble, as a few spectators became bored with a one-sided game and decided to amuse themselves. The main feature of the cricket was some fantastic bowling from Brett Lee, who finished with the unbelievable figures of 3–5 from six overs. Nathan Bracken and Stuart Clark also bowled superbly, reducing the home side to 6–33 after 12-and-a-half overs, and what we had thought was a very competitive total quickly became a colossal one.

Brett had a tailwind behind him, and he often clocked more than 150k as he made good batsmen jump and dive. When we batted, Chris Cairns got a few to fly, so they knew it was a dodgy wicket, and while I don't think their batsmen were scared, they were nonplussed and maybe a couple of them will be watching the replays of their dismissals a little grimly as they see what Bing's speed did to their techniques. Their supersub, James Marshall, came in at No. 5 to do a rescue job, but immediately he lost sight of a quick, straight ball and was lbw as he tried to duck out of the way. Hamish Marshall was bowled off the inside edge, while Craig McMillan was sharply caught at second slip by Mr Cricket, who just can't seem to keep himself out of the game at the moment.

Tuesday, December 9

Chappell–Hadlee Trophy 2005–06
Game Two (December 7) at Wellington: Australia 5–322 (50 overs: A Symonds 156, MJ Clarke 82*) defeated New Zealand 320 (49.5 overs: L Vincent 71, CL Cairns 60, JDP Oram 41, BB McCullum 48; ML Lewis 3–56) by two runs

GAME ONE MIGHT HAVE been one of our most decisive wins of recent times, but its sequel was totally different, a thriller that featured 642 runs and went down to the fifth ball of the 100th over. It was a contest that featured an explosive display from Andrew Symonds, with Michael Clarke offering strong support (their 220-run partnership was an Australian record for the fifth wicket, and just three short of the world record), a clever spin-bowling exhibition from Brad Hogg, some spectacular hitting from Chris Cairns, and finally some nerveless bowling and fielding from Mick Lewis, who was given the responsibility for the final over when New Zealand needed six to win with two wickets in hand. Mick has shown for Victoria in the ING Cup back home that he is excellent 'finisher', and he came through here by conceding only three runs from his first five balls of that last over. Then he put his own exclamation mark on the night by completing the run out of Kyle Mills that got us home.

The weather in Wellington in the lead-up to this game had not been good, to the point that for a while we weren't sure if there'd be any game at all. Meanwhile, as we were practising indoors, our manager, Steve Bernard, was seeking and gaining assurances from the authorities that there'd be no repeat of the crowd disruptions that marred the first one-dayer. One measure they adopted, to keep the first three rows of seats around the ground unoccupied, would have cost them a dollar or two, but I must confess to not being too concerned about that. I don't think I've ever been on a New Zealand tour where spectator trouble hasn't become an issue during the one-day matches. The best form of crowd control was Symmo's batting, which was so unique and dynamic I think everyone was spellbound. His first 50 took 70 balls, the second 39, the third 16 — all up, 156 from 127 balls, with 12 fours and eight sixes. Pup scored 82 from 77 balls and looked pedestrian.

Most of the acrimony among the Kiwi fans had been directed at Bing, whose bowling fortunes did a total somersault in the space of four days. Having conceded five runs in six overs at Eden Park, he conceded 85 in 10 at Wellington, as the New Zealand opener Lou Vincent went after him during his first spell, and then Brendon McCullum and Daniel Vettori hit the Kiwis back into the game by taking 18 runs off Bing's nine-ball final over, the 49th of the innings, a shocker that included two no-balls and a wide. Part of the problem was that from around halfway through the innings the field was saturated by the heavy evening dew, but we were ragged as the game reached its climax, even getting the number of fieldsmen inside the circle wrong in the second-last over. However, Pup's direct hit from point to run out McCullum off the third ball of the last over was slick and highly professional, and then Mick was bang on target two balls in a row and we managed to scrape home. Afterwards, Bing was really struggling with his breathing, a recurrence of the nasal problem that he thought he'd fixed earlier in the year, before the Ashes tour, and it was decided he'd return home to get the problem sorted out. Queenslander left-armer Mitchell Johnson has been called over as his replacement.

Monday, December 12

Chappell–Hadlee Trophy 2005–06

Game Three (December 10) at Christchurch: Australia 7–331 (50 overs: RT Ponting 75, BJ Hodge 59, MJ Clarke 71, MEK Hussey 88*; CS Martin 3–65) lost to New Zealand 8–332 (49 overs: SB Styris 101, BB McCullum 50*, SR Clark 4–55) by two wickets

BEFORE GAME THREE, THE squad for the first Test against South Africa was announced, and it was a case of one Clark in and the other Clarke out. Stuart Clark was included as the fourth fast man in the squad for the game at the WACA, with the batting remaining as it was for the third West Indies Test. Twenty-four hours after this announcement, Stuart took his first four-for in ODI cricket, in his fourth game, and Brad Hodge then continued his rise in international cricket by scoring his first ODI half-century.

These landmarks both occurred in another close, remarkably high-scoring affair that the Black Caps won by two wickets. This time, Mike Hussey was our batting star, slamming an unbeaten 88 from 56 deliveries (which kicked his career ODI batting average up to an amazing 151), but a Scott Styris century and a slogging 50 from 25 balls from McCullum got them home with an over in hand.

Mr Cricket just continues to amaze us. He has always had a sound technique, but early in his career he built a reputation as an opening batsman who needed all day to score a hundred, who sometimes seemed to struggle to hit the ball off the square. Not surprisingly then, for a few seasons he struggled as an opener in limited-overs cricket, but then he reinvented himself as a middle-order batsman with the ability to finish off an innings or timing a run-chase to the minute. Now, he's at a different level again, able to play that role but also hit the ball as hard and as far as anyone around. It's amazing what confidence can do for you! Once you've achieved something a couple of times, you know in your heart that you can do it, and then there's no stopping you.

There was a bit of that in New Zealand's total of 8–332, coming as it did so soon after their effort in Wellington. Their total was a new world record for the highest successful run-chase in the history of one-day international cricket, beating the 7–330 (pursuing a target of 327) we'd made against South Africa at Port Elizabeth in 2002. The Black Caps had needed 74 to win with just seven overs remaining and two wickets in hand, but even though the ground was tiny and quick scoring had been the order of the day and night, we should have stopped them.

TWO DAYS AFTER THAT dramatic game, Cricket Australia made what I believe will be one of the more significant announcements of the summer. Troy Cooley, my mate from the Mowbray Cricket Club who made such a name for himself as England's bowling coach during their Ashes win, will be finishing up with the Poms next May, after three years in that job, so he can return home and become Australia's bowling coach. The review Cricket Australia instigated at the start of this season identified the appointment of a bowling coach as a priority. I give full credit to them for one, acknowledging this, and two, signing up one of the best in the business. Troy has worked with Rod Marsh for a number of years, and Rod hasn't got a bad word to say about him.

I've known Troy, who's nine years older than me, since I was just a boy. He was one of the Mowbray blokes who took me under his wing, and I played a lot of club cricket with him. In 1993, we played some Shield cricket together, and two years later we toured Zimbabwe with the Tassie team. I have enormous respect for his knowledge of the game, and especially his understanding of bowling actions and bowling techniques and his ability to pass that expertise on to the bowlers in his care. It's exciting to think that we'll be working *with* him, rather than against him, and the fact that he has a detailed knowledge of the England players, especially their bowlers, can only be to our advantage.

Part IV

Winning the Moments that Matter

Australia v South Africa
December 2005

Wednesday, December 14

TEST SERIES AGAINST SOUTH Africa are invariably among the most competitive and enjoyable we play. The South Africans are proud, tough cricketers who approach the game in a similar way to how we go about things. For me, the Ashes will always be the No. 1 cricket contest involving Australia. India in India is also special, but even though Sourav Ganguly's team managed to square the series in Australia in 2003–04, traditionally these matches have not always been so tight. In contrast, in my time Australia v South Africa series, whether home or away, have always had an edge to them and the expectation is that 2005–06 will be no different.

While we were in New Zealand, former South African spinner Pat Symcox was talking up the coming confrontation. 'There are going to be a lot of harsh things said out in the middle,' he was quoted in the News Limited papers. 'I don't think either side is going to give an inch. South Africa will stand up to the Aussies this summer. Graeme Smith is strong-minded, Jacques Kallis is strong-minded; Mark Boucher, Makhaya Ntini, they are experienced ...'

Shane Warne and Glenn McGrath took it upon themselves to reply to such remarks, and the debate prompted the ICC to issue a warning to all players not to erode the spirit of cricket. They pointed out that the number of cricketers being found guilty of code-of-conduct offences was increasing, and while I agree that development is disturbing, I don't see Warney or Pidge making statements about what they are going to do to the South Africans as being against the best interests of the sport. They do it before every series, identifying the opponents they're going to target, because they like the challenge that comes with having to back up on the field what they've said off it. Shane especially has had a lot of success against South Africa in the past, a fact even Pat Symcox concedes. 'Warne has had it over us for a long time,' he said.

I'm not sure if the current South African players will be too happy to have been reminded of that fact.

DESPITE THE SUCCESS WE have enjoyed so far this season, most people see the games against South Africa as being the true measure of where we are as a team. We might have already proved to ourselves that we are still capable of playing better cricket than anybody else around the world, but if we fall short in the upcoming Tests that won't count for anything. On a personal level, playing key games against South Africa is nothing new, because such matches have already played an important part in my career, most notably when we toured there in early 2002. I went there on that tour as a 'veteran' of 53 Test matches and with a Test batting average of nearly 44, and in the second Test, at Cape Town, I played what was probably my most important innings to that point. We needed 331 to win, got them with six wickets down, and I finished 100 not out, reaching three figures and scoring the winnings runs with a six. It was my first second-innings century in Test cricket and I'll never forget the confidence and momentum it gave me. I went on to score another four Test hundreds in 2002 and six in 2003, building a momentum that has stayed with me till today. That game in Cape Town was an important one for us to win, not least because we needed that result to remain the No. 1 ranked Test team in world cricket, but also because we finally felt we put to bed for good the notion that we couldn't chase a target when the pressure was really on.

Immediately after that Test series, we won a seven-match one-day series 5–1, with one game tied. This was my first series as Australia's one-day captain, after Steve Waugh was controversially sacked, so it was reassuring for me that we won so decisively. We haven't played South Africa in a Test match or one-day game since that tour, so it is no wonder the sense of expectation leading into this series is so high. It's amazing to think that we haven't run into each other on the field in nearly four years.

We think the South Africans are vulnerable. For as long as I have played against them, everything about their cricket has been structured. When we faced them in one-day games, we could predict everything they were going to do. Shaun Pollock, for example, used to bowl at just about the same time in *every* game — with the new ball, a couple of overs around the 30-over mark, two more at the end. Jacques Kallis is one of the great players of the modern era, but because he tends to bat at the same pace whatever the circumstances of the game he can sometimes hold his team back, especially if less experienced team-mates see how he's going about things and think that's the way they should be playing as well. In the lead-up to this series, their captain Graeme Smith has been saying plenty, but most of it has been so predictable (we'll be disappointed if the Australians don't sledge us … they've lost their aura … they're weak against reverse-swing bowling … Warne and McGrath are getting old … etc, etc), it is as if he's reading from a script. It has made no impact on us.

The main by-product of his comments will be the extra pressure he has put on himself. He's also been critical of our middle-order batting, but maybe he doesn't know how well Mike Hussey and

Practising as if it was match day before the first Super Series one-dayer.

It took two balls from Andrew Flintoff before I got a smidgin of revenge for the Ashes loss — a six forward of square leg!

Our celebrations straight after I took the catch that ended Game One of the Super Series reflected the importance we placed on winning these matches.

South Africa's Jacques Kallis is run out (above) in the second Super Series ODI, and then ducks out of the way of a quick Brett Lee riser (left) two days later.

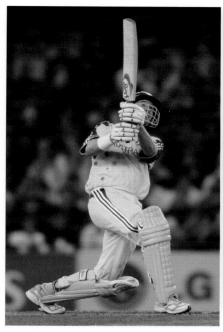

Mike Hussey hits the roof in Game Three.

Adam Gilchrist was named player of the one-day series.

The best spin bowlers in the game — Stuart MacGill, Shane Warne, Muttiah Muralitharan and Daniel Vettori — compare notes before the Super Series Test match.

Above: Michael Clarke is given out after the TV umpire couldn't decide whether he'd edged a bat-pad catch during the Super Series Test.

Right: Glenn McGrath and Shane Watson leave the SCG after our emphatic victory over the World XI.

Below: Matthew Hayden was in excellent form against the World XI in Sydney, making two of the three highest scores of the Test.

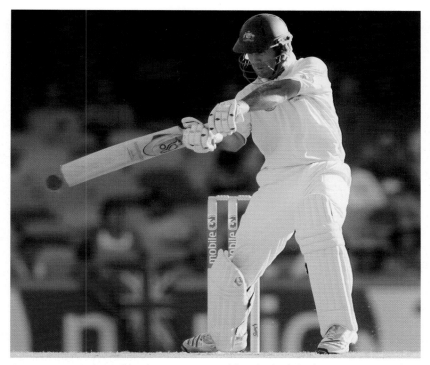

A square cut at the Gabba during my second hundred of the first Test against the West Indies.

Brett Lee has just bowled Jermaine Lawson, the final Windies wicket to fall in the first Test.

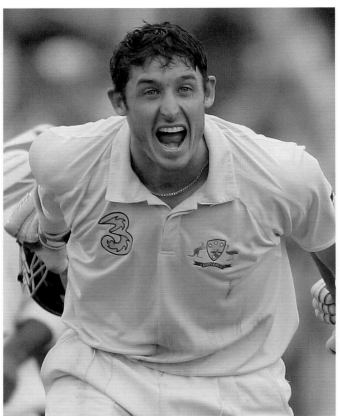

Left: Mike Hussey was very excited to score his maiden Test century in Hobart.

Below: Brian Lara has just broken Allan Border's Test run-scoring record during his double century at the Adelaide Oval.

Dwayne Bravo's stunning catch that dismissed Shane Warne during our first innings of the third Test.

As good as that catch was, Matthew Hayden's grab that dismissed Brian Lara in the Windies' second innings of the same game was even better.

Three images from the Chappell–Hadlee Trophy game at Wellington. Above: A Ponting pull shot. Right: Michael Clarke and Andrew Symonds during their big partnership. Below: Mick Lewis runs out Kyle Mills to give us a 2–nil series lead.

Brad Hodge are going, or doesn't understand that it is only a matter of time before Adam Gilchrist, who hardly scored a run in New Zealand, clicks back into form. Smith's comments about reverse swing aren't relevant because the ball doesn't reverse swing in Australia as much as it does in England (this is due in part to the balls we use here and also to the hotter, drier air), and anyway South Africa doesn't have a bowler capable of bowling reverse swing at the pace Andrew Flintoff, Simon Jones and Steve Harmison operated at so effectively in England. Smith might be averaging more than 54 in Test cricket, but I think he has to make some runs early in this series or he'll start to look a bit foolish. He is undoubtedly an excellent player with an ability to get big scores if he reaches 30, but we have made a point of targeting opposition captains in the past — because we feel that in doing so we can bring the rest of the team down with him — and our approach to Smith will be no different. We'll definitely be reminding him of his quotes whenever Pidge and Bing are charging in at him with the new ball, or when Warney is examining every aspect of his technique if he survives to face the spinners.

OUR MAIN CONCERN, THOUGH, is not what Smith is saying but that we get our own preparation for the opening Test right. This is especially true for the guys who have been involved in the Chappell–Hadlee Trophy series, as we are being asked to adjust quickly from one-day cricket back to Tests and also from the slow wickets of New Zealand to the extra bounce of the WACA. I don't feel this is as big a deal as others are suggesting — it always takes time to adapt when you play in Perth, because it is unlike any other pitch in Australia, and most of our guys have done it many times before. Almost certainly, we'll play Nathan Bracken, with Stuart Clark the 12th man. I believe the most important thing about playing in Perth is to not get obsessed about the conditions. Some bowlers, for example, get seduced by the pace and bounce of the WACA wicket and bowl too short, while visiting batsmen often look for more lift from the pitch than is actually there, which throws out their footwork and leaves them nailed on the crease, suckers for a catch behind or into the slip cordon.

For all that, my strong suspicion is that over the past five or six seasons the wicket hasn't been quite as quick as WACA pitches were in the 1990s, even if the bounce is still really good. I can't comment on this year's wicket, because with the Test still two days away I haven't looked at it. (I never see much point in examining the pitch until the day before a game commences.) Instead, I spent as much time as I could in the nets, getting used to the local conditions and savouring the competitive attitude of everyone in our squad. Today's training session was fantastic, as all of our bowlers went flat out against us batsmen. An optional training session is scheduled for tomorrow — which I sense at least most of the boys will attend — and then it'll be time for this Australian home season's main course to begin.

Tuesday, December 20

Australia v South Africa Test series
First Test (December 16–20) at Perth: Australia 258 (RT Ponting 71, BJ Hodge 41; M Ntini 5–64) and 8–528 declared (JL Langer 47, RT Ponting 53, BJ Hodge 203*, MEK Hussey 58, AC Gilchrist 44) drew with South Africa 296 (AB de Villiers 68, MV Boucher 62; B Lee 5–93) and 5–287 (JA Rudolph 102*, JM Kemp 55)

I NEVER THOUGHT I'D see the day when I'd be looking back on a Test match at the WACA and wishing that we'd played two leg-spinners. I'm writing totally with the benefit of hindsight, because we were tricked to a degree by the way the pitch looked beforehand (no different, on the surface, from the last couple of years), and if history was a good guide, it would have been the quicks rather than Warney who would have bowled us to victory. However, the wicket was actually very different from what we are used to playing on in Perth, especially on days four and five, and Stuart MacGill, working in tandem with Shane, might have made a difference.

I'd had no hesitation batting after we won the toss, and was very disappointed when we made only 258 in our first innings, being bowled out a good half hour before stumps. Everyone in the top five bar Matt Hayden got to 20, but no one made more than my 71, a knock I remember most for the fact that Makhaya Ntini struck me in the helmet with the first ball he bowled to me. It was a strange one, coming after Haydos was out in the second over. There was nothing weird or unexpected about the bounce of Ntini's delivery — the ball came back at me a little ... I saw it clearly ... and essentially froze. It flicked my gloves and hit me in the helmet grille. Afterwards, some people compared this incident to the recent Test at Lord's, when Steve Harmison cut my cheek with a short one that pushed the grille onto my face, but in fact this was more like the one I copped from an Indian opening bowler named David Johnson during a Test at Delhi way back in 1996. I'd been in for a little while on a slow wicket when Johnson bounced me, and again I saw it clearly and again I just froze, until at the very last second I managed to put my hand up and the ball hit me on the glove. The Harmison one was different: an excellent bouncer that caught me in two minds after I started to hook. Both times, in Delhi and here in Perth, it was strange how I reacted, but it wasn't a case of me not concentrating or not seeing the ball clearly. Nor do I think it's anything to worry about in terms of my batting technique. It'll probably happen again in 2014.

From that awkward start we batted ourselves into a position where we could control the Test, but then we lost our last seven first-innings wickets for just 78 runs, Smith and AB de Villiers added an unbeaten 38 in seven overs before the close of play, and we could have been in trouble, knowing how flat the pitch was becoming. However, our bowlers were outstanding on day two, and then Brad Hodge came out and turned his first Test hundred into a big one, grinding the tourists out of the game.

During our second innings, I had just arrived in the middle when their quick bowler Charl Langeveldt bowled a short delivery which I tried to pull through mid-wicket. Unfortunately, I hit the ball on the toe of the bat and it flew near Jacques Rudolph, who dived to take a spectacular one-handed catch. It looked like I'd creamed the ball when I swung at it, but actually it went quite slowly, though it still required some work for the catch to be completed. Then we discovered that the umpire, Billy Doctrove from Dominica (who once refereed a World Cup soccer qualifying tie), had no-balled the bowler for over-stepping the crease.

I was lucky, because replays showed that part of Langeveldt's front foot was actually behind the line when he delivered the fateful ball. Some people wanted to lampoon the umpire when this was highlighted, but I thought the incident just demonstrated how difficult this aspect of their job can be. Think about how quickly someone like Brett Lee bowls, and then think how difficult it must be to watch Lee's feet as he lets the ball go and then get focused on the other end before the ball gets there. I'm sure I've been dismissed during my career by a no-ball that wasn't called. Many is the time I've looked at the spike marks at the bowler's end after Bing has bowled a couple of overs at the start of a Test, when the pitch is new, and thought, 'He must have bowled half a dozen no-balls.' Yet not one delivery had been called. After that, Bing and the umpire both get into a rhythm, the bowler's front foot usually stays behind the line, and the game goes on.

My 'dismissal' would have left us at 3–91, a lead of only 53, early on day three. Instead, Justin Langer and I continued on until just before lunch, when Lang called for the physio after he felt a twinge in his hamstring. 'Just a tweak,' he told me, 'but let's be careful with the short ones for a while.' He came back after lunch with a runner but was almost immediately bowled, played on, for 47, and off he limped to wrap the leg in ice. At the end of the day, he had the leg scanned, which revealed a 6cm tear. Some 'tweak'! Lang's a tough bloke, but it looks like he'll be out of the Boxing Day Test, and probably the Sydney Test as well.

His replacement at the crease was Brad Hodge, and he was still batting more than a day later as he enjoyed his best moment in cricket to this point. It was terrific to see Hodgey make a hundred so soon after his Test debut. As it's been with Huss, there is something extra special about an 'older' guy coming into the team after a long first-class career and almost straightaway making a hundred. All that hard work really is worth it! Brad was 18 when he made his first-class debut for Victoria back in October 1993; now he became only the fifth Australian to turn his maiden Test hundred into a double ton and only the second Australian to score 200 in the third innings of a Test match (after Sir Donald Bradman, who did it twice).

I must confess I thought Brad would go well in this game. Before the Test, as I observed him in the nets, it struck me that he bats a little like Mark Waugh, Sachin Tendulkar or Damien Martyn, in that he is very well balanced, with his head very still, and he times the ball beautifully without ever moving his feet too much. However, not moving your feet in Perth can get you in trouble, so while he was working with the bowling machine, I stopped him and we talked for 10 or 15 minutes about what it takes to be successful at the WACA. I didn't want him to totally revamp his technique, just to be positive, which meant getting forward when he wanted to play forward, and back when he wanted to go back. Brad returned to his net and worked on getting his feet moving, and he carried that method into the Test, with fabulous results.

IT SEEMS TO ME that everyone outside the team believes I got the declaration on day four wrong, but I'll go to my grave saying that I didn't. In my view, a minimum 130 overs spread over slightly more than four sessions should be sufficient for any attack to bowl their opponents out in the fourth innings. Sure, by the time I called the batsmen in we'd reached the point where South Africa were never going to get the runs I'd set them, but I also had to measure what Hodgey getting 200 would mean to him as a batsman trying to establish himself in Test cricket, and also how it would boost the spirit of the entire team, as we shared his joy in reaching such a landmark. We are a squad that revels in each other's success. If someone doing something special wasn't going to cost us a Test victory, why not let it happen? We didn't fail to win the Test because I let Brad Hodge score a Test double hundred; we didn't win because the wicket was very batsman-friendly and we couldn't break a gallant and superb partnership between Jacques Rudolph and Justin Kemp on the fifth day. As I wrote, a second leg-spinner might have made a difference. But as things turned out, no matter how hard we tried, having 10 or 15 more overs to bowl at them wouldn't have mattered. Neither, I'm sure, would a more generous target have prompted the South Africans to throw their wickets away. It was a game destined to be a draw.

Adam Gilchrist, John Buchanan and I had been talking about the declaration for much of the day, and we never wavered from the view that somewhere around the tea interval was the way to go. In the period after lunch, Hodgey and Gilly actually scored more quickly than we anticipated, and we began thinking about closing not long after drinks, but four overs after the break Brad was 184 not out. The target kept growing, and he slowed as he approached 200, but we'd set the West Indies more than 500 in the Test at the Gabba and beaten them by plenty, and we believed there was more than enough time left to get those 10 wickets we needed to win this Test. A lot of thinking went into the decision, in the end it was 100 per cent my call, and just because the Test ended in a stalemate doesn't automatically mean it was wrong.

DURING SOUTH AFRICA'S FIRST innings, Shane Warne had sarcastically described Justin Kemp as the 'new Daryll' — a reference to Daryll Cullinan, who Warney often embarrassed during Tests in the 1990s. The sledge was picked up by the two batsmen, the fieldsmen near the wicket and (one assumes) the umpires, and also — we learned later — by the stump mike that is part of the live television coverage, but it didn't worry me. Kemp made only 7 (caught Hodge bowled McGrath) in that first innings, but he made his point on the last day when he came out during the 61st over and batted for much of the rest of the game, and with Rudolph kept out everything we tried.

Rudolph surprised us. Someone needed to graft for a long time if South Africa were going to force the draw, and he was the one who really put his hand up. He was right in the battle to the very last ball, fiercely concentrating as Warney kept going around the wicket to try to get a big turner to spin into him (a left-hander) and maybe get a bat-pad catch or bowl him through the gate as he tried to drive. We left him gaps in the offside field to try to tempt him into a loose shot, but he kept hitting everything in the middle of the bat. He showed a lot of skill, a heap of courage and plenty of mental toughness, a trait we admire. Saving a Test by batting for a long time is one of the most difficult assignments a batsman will ever face.

In the end, the wicket was too true, while the ball became old and dead as quickly as I have ever seen in a Test match in Australia. We were relying on Warney, but conditions were too flat even for him (though I reckon if the batsmen had relaxed even for a minute he'd have been through), and none of our quicks could conjure even a hint of reverse swing. Some reckoned I should have tried Hodgey or Symmo earlier, but there was no rough on the pitch for them to aim at and I really couldn't imagine how they were going to make a difference. It was one of those situations where we just had to persevere, keep attacking and be patient. On this day at least, Rudolph and Kemp were too stubborn for us.

IT SEEMS A SHAME to me that the Perth wicket, once so lively, now seems so lifeless, and I fear that its rapid decline is another indication that in this era of 'drop-in' pitches, the surfaces around Australia are losing their character. I was a little worried about the pitch in Adelaide, which held together much better than a traditional Adelaide Oval Test track, but put that down to the fact that we played a little earlier this season than is usual. It would be a tragedy if the grounds around the country become as one.

I know there is much for us to take out of this first Test. We dominated large parts of the contest, and indications are that we are facing an opponent who is going to spend much of their time during this series waiting to counter-punch. We expected the South African bowlers to be more accurate than the West Indians had been earlier in the season, and we also expected them to be conservative, though not quite as defensive as they actually were. It was something we talked about at some length in our team meetings before the Test — that they'd copy what the Poms had done by attempting to keep things tight, especially to batsmen such as Haydos and Gilly who are renowned for going after the bowling. Sure enough, after having a crack at the new batsman when he first came in, the South African bowlers quickly reverted to the defensive, firing in a lot of bouncers and often aiming well wide of the off stump with a fieldsman on the deep-point boundary and sometimes a third man as well. Such a strategy fits with their reputation as a cautious side, but whether it is best for them, I'm not sure. Graeme Smith had said beforehand that they were going to play 'brave' cricket, which implied that he'd recognised that they needed to be more aggressive, but as soon as any of us got off to a bit of a start, the slips disappeared and they reverted to type. Ironically, that cost them a couple of times, as potential catches went through where a third or fourth slip could have been.

Australia were the first side to consistently score at four runs an over or more in Test cricket, and as we were winning, too, it was inevitable that some teams would try to mimic us, while others would aim to rein us in. Such negativity might get you a draw or two, but if the batsmen facing defensive bowling recognise what's going on and refuse to commit batting suicide by playing illogical shots, then the pressure eventually goes back on the captain who has closed the game down. In the good old days, slowing a game's tempo also involved sending down as few overs as possible, which for poor teams made the tactic more attractive, but because these days you've got to bowl a minimum number of overs in a day and lost time can be made up, that's not much of an option. Instead, eventually, the defensive-minded captain has to do something or his side will be overwhelmed by the more positive force. It's rare for the team that starts a battle of attrition to win the cricket war.

Wednesday, December 21

BEFORE WE LEFT PERTH, the issue of spectators racially abusing the South African players became a hot topic, after their management officially complained to the ICC match referee, Chris Broad, and the head of the ICC's regional anti-corruption and security unit, John Rhodes, about some things the players had to endure during the first Test. Any person who has played international cricket for a few years knows that ugly taunts from the crowd are not unusual, so for the tourists to file an official report means that the WACA crowd must have really crossed the line.

We in the Australian team didn't know anything about any of these incidents until after the Test had finished, when our manager Steve Bernard was informed and passed a message on to me. I must admit I just don't get why spectators have to resort to racist slurs to get their point across, and support totally the ICC's mission to rid the game of racism, both on the field and off. Why can't the fans just enjoy the game for what it is? I think it is appalling that there is a need for increased security because the tourists feel threatened. Banter and sledging from home crowds aimed at touring teams can be funny, and cricket folklore is full of stories such as England's hated bodyline captain Douglas Jardine being told to 'leave our flies alone' by the fans on the old Sydney Hill. It happens all over the world. Indeed, this year we've copped plenty from crowds during the Ashes series and the Chappell–Hadlee Trophy matches. I remember having a full can of baked beans thrown at me in New Zealand one year, and a few years back Merv Hughes had a toilet seat lobbed in his direction. Indian fans in Cochin once amused themselves by throwing plastic bottles full of rocks at us. But all that is different from this issue. Racism has no place in international sport.

I was briefed by Cricket Australia before I spoke to the media this morning, but there was no script to keep to. When the first question on the subject was asked, right at the beginning of the media conference, I just responded as I feel. I know what's right and what's wrong. At this stage of my life, I don't see myself as being a cricket 'statesman' in the style of Steve Waugh or Mark Taylor, but I do think it is important that, as captain, I comment on important issues such as this one. And if I'm going to make a statement, I'm going to stick to what I believe in.

Saturday, December 24

JUSTIN LANGER'S REPLACEMENT IS the New South Wales opener Phil Jaques, who will be making his Test debut. Once that scan showed that Lang had done some serious damage to his hamstring, he was quickly ruled out of the Boxing Day Test, and Trevor Hohns actually announced Jaques' selection on the final day in Perth. I had no problem with this, because I had been briefed as to the scale of the damage to Lang's leg, but I am usually of the view that someone should never be ruled out prematurely, just in case by game day they are actually fit to play. Because the Melbourne and Sydney matches follow so soon after each other (Melbourne, of course, starts on Monday, with the SCG game beginning a week later), we asked Lang to come to Melbourne so he could work with Errol Alcott and give himself every chance to be right for the third Test, and sure enough now he is telling me he could have played here. I'm not going to get into that argument, preferring to focus on the new man, who I must confess I don't know a lot about.

I noted in the *Herald–Sun* yesterday that Steve Waugh had compared Phil to Adam Gilchrist. 'He can take attacks apart,' Stephen wrote. 'He can catch bowlers by surprise and I think people will be surprised how powerfully he hits the ball.' I do know that he scored a lot of first-class runs in Australia last season and has continued that form this year, and that everyone I've spoken to or heard from says he's an excellent player. I have seen him bat in a couple of ING Cup games on TV — including a match at the Sydney Cricket Ground around six weeks ago when he made 152 not out at better than a run a ball — and noted that his technique is slightly unorthodox and that he hits deliveries to different parts of the field from what most blokes would do. It will be good to see him bat in the flesh.

I guess it's a bit weird having someone in the team I haven't actually met, but this is not the first time it has happened during my career. I had never played against Jason Gillespie before he came over during the 1996 World Cup as a replacement for Craig McDermott, or against Scott Muller before he came to Sri Lanka as a replacement for Dizzy on our tour there in 1999. I'd also only played one Mercantile Mutual Cup game against Brett Lee before Bing made his Test debut in the Boxing Day Test of 1999. Still, it was hard for me to offer a strong opinion when we discussed our alternatives once Lang was ruled out. We could have pushed Mike Hussey up the order, as we did when Huss made his Test debut against the West Indies at the start of November, but in the space of seven weeks he has become a crucial part of our side, and with Brad Hodge also now established in the side no one liked the idea of disrupting the middle order. Everyone says Jaques is the real deal, so why not pick him?

We arrived in Melbourne on the evening of the 21st, and I ran into Phil for the first time at breakfast the next morning. Over the last couple of days I have quickly come to discover that he is a genuine cricket tragic who just loves batting, one of those players who would gladly spend all day, every day, in the nets if he could. He seems a quiet bloke, though that could just be that he's settling into a new environment. In that regard he's lucky in that there are a number of his New South Wales team-mates in our squad, who no doubt will help him settle in.

One of those Blues men is Stuart MacGill, who looks likely to come back into the team, with Andrew Symonds having more responsibility as the first-change seamer. If I'm batting against Stuey in the nets I can usually tell in five minutes if he's in good form; he can't hide the fact when he's struggling a little, but he's not struggling now. The MCG curator has been quoted in the papers as saying we should think twice before going into the Melbourne Test with two leggies (something about a 'slightly finer' type of grass on the pitch, which will suit the seamers), but I reckon Warne and MacGill will have a terrific time over the next couple of weeks.

MUCH OF THE LEAD-UP to the second Test has been dominated by talk about talk. First Shane Warne came out and suggested one of South Africa's biggest problems was that 'there is not a lot of imagination with their captaincy', and then Graeme Smith bit back by suggesting that Warney 'is finding it hard to accept Ricky Ponting as captain and team leader'.

It is not unusual for Shane to make public comments two or three days out from a big game, which can make life interesting for me, because I'm usually due to have a captain's media conference the following morning. Often, the first question I receive is about what Warney said the day before. But it really doesn't worry me, even if making such provocative statements is not my go. Shane, as I've said before, likes the confrontations his remarks cause, and he knows they often put his opponents under pressure, which can't be a bad thing.

Smith's comments, in contrast, were just silly, as he tried to regurgitate some stories that had first surfaced during the Ashes series. There was a rumour about that Shane and I had to be separated by team-mates at Edgbaston after we had an argument over my decision to send the Poms in. It was total rubbish, but that didn't stop it being run as a lead story in papers in England and Australia.

For me, as I read what Smith was saying, I couldn't help thinking to myself, 'Is that the best you can do?' I like our chances in the Boxing Day Test.

Friday, December 30

Australia v South Africa Test series
Second Test (December 26–30) at Melbourne: Australia 355
(ML Hayden 65, RT Ponting 117, MEK Hussey 122; A Nel 4–84) and 7–321
declared (ML Hayden 137, A Symonds 72) defeated South Africa 311
(AB de Villiers 61, HH Gibbs 94) and 181 (SM Pollock 67*; SK Warne 4–74)

CHRISTMAS DAY IS A special time for the Australian cricket team. After a morning with your immediate family, our cricket family — which means not just players and partners but also kids and in some cases parents — gathered together in a private room at Crown Casino for a lunchtime party that has become a tradition, something we all look forward to. After that — like most Australians on Christmas Day, I reckon — most of us returned to our rooms and had a sleep in the late afternoon.

Between the first present being opened and the lunch at Crown, many of us headed across to the MCG for an optional practice and a look around. My wife Rianna came down with me, because she wanted to walk out onto the famous ground and have a look at it from the middle. Kellie Hayden was there too, with little Gracie Hayden, and while Rianna and Kellie stopped to take in this awesome stadium — which now has a real Colosseum feel to it after the major revamp that is all but completed in preparation for the Commonwealth Games in March — Gracie and I mucked around together. When I did stop to take in the surroundings, I got myself a little confused thinking about the various player entrances we have used in the past few years as parts of the reconstruction were completed and we used alternative change rooms. I also tried to come to grips with how different the ground feels when it is a football venue, when the goalposts are located just behind deep point and just forward of deep square. One intriguing fact about today's set-up is that the drop-in pitch has been positioned at a slightly different angle to the old pitch. Warney actually pointed that out — it's one of those situations where at first you don't notice the change but once you do it gets more disconcerting every time you look at it.

BY THE FOLLOWING DAY, Boxing Day, that pitch was very much the centre of everyone's attention. A few of us had commented, when we first looked at it, on the amount of grass on the wicket, and we also noticed that the soil underneath that grass was very dry and cracks were already forming in the surface. The days leading into the Test have been sweltering, so there was plenty of conjecture as to what the wicket would look like on game day, but we were still startled when the covers were removed to reveal a pitch of black, saturated soil and long (by cricket-pitch standards) grass. Clearly, a lot of water had been hosed into the pitch, but now it seemed there was no way we were going to start on time.

Both captains thought we had to wait, as did the umpires, but the MCG curator, Tony Ware, thought we were over-reacting. I thought he was wrong, as were the commentators who were very quick to agree with him after it was announced that the start would be delayed by 30 minutes. The fact that once the pitch dried out it would most likely suit the spinners meant that we were always going to play both Warne and MacGill, which also meant that if we won the toss we'd have to bat first. But we'd be doing so on a pitch that might do anything in the first hour. We did win the toss and at stumps Graeme Smith said that he would have batted first as well, but frankly I doubted that — it is not in South Africa's style to be so bold and they had gone into the match with three quicks plus Jacques Kallis, who is a better-than-average fast-medium bowler. The pitch was tricky in the first half hour, which unfortunately was long enough for Phil Jaques to have a very difficult and unsuccessful debut. Matthew Hayden and I managed to get through to lunch, and after that we seemed to play ourselves into a position of strength, reaching 2–162 at tea. That score, of course, gave the critics a chance to knock us for our concern about the wicket at the start, but I thought it was more a case of Matty and I batting really well, and the South Africans not taking their chances, most notably when I edged the third ball I faced straight to where third slip should have been, and then when I was on 17, when Andre Nel spilt a sitter at mid-wicket.

There might have been some logic to Smith putting two slips, a gully and a 'floating' slip, sort of halfway between second and gully, when I first came to the middle. Because the wicket was so damp, it might have been more likely that an edge would have gone squarer than it usually would on the first morning of a Melbourne Test. And it was just his luck that the snick would go through the gap. His body language straight after strongly suggested he was thinking about what-might-have-beens, and I was happy to point out to him just how 'unlucky' he'd been, but later I couldn't help but ponder how, when the Poms were juggling the positioning of their slips fieldsmen during the Ashes series, their switches always seemed to work. Cricket can be a game of centimetres.

ONE OF THE FEATURES of the opening day was the reception given to Brad Hodge when he walked out to play his first Test innings on his homeground MCG. I know how worked up I can get before a Hobart Test, so it was no surprise that Hodgey was really nervous, and I don't think his anxiety would have been lessened by the din created by the big crowd on that first afternoon. He was coming off a double hundred in his previous Test innings, so it was no wonder they 'claimed' him so enthusiastically. I heard someone say later it was at least equal to the roar Dean Jones used to get when he walked out to bat back in the early '90s when Deano was Victoria's favourite son.

I thought the conditions were difficult until well after lunch, which made this one of my best hundreds, but my joy was tempered by the fact that we lost six wickets in the final session, finishing at just 8–239. The wicket had dried out a lot by late in the day, yet that was when the South Africans played themselves back into the game, which set up a situation where Mike Hussey had to play one of the great Test innings to get us back on top. He came in after Brad was dismissed soon after tea, and by stumps was 23 not out, having faced 87 balls. Nine runs into day two, Stuart MacGill was bowled by Ntini, and soon after Hussey was dropped by Kallis in the slip cordon, but from that shaky beginning Huss went all the way to 122, adding 107 for the last wicket with Glenn McGrath, of which Pidge made 11 not out.

To hit boundaries in that situation, batting with the No. 11 and with most of the field back on the boundary, is not easy. To hit a number of sixes in such circumstances takes courage, because if you don't quite hit it you're caught on the boundary. It also takes guts to let your partner face a few balls at different times — it is amazing how some players have an innate ability to judge this tactic brilliantly while others put their faith in less-accomplished team-mates at exactly the wrong moment. In this case, it wasn't as if Huss and Pidge were going from 500 to 600; this was a critical partnership, because we knew that a total of 250 or 270 would be inadequate, that even 300 was probably not enough. When Stuey was dismissed, Huss had hit four fours. He finished with 14 fours and four sixes, being particularly severe on their left-arm spinner Nicky Boje.

Graeme Smith didn't want to bowl Boje on that second morning, and held him back until Huss was 89 and the last-wicket stand was already worth 67. After a couple of singles, Huss smashed Boje over the boundary rope at mid-wicket; next over, he hit a two, then one to reach his hundred and then another big six to celebrate. An over from Nel later, it was lunchtime, and the buzz across the ground underlined the fact that the mood of the game, probably the entire series, had changed. We had let an early advantage slip away, then recovered through the efforts of one very special player. The effort typified a key characteristic of the great Australian teams of recent years: we've managed to get ourselves in just as much trouble as our opponents in various games, but while others might submit in such situations, we have always backed ourselves to not just escape, but to turn the game on its head. Part of this comes from the incessant self-belief that has been instilled in us over the past 15 years, and part of that comes from the fact that having done it before, we know we can do it again. It was important this season that we restored that confidence, which was dented in England, no doubt about it. Huss' role in this revival has been significant.

ONE EXTREMELY SAD ASPECT of this Test occurred on the second morning, when we learned that Kerry Packer had died at his Sydney home on Boxing Day. Mr Packer is best known in cricket as the entrepreneur behind World Series Cricket, but on a personal level I knew him more as a committed supporter of the game — something that was apparent to me as a fan in the 1980s and especially as a first-class and Test player since the early '90s. Of course, WSC accelerated the growth of player payments, which the generations of international cricketers since 1977 are eternally grateful for, but I think he should be remembered by the game for much more than that — so many innovations had their genesis in WSC, including night cricket, coloured clothing and quality television coverage. One-day international cricket, which I grew up on as a kid, wasn't truly accepted in Australia until Mr Packer pushed it.

Both teams observed a minute's silence before Tuesday's play, and throughout that day you could sense that many people had been really affected by the news. Cricket Australia chairman Creagh O'Connor said Packer had to be ranked alongside Sir Donald Bradman as one of the giants of Australian cricket, a man who had influenced the shape of the sport. 'That cricket is today taken for granted as a natural part of the Australian way of life is in no small measure due to his influence,' he said in a statement.

I met Mr Packer on several occasions, discussing not just cricket with him, but also golf, another shared passion. I didn't know him as well as some guys in the Australian team, especially Shane, who was very close to him, but I am fully aware of Mr Packer's impact on the game and his influence in cricket circles, and I also came to realise over the years how much the cricket people who worked with him respected him and enjoyed his company. 'Kerry Packer's one of the all-time great thinkers and figures of Australian cricket,' I said when I was interviewed by Channel Nine before play. 'It's an extremely sad day for the whole cricket community in Australia.

AT LUNCH ON DAY three, South Africa were 5–226 in reply and the Test was evenly poised. The on-field highlight of the first session for us was the way Brett Lee softened Jacques Kallis up beautifully: first the bouncer that rattled his helmet, then the fierce yorker that shattered his stumps; off the field, we were taken by the way Phil Jaques skipped the lunchtime cuisine so he could go out to the nets for 20 minutes and hit a few throwdowns (as I said, he's a real batting tragic!). Back on the ground, the score reached 5–260, with Herschelle Gibbs and Mark Boucher going along well, but then Andrew Symonds stepped up, getting three big wickets — Boucher, Gibbs and Shaun Pollock — for seven runs in the space of 21 deliveries, and the game turned our way. This was the start of a remarkable 24 hours in which Symmo turned from likely Test discard to everyone's hero, and there wasn't a person in the Australian dressing-room who didn't love every minute of it.

There'd been a lot of talk about Symmo's role in the team, with too many people suggesting he was one of those allrounders who wasn't quite good enough to be a Test batsman or a Test bowler. In his first five Test innings of the summer, he'd scored 48 runs, and before he took those three wickets he'd taken one in his past three Tests. I didn't agree with the knockers, but there was no disputing that his mediocre form since he came back into the team had given the critics plenty of ammunition. I was hoping he'd have a breakout game, when the natural talent he often displayed in one-day cricket would shine through, and the confidence he got from those wickets and the state of the game when he went out to bat on day four were perfect for him. He was able to play his shots, bat *his* way, and he finished with a spectacular 72 from 54 balls. Half his runs came from sixes, he added 124 for the fifth wicket with Haydos in 15 overs, and the big hitting meant I could declare 45 minutes before tea. Better still, we took six wickets before stumps and the game was as good as over. We'd won the moments that mattered, another of those traits that separates the good teams from the great ones.

We were firmly of the view that with the pitch cracking up and Warne and MacGill both ready and able, four sessions would be plenty of time to bowl the South Africans out. The outfield here was slower than Perth, so the fact that the target was 'only' 366 didn't worry me at all. The big wicket was Kallis, and who would get him but Symmo, of course, caught behind by Gilchrist to make them 4–64. It was a dismissal I attributed to the state of the game, with the great batsman jabbing at a ball in a way I doubt he would have done if the fate of his team hadn't depended on him. Funny thing was, even though it looked like a nothing sort of ball that induced a nothing sort of shot, afterwards I read a report that described the delivery as 'an outswinger pitched in just the right spot'. It actually didn't swing at all, but now that Symmo's a star again, there is nothing he cannot do.

SYMMO FINISHED WITH 2–6 from four important overs in that second innings, but the two main men remain McGrath and Warne. Despite Brett Lee's often imposing form since Brisbane, Pidge is still our 'go to' man, whatever the situation. When we desperately need a wicket or I want a bowler to tie things up, he is the bloke I turn to first. Here he demonstrated again how much he loves the challenge of confronting the best players in the opposition, by getting Smith to drive at a ball that moved away off the seam after two or three overs where he gave the South African skipper absolutely nothing. This dismissal came in the over after Warney had spun a leg-break across de Villiers, who edged a catch to Gilly. Suddenly, South Africa were 2–45 and sliding to defeat. The next day, when we needed four wickets to wrap up the Test, I decided to open the day with our two leggies, and Pidge didn't get an over for 90 minutes. I wouldn't have done that in a crisis. When he did come on, he promptly took 3–17 and the game ended six balls after lunch.

What's his secret? Pidge makes batsmen think that they have to do something out of the ordinary to score off him, that their natural games are not enough. The great West Indian, Curtly Ambrose, was the same. In a way, this game plan is not very complicated, but not many bowlers can do it as consistently and effectively, or with greater cricket intellect, as McGrath. He knows his game extremely well, and knows, too, that he doesn't have to change, that the methods that have made him a great bowler will keep getting him wickets.

The one thing he has always had is unexpected bounce off the wicket. He is constantly surprising batsmen with that extra bounce, has been doing so for more than a decade. Batsmen who have been in for a while have often been surprised in this way, while a number of very good players — England's Mike Atherton probably being the most notable example — have never come to terms with that bounce, or the way Pidge keeps hitting the seam on or about off stump, always pitching the ball on that length batsmen hate, where they're not sure whether to go forward or back. When I face him in the nets, I'm always thinking, 'Do I go forward? … But it might nip back and hit me in the guts … Should I go back? … Or let it go? … If I do, it'll nip back and trap me in front.' You can't process all that in the time he gives you, ball after ball. There's never much to drive. The pressure builds and builds, and eventually gets to the batsman and gets him out.

Warney was singled out for over-appealing by the South African coach, Mickey Arthur, after the fourth day's play, but we thought they were clutching at straws. 'I think they do it and they master it,' Arthur said when asked if Australia pressure the umpires. 'Warney is a master and he has an aura about him. He's a world-champion bowler and if we had bowlers like that we'd be placing the pressure on them, too.'

We have heard this line before from opposition coaches talking to the media, but never to our face from an umpire or a match referee. In this case, we were frustrated by the umpire from Pakistan, Asad Rauf, who kept telling us that lbw shouts against the left-handed Ashwell Prince weren't out because the ball was hitting the pad outside the line of the off stump. But Prince wasn't offering a shot, so he could be out in such circumstances.

I reckon we were entitled to seek a clarification, and I don't think we overdid it. We do appeal every time we think something is out, and we never realised there was anything wrong with that. Furthermore, it's the nature of Shane's bowling — always at the batsmen, rarely delivering a loose ball, bowling a mixture of sharply turning leg breaks and sliders that go straight onto the stumps or the batsman's pads — that there is often going to be a chance for an lbw, a caught behind or a bat-pad catch. People like Mickey Arthur need to remember that.

THE TEST ENDED ON a bitter note after a misunderstanding involving Warney and Makhaya Ntini threatened to blow up into an incident. Earlier in the Test, a couple of local comics, Glenn Robbins and John Blackman, both mates of Shane, had come down to our dressing-room. One of Blackman's many claims to fame is that he was the voice behind 'Dickie Knee', a popular character from the old TV show *Hey Hey! it's Saturday*, and by coincidence Ntini had suffered a knee tendon injury so serious it looks like his tour of Australia is over. On the last day, just before lunch, McGrath had Nel caught behind, which brought Ntini and a runner to the middle, and as he limped out someone made a joke about him having a 'dickie knee'. Then, just before Pidge came in to bowl his first ball at the new batsman, Warney at first slip yelled out, 'Let's get one for John Blackman!'

Ntini heard the end of that, and spun around and told us exactly what he thought of it. For the four balls until lunch, he angrily kept telling us to be careful with the 'black man stuff' and he continued this as we walked off the field for the break. When play resumed, Stuey MacGill had the first over and fifth ball Ntini was back on strike. I went in to bat-pad on the offside and when he brought the matter up again I told him that no one had said anything racist, that it was all a misunderstanding and he should get over it. He only lasted two balls, and was clearly still upset, so I decided that when I got a chance I'd speak to Graeme Smith and explain exactly what went on. And I must admit that the more I thought about it, the more I realised that while there really wasn't anything in the comment, I could see why it had caused offence. I also knew it was going to be hard to explain, especially to South Africans who almost certainly had never heard of *Hey Hey!*, John Blackman and Dickie Knee.

The opportunity came after the presentation, when we were in the tunnel that leads down to the dressing-rooms. I shook Graeme's hand and asked him if I could have a moment, and we went though the issue. I'm not sure if he believed me, and we were both waving out hands about as we made points, but the exchange never became angry or bitter. Rather, it was such a bizarre incident that it took a while for me to explain things properly and then for Graeme to remind me why such a remark could cause such acrimony. We left on good terms, only to discover that a Channel 10 cameraman had filmed the discussion and soon there was a story circling about the 'ugly' incident. It was nothing of the kind.

Part V

My Test Centenary

**Australia v South Africa,
Third Test, Sydney
January 2–6, 2006**

Saturday, January 7

Australia v South Africa Test series

Third Test (January 2–6) at Sydney: South Africa 9–451 declared (JH Kallis 111, AG Prince 119, SM Pollock 46) and 6–194 declared (HH Gibbs 67, JH Kallis 50*) lost to Australia 359 (RT Ponting 120, MEK Hussey 45, AC Gilchrist 86; A Nel 4–81) and 2–288 (ML Hayden 90, RT Ponting 143*) by eight wickets

AS AN ACHIEVEMENT, I rate playing 100 Tests right up there among the most special of my career. It's a long, long way from being a 'one-Test wonder', a badge of honour that says I am capable of consistently succeeding at the highest level.

The best dreams are the ones that come true, and this one has been fantastic. For as long as I can remember, the thing I most wanted to do was play cricket for Australia. Either that, or play football for North Melbourne (now the Kangaroos). When I was very young, growing up in Mowbray, Dad reckoned I was going to be a better cricketer, but I loved playing footy, and wasn't so sure. In my teenage years, however, cricket really took over, and I left school at 15 so that I could go straight to the Cricket Academy in Adelaide. I really wanted to give myself every chance to be a Test batsman. I hit as many balls as anybody and spent my spare time analysing the better players at the Academy and the international stars, too. Anything to improve my game.

While I can't call myself a real student of the game's history, in my youth I did devour every contemporary cricket book on the market. The Channel Nine *Wide World of Sports Cricket Yearbook* was a staple Christmas present, and I rarely missed reading the latest cricket magazine. I wanted to learn as much as I could about the players I saw on the television, why they were special, what made them different? The two I loved watching most were Kim Hughes in the early '80s, and then David Boon, who was, of course, a hero of mine simply because he was from Launceston. The fact that he was also a superb batsman only added to his huge appeal. My most vivid memory of a job I had working the scoreboard during a Shield game at the Launceston Oval is of 'Boonie' batting out in the middle. Later, there were coincidences between his career and mine that went beyond our mutual birthplace: he had made his debut for Tasmania at age 17; in my first-class debut game, against South Australia in Adelaide, I was 15 days younger than he had been when he first played for Tassie, 14 years before.

The start of that initial game was very traumatic for me, simply because I slept in on the morning of the first day, missed the warm-up, and only just made it to the ground before the start of play. Three years later, in Perth, I set *two* mobile-phone alarms, plus the alarm on the clock-radio next to my bed and had my parents ring me to make sure the same thing didn't happen before my debut Test match. The 10 years since have raced along, but even so they have shaped me as a cricketer, and one or two moments — such as when I've been dropped or the couple of times I've found myself in trouble over off-field incidents — have toughened me up as an individual. The overall experience has made me a smarter, more mature person than I otherwise would have been.

BOONIE FINISHED UP APPEARING in 107 Test matches, and I've always seen him as the bloke who forged a path for me to follow. I was in Port-of-Spain in Trinidad in 1995, on my first tour with the Australian Test team, when he played his 100th Test. At the time, it didn't occur to me that he was doing anything *that* special, even if he posed for photos in the hotel pool holding an exotic cocktail and wearing his whites and his baggy green. If you'd asked me then, as a fairly naïve 20-year-old, I probably would have said that there really shouldn't be any difference between your 99th Test match and your 100th. To be honest, I'd have said the same thing earlier this season. But I know now that there is a difference.

I was much more nervous in the lead-up to this Test than I had been for any of my Test matches of the last few years — even my debut as captain, or a game when my place in the side was on the line. The anxiety before an international in Hobart is different; that is about not wanting to let people down. As the day of my 100th Test drew closer I kept telling myself that I just had to prepare as well as I could and then, hopefully, go out and make some runs. If something unusual happened, I had to be ready for it, and then adapt and fight through. These are the sort of 'checkpoints' I think about before every game. But on top of this, this time I found myself putting more and more pressure on myself to succeed, because I desperately wanted my performance to match the occasion.

Sure, in one sense, 100 Tests is only a milestone. However, it was one that filled me with a truckload of personal pride. One hundred Test matches! I thought about the Australian players who had got there before me: Allan Border, David Boon, Steve Waugh, Ian Healy, Mark Taylor, Mark Waugh, Shane Warne, Glenn McGrath. All had played Test cricket in the last 15 years, which reflected the fact that the 100-Test landmark is mostly a modern phenomenon, a product of the often heavy schedules that have us playing many more games than did the champions of the past. But I thought also of the quality of each of these centurions

— as men as well as cricketers — and felt humbled that I was about to become a member of their club. This is where my nervousness came from. Subconsciously, I was convinced that I had to succeed in this match to prove I was worthy of the acclaim that comes with reaching this particular Test century. There'd never be another 100th Test for me, so I had this crazy now-or-never impulse driving me that I *had* to have a productive game.

As it turned out, the Test evolved into a brilliant one for me, as I became the first man to score a hundred in each innings of his 100th Test and we won the match and the series. I guess I had every right to dwell on all the runs I scored, but as I revelled in this outcome, it was the *win* that clearly mattered most to me. The centuries were terrific. The way the SCG crowd cheered for me was brilliant. I loved the fact that because the game was in Sydney, I was able to share the moment with many people who are very close to me, including my family from Launceston, who came up and finally proved for good that the old jinx was a furphy. However, as Justin Langer led us in another rousing rendition of *Under the Southern Cross I Stand*, I felt this immense joy about the way we'd prevailed. That's what I'll always remember first about this Test match.

If I'd batted as well and scored as many runs as I did, but we'd lost, my 100th Test wouldn't have been the same. It was not as if my pre-match mindset had clouded my judgment. My nerves were understandable and no bad thing. But it was still nice to be reminded that cricket is first and always a team game. And when you win, it's wonderful.

I REALLY HAD TRIED to do the same thing before this Test as I had before other games. As usual, the guys ensconced at the team hotel in the city grabbed a prime vantage point for the New Year's Eve fireworks, but I had a quiet one, staying at home with

Rianna. This is in keeping with my policy of trying to keep things low-key in the lead-up to an important match. There had been plenty of requests for photo shoots and one-on-one interviews, but I tried to avoid this sort of thing as much as I could, purely because I was keen to make the lead-in to this game as normal as any other. January 1, 2006, the day before the game was due to begin, was the hottest day in history, to the point that just going down to the SCG was gruelling, and we didn't stay there for long. About the only bloke really keen for a net was Lang, who wanted to prove that he was totally over his torn hamstring. He did that comfortably, which means Phil Jaques' Test career is on hold for the moment, while our opponents made two changes from the team we beat in Melbourne: paceman Charl Langeveldt and Test debutant off-spinner Johan Botha come in for the injured Makhaya Ntini and the sacked Nicky Boje.

The pitch looked a pretty typical Sydney wicket, but the heat must have got to it, because when we arrived at the ground for the start of the Test it was pretty damp. In something of a repeat of what had happened in Melbourne (though not as extreme), it looked as if the ground staff had put plenty of water into the track to stop it baking dry.

Furthermore, the weather had turned full circle, and at the time the Test was scheduled to begin it was drizzling and the toss was delayed. We could see that grass was starting to sprout through the surface, and with the temperature much cooler than it had been 24 hours before and rain about, it was going to be quite difficult for whichever team had to bat first. I never thought I'd see the day when I'd have to think (even for a second) about what to do if I won the toss at a Sydney Test. Of course, with the pitch likely to dry out and with Warne and MacGill in our team there really wasn't any alternative to batting first, but it was still weird to even ponder the thought. After we took an early lunch, Smith won the toss and made the same decision we would have done, then it was time for the national anthems and a ceremony in which Cricket Australia presented me with a specially framed baggy green cap for my 100 Tests. Finally, the big match was underway.

My parents, Graeme and Lorraine, sister Renee and her husband Greg had flown into Sydney that morning, and we'd tentatively scheduled dinner for after the first day's play (unless I was due to bat the following morning, in which case I'd be having another quiet one at home), but the mere fact they were coming proved that something important was happening. Mum and Dad don't venture out of Launceston to see too many of my games, though they did head to Perth back in 1995–96 for my Test debut and they have seen a few one-day internationals at the MCG. This time they were seated very comfortably with friends, family and sponsors in a box that had been kindly provided by the Sydney Cricket and Sports Ground Trust, and during the Test they were visited by a number of notable sporting identities and at one point by no less than Prime Minister John Howard and his wife Janette. I was very grateful Mum and Dad had made it and that the SCG had looked after us all so well, but the jinx was still an issue when the Test started and, sure enough, I spilt an easy catch at second slip off the last ball of the third over. If you'd told me then I was going to make a pair and we would lose by an innings, I would have believed you.

The ball zipped around early, and we snared three wickets before the total reached 100, but after that the pitch settled down and Jacques Kallis and Ashwell Prince batted extremely well to get to 3–230 by stumps. Prince is a fighter, as a batsman and in the field, too, though he is one of the players who is never going to tear you apart, while Kallis was Kallis, technically superb but never totally dominant. On day two, their innings ploughed on to 9–451 before Smith closed, with our two leg-spinners both conceding more than 100 runs on a deck that was getting flatter and flatter. When we lost three wickets before stumps things looked a little awkward for us, but Mike Hussey stuck with me the next day while we put on 130, and then Gilly strode out to play one of his specials. He belted 61 runs from his last 46 balls and added 133 for the last three wickets with Brett Lee, Stuart MacGill and Glenn McGrath. We were back in the game.

I felt comfortable throughout my innings, even when those early wickets fell and we were under pressure. The start of the third day had been delayed because of more drizzle, but when play finally commenced an on-drive off Langeveldt's bowling soon set me on my way. In the next three-and-a-bit overs he bowled to me I hit him for three more fours and a six, and the mood changed as Smith went on the defensive and Huss and I settled in. It probably wasn't until I got into the 90s — when I started worrying about stuffing up this unique chance to get a hundred in my 100th game — that I got myself in trouble. On 92, I edged a ball from Langeveldt at catchable height through a gap in the slip cordon and next ball survived a very tight lbw shout; my nerves might have affected my partner, as he was caught by Boucher after edging a doosra onto his pad when I was still three short of the century. This was Johan Botha's first Test wicket. All of 20 minutes later, Andre Nel aimed one at my pads and I pushed it wide of mid-on for my hundred. On the big screen, it was recorded that I had become the sixth batsman to score a century in my 100th Test — after Colin Cowdrey, Gordon Greenidge, Javed Miandad, Alec Stewart and Inzamam-ul-Haq — and it was the first I knew that these guys had performed this feat. My preoccupation before the game had not been with making hundreds, just making runs.

Heavy rain on day four meant we spent most of the day in limbo. During this down time the lads might do any one of a variety of things: listen to their iPods, read the papers, watch replays of past matches on the TV monitors, change grips on bats or spikes on boots. Brett Lee might get out his guitar, Warney could organise a card school, while others might discuss an ailment with Errol Alcott. Meanwhile, in the away-team dressing-room, Graeme Smith was stuck with a real dilemma. He needed to win the Test to square the series, but as the rain kept falling and more time was wasted (from his perspective) the only way he was going to win the game was to risk losing by setting us a realistic target. On such a flat wicket, there was no way he could bowl us out unless he gave himself a reasonable amount of time to do so *and* we were going for our shots. We knew he'd be bold, and sensed that — because the South Africans' natural instinct is to be conservative — he might even overdo it, as if to prove he can be as adventurous as the next guy.

At the start of that final day, South Africa were 3–94, a lead of 186. Kallis was 14 not out, having already faced 47 balls, and Prince was yet to score. During the warm-ups, I got all the boys together and we talked at length about how the game was going to unfold. I told them that in the perfect world, this is how it was going to happen . . .

Our job was to keep it tight in the morning, and try to make Kallis play in a way that was foreign to his usual method. In fact, I believed he'd keep going the way he always did. McGrath and Warne opened the bowling, and they set out to make it as hard for him to hit runs as possible, and while a couple of his team-mates attempted to blaze away, Kallis scored only 36 from 49 balls. Just as we'd hoped, Smith was forced into a corner (he ended up asking us to get 287 runs in 76 overs), and from the moment the declaration came we were playing to win. Matt Hayden and I put the pressure on, the South Africans wilted, and we ended up getting home with eight wickets and 15-and-a-half overs to spare. Throughout this innings, I never felt as though we were scoring all that rapidly, or even that much was going on around me, until suddenly we were on the verge of the win. It's a bit weird when you get into this 'zone' when you're batting — the pressure, the noise of the crowd, even the sense of the occasion all seem to dissipate — yet you never lose sight of the ultimate objective. You're in a groove and it's beautiful. I was very animated after I hit the winning four, and part of that was about the fact that the entire last day worked out precisely as I'd hoped, almost as if I'd written the script. My 100th Test had ended like a dream.

DURING HIS PRESS CONFRENCE after the Test, Graeme Smith was talking up his team's chances for the return series in South Africa in March and April. 'When we get back home in front of our supporters, we're going to play for a win,' he said. 'We're going to back ourselves, we're going to be confident, we're going to stand up and we're not going to back down. Certainly, when Australia come to South Africa it's going to be one of their toughest times ever.'

This all sounds fine, and I know Smith was trying to stand up for his team and show that they had no fear of playing us, but that sort of bravado doesn't count for anything if you can't back it up with actions. His declaration on the last day in Sydney had been bold, but then his bowlers let him down, whereas we had got just a sniff of the victory and then devoured the opportunity. Psychologically, the results in both Melbourne and Sydney had been huge for us. It's always how you play your cricket, rather than how you talk, that really matters.

There were a few negatives to come out of the game — Johan Botha was reported for having a suspect action, while Brett Lee and Glenn McGrath have been asked to open their wallets to pay fines after they were charged with dissent. In Botha's case, I can't do any more than feel sorry for the guy, and hope that he can sort through his problem during the VB Series, while I believe our guys fell victim to 'back-to-back Test syndrome', something that can be especially prevalent towards the end of an important series. This shouldn't be an excuse, but the guys were tired after competing in two Tests in 12 days, and when things didn't go as they wanted, their frustration showed. It's not the first time it has happened in a Sydney Test, but in the future I hope we are more aware of the possibility of tempers becoming frayed, so it is less likely to occur.

I don't like having members of my team having to defend their conduct at disciplinary hearings, especially as we have been working hard over the past couple of years to adhere to the 'Spirit of Cricket' code that Cricket Australia's contracted players wrote back in October 2003. The basic tenet of that document was that we would play our cricket 'hard but fair', respecting our opponents, the umpires, ourselves and the game. It's a creed we want to stick to, and not just when it suits us.

Depressingly, for the third Test in a row there were reports of racial abuse coming from the crowd, this time on the third day when Andre Nel was targeted. This is becoming a major problem, one that cannot be excused or ignored just because it is coming from a tiny, stupid group of idiots. I wish these people making gooses of themselves could recognise the difference between good-natured barracking, which can be funny, and racist remarks that don't amuse anyone. I have no idea what the complete answer is, because it's a slight on society not just sport, but I totally support any moves Cricket Australia instigate — such as extra security in the problem areas and culprits being immediately ejected from the ground — that might lead to the trouble disappearing from our game.

Part VI

Crash! Boom! Bang!

Australia v South Africa, Twenty20 International, Brisbane January 9, 2006

Tuesday, January 10

Twenty20 International

At Brisbane (January 9): Australia 3–209 (20 overs: DR Martyn 96,
A Symonds 54*) defeated South Africa 114 (18.3 overs: NW Bracken 2–9,
ML Lewis 2–18, JR Hopes 2–26, A Symonds 2–26) by 95 runs

I DON'T THINK I really like playing Twenty20 international
cricket. I know it is cracking entertainment for the fans, I can see
how it could be good fun, and as a means of attracting new
spectators to our game — maybe with the odd international
game and by having state teams playing a short competition in
the way Twenty20 cricket is played in England — I think it has
value. My problem with it, I think, is that I can't a play a game
of cricket in which I'm wearing my national team's colours, and
my opponents are wearing their national team's colours, and
treat it as being *just* fun. Last year in England, I described our
game against the Poms at Southampton as being a 'bit of a
laugh', but that was really just an off-the-cuff remark aimed at
deflecting attention from the fact that we lost. In truth, we were
humiliated, losing by 100 runs. I didn't enjoy that at all.

It's all very well to say that as professionals trying to do the best
by our sport we have to treat Twenty20 internationals seriously,
but I'm not sure the game lends itself to being played too seriously.

As a batsman, you're required to swing away from the very first ball, and as a bowler your aim is to concede something like 40 runs from your four overs. That's hardly cricket as we know it. Yet because life in the 21st century is moving so quickly and people only have so much spare time in their day, I know that we are going to have to embrace it eventually, which means discovering the best way to play it. For me as captain this starts with trying to determine what to do when I win the toss. I remember the first Twenty20 game Australia played, during our tour of New Zealand last season, when the coin went up and suddenly I had this horrifying thought: 'What am I going to do?' Of course, I called correctly, and I looked Stephen Fleming in the eye and said confidently, 'We'll have a bat.' Buggered if I know what I was really supposed to do!

Before last night's game at the Gabba we did talk tactics, if only briefly. The general consensus was that there is an advantage in batting first, perhaps because it is better to swing the bat hoping to score as many as you possibly can, rather than with the knowledge that you need a specific number of runs per over to win. A number of blokes in our side have appeared in Twenty20 games while playing county cricket, so they had some experiences to share, but it was funny how it quickly became evident that different counties approach the game in different ways. Some captains apparently prefer to win the toss and then send their batsmen out to hit out from ball one. Others want to bat normally for the first couple of overs, and get most of the runs at the end of the mandatory 20 overs. There are bowlers who reckon it's best to fire in yorkers aimed at middle stump every ball, while others are just as adamant you've got to change it up all the time, so the batsmen never get into a rhythm. As we play Twenty20 more, we'll work out our own way to play it; for the moment, we decided that when we were bowling we'd treat it like an abbreviated one-day game. The guys who operate best with the new ball, such as Nathan Bracken, would bowl at the start of the innings, and I'd save a bloke such as Mick Lewis, who showed in New Zealand that he's proficient during the final overs, to bowl at the finish.

As for the toss, again I opted to bat first, still with no real personal belief that this was the way to go. Damien Martyn promptly went out and made my decision look brilliant by playing a classic smashing innings of 96 from 56 balls, on a pitch that had some pace and bounce in it, perfect for the occasion. Given it was Twenty20, I'm not sure whether this knock will help Marto's chances of getting back in the Test squad, but it was still a nice opportunity for him to remind the cricket community of what a sweet timer of the ball he can be. I'm also sure he enjoyed making some runs in front of a vibrant full house, but the locals didn't get really excited until the local hero, Andrew Symonds, went on a rampage.

This game featured a number of gimmicks, including our specially designed uniforms for the night that came complete with nicknames rather than surnames on the backs of our shirts. Graeme Smith and I were both 'miked up' so we could interact with the television commentators, though this was only on a limited basis after I raised a couple of concerns. I didn't like the concept of the microphone being switched on throughout the innings, as I've had enough experience with stump mikes to know that some things that are said on the field should stay on the field. I also didn't like the idea of me having a chat with one of the bowlers about what I wanted him to do, and that information being broadcast straight into the opposition dressing-room. But I was happy to answer questions between overs, and it was good to hear from Ian Healy and Michael Slater in the commentary booth as we charged to an emphatic victory.

The tourists' catching in this game was ordinary, but we were excellent, with Mick Lewis' tumbling effort to dismiss Shaun Pollock the highlight. I also enjoyed my direct hit which ended Jacques Kallis' innings, and took some pleasure out of the fact that none of our bowlers got belted and we bowled the South Africans out. Afterwards, I sensed that many people who came along quite liked the idea of the evening's entertainment being over in around three hours, and from what I understand, that is the game's great appeal in England — that with their long twilights you can start a game in the late afternoon and it's over before the last ray of sunshine is gone.

It was also very nice to send the ground-record crowd home happy, but even with all the smiles about I still couldn't help thinking that Twenty20 is not really my game. Certainly, if we played a lot of it, I think cricketers and spectators alike would get sick of all the slogs, the sixes and the bowlers going for plenty. It's a game that could get old very quickly. One international game a season, maybe even an international tournament once every four years, might be all right, though. If that's all there is, maybe I will get to like it. Eventually.

Part VII

The VB Series

Australia, South Africa and Sri Lanka
January–February, 2006

Saturday, January 14

VB Series

Game One, at Melbourne (January 13): Australia 5–318 (50 overs: SM Katich 60, DR Martyn 70, A Symonds 66, MJ Clarke 45*) defeated Sri Lanka 7–202 (50 overs: MG Vandort 48, DPMD Jayawardene 50) by 116 runs

IN ONE SENSE, TROY Cooley, my mate who became the England bowling coach, was the first former team-mate of mine to become a coach for an overseas Test side. However, Tom Moody, who is now in charge of the Sri Lankan team, is the first former Australian comrade who has faced us as an opposition *head* coach. I played a number of one-dayers for Australia with 'Moods' between 1996 and 1999, including all our crucial games at the 1999 World Cup. I'm sure the Western Australian blokes could offer a better opinion than me as to his ability as a mentor, because his record in the Sheffield Shield was outstanding, but I know he was a good influence when he was in the Aussie squad and he was also a very shrewd captain whenever I played against him. It doesn't shock me at all that he has become an international coach.

Like most blokes who've been around the international cricket scene for a long time, Moods is pretty comfortable with the media game, so it was also hardly surprising that he'd have his 20-cents' worth about the banter that had been a feature of our games against South Africa. I'm sure he'd like to minimise the attention on his young side for as long as possible, and what better way to do that than to keep the press boys writing about the rivalry between his two opponents in the VB Series. The Sri Lankans will focus on their cricket, Moods told reporters before the opening game of the competition, and leave the 'verbal' to Australia and South Africa. He dismissed his own team's ordinary recent performance in New Zealand, when they lost three one-dayers out of four, saying that all three teams in the VB Series were starting from scratch. 'We've got talented cricketers,' he said. 'We respect that Australia's got those as well, but why can't we win?'

Unfortunately, if the opening game of the tournament — in which we overcame a mediocre start to win comfortably — is any guide, the Sri Lankans might have a tough time over the next few weeks. They are without their outstanding opener Sanath Jayasuriya, who is injured, for at least the first couple of games and their defeat in this game was their 10th in their last 12 ODIs. They seem a bowler or two short, and their batting tactics were basically weird.

WE'D LEFT STUART CLARK and newcomer Brett Dorey out of our final XII for this match, with Brad Hogg the supersub. Dorey is an interesting character, who comes into the Aussie one-day squad as the leading wicket-taker in the Pura Cup so far this season, but via an unlikely route before that. He'd played junior rep cricket with Western Australia, before heading off to Europe on a working holiday that had him employed at one stage as a bodyguard to the children of a rich Russian businessman, until he returned home in 2004 to resume his cricket career. He's a tall bloke, around 200cm (6ft 7in), with a bowling action that suggests he'll get some good bounce in the right conditions, but he's another bloke I never faced in a game before he came into the Australian squad. The selectors preferred him to Mick Lewis for our VB Series squad, despite's Mick's game efforts in the Chappell–Hadlee series. Damien Martyn and James Hopes, who missed the games in New Zealand because of injury, also came back into the squad, replacing Brad Hodge and Cameron White, and with Brett Lee fit and firing there was no room for Mitchell Johnson.

We were 2–58 after I was dismissed in the 12th over, bowled after an unsuccessful charge against their opening bowler Ruchira Perera. He was sending down slowish off-cutters, which were grabbing the wicket and bouncing a little, and one or two had hit me on the typing finger of my right (bottom) hand. If he keeps pitching there, I thought to myself, he's going to be tricky to get away, so I tried to hit him down the ground to put him off his game. It didn't work, but that's not to say my counter-attack was wrong — it was the kind of calculated risk you have to take in one-day cricket.

Fortunately, all the batsmen after me contributed, though Michael Clarke caused a bit of grief when he got in the way of an Andrew Symonds straight drive and the rebound lobbed to the mid-wicket fieldsman, Tillekeratne Dilshan, who completed the catch. Symmo walked off with a wry smile on his face, signalling to his great mate Pup that he owed him a beer or two, but the Sri Lankans weren't laughing for long, because Mike Hussey promptly strode out to smash 34 from 29 balls, Pup finished with 45 from 39, and 77 runs came from the final 10 overs. In reply, the Sri Lankans seemed to get their batting order wrong — Mahela Jayawardene batted six and skipper Marvan Atapattu was at seven — and having scored only 103 runs from their first 30 overs, they had no chance. The most peculiar innings came from their not-so-super sub, Michael Vandort, who was making his ODI debut when he replaced Muttiah Muralitharan (0–67 from 10 overs) at the end of the Australian innings.

Vandort came out at No. 3 and scored an extremely tedious 48 from 117 balls. I know he is a young guy trying to find his feet in the international game, but by batting the way he did he gave his team no chance of winning and set up a situation where the runs scored by Jayawardene and Atapattu were cheap and meaningless. After the game, Gilly and I were talking to the Sri Lankan coach and we 'congratulated' him on the way his team had used their supersub. Next time, Moods replied tongue very firmly in cheek, we might see something different. We've been led to believe that if anyone in their team bats like that again they'll become the first player in cricket history to be run out by their own coach sprinting onto the field, picking up the ball, and hitting the stumps with a direct throw from near the boundary!

Monday, January 16

VB Series
Game Two, at Brisbane (January 15): Australia 228 (49.5 overs: MEK Hussey 73, B Lee 57; SM Pollock 3–30, AJ Hall 3–43) lost to South Africa 5–231 (48.5 overs: HH Dippenaar 74, MV Boucher 63*) by five wickets

IN THE OLD DAYS, IT was the first game of the one-day triangular series that sorted Australia out, as we struggled to adapt quickly from Test to one-day cricket. This time, however, it was our second match, against South Africa in front of another record crowd in Brisbane, that caught us out. We batted poorly, losing our first six wickets for just 71 before Mike Hussey and Brett Lee dragged us back into the game, but 228 is rarely a winning total these days and Mark Boucher and Justin Kemp got them home with seven balls to spare.

After our 2–0 win in the Test series and our opening VB Series victory against Sri Lanka, I sensed that some observers were assuming we'd handle South Africa pretty easily, but these people should have remembered that in 2005 Graeme Smith's team actually went an impressive 20 ODIs in a row without defeat (17 wins and three no-results). That is just one short of the world-record sequence we established in 2003. So we were ready for a tough contest in front of another ground-record crowd, whose support for us was constant and fantastic, but as it turned out there wasn't too much in our performance for us to get excited about other than the way Huss and Bing batted.

Huss has taken over the role Michael Bevan used to have, batting brilliantly with the late order and getting the absolute most out of his innings even if the early batsmen have struggled. He also offers an added advantage over 'Bevo' in that he can smash the bowlers as well, if that's what the situation warrants. Some people have suggested that we should push him up the order in one-day cricket, to give him more time at the crease, but I love the way he has been finishing innings for us. I'm not saying that Huss is as good as Bevo yet, but he's definitely not too far behind — which makes him exceptional.

The other thing about Mr Cricket is that not only is he doing it on the field, he's a top bloke to have around the team. He makes the most of every minute; whether it's gym work, practice or a recovery session, he's always the first one there and the last to leave. I love that sort of attitude. The way we have trained and played since returning from England is clearly different from how it was and the refreshing presence and added zeal Huss adds as a permanent member of the Test and one-day squads has certainly helped in this regard.

Bing bats so well in the one-dayers now that he's almost entitled to be rated a genuine allrounder. He hit three sixes during his innings, and also survived a blow to his jaw after he misjudged a short one from Jacques Kallis. With the ball, there were times early on when he and Glenn McGrath looked a bit too good for the South Africans, especially Boeta Dippenaar, who took 75 balls to get his first 50 runs and finished with 74 from 115. Mark Waugh rang me this morning, wanting to know why we'd run Dippenaar out when we did. Had he remained instead of being the fifth wicket to fall — when South Africa needed seven runs an over — Kemp wouldn't have been able to come out and hit so effectively. Thus, 'Junior' argues, we might have hung on.

Adam Gilchrist was dismissed by the first ball of this game, and then he found himself reported for the way he reacted to umpire Aleem Dar's refusal to go to the video on a run-out appeal when the South Africans batted. However, neither of these events had anything to do with our decision to give him a rest after the game — that had been built into his schedule a while ago. Gilly missed last week's Twenty20 game, but as a 'marquee' player returned for the launch of the one-day home season, so now is the chance to give him the break from the heavy workload he carries each season.

I'm all for this sort of 'rotation' of the senior players. Pidge missed the Chappell–Hadlee back in December and we'd wanted Gilly to have a short spell then as well, but Cricket Australia ruled otherwise. I'll also be taking a break myself before the one-dayers are over, as much to perk myself up mentally as physically. In my view, time with your family and doing very little (and in my case hitting a golf ball) has to be good for cricketers who are on the road, whether home or away, playing Tests and one-day matches for many months at a time. And I reckon it has to be a complete break, not just a game off while you remain with the squad, a bit like when a player on a tour of England gets a few days away while the team is playing a county game. If you are still there — going to practice, doing the warm-up, in the dressing-room on game day with your gear on, doing press interviews, maybe taking the drinks out — you may as well play. Unfortunately, there are people in the media who don't agree with the whole rotation concept, so we have to cop some criticism any time one of the senior players steps away from the squad.

New South Wales keeper-batsman Brad Haddin has substituted for Gilly 10 times in the past two years, and he'll do so again in our next two matches, against South Africa in Melbourne and then Sri Lanka at the SCG.

Wednesday, January 25

VB Series

Game Three, at Brisbane (January 17): Sri Lanka 6–282 (50 overs: J Mubarak 61, KC Sangakkara 88) defeated South Africa 188 (44.2 overs: JA Rudolph 53, MV Boucher 62) by 94 runs

Game Four, at Melbourne (January 20): Australia 245 (49.2 overs: PA Jaques 94; AJ Hall 4–35) defeated South Africa 186 (47 overs: HH Dippenaar 41, SM Pollock 46; B Lee 5–22, GB Hogg 3–32) by 59 runs

Game Five, at Sydney (January 22): Sri Lanka 7–309 (50 overs: ST Jayasuriya 114, KC Sangakkara 78, DPMD Jayawardene 56) defeated Australia 258 (50 overs: MJ Clarke 67, BJ Haddin 41, JR Hopes 43; CM Bandara 4–58) by 51 runs

Game Six, at Adelaide (January 24): South Africa 5–263 (50 overs: HH Dippenaar 125*, HH Gibbs 68) defeated Sri Lanka 8–254 (50 overs: TM Dilshan 82*, DPMD Jayawardene 52) by nine runs

IN THE SPACE OF three days, Friday to Sunday, we experienced the happy and sad of the one-day game. First, under a closed roof at the Telstra Dome and on a pitch with a little uneven bounce, we handled the South Africans comfortably, largely on the back of an excellent innings from Phil Jaques (brought into the side because Simon Katich had a minor groin injury) and then a fantastic opening bowling display by Brett Lee and Glenn McGrath. Our opponents could score only 34 runs in their first 15 overs, and Bing finished with 5–22 from 10 explosive overs, underlining the fact that he is really in control of his game these days. I described him immediately afterwards as the best one-day opening bowler in the world, on the basis that no other quick in the limited-overs game so consistently gets wickets with the new ball. When he is bowling the way he is — fast and swinging the ball — no batsman could enjoy facing him. And because he has his game in such good shape at the moment, he's really enjoying the extra responsibility that has come with being the second most experienced bowler in the side, and that is reflected in the way he is bowling.

Unfortunately, 48 hours later, in Sydney, Bing couldn't immediately live up to the praise I'd given him, largely because Sanath Jayasuriya (who had recovered from his shoulder problem in time to score his third consecutive hundred in ODIs at the SCG) and Kumar Sangakkara were superb, spearheading a magnificent batting exhibition by the Sri Lankans that took them to their second highest ever one-day total against Australia. Their win also opened the competition right up. Nathan Bracken bowled really well into a stiff wind, but our support bowlers, Brett Dorey and James Hopes, went for plenty, and no one made the big score we needed if we were going to get close to 300 ourselves. Now, all of a sudden, with only two wins from our first four games, we are no certainty to make the finals.

After the game, I had an extended chat with the selectors, during which we focused on the way we bowled — both in this match and at various times over the past few games. I'm not sure some of our bowlers are adapting very well to varying situations and conditions; I think the quicker bowlers need to vary their pace a little and run their fingers across the seam more often to change things up a bit. This sameness about our bowling certainly needs to be eradicated, not least because next year's World Cup will be played in the West Indies, where many of the pitches we've seen on recent tours have been dry and slow.

JANUARY 19, THE DAY before the game at Telstra Dome, was a special one for me, because this was when the Kangaroos AFL club announced that I have been appointed as their new No.1 ticket-holder. I've been a fan of the Roos for as long as I can remember, from the days back to the late 1970s when they were North Melbourne and one of the strongest clubs in the VFL competition. While I have never regretted for a moment my decision to concentrate on cricket, there have certainly been times when I've dreamt about running out onto the MCG or even their old home ground at Arden Street wearing the famous blue-and-white vertical stripes. These days, I go to as many games as I can, even though I feel like I've developed into something of a jinx. On one occasion last season, I was invited down to the rooms before the game to watch the boys prepare, but things went badly from the moment I accidentally turned the lights off while the team was doing its warm-up. On the field, they got belted and I took much of the blame!

I'm not sure if it's right to say that I'm obsessed by the club, but I'm certainly a very passionate supporter and it is definitely true that while on tour I have sometimes gone to extreme lengths to keep track of the team's fortunes. I've heard stories of cricketers of the past having newspapers mailed to them each week during tours so they could keep up with their favourite team, so I guess I'm lucky we have text messages, DVDs and the internet, but it still can be frustrating when I'm on the 'wrong' side of the world and the Kangaroos are involved in a crucial match. There was one occasion in India when the hotel we were staying in had a television in the room but no DVD player, and I had just received a package containing a copy of the Roos' four most recent matches. The choice was to wait until we moved on to our next location, or go out into the streets and buy a DVD player. Of course, I went for the latter option. Really, there was no alternative.

BEFORE THE GAME AGAINST Sri Lanka on January 22, we had decided — with Gilly coming back into the team for our next match in Adelaide on January 26 — that if I was going to have a break it would have to be now. But when this decision was revealed to the media *after* the Sydney game, there was something of an outcry, for three reasons. One, because we'd lost twice, some people have made it clear that they do not believe this is the right time to be playing with anything less than what they perceive to be a full-strength outfit. Two, there is an argument that fans are being short-changed by not seeing the very best Australian team every time we take the field. Three, some patriots feel it isn't right for the Australian captain to be absent on Australia Day.

We believe that to accept the first argument is to ignore the advantages that can come with me having a short spell. We know from experience that after weeks and weeks of often relentless cricket, frontline players do start to make bad mental errors that can prove costly to the team. A couple of mistakes brought on by mental tiredness can be disastrous for a batsman, reducing his confidence, perhaps initiating a bad run of form and impinging on the team's performance. We want to avoid this happening to me, but with the media starting to complain, it has been decided that, as a contingency plan, if we lose our next game I'll be playing in Perth next Sunday. However, if the boys do win in Adelaide, I won't link up with them again until they return to Melbourne for the game against South Africa on February 3.

The second criticism is valid to a degree, but unavoidable in modern sport, and I think cricket fans have to be educated about this. Supporters of the top football clubs in Europe have become conditioned to their teams not playing at full strength in every game because of packed schedules that feature a number of elite League and Cup competitions. If you go to an Arsenal match there is no guarantee you will see their gifted French striker, Thierry Henry. The same is true of American baseball, where almost all the best players are rested from time to time. The New York Yankees' great shortstop, Derek Jeter, plays in most of their games, but not all of them. This scenario will become more prevalent in cricket as long as the itineraries remain as crowded as they are at the moment.

The third knock on my time off — that as Australian captain I should be playing on our national day — is, frankly, the hardest one to defend, though I feel I am something of a victim of the way the program has fallen this summer. There just isn't a perfect spot in January for me to take some time off. The captain and vice captain can't take a break at the same time, and last week we felt Gilly's need for a break was greater than mine, because of the stress that comes with being the best keeping/batting allrounder in the world. So when I have my brief spell is largely determined by when Gilly takes his. I think the time off is worthwhile and something I want to repeat in future seasons, but given the stick Cricket Australia and I are beginning to cop, somehow I don't think the captain will be missing on Australia Day next season.

Monday, January 30

VB Series

Game Seven, at Adelaide (January 26): Sri Lanka 8–218 (50 overs: A Symonds 3–48) lost to Australia 5–219 (48.3 overs: SM Katich 52, DR Martyn 46) by five wickets

Game Eight, at Perth (January 29): Sri Lanka 8–233 (50 overs: DPMD Jayawardene 69, RP Arnold 56) lost to Australia 4–237 (41 overs: AC Gilchrist 116, SM Katich 82) by six wickets

I KNOW THE TIME I have been spending with Rianna and occasionally on the golf course has been good for me, and I think Gilly showed to some extent in Adelaide (34 from 33 balls) and totally in Perth (116 from 105) that the days he spent away from the team didn't do him any harm either. His century at the WACA, in which his first fifty and second fifty each occupied 44 deliveries, was a Gilly special that featured four big sixes, had his hometown crowd chanting his name and was the ideal Sunday-night entertainment for TV viewers across the country, of whom I was one. His previous six innings in ODI cricket had brought him only 58 runs, but here all the trademarks shots were back, and I could tell there was a sense of relief as well as excitement in his grin and punch of the air as he celebrated his hundred.

We are now in a position where it is almost impossible for us to miss the finals. We'd have to not just lose, but be thrashed in our last two games for us to fail to qualify.

I WAS VERY GLAD the boys came through in these two games, not least because it got the media off my case. For four days after the loss to Sri Lanka in Sydney, I had a photographer from one newspaper following me everywhere. The boys had to overcome 40°C heat to win in Adelaide on Australia Day, while in Sydney the weather was much milder, which gave people a chance to imagine me relaxing while the team sweltered. The purpose of the time off was to get away from cricket, to recharge the batteries, so I deliberately didn't pick up a bat during this time, which provided the papers with more ammunition. A newspaper story on January 27 was accompanied by a selection of photographs, one of which was of a young spectator at the Adelaide Oval holding a makeshift sign that read, 'Where's Ricky?' The others were all of me, with a caption that read: 'Ricky Ponting enjoys his Australia Day playing a round of golf, lunch with the missus, stroll to the shops and a nice strong cuppa.' The story itself began . . .

> CRICKET fans vented their anger at selectors in Adelaide yesterday as Australia beat Sri Lanka without their holidaying captain.
> As Ricky Ponting was spotted enjoying Australia Day at Cronulla with his wife after a week of golf and lazy strolls, the South Australian fans were less relaxed about missing seeing the world's top batsman play . . .

The clamour wouldn't stop. One former Australian captain, Mark Taylor, was quoted as saying that giving me a break was 'dangerous', while another, Steve Waugh, supported the rotation policy but then argued that the rotation should not include the captain. 'If anyone has a need to recharge, it would have to be the captain,' he wrote in an article that appeared in the News Limited papers. 'But that's exactly why you are the captain — because you are the benchmark for resilience and mental toughness, and seen by the team as almost indestructible. To be having a rest at a crucial juncture in the limited-overs series is tempting fate and opening the door to both Sri Lanka and South Africa, who will see this move as a lack of respect and be motivated by it.'

I respect Stephen's views on sport and competition enormously, but my counter to him is that I believe our blokes are mature enough and confident enough in their own ability to not think less of me because I've taken a break. They appreciate that the motivation behind the move is not to destabilise the team's performance, but to bolster it in the long term. In this context, I liked the line of Brad Hodge, who batted three in Adelaide and Perth, and was reported as saying of the controversy: 'We were just joking about it before. Even the prime minister had a few weeks off over Christmas, while Ricky was busy making a century in Melbourne and a century in each innings in Sydney . . . if Ricky needs a couple of days' rest, then he knows exactly what he needs himself and he'll come back ready to fire.'

The South Africans got into the act by getting the chairman of their selection committee, Haroon Lorgat, to cheekily reveal that unlike Australia, they were going to play their 'best XI' in every match, because — given that the VB Series table was so tight — every game was important. The strong implication, of course, was that we didn't think the games were important, which is not true at all. We believe we have a strong enough squad to cover for my absence, Gilly's absence, Glenn McGrath's absence, anyone in the team's absence, and that the team will be better off in the long run. 'I'd like to rest Graeme [Smith],' Mr Lorgat said, 'but he's not the only one. I'm a little worried about "Polly" [Shaun Pollock], too. But these are all must-win games, and you simply have to pick your strongest XI for "must-win" games. That's why Polly has played in all of them. And at the moment Graeme is still a part of our strongest XI.'

I'm not sure just how much comfort Graeme Smith would have taken from that final comment.

The next day, January 28, one over-excited Sydney-based columnist wrote that in giving me a break the Australian selectors and Cricket Australia had 'completely lost the plot' and had become 'arrogant' and 'apparently blind to the desires of the Australian public'. It was all getting ridiculous, but fortunately the two good wins the team managed in my absence calmed everyone down, and my guess is that the controversy will quickly be forgotten. I really believe that in future seasons the captain having a mid-season break will be accepted as the sensible move it is, and never again cause anything like the drama it has over the past few days. It just needs everyone to realise that in 21st-century international cricket, some things have to work differently from how they did in the past.

Thursday, February 2

VB Series
Game Nine, at Perth (January 31): Sri Lanka 221 (50 overs: ST Jayasuriya 86; GC Smith 3–30) lost to South Africa 5–224 (45.1 overs: GC Smith 41, HH Dippenaar 87; M Muralitharan 3–44) by five wickets

THE SOUTH AFRICANS HAVE been doing it tough over the past few weeks, with Jacques Kallis recently becoming the third prominent member of their squad, after Makhaya Ntini and Andre Nel, to return home early from their tour because of injury. Kallis has a shoulder problem. Despite these setbacks, I doubt their supporters would take too kindly to them failing to qualify for the VB Series finals, so their comfortable victory over Sri Lanka in Perth was an important one for them. It leaves them second on the table, with 12 points from their five matches (a team receives four points for a victory, with a bonus point on offer if a team can attain a run-rate of 1.25 times that of the opposition in achieving that win). We have 18 points from six games, and Sri Lanka nine points from seven, so with each team scheduled to play eight qualifying games we are now certain of our place in the finals. South Africa must win one of their last three games — against us in Melbourne and then Sydney, and finally against Sri Lanka in Hobart — to join us.

I rejoined the team in Melbourne last Tuesday, and have been really pleased with the way I've trained since then. It's not as if I'm spending hours in the nets, though, because I've never been a bloke who feels he needs to face a thousand balls at practice to maintain or regain form. I always want to be as mentally sharp as possible, and I think I've regained that state of mind now. Indeed, if the critics knew how well I'm feeling, compared to how I was going a week ago, I'm sure they'd change their minds immediately about the whole concept of having a mid-season freshen-up.

One of the most disappointing aspects of the cricket during my time away was that the issue of racial abuse by Australian spectators re-surfaced, especially following the games in Perth. The Chief Executive of the South African Cricket Board has come out suggesting that the situation is so dire that they might have to boycott future tours of Australia, while the Sri Lankans have also complained about some incidents, most of which involve insults aimed at Muttiah Muralitharan by cowards in the crowds. You'd think the mugs would want to enjoy watching the bloke bowl rather than hurl abuse from the other side of the fence. It's appalling that these episodes are recurring. As I've said repeatedly, there is no place at any cricket venue for racism of any kind. That goes for players and spectators alike — racists are not welcome in cricket. I think the game should adopt a zero-tolerance approach in the hope that such a policy can stamp the problem out as quickly as possible. It doesn't matter that there is only a minuscule number of people involved. We need to kick them out of the grounds and make sure they're never allowed back in.

THIS MORNING, WE HAD an official team practice, and straight afterwards I took up an offer to sail on ABN AMRO ONE, the boat that is currently leading the Volvo round-the-world ocean race. The boat had been in dock at Port Melbourne since arriving from Cape Town last month, but recently returned to the water as the first step in preparations for the next leg of the race, from Melbourne to Wellington, New Zealand. Just before we headed out this afternoon, a healthy breeze arrived — getting up to 20 knots, I was told — which chopped up Port Phillip Bay and made for a lively and interesting time.

The power of the boat was remarkable, but what really struck me was the way the skipper and his nine-man crew worked as one as their awesome machine cut through the water. When these blokes get down to action, everyone knows their task. I can't imagine too many sports in which the role of the skipper is so crucial — in full race mode I imagine he needs a total understanding of how the boat, the crew, the weather and the ocean behave, and at the same time his crew must have total trust in his judgment. In this sense, there are parallels with my own team sport, in that if one ingredient in the mix is flawed, the success of the whole operation is jeopardised.

As I kid in Launceston, I spent plenty time on or near the water, fishing and sailing, but that was nothing like this. For a while, the skipper, Mike Sanderson, gave me a chance to take the helm, and while I was keen to see just how fast the boat could go I still felt as apprehensive as I've ever been on the cricket field. The sense of responsibility when you are behind this particular wheel is total, and I asked a lot of questions and concentrated as hard as I've ever concentrated in my life. When I told Mike about how shaky I felt, he replied, 'Imagine how nervous I'd be if I had to stand up to some of the fast bowling you guys face.' All we could do was laugh and agree that we'd both probably be better sticking to what we're best at.

I also had the chance to meet a couple of young Australian guys who are part of the crew of ABN AMRO TWO, which is also competing in the Volvo ocean race (and currently running second). It was a brilliant afternoon; one of those experiences that remind me how lucky I am to live the high-profile sporting life I do.

Monday, February 6

VB Series

Game 10, at Melbourne (February 3): Australia 7–281 (50 overs: RT Ponting 53, A Symonds 65, MEK Hussey 62) defeated South Africa 9–201 (50 overs: J Botha 46; B Lee 4–30) by 80 runs

Game 11, at Sydney (February 5): Australia 6–344 (50 overs: AC Gilchrist 88, RT Ponting 72, DR Martyn 79, MEK Hussey 47*) defeated South Africa 6–287 (50 overs: HH Gibbs 46, MV Boucher 76) by 57 runs

OUR ORIGINAL INTENTION WAS for Brett Lee to also have a break before the finals, on the basis that while he's been in red-hot form we still need to be wary of him suffering a burnout from all the stress he puts on his body, but just before our game in Melbourne last Friday night, we received the ghastly news that Glenn McGrath's wife Jane might have suffered a recurrence of the cancer she had fought so bravely for the last few years. Naturally, Pidge headed straight for the airport, while Bing stayed with the squad and bowled beautifully at Telstra Dome and pretty well on a flat track in Sydney, as we confirmed our place at the top of the VB Series qualifying table with two decisive wins.

The victory in Melbourne was a comprehensive one, with most of the batsmen contributing (especially Symmo and Huss, who added 109 at nine runs an over), and then the bowlers reduced the South African top order to 4–69 in the 20th over. Brett started their collapse by getting Graeme Smith lbw with the second ball of the innings, continuing Smith's difficult summer. It's not so much that I'm enjoying watching the South African captain struggle, because there is always a certain pain in seeing a fellow professional go through such hard times, but there is certainly a great deal of satisfaction in seeing him unable to follow through on the big statements he made earlier in the season. In the main, we've played superbly against him and his team, and it's funny how, as the summer's gone on, he's quietened down so much. Perhaps he's missing Warney? Much more likely, the run of defeats in the Tests, the Twenty20 and now the one-dayers has exhausted much of his bravado. His body language keeps reminding us that he's under pressure, and it's essential — given that we'll be seeing plenty more of each other before 2005–06 is through — that we keep him like that until our upcoming tour of South Africa is through.

Smith's team still had an outside chance of victory in Melbourne when Brett began his eighth over, but in the space of six balls three wickets fell and the game was over. The first of these was a bit special, when Justin Kemp swung Bing high down to fine leg, where James Hopes back-pedalled, took the ball above his head and held on despite whacking the back of his head on the Telstra Dome turf.

The star in Sydney was Adam Gilchrist, who first continued his batting revival by smashing 88 from 66 balls. But he was hardly alone, as every Australian batsman who reached 40 scored at better than a run a ball, and we finished with the second highest total achieved in an ODI at the Sydney Cricket Ground.

Then, when South Africa began their reply, Gilly produced a stunning catch to dismiss Smith off the first ball of the third over, and from that moment the result was never in doubt. Afterwards, I spoke about how much more dangerous a team we are when Gilly is in such spectacular form, because it takes much of the pressure off the rest of the batting order. We can play our own games, knowing that if we do so after Gilly has provided the platform, then we are almost inevitably going to finish with a substantial total. Having him in our line-up and firing gives us an advantage that no other international team can match.

AFTER SOUTH AFRICA DEFEATED Sri Lanka in Perth last Tuesday, Tom Moody was philosophical. He knew the result meant that South Africa only needed to claim one of their last three matches and his men were out of the finals, but rather than be glum Moods was talking up his inexperienced team, saying that if the senior blokes — Muttiah Muralitharan, Sanath Jayasuriya, Mahela Jayawardene, Kumar Sangakkara, Marvan Atapattu and Chaminda Vaas — did their job and the younger guys continued to improve, he thought they could even win next year's World Cup. Typical of a bloke who played in the Aussie teams of the late '90s, Moods is aiming high. 'We've got another year to develop as a team and learn as a team,' he told reporters during the post-game media conference in Perth, before praising the ability of some of his up-and-coming cricketers, specifically nominating batsman Jehan Mubarak, paceman Nuwan Kulasekara and batsman-keeper Upul Tharanga. I guess these guys and a couple of other promising players in the Sri Lankan squad remain largely unknown to all but the keenest Aussie cricket followers, but I suspect it might not be that way forever.

In fact, this evolution might happen faster than even Moods expected, because after our two wins over South Africa in the past three days, the Sri Lankans now find themselves as slight favourites going into a virtual one-match play-off tomorrow in Hobart for the second spot in the finals. Graeme Smith's team seemed pretty demoralised after our batting bonanza in Sydney, more like a team that wants to get home so they can regroup before we arrive there later this month, rather than one burning for a quick form reversal. It won't surprise me one bit if we get to see Tom Moody again before this Australian summer is through.

Wednesday, February 8

Allan Border Medal Night (February 6)

Allan Border Medal: Ricky Ponting
Test player of the year: Shane Warne
One-day international player of the year: Mike Hussey
State player of the year: Phil Jaques
Bradman young cricketer of the year: Dan Cullen
Women's international cricketer of the year: Karen Rolton

VB Series

Game 12, at Hobart (February 7): Sri Lanka 9–257 (50 overs: MS Atapattu 80, KC Sangakkara 62; AJ Hall 3–50) defeated South Africa 181 (43.4 overs: GC Smith 67; CM Bandara 4–31) by 76 runs

THE ALLAN BORDER MEDAL — where Australian cricket's overall player of the year, based on performances in Tests and one-day internationals, is revealed — is always an exciting time, if for no other reason than it's the one night of the year when we get dressed up, our partners get dressed up, and we can go out, relax and have some fun. But given its scheduling this year, just before the VB Series finals, we weren't able to truly 'let our hair down', which might have been lucky given that the organisers decided to make the drink a central theme of the night.

First, everyone's favourite, Dougie Walters, was invited up on stage to share some funny stories that all seemed to involve alcohol. Then England's former left-arm spinner, No. 11 batsman and dud fieldsman, Phil Tufnell, gave a little routine from London while leaning on a bar. And through the night, it seemed as if every presenter made a crack about Andrew Symonds' late night on the tour of England last year, which had resulted in a two-match suspension. It was funny the first time; the second time, less so; and eventually it just got boring.

When I accepted the Border Medal, I said that the guys on my table were 'pretty fired up' about some of Tufnell's one-liners, and suggested that these wisecracks had 'certainly made us a bit hungrier to take on the English'. Truth be told, I can't imagine his name being mentioned in any of our pep-talks over the next 12 months, but the next morning, when I was required to do more media interviews, the most popular questions involved Tufnell's gags, the drinking jokes and my reaction to them. I decided to let the world know that I wasn't happy about the overall content of the night, but the general response to that was that I needed to lighten up. I guess I set myself up for a fall in this regard, because what invariably happened was that that the TV and radio commentators started replaying one of Dougie's stories or part of Tufnell's sketch, then my criticism, and I was made to sound like a whinger without a sense of humour. In isolation, each of the jokes was funny, but it was the fact that it went on and on that annoyed me, especially as the Border Medal is supposed to be a celebration of Australian cricket and what the Australian team has done in the past year (and though we lost the Ashes, we still did some good things). In a way, it's *our* night, but instead, in my opinion, it became a piss-take a little too often.

Ironically, the competition for the one-day player of the year only made it worse. Four players finished level at the top of the voting, and Symmo — who scored 963 runs and took 26 wickets in the ODI matches on which the votes were based — was one of them. The first tie-breaker in this situation was the number of 'three votes' (as best Australian player of the game) each player received, and Symmo had the most of those. However, because of that two-match ban the team imposed on him in England, he was unable to claim the award for the second year in a row. He had actually put his hand up and insisted this be the case, because he — like everyone in the Australian set-up — knows that we are fair dinkum about adhering to the Spirit of Cricket and we want everyone to be aware of our attitude. But no one said anything about this during the night because they were too busy cracking another drinking joke. Next day, whenever the one-day award was mentioned, so too was the fact that Symmo was ineligible ... because he'd been on the drink.

Of course, awards like this are not the reason we play the game, but it was still nice to claim the Border Medal again (I'd previously won in 2004). I must admit going into the night I thought Mike Hussey would win, mainly because he has put in some fantastic performances in both versions of the game, whereas my one-day form hasn't been that good and most of my best Test performances have been in games where other guys have also done well. With the votes being awarded on a 3–2–1 basis (three votes to the best player), the guys who should poll well are the ones who stand out on a consistent basis. Huss had to settle for the one-day player award — winning on a countback after he finished level with Adam Gilchrist and Brett Lee — and Warney won the Test player award quite comfortably, not least because of his stunning 40-wicket performance in the Ashes series and his record-breaking 96 wickets in the 2005 calendar year. Shane actually finished fifth in the overall Border Medal count — an amazing result given that he no longer plays in the one-day internationals.

NOW IT'S TIME TO look forward to the VB Series deciders — a best-of-three affair featuring games in Adelaide, Sydney and, if required, Brisbane — in which we will be facing a Sri Lankan team that handled the South Africans quite comfortably in Hobart. The big surprise was that the man of the match in that final qualifying game was a Sri Lankan spinner but not Muttiah Muralitharan. Malinga Bandara was their supersub, and wasn't even introduced into the game until the 20th over of the second innings, by which time South Africa were 3–87 chasing 258 to win. Four overs later, Bandara came on to bowl his wrist-spinners, dismissed Graeme Smith with his seventh ball, and 58 runs later Sri Lanka were through to the finals.

Wednesday February 15

VB Series Finals

First Final, at Adelaide (February 10): Sri Lanka 8–274 (50 overs: MS Atapattu 53, KC Sangakkara 83; NW Bracken 3–61) defeated Australia 252 (49.1 overs: SM Katich 56, MJ Clarke 80; M Muralitharan 3–40) by 22 runs

Second Final, at Sydney (February 12): Australia 5–368 (50 overs: RT Ponting 124, A Symonds 151, MJ Clarke 54; WPUJC Vaas 4–56) defeated Sri Lanka 201 (36 overs: DPMD Jayawardene 50, RP Arnold 64*; NW Bracken 4–30) by 167 runs

Third Final, at Brisbane (February 14): Sri Lanka 9–266 (50 overs: KC Sangakkara 59, DPMD Jayawardene 86, RP Arnold 76; NW Bracken 3–44) lost to Australia 1–267 (45.3 overs: AC Gilchrist 122, SM Katich 107*) by nine wickets

WHEN I WAS A BOY, reading my *Wide World of Sports Cricket Yearbook* in the days after Christmas, the one-day internationals in Australia were just as important to me as the Test matches. I can still picture the various uniforms the Aussie players wore, the big hits by men such as Rod Marsh, Kim Hughes, Allan Border and Simon O'Donnell, and the way the West Indies seemed invincible whenever they were in Australia, which seemed like every other year. Because I'm of the generation who grew up with one-day cricket, I know how much many people, especially youngsters, look forward to it and have never been one of those people who think it's bad for the game. On the contrary, I know it's brilliant for the fans and I also know that it can often be brilliant for the players.

Having said this, I'm not convinced that we have the programming of one-day international cricket in Australia absolutely right. Yes, it must always be a major feature of Australia's summer of cricket, the games in themselves are terrific, and each year we look forward to the big crowds that get behind us all across the country. However, in recent times there has sometimes been a feeling that just before the finals the momentum of the competition is petering out, that the last couple of matches are too much of a good thing, which suggests to me that the schedule needs looking at. I know the tournament developed along these lines this season — our last game against South Africa in Sydney seemed like one too many and there really didn't seem to be too much public interest in the result of the game in Hobart. A lot of people on the mainland expressed surprise at the defeat of the South Africans, but not too many saw it happen.

This season's VB Series finals went to a third game, but still didn't *totally* capture the public's imagination. It seemed some fans might have been suffering from burnout. We've reached the stage where leading players are seeking a break from the schedule during the season, but for the fans there is no let-up. There were empty seats at the Adelaide Oval for the first final, while the crowd for game three, the tournament decider at the Gabba, was significantly smaller than it had been at the same venue for the Australia–South Africa Twenty20 game a month earlier (though it must be said that, because it was the third game in a best-of-three finals series, there was no certainty until two days before the game that it would definitely be on). My view is that the one-day competition would not lose anything if each team played each other three times, as occurred in 2004–05, rather than four, as was programmed this season. This would ease the pressure on the Australian players, many of whom have already appeared in five or six Test matches (or, as was the case this season, seven Tests and six one-dayers), and also make every game a major attraction, because it is more likely to have an impact on the make-up on the finals. The other advantage for us players if this happened is that, as I commented in my diary last year, a slightly briefer program would have the benefit of making our overseas schedules more manageable, because our opponents quite rightly expect us to play the same number of ODIs in their homeland as they are asked to play here.

While I'm making suggestions, I also wonder if we need to be locked into the triangular format that has been a feature of the one-dayers in Australia since 1979–80. Perhaps two head-to-head battles, one in a 'block' of games early in the season and one later, and not necessarily featuring the same opponent, might be an option worth exploring.

I must stress that I am not suggesting that the VB Series games do not matter. But neither do I think that we should automatically do next season and in the seasons after exactly what we have always done in the past. As I have often said, the fact that every Test and one-day international is important has been drummed into us by our predecessors; you'll never see an Australian cricketer giving anything other than his best when he is wearing the baggy green or one-day yellow cap. The guys in the current one-day squad who have been around for few seasons also have vivid memories of the 2001–02 VB Series, when we failed to make the finals. That calamity cost Steve Waugh the one-day captaincy. Everything we do — even resting players so they stay sharp — is about the Australian team operating at its optimum level in every single match. Whenever we are asked to play, the guys wearing the Australians caps will aim to play the very best cricket we possibly can.

WE STARTED THE 2005–06 finals series badly by throwing away the first game in Adelaide with some shocking running between wickets, but ended it spectacularly well, on the back of another Gilly classic at the Gabba. In between, Symmo and I had a day out against the Sri Lankan bowlers in Sydney, and the overall result became a very satisfactory exclamation point on what has been a brilliant home season.

I'm not really sure what happened in the first final. When we batted, poor calls and ordinary judgment suddenly became contagious. This said, I have to give credit to Sri Lanka, whose bowlers and fieldsmen kept things tight as we were struggling to get the ball through the infield. We just didn't respond well to the pressure that resulted from the successful implementation of their game plan. This is definitely not the same Sri Lankan team we faced at the start of the tournament, and their improvement is a credit to all involved.

We'd done okay to keep them to 274 from their 50 overs on a beautiful Adelaide Oval batting wicket, though annoyingly they did hit 54 from the last five overs, but then no less than *five* of our top seven batsmen were run out, me without even facing a ball after a mix-up with Simon Katich. Amazingly, one of their fieldsmen, Tillakaratne Dilshan, was involved in four of the run outs, the highlight being the direct hit from cover point that was the undoing of Damien Martyn. This is the first time Australia had lost a VB Series finals match (or its equivalent) since 1997–98, Steve Waugh's first year as one-day captain, when we won the finals by two games to one.

It's very rare for a run out to be just one batsman's fault. In my case, I'd come out after Gilly had been caught in the deep off the first ball of Nuwan Kulasekara's second over, the 11th over of the innings. Kato was kept scoreless for the next four balls, and then took a single, keeping me off strike. The first ball of the next over, bowled by Chaminda Vaas, struck him on the pad and the ball dropped down on the offside. I saw where it had gone and knew there was a run there, but Kato didn't know where it had bounced to and your first instinct when that happens is to protect your stumps. By the time he discovered where the ball had gone and realised I was running we were close enough to whisper to each other, while Dilshan had dashed in, picked up the ball and was running to break the stumps at the non-striker's end. Both Kato and I should have been more aware of how the other man was thinking. Adelaide Oval might only have a short boundary from the middle to the entrance to the dressing-room, but let me assure you it's still a mighty long walk when you've been dismissed without facing a ball. From 0–51 after 10 overs we crashed to 3–64 in the 15th, and despite Michael Clarke's run-a-ball 80 an Australian victory never really looked likely from the time the run outs started happening.

IF THE FIRST FINAL was something of a disaster for us (not because we were defeated, but the manner in which we lost), the second game was a beauty, though it started almost catastrophically when we lost three wickets in the first three overs of the game. Andrew Symonds and I were left to revive the innings, which we did in pretty amazing style, adding an Australian record 237 for the fourth wicket before I was dismissed in the 41st over. Symmo went to his second 150 in ODI cricket, only the second Australian (after Adam Gilchrist) to do so, and we finished with the highest total ever achieved by Australia in ODI cricket, beating the 2–359 we hit in the 2003 World Cup final and the 5–359 we hit against India in Sydney in the 2003–04 VB Series finals.

A key moment in the partnership came early, when I felt Sri Lanka made a mistake in the way they used their power plays. This is not something I am saying with the benefit of hindsight — I actually told Symmo the moment it happened that I thought they'd offered us a chance to take control of the game — but it did represent a rare instance where the power plays were a factor in the outcome of a one-day game.

The 'power play' fielding restrictions — two five-over blocks where only two fieldsmen can be positioned outside the circle — are required to be implemented, at the fielding captain's discretion, at any point after the first 10 overs of the innings. (The mandatory two-fieldsmen-outside-the-circle restrictions that used to apply to the first 15 overs remain in place for the first 10 overs of the innings.) This concept was introduced by the ICC to try to disrupt the mechanical, often boring nature of many one-day innings, between the 15th and 40th overs, when batting sides often seemed content to score at five or six runs per over and the bowling sides were happy to let them. What usually happens now is that the fielding captains use their power plays one after the other, from overs 11 to 20, which means that the rigid nature of the games is maintained. But it is hard to argue with this from a captaincy point of view, because it is invariably the logical time to do it. The usually unpalatable alternative is to wait until later in the innings when the batsmen are looking for quick runs and having only two fieldsmen to protect the boundaries is simply not enough.

Here, though, Sri Lankan captain Marvan Atapattu opted not to use his second power play at the 16-over mark. At the time, we were 3–84 and going okay, but it was a short-term defensive move on their part at a time when the game was evenly poised. 'They shouldn't be doing it this way,' I said to Symmo. 'They should be forcing us to try to hit over the top.' With the fieldsmen back, we scored 32 runs from the next seven overs without taking a risk, and then Atapattu decided he couldn't wait any longer. Forty-one runs came from the next five overs while only two men were on the boundary, of which Symmo scored 23 runs from 13 balls, and a surge was created that the Sri Lankans could not control. These tactics also meant that Murali couldn't bowl when he wanted to, and he was eventually hit so often he finished with an ugly 0–99 from his 10 overs. (We would have liked to take him for a hundred, not to embarrass the great bowler but because it would have represented an outstanding *team* achievement.) Having scored 42 from his first 53 balls, Symmo belted another 108 from his last 72, putting on a dazzling exhibition that showed just how much he thinks about his batting and his game compared to the largely instinctive way he played a few short years ago. Later, he said to me that this partnership will be one of the things he'll look back on most fondly when his career is over. It'll be the same for me.

A controversial moment came when I was on 57. The Sri Lankans weren't happy after I refused to accept Mahela Jayawardene's word that he'd caught me at backward point, but I had a clear view and knew that he was mistaken and the ball hadn't carried. I think when the incident happened a number of people wanted to call me a hypocrite, because I have been campaigning strongly for everyone to believe the fieldsman when it comes to inconclusive 'bump-ball' catches — because the video replay rarely offers indisputable evidence. But to me this was different. I wasn't in any doubt as to what happened — it wasn't an inconclusive catch; the ball hit the ground before Mahela caught it — and in such circumstances I believe I had every right to stand my ground. I'm not suggesting he was cheating, just that he'd made an honest mistake, which is very different. If I hadn't been 100-per-cent sure and Mahela had said he caught it, I would have walked off without argument. Atapattu was particularly angry with the umpires, but a few overs later someone from the Sri Lankan dressing-room came out and told the fieldsmen that the replays had clearly shown that it wasn't a catch, and after that Mahela made a point of coming up to me and apologising. For me, that was the end of the matter.

LAST OCTOBER, IN THE second Super Series one-dayer, Gilly belted a hundred from a record-low 73 deliveries. Three-and-a-half months later, in the third final of the VB Series, he went six balls better, turning a game that at the change of innings had looked like it might be a tight one into a one-sided romp. All up, Gilly crunched four sixes and 13 fours, with one six returning to earth in the second tier of the grandstand; his first 50 came from 38 balls, and we reached 100 in the 18th over and 200 in the 33rd. The result was so assured and the hitting so clinical that just before the end the crowd of 26,139 were amusing themselves by starting Mexican waves and throwing paper cups onto the field. Lost in all this was an excellent knock by Simon Katich, who reached his own century off 136 deliveries, having taken 31 balls to score his first nine runs.

Gilly was very animated when he reached his hundred, showing just how much he enjoyed proving wrong those critics who'd claimed a couple of weeks ago that he was no longer worth his place at the top of the order. Kato was similarly pumped with his hundred, which came at the end of a summer when he'd been constantly under pressure to retain his place in our one-day side. And lost in the excitement of the blazing batting was the earlier effort of Nathan Bracken, who took four wickets — including both openers, Jayasuriya and Atapattu, in his opening spell — and confirmed once again how well he bowls at the Gabba. Bracks took a total of 11 wickets in the three finals (the next best on either side was Stuart Clark, with five) and impressed everyone in the Australian set-up with the way he added some variety to his bowling, especially the way he started bowling more cutters, in the second half of the tournament.

I was delighted to be out there at the finish, hitting Dilshan to mid-on for the winning single. Earlier, I'd taken one of my more improbable catches — back-pedalling from mid-wicket after Russel Arnold had miscued an attempted hit off Bracks and then sticking out one hand to complete the catch as I dived backwards — so it was a good day and night for me. I must confess that the fielding effort wouldn't have looked so good if I hadn't slightly misjudged it, but later it was described in some quarters as the 'catch of the season'. When people asked me later if it was that good, I pointed them back to Matthew Hayden's slip catch that dismissed Brian Lara in the Adelaide Test. That one was *really* special.

And so ended what was for us an up-and-down one-day season. We'd been terrific in the Super Series, good in parts in New Zealand, ordinary early but excellent during the latter stages of the VB Series qualifying tournament, not so good in the Adelaide final and the first three overs in Sydney, but from there to the end of the third final we were very good. The one constant was that we *always* worked hard, which meant that when the important moments in the games arrived we were usually ready for them. To finish with a 13–4 win–loss record for the ODI season represents a fair reward for our efforts

Now I'm pumped up about the idea of heading to South Africa to resume battle with Graeme Smith and his team. This is a little strange in that, if you'd asked me a month ago, I doubt I would have said I was going to feel quite so excited. I reckon there might have been something in those short breaks Gilly and I enjoyed, after all.

Part VIII

Losing Our Momentum

**Australia in South Africa
One-Day Internationals
February–March, 2006**

Tuesday, February 21

BECAUSE THE VB SERIES finals went to a third game, we were left with a five-day break before we were required at the airport yesterday for the flight to South Africa. In that short time, I suffered from the golf bug so badly that I was up at 6am some mornings so I could fit in nine holes before breakfast; otherwise, I took it fairly easy because I know the next 10 weeks — when we play one-dayers and then Tests against South Africa, and then Tests and one-dayers against Bangladesh — will be full on. This intensity won't be confined to the field either, with indications about that the South African crowds might want to return in kind some of the abuse their players copped from a few rogue Australians during their tour here. A couple of the South African players have intimated in the media that they wouldn't mind if this was the case. The playing side of the tour starts with a Twenty20 match on Friday in Johannesburg, where the fans have got on our backs before, so it could be an interesting start. When we were there in 2002 we had to get a cover placed over the players' walkway from the dressing-room to the field to stop people spitting at us and pouring drinks over us. I have no doubt that this time the atmosphere will be lively.

For the first few overseas tours I went on, especially when I was going to a country I'd never seen, just getting to the airport before the long flight was genuinely exciting. Nowadays, however, I've seen so many departure lounges, this side of my sporting life has become a chore. The cricket is still exciting, the travelling isn't. Packing and unpacking a suitcase, checking in, collecting bags, getting your room key, another flight, working out time differences so you can phone home at the right time . . . it's all part of the lifestyle but it's rarely fun. Fortunately, Cricket Australia really look after us now (any journey over three hours is business class, for example), and the coaching staff have put a lot of thought into how we travel. We need to land in the best possible physical condition, because it's never a case these days of us having a lot of time to get over a flight. In what seems like no time at all, we are invariably playing our opening match of a new tour. We don't drink alcohol on the flights any more, mostly water, and we try to sleep at the times that will have us ready to go whenever we get there.

Since I've become captain, it's become almost natural to find myself sitting next to Buck for much of a flight, because either he wants to talk to me or I want to talk to him. This one was no different. There is always some aspect of our planning we need to go over, a new concept to discuss, a strategy to review. Our coach always has our training mapped out for the next few weeks, and he might want to get an idea of potential team line-ups for the upcoming games, so he can be as well prepared as possible. Or he might have found something in a piece of footage Richard McIness, our performance analyst, has prepared for him (Buck has years of cricket video stored on his laptop). There is always so much time to kill on those flights, so it'd be silly not to make the most of it. For the other players, there is not much cricket talk, just their individual ways of killing the time — in-flight movies, cards, books, sleep. Some guys might seek some time with the coach or captain. We're all used to it and we always get there eventually.

THE SELECTION OF OUR squad for the first part of the South African tour — a Twenty20 game and then five one-day matches — was reasonably predictable. Shane Watson has recovered from his shoulder injury, and was preferred to his Queensland team-mate James Hopes, while with Glenn McGrath unavailable, Mitchell Johnson and Mick Lewis made it ahead of Brett Dorey and more experienced pace bowlers such as Michael Kasprowicz, Jason Gillespie and Andy Bichel. This preference for younger guys underlines for me the fact that the make-up of this one-day touring party has been determined with next season's World Cup in mind. The full squad is: Ricky Ponting (captain), Adam Gilchrist (vice captain), Nathan Bracken, Stuart Clark, Michael Clarke, Brad Hogg, Michael Hussey, Mitchell Johnson, Simon Katich, Brett Lee, Mick Lewis, Damien Martyn, Andrew Symonds and Shane Watson.

The side contains a nice blend of youth and experience (I say this based on the fact that in modern cricket, with players' careers extending well into their 30s, any player aged less than 30 is relatively young). I was pleased to see Watto back. My often-stated theory is that the most competitive sides at the World Cup will be those with high-class allrounders, and Shane remains the most likely man to fill that role for us. He's a terrific athlete, who I'd describe right at the moment as a very good batsman, handy bowler and excellent fieldsman. He was in good nick during the Super Series, and also showed glimpses of his enormous natural talent in the Gabba Test against the West Indies before he hurt his shoulder, but now is the time for him to step up and really make a statement in the international game.

The selection of Mitchell Johnson did cause some debate back home, with Geoff Lawson, the New South Wales and Australian Test bowler turned commentator, calling it an 'absolute disgrace'. I thought that was just silly. Mitchell is something of a rarity — a tall left-arm bowler with genuine pace — and this tour provides an excellent opportunity to give him a few games at the highest level and see what he's capable of. He is a guy who can swing the ball, which makes him potentially an impact player, the sort of cricketer who doesn't come along every day. I see his selection as an investment that might pay a big dividend not too far down the track.

There has also been some comment from Sydney over the non-selection of Phil Jaques, and chairman of selectors Trevor Hohns added to the debate by suggesting Jaquesy needs do a bit more work on his fielding. Frankly, I'm not sure about this, but I do know that during the summer, whenever Phil was with the Australian team, he was doing everything possible to develop his skills in this area, and I wonder about what a remark like this might do to his mindset next time he is fielding for Australia. This said, we are all aware that in modern cricket it is almost a fundamental requirement that you are capable in the field, and we always use our fielding standard as an indicator of how we are going as a team. Since England, this has been the area we have improved most dramatically.

It was strange arriving without Pidge, though we all know why he isn't here. Purely from a cricket perspective, we strongly wish he was, but it's not about cricket — we are happy that he is staying home where he is most needed. When someone who has been around the team for a long time is suddenly not there, the dynamic inevitably changes, and this is especially so when the absent individual is a great player and an outgoing bloke, both of which Pidge most definitely is. But no matter who it is that is left behind, a change in personnel has a positive side, because of the freshness and energy the new man inevitably brings to the group. For the senior guys, there is also the pleasure that comes with being able to welcome a newcomer and show him how everything works. The point I have made to the quicks who are here is that with Glenn missing they have an opportunity to stake a claim for the World Cup. With there seeming to be little likelihood of our great fast man being back for the South Africa Test series, there is also a huge, more immediate chance on offer there. As things stand, my preference would be for an experienced bowler to be brought into the Test squad once it is confirmed that Pidge is definitely out — probably Kasprowicz or Gillespie, who have both been taking plenty of wickets in the Pura Cup. But maybe one or more of Bracken, Lewis, Johnson and Clark can turn my opinion around.

Thursday February 23

WHILE SOME PEOPLE SEEM to have forgotten how good a one-day team the South Africans were in 2005, we certainly haven't, and with players such as Makhaya Ntini and Jacques Kallis expected back during the upcoming series, we know we'll be in for a tough contest. It might be a bit spicy, too, especially if an interview with Mark Boucher that was published in the *Wisden Cricketer* just before we began our 14-hour flight to Johannesburg is a good guide to how the South Africans are thinking. Boucher made some provocative comments that included this line: 'I hope our public give them a bit of stick because we've taken a serious amount.' I can't see how such a remark can help anyone, because he knows as well as everyone else that the racial abuse problems in Australia, while very real, came from just a few ugly people, and hardly reflected the mindset of cricket fans in general or the broader Australian community. However, two days after Boucher's comments were published, Andre Nel described Australian cricket followers as 'the rudest fans I have ever come across'. Maybe this is their way of trying to get the home crowds behind them, but to me taking such a negative line seems a strange way to do it.

Boucher also claimed that some 'nasty things' were said on the field during the games in Australia, and that while we shared a few beers after the Test series, he felt those beers were drunk 'for the sake of it because that's the right thing to do'. He must have been in a good mood when he did the interview, because he also said, 'I have lost respect for one or two of their players.' My suggestion is that he gets a thicker skin. There was an edge to the games at times when they were in Australia, as there has been in Australia–South Africa matches for as long as I can remember, but nothing spiteful, and I felt that the exchanges definitely went both ways.

I know Justin Langer, who is still in Australia and who had a brief run-in with the South African keeper during the Sydney Test, has publicly described Boucher's comments as 'stupid', and John Buchanan pointed out after we landed in Jo'burg that 'our record over the last while has been pretty well exemplary, with just the odd incident, and we hope to leave the tour unscathed'.

Elsewhere in his interview, Boucher said, 'Every tour I've been on to Australia, about a month or two before, we start talking about the way they play. We build it up way too much.' I found this more interesting than his complaints about crowd and player behaviour. Talk, usually from South Africa, about the psychological advantage we have over them has been around for so long it must be true. Some of the tight Test matches of recent times we have prevailed in, even the Tests we won in Melbourne and Sydney this season, certainly offer evidence of this, as do one-dayers like the two famous games we won at the 1999 World Cup that cost South Africa a spot in the final. It's important we maintain this grip on them.

It wouldn't surprise me if they do over-analyse things. It's actually easy to do when things aren't going completely right; it's something we might have been guilty of during last year's Ashes Tests, when we became a little consumed by all the comment about how well English players like Pietersen and Flintoff and Jones and Harmison were going. More than once, I said at team meetings, 'We are worrying too much about what they are doing and getting away from the way we play, from what has made us so successful over the years.' I felt this was especially true of our batsmen. It's something that can be difficult to stifle once you start doing it. Yet it wasn't as if we hadn't been challenged before; we've faced some excellent attacks over the years and had great successes against them, but England, for some reason, were different, perhaps because the ramifications of a loss — given that we'd held the Ashes for so long — were so dire. Since then, we've learnt our lesson, and I don't think we'll fall into the same trap when the Poms come to Australia next season.

BOUCHER'S COMMENTS CAUSED SOMETHING of a storm, but Adam Gilchrist opted to ignore the negativity when he was met by reporters. 'Everyone seems so genuinely happy to have us here and the hospitality is second to none,' he said. This is something I've picked up on, too — that many locals are genuinely glad to see us. Could this be related to a vibe I'm also getting that many of the South African players are not quite as popular with some of their own supporters as they might think? It seems they might have been whingeing a bit too much, when they should have been focusing on their own games. I've had quite a few people approach me to express their hope that we put the home team in its place before this tour is through.

Maybe it is because we are in Johannesburg, a city that has a reputation for violent crime and where we are advised to be careful whenever we venture out of the team hotel, but I can't help thinking that the South African cricketers asking their crowds to be hostile just isn't clever. My fear is that too many inflammatory statements could lead to an explosive atmosphere that would tarnish rather than add to the cricket. I don't think we've reached that stage yet, but maybe a few people do need to calm down. At our team meeting tonight, on the eve of the Twenty20 international, I tried to play down the edgy relationship between the two teams, though I did remind the boys that we must never get distracted by anything unexpected or bizarre that might come from the crowd. South Africa has always been a pretty tough place in which to play one-day cricket, not least because the local supporters can be as loud and fervent as any I've experienced around the world. But we've overcome that home support on previous tours. 'If the fans go quiet,' I said, 'that'll mean we're playing well.'

We're going to use similar tactics in tomorrow night's game to how we played in the Twenty20 game at the Gabba. We'll bat first if we win the toss and arrange the bowling order as if it was a mini 50-over game. This is even though I'm not convinced that batting first will be an advantage, especially in Jo'burg. The ball traditionally moves around here, so we'll be putting our faith in our five pace bowlers: Lee, Bracken, Lewis, Clark and Watson. At training during the past couple of days, in the nets that are located on the rugby ground out the back of the Wanderers, the ball has been swinging, though it has been impossible to get a true measure of what might happen on game day because the practice wickets were saturated — a situation the groundsman blamed on the South Africans, who had apparently been on them the day before when it was raining, so he couldn't cover them until it was too late. The bowlers had to be careful, and the batsmen were reluctant to have a serious net.

It has been quite humid here, with a lot of rain about, so maybe the batsmen will be at a disadvantage. A Twenty20 game played in conditions that traditionally suit the bowlers might be interesting, but the ground here is still small, the outfield is invariably slick, and the bats will be swinging. Most likely, there'll still be plenty of runs belted.

A STORY THAT HAS received plenty of coverage in recent times has been about the Kookaburra bats that Mike Hussey, Brett Lee and I, among others, are using. The controversy first raised its head last October, before the Super Series, and a few days back the Marylebone Cricket Club in London, which is still the body responsible for the laws of the game, ruled that the bats were illegal, apparently because they believe that the carbon graphite stickers on the back of them increase their power. I must say this decision astonished me, and I know that the blokes at Kookaburra are going to have the bats independently tested to prove there is nothing wrong with them.

My bat is known as the 'Kahuna', while the blade Huss and Bing use is the 'Beast'. As it stands at the moment, we can use our bats during the one-day games here in South Africa, but not in the Test matches that follow, so my plan is to continue with them as is for now, and then get the stickers removed before the first Test. It's frustrating that some people are suggesting that Kookaburra are doing something akin to 'corking' bats in baseball, because I know from experience that the stickers have made absolutely no difference to the bats' performances. Why? Because when the concept came up, I had the bats I was using (and I loved) sent away to get the stickers put on, and when they came back they didn't perform any differently. The bats were still fantastic, that's for sure, but none of their quality came from the 0.6mm thick piece of carbon graphite stuck on the back of them.

I'm very fussy when it comes to my bats, because owning a great one can make so much difference. There is also no doubt that the bats the top cricketers use in the 21st century are superior to those of the past. When I first started in first-class cricket, I was using bats that weighed around 2lb 6oz (1.08kg) and there was no way I could just stand straight at the crease and drive a quick on the up-over mid-off unless I hit the ball right in the middle. Nowadays, I use a slightly heavier bat, around 2lb 9oz or 2lb 10oz, but it 'picks up' lighter and has a broader sweet spot.

For the last five or six years, whenever I have needed new bats, I have sent over an old one I really like to the bat maker in India, where the Kookaburra bats are produced. What I need are precise replicas of that bat, and the designer will go through piles of willow to find exactly what I'm after. It's not just about the shape or the weight of the blade either — the relationship between a batsman and his bat is a very special one, and looks are important, too. My favourite bat becomes like an old friend, providing me with added confidence when he accompanies me to the middle; it is remarkably reassuring in a pressure situation to get into my batting stance and then look down at the familiar features of my bat before I look up to watch the bowler in his run-up. The best bats are the ones that never let you down when you wind up for a drive or try to hook the fastest bumper. For me, it's like being on the tee of a par-five with my big driver — I feel so much more assertive with that club in my hand than I do if I'm playing safe with a five wood.

The faces of my bats always have a contrast: the timber towards the outside edge, two or three centimetres wide, is redder than the rest of the blade. This red willow is the softest wood in the tree, and my view is that the softer the wood, the better the bat. These bats with the softer timber don't last as long, but they perform better. On most tours, I like to take four or five bats with me, though in England — where the balls are harder — you need a few more. As a rule, you break more bats in one-day cricket, when you might swing hard at balls that are going to hit down near the toe of the bat, or up close to the splice, so if there are a lot of one-day games in a schedule I might make room for a couple more bats in my kit, too. One thing I will never do is use my 'Test bat' at training — it's too precious for that. If it's going to break, I want it to break out in the middle, after I've got the maximum use out of it in game situations.

The first 'serious' bat I owned was a Duncan Fearnley size five, which was followed by a David Hookes-autograph Gray-Nicolls 'scoop'. My association with Kookaburra began nearly 20 years ago, at a time when there was a state-wide one-day competition in Tassie called the 'Kookaburra Cup'. I was 11 years old, and made four hundreds in five games in the under–13s component of that competition, and then made two hundreds in the under–16s. After that, a bloke called Ian Young, father of the future Tasmanian and Australian player Shaun Young, called a good mate of his, Ian Simpson, who was also a senior marketing figure at Kookaburra, to tell him about this young kid from Mowbray who was scoring all these runs in the competition they were sponsoring. I was introduced to this gentleman during the final of the Kookaburra Cup at the NTCA Ground in Launceston; the result was that he organised for some bats, pads and gloves to be sent to me, and I've been using their gear — graphite stickers and no graphite stickers — ever since. When a few people in the media started insinuating that Kookaburra and I were basically cheating by using the bats that have been so kind to me, I got really angry. It wasn't like these people were attacking my family, but it was close.

Twenty20 International

At Johannesburg (February 24): South Africa 4–201 (20 overs: GC Smith 89*, HH Gibbs 56; ML Lewis 2–31) defeated Australia 7–199 (20 overs: GB Hogg 41, B Lee 43; AJ Hall 3–22, RJ Peterson 2–29) by two runs

IT DOESN'T SEEM LIKE three years since we were out in the middle of the Wanderers Stadium, singing our team song after winning the 2003 World Cup final. This ground will always be a special place for me because of that remarkable day, as it will be for all the Aussie guys who were there. This time the stakes were much lower, but though Twenty20 might essentially be entertainment, and we'd hardly prepared for the game as if it was a Test match, there was still something to be won and lost tonight. As it turned out, we were outplayed for most of the game, but near the death a frantic seventh-wicket partnership between Brad Hogg and Brett Lee almost got us back into the game. We needed 19 runs from the final over, and though eight runs came from the first three balls, the next two deliveries yielded only two more, which made the Bing's big six off the last ball of the match meaningless.

The South Africans had picked something like a 'specialist' Twenty20 team, if such a thing is possible, while we were without Andrew Symonds, who strained his left hip-flexor muscle at training yesterday, and Mike Hussey, who didn't leave Australia with the rest of us so he could be with his wife when she gave birth to their second child, a boy named William Oliver. Indications are that Symmo will miss at least the first couple of games in the one-day series, which begins in two days' time, while Huss is due in South Africa tomorrow.

I know that some 'old timers' might have been shaking their heads at Huss being allowed to stay behind as he did, but it was a 'no-brainer' as far as I was concerned. In my view, the members of our team should always be given the chance to put major family events such as births, bereavements, illnesses and so on before their cricket, without it being held against them in any way. Of course, in doing so a player might be offering an opportunity to the team-mate who will play in his place, but the other side of that is that the affected cricketer would hardly be able to perform at his best if he was made to play while his mind was elsewhere.

In this case, Huss was on the plane the day after his son was born, but for me it wouldn't have been a problem if he'd opted to stay another day or two. In fact, the joke among the team has been that Huss, being the cricket tragic that he is, would have tried to arrange the birth and the flight so that he could have made it in time for tonight's game. We can picture him wearing his 'yellows' under his team suit so that he could look the part as he walked through customs and into the arrivals lounge, and then he'd hail a cab, bolt to the ground, take off his civvies like Superman, and run straight on to the field.

The sell-out crowd for the Twenty20 was boisterous and not put off in the least by the fact that the start of the game was delayed by a couple of hours. It did appear that many of the spectators had read the Mark Boucher interview and decided to follow the keeper's instructions, and the noise they generated was made even more intense as it echoed off the big, steep grandstand and scoreboard that dominate one side of the Wanderers Stadium. This made for an atmosphere more football crowd or rock concert than cricket match. It was immediately obvious that the South Africans were going to try to use this game to ignite their home season — a little like England did with the Twenty20 game that launched our Ashes tour last year — and in this regard they must have been delighted with the batting of Graeme Smith and Herschelle Gibbs, both of whom looked to be in much better touch than they had been in Australia.

For me, though, the game was ordinary. In Australia, we played under a rule that stated that the fielding restrictions were in place for the first six overs of the innings, so as soon as the sixth over ended, with South Africa 1–48, I started waving blokes back to the boundary. Quickly, the umpires told me that over here the restrictions applied for the first seven overs, which had me wishing that someone had told me that before the game started. It didn't change my tactics at all, but it did have me wondering what other rules might have been altered. When we batted, Adam Gilchrist and I were out before the end of the fourth over, both lbw to Andrew Hall, and both very unlucky.

Hall, a medium-pace seamer, was the best of the South African bowlers, and his success underlined something about the wickets we might be confronted with during this tour. You're always looking to learn things, and this might actually turn out to be the biggest lesson we pick up from this game. We have been told since we landed in Jo'burg that pitches across the country don't have as much pace in them as they once did, and there has been talk in the press that the local curators might try to rig the Test wickets to thwart Shane Warne. This deck was certainly dry and slower than the Wanderers pitches we've played on in the past, and if it's typical of tracks we're going to play on Warney should be okay, but we might have to reassess the make-up of our bowling attacks. There might be fewer opportunities for the swing bowlers than we originally expected.

AT A MEETING BEFORE the Twenty20 game that involved the ICC match referee Chris Broad, Graeme Smith and me, we came to a decision not to use the supersub rule in the one-day matches on this tour. As things stand, the rule is still an official ICC playing condition, and we will have to nominate a substitute, but we've effectively settled on a 'gentleman's agreement' not to use the sub during any of the games.

This suits me fine. I think most people around the cricket world have concluded that the rule is flawed. By being obliged to name your supersub before the toss, rather than after, winning that toss becomes unduly important. If you nominate a bowler as your supersub, but then lose the toss and have to bowl first, your sub is often of little value, sometimes even useless. In such circumstances, you're effectively playing 11 against 12. This happened in Perth during the VB Series, when Brett Dorey was the 12th man but Sri Lanka won the toss and Brett never got involved.

If they are to keep it, the ICC need to at least amend the rule, so that the supersub is nominated after the toss. My strong preference for a while has been for it to be scrapped altogether. We learnt recently that they have decided that the supersub won't be used in any ODI series after March 21, and definitely not in next year's World Cup, so to Chris, Graeme and me it makes sense to play here by the rules we'll be using during important games in the near future, rather than continuing with a system that will, for the next 12 months at least, be obsolete.

The two five-over power plays will remain in operation. I'm not dead against this innovation, but I wonder whether the power plays would work better if one of them was given to the batting team. This was an idea floated by Daniel Vettori during last year's Chappell–Hadlee series. Either that or maybe they could force the bowling team to use one after the 30-over mark.

The power plays were introduced to try to bring some variety to one-day cricket, but it appears the lawmakers have to go a step further if they want them to achieve something like what they were designed for. Or maybe they just have to accept that cosmetic changes such as supersubs and power plays are really not going to make much difference; that if there is a problem with one-day cricket then it is the participants' responsibility to fix it. My opinion has always been that if we players approach one-day cricket in the right way, and don't restrict the limits of how we play and what we can achieve, who knows how thrilling the game can be?

Saturday, March 4

One-day Series

Game One at Pretoria (February 26): Australia 8–229 (47 overs: MJ Clarke 53, MEK Hussey 56; SM Pollock 3–23) lost to South Africa 4–207 (37.3 overs: GC Smith 119*, AB de Villiers 43) by six wickets (Duckworth/Lewis method)

Game Two at Cape Town (March 3): South Africa 7–289 (50 overs: HH Gibbs 66, MV Boucher 42, JM Kemp 51) defeated Australia 93 (34.3 overs: M Ntini 6–22, A Nel 3–30) by 196 runs

ONE THING THAT'S WORSE than being captain of a losing side is being captain but not part of a losing side because you're injured. That is the fate that befell me for the first two games of this one-day series. The injury was, in basic terms, an 'abdominal strain'. It wasn't actually a major tear or anything like that, but because I managed to hurt a muscle that is central to all my movements it was always jabbing at me, always reminding me that I wasn't able to sit up, sneeze or even sleep the way I wanted to, let alone bat, bowl, field or run.

With Symmo (hip-flexor strain) and Stuart Clark (bruised rib) also unavailable, we were down to 11 fit players for game one of the one-day series. At least the selection of the side was easy, and we were lucky they'd ditched the supersub concept because I have no idea who would have been the 12th man if it had still been in operation. The best positive I could come up with when the press asked me about my injury was: 'It is a good opportunity for some of the guys to move up the batting order and show us what they can do.' I guess that was true.

The manner in which I damaged my gut was bizarre. On February 25, the day after the Twenty20 game, we had travelled the 50 kilometres from our hotel in Johannesburg to Pretoria for a session at the ground that would host the first ODI 24 hours later. After we arrived at the ground it was announced that we were going to pay a lot of attention to our warm-up and stretches, to make sure there was no stiffness left over from the long bus trip. We must have spent a good half hour stretching, then we walked a couple of laps, then a jog, some run-throughs before we were allowed to head for the nets. But just as the first guys were putting the pads on, it started to rain, so we had to pack up all our gear and dash up into the change rooms, from where we could get a good view of the rain pouring down.

Some blokes wanted to hang around and hope the rain would stop, others decided they didn't need a hit all that badly, while a few us headed for the indoor nets. Once there, I had to wait for about 10 minutes before I found myself facing Mitch Johnson bowling with a brand new white ball on some very bouncy artificial turf and with a very white background right behind his bowling arm. These were hardly match-like conditions, but I still felt I needed to have a hit.

After he'd bowled maybe a dozen balls, Mitch bowled one that pitched on a good length and started swinging into me. I went back on my stumps as the ball bounced and kept ducking, and as I tried to hit it away into the legside I also jumped in the air and hunched my body forward. You try doing all this at once! In doing this contortion I put too much pressure on the right side of my abdomen, and straightaway I felt the muscle rip. Initially, I hoped

In the first Test against South Africa, at the WACA, Brad Hodge (left) turned his first Test century into a double ton. However, a day later, Jacques Rudolph (photographed with Mark Boucher at the end of the Test) played a superb defensive knock that earned his team a draw.

With my wife Rianna at the Melbourne Cricket Ground on Christmas Day 2005.

Above: With Grace Hayden at the MCG, 24 hours before the start of the Boxing Day Test.

Above right: Ashwell Prince has just been caught Ponting bowled Warne in South Africa's first innings in Melbourne.

Right: Glenn McGrath congratulates Mike Hussey on his fantastic century during their critical stand on the second day of the second Test.

Above: Brett Lee has bowled Jacques Kallis at the MCG.

Above right: Andrew Symonds gets excited as his Test career finally takes off. Here he's just trapped Mark Boucher lbw; soon he had two more wickets, and the following day he scored 72 from 54 balls.

Right: I've just scored a hundred in my 100th Test.

A victory leap that confirms my 100th Test has ended just the way I wanted it to.

Punter and BJ (Brad Haddin) at the Gabba during the first Twenty20 international to be staged in Australia.

Nathan Bracken (left) and Glenn McGrath prepare for the start of the VB Series.

At the helm of ABN AMRO ONE on Port Phillip Bay — an awesome experience.

The winners on Allan Border Medal night: (from left) Phil Jaques, Dan Cullen, me, Shane Warne, Mike Hussey and Karen Rolton.

I'm about to be run out without facing a ball after a mix-up with Simon Katich during the first VB Series final in Adelaide.

I'll always remember my hundred in the second VB Series final as one of my favourites — scored in front of a full house at the SCG during a long and very enjoyable partnership with Andrew Symonds.

The third VB Series final at the Gabba turned into a celebration for the Australian openers, Adam Gilchrist (left) and Simon Katich.

Above left: In the nets at Johannesburg at the start of our South African adventure.

Above: Coach John Buchanan and I face the men and women of the press during the opening media conference of the tour.

Left: Last pair Stuart Clark and Mick Lewis have just scored the winning runs in Game Four of the one-day series in South Africa, levelling the rubber at 2–all with one to play.

it was a cramp of some kind, but I knew it wasn't, so I walked out of the net and back to the dressing-room, where I threw my gear all over the place and carried on for a minute. I told Errol Alcott what happened, he pushed and prodded around my side and stomach, we iced it for a little while and then I got changed so we could go to the hospital back in Johannesburg and I could have an MRI scan.

ERROL WAS A RUGBY league man who had little experience in top-level cricket when he first won the job as the Australian physio in 1984. He reputedly earned his nickname of 'Hooter' on one of his first days in the new job by innocently asking, 'What time does the hooter go?' when he wanted to know when the day's play ended. (In league, the siren that sounds to signify the end of the game is colloquially known as the 'hooter'.) When I was injured in Pretoria 22 years later, he was in the dressing-room looking after a couple of our blokes, but somehow he was expecting me when I walked in. I don't how he does that; it's like the uncanny way during a game when he seems to be running out of the dressing-room and onto the field when a guy gets hurt even before the injury has been suffered.

When I was right to go, we jumped into a police car for the trip to the hospital, a journey completed in world-record time. Why a police car? The Aussie team always travels around Jo'burg and the surrounding areas with a police escort, and in this instance the car was waiting for training to finish so they could accompany us back to our hotel. The alternative for Errol and me was to take the team bus, but obviously that would have meant a much slower journey and inconvenienced everyone else, so once it was determined that the police car could get to the hospital and back in time to escort the bus home, Hooter and I were on our way, siren blazing.

The MRI confirmed that this was easily the worst muscle tear I've ever had. Most of my problems in the past have been minor ailments with my lower back and hips. At first, Hooter described this injury as 'three weeks', as in three weeks off (a diagnosis that was confirmed by Dr Trefor James of Cricket Australia, after copies of the scans were emailed to him in Australia), but straightaway, we went to work on the injury — mostly ice treatment for the first couple of days, then he was into the damaged area, gentle to start with then firmer as the stomach muscles started to loosen up. Like a lot of physios, with Hooter there's never any machinery around; it's all hands-on stuff and somehow it's impossible to fool him. The danger is to try to do too much too soon, and early on I kept thinking I might be healthier than I actually was, but quickly I'd remember that Hooter has been a master at getting players back on the field as soon as possible, but no sooner, for more than 20 years. He didn't let me down. I actually thought I was close enough to right to be able to play in the second one-dayer in Cape Town, and had a reasonably pain-free net the day before the game, but our physio's firm advice was to give it a couple more days. I would have been mad not to listen to him. But unless something unexpected happens overnight, I'm a certain starter for game three tomorrow.

Hooter has a better grasp of how a team needs to function than just about anyone else I've met, and his overall cricket experience has been so rich and rewarding, there can't be too many blokes alive with a better understanding of what makes Test cricketers tick. He knows how to get blokes together and can recognise immediately when the mechanics of the team aren't functioning as smoothly as they should be. Maybe this has something to do with the fact that when he began his life as a cricket physio the Aussie team wasn't going well, and in the past decade we've been very successful, so he's seen both sides and can recognise what makes the difference. He is also a shrewd observer and a good listener, with an almost unique ability to keep confidences while at the same time letting the team hierarchy know the things about injuries and mindsets that they *need* to know. While he might have come into the Australian set-up without any high-level cricket experience, he's still made many telling contributions over the years that have nothing with do with his medicine.

I remember in the Caribbean in 1995, my first big tour, when Hooter stood up and basically ran a team meeting, giving a stirring speech that focused on the shift in balance that was occurring between the two teams. The West Indies were now the 'hunted', he told us, and we were the 'hunters', which is always the better position to be in. He had recognised that many of the guys in the team who had been defeated by the Windies in the past still had something of a mental block about the idea of beating them, and he wanted to set that straight. I was 20 years old and have never forgotten it, not least because guys like the Waugh twins and Glenn McGrath then stood up to the best the West Indies could throw at us and we won back the Frank Worrell Trophy.

WHEN I'M PLAYING, AND especially when I'm due to bat, I'm not a particularly good watcher of cricket, mainly because I know that eventually the process gets me mentally tired and seeing things that might not be there. But when I'm not directly involved in the game, I do closely observe what's going on. In these first two one-dayers, when we were in the field I focused on how Adam Gilchrist was using the bowlers, the field placements and the body language of different players. Before the games began, I still led the team meeting as I usually do, but once the match began I left Gilly alone. Going into this series, his record as skipper was quite exceptional: six Tests as captain for four wins, one draw and one loss, and 11 ODIs as skipper for 10 wins. Even with these two losses here, in charge of a much-weakened team, he has one of the best captaincy success rates of all time in international cricket, and leadership in one-day cricket is often instinctive anyway, so it was hardly necessary for me to be overloading him with my opinions. Instead, I made sure I was available if he wanted to ask me questions, and otherwise tried as best I could to fill that non-player's support role that has often been a crucial factor in the Australian team's success.

It certainly wasn't Gilly's fault that the team was beaten in Pretoria and Cape Town. Graeme Smith dominated the first game, carrying on from the Twenty20 encounter and re-establishing himself as a key figure at the top of the South African batting order. That he has fought back in this way says something about his character, because we'd talked about the need to stay on top of him, yet he'd countered our best efforts to keep him down. He has obviously thought about his game and now it might be time for us to think about ours, though I still believe if we can be as relentless in our bowling to him as we were in Australia, mostly chiselling away at or just outside his off stump, then we can wear him down. There is still an awful lot of pressure on him to live up to the big statements he made earlier in the season. The rain that interrupted the game twice — at the 40-over mark of our innings and then when they were close to victory — didn't have a major impact on the game, though under these circumstances, with the outfield damp and the South African innings reduced to a maximum 41 overs, Brad Hogg's ability to bowl eight overs of wrist-spinners for just 30 runs was a good effort.

About the only other positive we could take from the two matches was Michael Clarke's batting at Pretoria — he came in at 3–25 and played beautifully, hitting everything in the middle of the bat. Mike Hussey also went okay, but we're used to that. These two digs apart, our batting was mediocre in game one and dreadful in game two, when Makhaya Ntini looked like a superstar. To collapse to 4–7 in the 10th over and get bowled out for less than 100 in 34.3 overs when our opponents had scored 7–289 was very poor, and we couldn't use the excuse that we were short-handed any more because Phil Jaques had been flown in to give us a full complement of batsmen. I guess it was a hard ask for Phil to go pretty much from the airport to the middle in the second over to face a fired-up Ntini, even though I know he was grateful for the opportunity. He lasted only four balls before he was caught by Justin Kemp at second slip. Now, as I'm likely to be right for tomorrow's third one-dayer at Port Elizabeth, Jaquesy will probably be heading straight back to Australia — hardly the South African adventure he would have hoped for.

I don't like making excuses, especially when we have just been embarrassed in the way we have, but it is true that the practice facilities we've encountered so far on tour have not been perfect. From the moment we landed back in Australia after the Ashes series, we recognised that getting our practice right was going to be a key component in our revival, and throughout the home season we were committed, focused and excellent on the training grounds. However, for reasons beyond our control, most of them weather-related, we haven't been able to do that here. I'm confident that once we get our preparation right, this tour will turn around. As an example, Brett Lee, who has gone for 1–110 in 18 overs so far in the one-day series, mentioned to me tonight that he is struggling to find his rhythm, but I'm not concerned by that because he knows his game now and if he can have more game time and a good workout in the nets he won't be out of sync for long.

As a team, what we need to do as soon as possible is arrest the momentum the South Africans have built up. Whether we bat or bowl first in game three, we've got to be assertive from the jump and put the pressure back on them. If we don't, this one-day series might already be over.

Wednesday, March 8

One-day Series
Game Three at Port Elizabeth (March 5): Australia 6–254 (50 overs: SM Katich 49, RT Ponting 62, DR Martyn 51) defeated South Africa 230 (47.2 overs: AB de Villiers 68, SM Pollock 69; B Lee 4–48) by 24 runs

ST GEORGE'S PARK AT Port Elizabeth is a place where the Australian one-day team has not played particularly well in the past, yet its win–loss record there is exceptional: eight games (including yesterday) for seven wins. My first ODI at the ground came in 2002, when we conceded 326 in 50 overs but still won after Gilly got our reply off to an absolute flier. During the 2003 World Cup, it became a lucky venue for us, yet against both England and New Zealand we batted poorly before Michael Bevan and Andy Bichel rescued us, and in the semi-final against Sri Lanka, Andrew Symonds (who scored 91) was the only one of our batsmen to get past 40. I've never really enjoyed batting there, because the pitch is slow and as a consequence shot-making is not easy. Game three of this one-day series last Sunday was no different, in fact it might have been worse, and the combination of the slow wicket and my lack of practice over the past two weeks had me scratching around early. I started to middle a few towards the end of my innings, but the 62 runs I scored from 82 balls was still my slowest half-century in ODI cricket since I took

95 balls to score 66 when I was helping to make sure we beat Bangladesh at Canterbury back in June.

I was much more pleased that I stuck around than disappointed that it wasn't my most stylish knock, not least because I was hardly the only batsman to struggle with the pace of the wicket. It was a beautiful day and another full house was in attendance, but from a batting perspective, it was a game for grinding. We knew pretty much from the first ball that the track was going to get slower and slower, so in this sense we were probably lucky that South Africa sent us in. The mistake would have been to go too hard, too early, but though we never set ourselves a specific target (my view is that to limit yourself in this way can be counterproductive — if a ball's there to hit, you still hit it), in the back of our minds we knew that what would normally be regarded as a 'reasonable' total might actually be a match-winning one.

For the first two-thirds of the innings, we scored at four runs an over, before mounting an assault that amassed 84 runs in the final 10 overs, 45 in the last five. For me, this was good, controlled batting. It's become almost an accepted maxim in one-day cricket that if you have wickets in hand at the 30-over mark, you'll double your score; in this case, we did even better than that, going from 2–120 to 6–254, so we knew we'd done okay. Mike Hussey's 22 from 10 deliveries, including two sixes over mid-wicket, proved to be a crucial cameo.

With the ball, Brett Lee was more like his usual self, getting two wickets early (including Graeme Smith, caught behind pushing a little tentatively) and two more in the 45th over to seal the victory. In between, Shane Watson and Michael Clarke bowled really well on the slow wicket, and while Brad Hogg didn't contribute with his bowling, he did take a freakish catch at long-on to dismiss AB de Villiers. This effort was a bit like the one I took against Sri Lanka at the Gabba in the third VB Series final, only more important. Shaun Pollock and de Villiers had hit the home team back into the game, before Pollock was bowled by Watson in the 43rd over, when the required run-rate was almost nine runs per over. Five balls after that dismissal, de Villiers went for the glory shot off Clarke and — typical of this pitch — didn't quite get it. Hoggy's first reaction was to run in, but then he realised he'd misjudged it, so he back-pedalled . . . back-pedalled . . . and then stuck his left hand over his head and behind him, and came up with a stunning catch.

It was a great moment for a great team man. It's really not Hoggy's style to do the spectacular, and I don't mean that in a derogatory way. There is just nothing flashy or fancy about his cricket, but since Shane Warne stopped playing ODI cricket in 2002–03, Hoggy has kept doing the job with the ball, been more than handy with the bat and is always very good in the field. He can be hard on himself if he bowls a bad ball, but at the same time you can certainly tell he's enjoying himself when he plays for Australia and that he's very proud whenever he's wearing his national team's colours. In an era when we've had a lot of very good men play one-day cricket for Australia, his contribution has probably been undervalued by everyone except his team-mates.

WE NOW FIND OURSELVES in Durban preparing for game four on Friday, and it seems Andrew Symonds will be right to play. It's funny how things can change — two-and-a-half months ago, it seemed like everyone was campaigning for Symmo to be booted out of the Test side; after a couple of one-day losses here he has now been identified as the key man to revitalise things. There is no doubt that when it comes to limited-over cricket, Symmo is close to the complete package; perhaps only Andrew Flintoff can offer more when you consider the best allrounders' ability to make an impact with the bat and ball and in the field. Our hope, of course, is that Symmo can have a similar sort of impact in Test matches, and with the announcement yesterday of the Test squad for the series that follows the one-dayers, he will continue to get that chance. With Shane Watson fit again, there was always the possibility that he would have been given the allrounder's spot, but it would have been hard to leave Symmo out after his Boxing Day Test heroics and excellent one-day batting form. And unfortunately there just wasn't room for both of them.

There were a couple of surprises, the most notable being the choice of Damien Martyn and Michael Clarke in front of Brad Hodge. No doubt, Hodgey was very unlucky, but he hadn't quite put his stamp on the No. 4 spot since he made that double ton in Perth, and Marto and Pup have batted well in the one-day games we've played since then. I envisage Marto coming back into the Test XI at four, and I'll be surprised if he doesn't do the job for us. I thought he was stiff to be dropped in the first place, and rate him as one of the most underrated players in Australia over the past few years, yet for some reason, while other blokes have had their excellent performances celebrated, many of Marto's best efforts have slipped under the radar. When he's firing, he's as good as anyone.

With Glenn McGrath unavailable, Michael Kasprowicz, Stuart Clark and Shaun Tait were given the fast-bowling places behind Brett Lee. Kasper is currently the leading wicket-taker in the Pura Cup back home, and with Pidge out his experience will be invaluable, while Shaun has apparently shown in his last couple of games that he's over his shoulder injury and back to full pace. The last spot was probably between Stuart and Nathan Bracken, and the slow wickets we've encountered on tour were probably what got Stuart over the line.

The Test squad was announced on Tuesday, and from what I gather the reception it has received back home has been 'mixed' — especially in Melbourne, where a lot of people are upset about Hodgey's omission. Such is the life of a selector when there are more players in contention than places to fill. The following day, when we were on the bus returning from training, the selector who is 'on duty' with the team at the moment, Andrew Hilditch, revealed to me our line-up for Friday's fourth one-dayer. The thing that stood out immediately for me was that, with Symmo coming back, Shane Watson is the guy to miss out. It was a double whammy for Watto — no Test place one day, out of the one-day team the next.

Even though I'm not a selector, I know some guys want to have a yarn with the captain if selection decisions go against them, so while Andrew was the guy who originally informed Watto of his demotion, I did have a good talk to him after that. I emphasised that he hadn't been cast aside for good, but had lost out in this case because a very good player had been picked ahead of him. And there were also the experiences of a number of guys — Martyn, Kasprowicz, Symonds, Clarke, et al — over the past six months that emphasised the point that opportunities often come and go quickly. The key for any player out of the team is to be ready when the next big chance arrives. Watto wanted to know what he needs to change, but it is my honest view that he doesn't have to go away and do any more than what he has been doing. He already works as hard on his game and his fitness as any cricketer I know. I remember clearly from my time on the outer in 1996–97 and 1998–99 that being patient is never an easy thing for an ambitious cricketer who has tasted life at the top level. But patient and ambitious is what Shane needs to be.

Saturday, March 11

One-day Series

Game Four at Durban (March 10): South Africa 9–246 (50 overs: HH Dippenaar 101, SM Pollock 53*) lost to Australia 9–247 (49.1 overs: AC Gilchrist 45, SM Katich 46, A Symonds 76; R Telemachus 3–34) by one wicket

LAST NIGHT'S BATTING EFFORT was hardly one of our finest — poor selection being a feature as we collapsed from 0–87 in the 18th over chasing 247 to almost throw away a game we had to win — but at least we still sneaked home with the victory and have tomorrow's decider to look forward to. Of all the batsmen to make a mistake, I was as guilty as anyone, trying to drive Roger Telemachus on the up two balls after Damien Martyn had edged a good one through to the wicketkeeper. Fortunately, Andrew Symonds marked his return to the side with an outstanding innings of 71 and then our last three, Nathan Bracken, Stuey Clark and Mick Lewis, scrounged the final 29 runs to get us home.

It was a terrific return to the team for Symmo, but he would have been disappointed with the way he got out, trying to win too quickly when he had control of the game. Mick was the golden boy for us again in the final over of a big game, getting the necessary two runs through mid-wicket. Earlier, he'd bowled really tightly, especially in the 49th over of the South African innings, when he conceded only five runs at a time when Shaun Pollock was swinging at everything. Following his efforts in the Chappell–Hadlee Trophy series, he is making a name for himself as being able to finish games off.

When Bracks had been bowled by Andrew Hall in the 48th over, we still needed six to win, setting up a thrilling finish. Fortunately, our last pair held their nerve. The crowd, of course, would have been very disappointed with the loss, but they must have been engrossed with the tense finish and could hardly have complained about the value they got for their money. So it seems such a shame that Graeme Smith decided to try to cloak the fact that his team had thrown away a 2–0 lead in the rubber by accusing us of 'choking'. I don't think there is a sportsman or sportswoman in the world who appreciates being tagged in this way, especially when the evidence to support such a cheap shot simply doesn't exist.

'I thought they were the team that were choking, if that's the word, under pressure a little bit at the back end,' Smith reputedly said. He had been dismissed for 1 in the second over, caught behind again by a good outswinger from Bracken. He'd actually captained his team pretty well in the field, but the fact remained that he and his bowlers couldn't take that crucial last wicket when they needed to.

'He said that, did he?' I responded when the reporters read back Smith's quote when it was my turn to face the media. If any team had been choking out there it would have been the one that lost the game and the 2–0 advantage they'd once had in the series. 'They can say whatever they like,' I continued, with a mixture of anger and bemusement. 'If they want to keep talking it up and losing games, then fine.'

I don't know if this all amounted to the 'bitter slanging match' the papers described it as the following morning, but as I walked back to our dressing-room, I couldn't help wondering why the South African captain kept putting such comments out there for public consumption. Game five is a sell out, so they're not going to increase ticket sales, and Smith must know they aren't going to change the way we play or think. His comments seemed as misguided as were Mark Boucher's remarks from two or three weeks ago, even if the South African keeper is now saying his words were 'twisted'. I guess they're trying to talk themselves up by talking us down, but if these statements put pressure on anyone, surely it's on the blokes who make them.

Monday, March 13

One-day Series

Game Five at Johannesburg (March 12): Australia 4–434 (50 overs: AC Gilchrist 55, SM Katich 79, RT Ponting 164, MEK Hussey 81) lost to South Africa 9–438 (49.5 overs: GC Smith 90, HH Gibbs 175, MV Boucher 50*; NW Bracken 5–67) by one wicket

IT'S BEING TALKED ABOUT as the greatest one-day game ever, and I guess if nearly 900 runs have been scored, in one way it could be seen in that way. But frankly I don't think it was. The game was thrilling, dramatic and unique, and it featured some of the most fantastic hitting I have ever seen. The atmosphere was frenetic and desperate, as the packed, parochial crowd helped get South Africa across the line. It was one of those defeats when you have to tip your hat to the opposition, because they had to do a lot of brilliant things to win. However, for a cricket match to be truly great it surely needs to have some decent bowling as well, and just about all the bowling in this game was abysmal.

What happened? Over the past couple of seasons we in the Australian team have often talked about the importance of momentum — how vital it is to ride it, how devastating it can be if you can't arrest it when it's working against you. Never has that been better demonstrated than here. In both innings of this game, the batsmen starting hitting from the jump, it worked for them, they kept going with the flow and the bowlers couldn't cope. Throughout, as both teams powered towards 400 and beyond, I couldn't help thinking that all that was needed from a fielding team's perspective was for a bowler or two to go back to the fundamentals — line and length, varying pace, bowling to a field and, most importantly, trusting their own ability — and the deluge would stop. But it didn't happen. Instead, it was a bit like one of those multiple collisions on a fog-bound motorway, where car after car runs up the back of the one in front until dozens of vehicles are mangled together. The mistakes kept coming, and no one thought to slow down, play safe and get things right. Another appropriate analogy is with the golfer who is usually accomplished on the greens but then starts missing short putts. As the pressure in his mind grows, he starts killing himself with thoughts about how small the hole looks, and he keeps missing them. Here, when the bowlers needed to keep their nerve and land the ball in the right spots, instead they persisted in feeding the batsmen's strengths. All the adrenalin in the Wanderers Stadium made the batsmen superheroes, while pressure and anxiety turned the bowlers into lambs for the slaughter.

Another key factor was the 'no fear' mentality that has become a feature of modern batting. Sachin Tendulkar embodied this at his greatest, especially in the one-day game, as do players such as Adam Gilchrist, Matt Hayden, Virender Sehwag and Kevin Pietersen today, and as did Graeme Smith and Herschelle Gibbs from the first deliveries they faced in this match. Smith smashed his 90 from 55 balls, while Gibbs was phenomenal in blasting 175 from just 111 balls, with 21 fours and seven sixes. Think about that: over the course of his innings, his average for fours and sixes was better than one every four deliveries. On the night, these two guys were way too good for us.

The plethora of excellent batting wickets we have seen in recent years is one reason for the success of this no-fear approach; another is the quality of the bats we are now using; and a third is that one-day cricket and now Twenty20 cricket have taught the top batsmen that they can get away with hitting out so long as their eye and technique are in top working order. The result of all this is that the bowlers are the ones under pressure; they feel they have to bowl the perfect ball every ball or they are going to get belted, and not many of them enjoy bowling in such circumstances. What this game emphasised is that there has been a revolution in the art of batting over the past decade that I don't think too many bowlers have kept up with, which means that in the future we'll probably see more batting exhibitions like the two we saw yesterday. It will be very rare for it to happen in both innings of the same game, as happened here — and it should not be forgotten that with Jo'burg being 1700 metres above sea level the ball does fly and the outfield at the Wanderers is like the greens at Royal Melbourne — but I have absolutely no doubt that the 400-run barrier in a 50-over innings will get broken again. It could even be that some team will crack 450 one day, and a batsman will get 200 on his own, unless the bowlers of the world can meet the challenge and pick up their one-day games.

THE IRONY OF THIS momentum factor is that it was us who went into the game with all the positives flowing our way. We'd fought back from 2–0 down to level the series, and the South Africans' body language and Graeme Smith's silly post-game comments after game four strongly suggested that they thought their chance of claiming the rubber had gone. Then, after we won the toss, we got off to a real flier, scoring our first 50 in the eighth over and reaching 100 with just one wicket down halfway through over number 17. It was the perfect platform: it gave me time to get my eye in (just four singles from my first 12 balls) and then I went for it big-time and never stopped until I was dismissed after facing 105 deliveries.

The last time I'd batted here in a one-day international was the 2003 World Cup final, when I made 140 not out from 121 balls. This was just more of the same in that everything came off, almost unbelievably. Through the middle overs, Mike Hussey did the same thing and we added 158 in 15.4 overs, with runs coming off just about every ball, fours or sixes coming every over. The bowling was poor — at one point I hit Jacques Kallis forward of square for six and he bowled pretty much the same delivery next ball, so I hit him for six again; later, Roger Telemachus bowled four no-balls in a row — but even so, when I was dismissed in the 48th over, just after the innings total raced past 400, I walked off thinking that, in terms of pure ball-striking, I couldn't bat any better. The six I slugged up to where the camera crews were perched in the top deck of the grandstand was the biggest hit of my life. As I had been on the last day of my 100th Test, I was in a zone where I could almost sense what they were going to bowl next, and I felt as if the sweet spot of my bat was a metre wide. I have no idea how you get in that mindset, but when you do it's like when you catch a big wave in the surf. All you can do is get on it, love it, and ride it for as long as you can.

As soon as I got back in the dressing-room, Gilly had a go at me for getting out when I only needed 10 more runs to break Mark Waugh's Australian record for the highest score in an ODI. I must admit I didn't know what Junior's score had been, but Gilly did because he'd been dismissed for 172, one short of equalling the mark, at Bellerive in 2003–04. While this friendly discussion was going on, Andrew Symonds was clobbering 27 from 13 balls at the end of our innings, but it was as if no one noticed because fours and sixes had become so commonplace. The crowd was nonplussed, we were exhilarated, and in the dressing-room John Buchanan was in a very satisfied mood. He is a coach who likes to challenge us to never limit our ambitions, and he had told us many times that 400 runs in a one-day innings is not impossible. For Buck, this was a red-letter moment. And then we ruined it for him.

In the break between innings, the mood in our dressing-room was excited. I wouldn't say we were cocky. I stressed the point that there was still a game on the line and a series to be won, and asked the boys to forget about the scoreboard and have pride in their personal performance. We knew that South Africa would have a go because they had no alternative, and I have seen plenty of instances where a substantial target is actually harder to defend than a small one, because the chasing team starts well and soon becomes hopeful of winning rather than fearful of losing. Hope can build; fear destroys. Of course, I was concerned that they might get on the same sort of roll that we had. But being honest, it never really occurred to me that we would lose. I thought we were better than that.

As it turned out, Smith and Gibbs smashed us so well we might have been lucky to take the game into the final over. At the 30-over mark, South Africa were 2–279, a run-rate of 9.3 runs an over. Gibbs was 156 not out, and from there they 'only' needed to score at 7.8 runs an over to win the game. But Gibbs was flying so fast that he couldn't help himself, and after hitting Symmo for two straight sixes he hit a catch to long-off and the game was back to something like even-money. But from this point Mark Boucher batted very well, while Johan van der Wath hit a crucial 35 from 18 balls (including three sixes in a sequence of six balls) from overs 43 to 47 after the required run-rate had blown out to 11 runs an over. We tried to protect the short boundary on the scoreboard side, we emphasised the need to bowl yorkers, we even spent a few overs bowling well wide of the off stump with four men deep on the offside boundary, but it didn't matter. The runs kept coming.

Van der Wath's third six came in Nathan Bracken's eighth over, which cost 14 runs. Other than that one over, Bracks sent down nine overs for 53 runs and five wickets, and was the one Australian bowler to go okay, but his night was wrecked when he dropped Gibbs at mid-off off Mick Lewis' bowling when the danger man was 130. Poor Mick finished that over, his sixth, with figures of 0–54; his next four overs went for 18, 16, 9 and 17 and he became the first man to concede 100 runs in a 50-over ODI. I know I'll be criticised for persevering with him, but we needed a couple of good overs of yorkers and I felt he was the right bloke for that job. He's been good for us in similar circumstances, but on this crazy night, it didn't work out.

The stress I felt near the end of the innings was something I'm not sure I've experienced before. A sense of gloom pervaded the team as we made error after error, and I was as fearful as anyone of making the next mistake. Van der Wath's innings ended when he when he hit a catch to me at extra cover. The out meant they needed 35 from the last 21 balls, but ridiculously they did it fairly easily, even though Bing gave them a bit of a scare when he dismissed Andrew Hall off the third ball of the 50th over when they needed two to win. We needed to keep No. 11 Makhaya Ntini on strike, but first ball he got a single to third man and then Boucher hit one more four to long-on and the series was lost.

I HATED THE FEELINGS of helplessness and embarrassment I experienced during that South African run-chase. The idea of being captain of the team that had just conceded a world record total didn't thrill me one bit. So when I saw the people in our dressing-room clapping the South Africans off the field and in my eyes not looking too disappointed at all, I just lost it. I'm sure our support staff would say they were simply caught up in the occasion and were being sporting losers, but in the blur of such a dismal defeat I didn't see it that way. Instead, as soon as the dressing-room door was shut, I sailed into the biggest spray I expect I will ever deliver as Australian captain.

I told the team that not being able to defend such a score was simply unacceptable. If they weren't embarrassed, they bloody well should be. As captain, I roared, the buck stops with me, but there was no way any member of the squad was going to duck his individual responsibility for such a dreadful performance. Later, at the presentation, I was offered a joint man-of-the-match award with Herschelle Gibbs, but I didn't want it. I didn't want anything positive to come out of the loss. Because it was the end of the series, the two teams got together for a drink, but though I stayed around for a little while I didn't have a beer because it didn't seem right. Usually, after a hard-fought series, a beer tastes all right even when you lose, because it represents something of a prize for the effort you've put in. But I didn't feel like we'd fought hard or that we deserved any reward.

I've never taken a defeat harder. I just can't believe that we lost the unlosable game. If being so distraught and angry means I'm not a cricket romantic, then I plead guilty. I have tried to focus on the good things we did when we batted, but they truly don't matter to me any more. I'm sure I don't feel this way because I'm more competitive than the other blokes in the team — I've seen them in muck-around games at practice as well as on the sporting field to know how much winning means to them, and how much pride they usually have in their performance. I expect everyone else to feel the way I do, and I think most of them do. Losing is one thing; losing as limply as we did is another. That night, whenever I sensed that one or two people in the squad might not have been as disillusioned as I felt, the anger returned and I was best left alone.

NOW THE RESULT IS being described in various quarters as South Africa's equivalent of England's Ashes victory. Everywhere I go — to breakfast, to buy a paper, wait for a lift, check out of the hotel, walk to the bus — people want to talk about how exciting and uplifting it all was. I smile weakly and agree it was a great game, but the truth is that it wasn't great for everyone. I know one-day cricket is different from Test cricket, and that there will be significant changes in personnel for the upcoming matches, but I can just imagine how pumped up Smith's team and the entire South African cricket community will be going into the first Test on Thursday. After what had happened in our matches in Australia and after fighting back from 2–0 down, we had a chance to get all the momentum flowing in our direction for a series that means a lot to us. Instead, we blew it in the most ugly and unimaginable way.

Of course, some very experienced hands have joined us for the Test matches, notably Shane Warne, Justin Langer, Matthew Hayden, Stuart MacGill and Michael Kasprowicz. These guys are experienced enough and ambitious enough not to be affected by the result of a one-day game, though I do wonder what it will do to some of the guys who played last night and will be saddling up again on Thursday. I guess it be a good test for them, so maybe something productive will come out of the debacle. The arrival of fresh faces when Test and one-day series overlap always rejuvenates the men who play both forms of the game, and I think that process is going to be more important than ever this time. I'm not going to allow myself to think about what-should-have-beens, and I need everyone else to do the same. So when we had our first meeting with the Test squad this morning and our coach started talking about the positives we could take out of the last night's game, I quickly cut him off.

'Buck,' I said flatly. 'I'm not hearing one more thing about that game. That game is done, over, done with. It's one-day cricket. We've finished with one-day cricket. We're into Test cricket now. We're starting afresh. Everyone's got to forget about that game.'

Part IX

Three in Three

Australia in South Africa
Test Matches
March–April, 2006

Wednesday, March 15

THREE TESTS IN THREE weeks. That's what we're facing, the first of them starting just four days after the nightmare that was that fifth one-dayer. It's a tough program, and the fact that both teams are going through the same experience doesn't make it any less arduous. For the guys who'd come through the limited-overs series, I felt we only had a day — and a travel day at that — to regroup before we had to get full-on into Test mode. Ideally, ridiculous as it seems, we had to start preparing even earlier than that.

For the South Africans, game five is still everything. Ticket sales for the first Test took off from the morning after Boucher hit the winning four, and there is currently sustained and passionate debate across the country as to whether this or the 1995 Rugby World Cup triumph was a bigger moment in the nation's sporting history. We travelled with the South African team on the same flight to Cape Town, and it was clear from the dusty looks on some of their faces that they'd been up most of the night celebrating. More surprising, given there was a Test match not too far away, a few of them continued the revelry on the plane. Maybe they thought this was a way of sticking it up us, but I couldn't help thinking that they were doing us a favour. By the time we touched down I was beginning to think we'd be going into the first Test in better shape than our opponents, and that belief was accentuated when we heard whispers that the party was still going on last night, just 36 hours before the start of the Test series. It's amazing the boost such knowledge can give you — it's like we've been given a free kick before the first bounce — and this plus the cool assurance that the experienced Test boys have brought to our camp means that I can now write with some confidence that the one-day disaster won't damage our psyche. As I pondered the defeat the night it happened, with the post-game buzz everywhere, I was fairly sure it would.

SHANE WARNE HAD CAUSED something of a stir when he landed here just before the last one-dayer, by offering more of his opinions on Graeme Smith and his men. Smith had 'made a fool of himself' in Australia, Shane told reporters, while the team had put in the 'worst performance ever' by a South African side. These comments were inevitably lost for a while in all the excitement of game five, but I still found myself (again) having to respond to Warney's statements when it came to my turn to face the media in the lead-up to the first Test. I even made a point this time of saying how much fun that process can be. I was also asked if I would have liked to have had the great leg-spinner bowling for me when South Africa were going so well in pursuit of 435. I sensed what they were after, and tried to downplay my reply, saying simply, 'It would have been nice to have Warney out there.' If they'd asked about Glenn McGrath, I would have said it would have been nice to have him out there, too. There is no captain alive who wouldn't want the best spinner the game has ever seen or the best pace bowler of recent times bowling for him, in the backyard, a Test, a one-day, whatever the circumstances. Of course, my response set off a chain reaction, with the story going around the cricket world that Ricky Ponting *wants* Shane Warne back in the Australian one-day side. That is not what I said, but it doesn't seem to matter. I can only hope the guys who bowled in the game at the Wanderers won't react badly to the 'Punter Wants Warney' headlines that were wired around the world.

The notion that during the series the South Africans would tailor the first-Test wicket to nullify Shane was another story that wouldn't go away. Yet when we turned up at Newlands in Cape Town yesterday, two days before the series was set to begin, I was surprised to learn that the locals were not happy with the look of the pitch. The surface was 'too dry', they complained. I had to check it out, and it sure looked like it was going to turn, which actually fitted with a conversation I'd had with the groundsman when we were here for the second one-dayer. I was thus making plans for us starting the Test with both our leg-spinners, but when we returned to the ground today, and I went to check out the wicket with John Buchanan and Merv Hughes, the selector on duty, it had changed appearance quite remarkably. The South African coach Mickey Arthur had said publicly that he wanted a wicket with some grass on it and sure enough plenty of water has been poured into it in a short period of time and now a layer of grass is coming through. But the grass is brown in colour, not green, and when I tapped a bat on the pitch it felt spongy, like Plasticine, with no bounce.

It's ironic, given that just a couple of days back we were all rocking along at eight-and-a-half runs an over, but I reckon this Test might evolve into something of a war of attrition. I can picture South Africa trying to drag the game out, by grinding out their innings when they bat and trying to make us bat for a long time in order to score our runs. I doubt they'll let us get away with too much, and on this pitch the risks involved in trying to score quickly might be too great. Batting will probably be about constructing an innings, and knowing that when you walk out to the middle you've got six hours in any one day in which to occupy the crease. Some shots might have to stay in the locker, too, at least until a batsman is well set. For the bowlers who were in the one-dayers, it's going to be a lot different to sending down just a maximum 10 overs in a day, maybe in three spells. I can see some bowlers being asked to do a lot of work, and it could be the guys who persist best who make the biggest impact.

There is some wacky gossip about, too. I'm supposed to have a broken finger that's going to keep me out of the Test, according to some reports, while Brett Lee is also in doubt, though I'm not even sure what his ailment is. Neither of these yarns is true, but it is a fact that we are concerned with Bing's workload. He didn't get the break at the end of the VB Series that we wanted him to have, and he's basically been going full time since the start of the Ashes tour. He loves coming to practice and working on things, and he also wants to bowl all the time, so occasionally we have to advise him to slow down. But he's such a great athlete; it's almost natural for him to be going all the time. Our new physiotherapist, Alex Kountouris, who has taken over as planned from Errol Alcott for the Test-match leg of this South African tour and the games in Bangladesh that follow, will have to keep an eye on him. Alex was the chief physio for Sri Lanka for six years before becoming Errol's understudy with the Aussie team in 2003, so we're very familiar with his work and are very comfortable having him on board.

The travelling Aussie media is guessing as to whether we'll go into the game with both Warney and Stuart MacGill bowling after Bing and Michael Kasprowicz, or if we'll pick Shaun Tait for his pace, instead of the second spinner. But if they saw what the pitch now looked like, I think they'd be reassessing their opinions. The South Africans have shown their hand by recalling a finger-spinner, Nicky Boje, and choosing the medium-pace seamer Andrew Hall. We also need a guy who can move it off the seam, and keep it pretty tight for over after over. I can't help thinking that Glenn McGrath would be brilliant on this wicket.

With this in mind, I'm pretty sure we're going to play Stuart Clark. He was carted like everyone else at Johannesburg, but he was impressive in the earlier games, especially at Port Elizabeth and Durban, and with his height and the movement he can get off the pitch he is similar in style to Pidge. He is six months past his 30th birthday, and has been playing first-class cricket since 1997–98, but like a few other 'young veterans' who've joined the Test squad in recent seasons, at a time in their careers when they might have thought the opportunity was gone, there is a real enthusiasm about him that helps us all. He goes by the nickname of Sarfraz, which comes from the day early in his career when someone remarked that his short-stepping run-up closely resembles that of the famous old Pakistan opening bowler, Sarfraz Nawaz. Because he's has been with the Aussie one-day squad, Stuey hasn't played a first-class match since late November, but I don't think that lack of long spells in match conditions will worry him. It's just another reality of the modern game — with one-day games so prevalent and Test tours no longer featuring many (in some cases any) three-day or four-day games — that some people have to get used to.

Sunday, March 19

South Africa v Australia Test series
First Test (March 16–18) at Cape Town: South Africa 205 (SR Clark 5–55) and 197 (JA Rudolph 41; SR Clark 4–34) lost to Australia 308 (ML Hayden 94, RT Ponting 74, A Symonds 55) and 3–95 by nine wickets

I THINK THIS WAS one of our better Test-match victories of recent times. It wasn't so much about coming back after the one-day fiasco, more about reasserting ourselves again in a tough environment. We lost the toss, it was an awkward pitch, we were without Glenn McGrath, it was our first Test on foreign soil since the Ashes series, the pitch wasn't supposed to suit us, but we still won in three days. There was the joy of one member of the squad taking nine wickets on his Test debut, while a couple of popular veterans came back into the team for the first time for six months and also made a contribution. It was a good game and a great win.

The wicket wasn't flash. It was one of those tracks where you never felt you were truly in and where it was almost impossible to bowl a straight ball. When we were chasing 95 to win on the third afternoon, Makhaya Ntini was almost impossible to play, as he got the ball to sidestep all over the place. Justin Langer and Matthew Hayden were fantastic then, getting us to 71 before a wicket fell.

Back on the first day, after Graeme Smith won the toss and batted (I would have done the same), all but two of the South African batsmen reached double figures but none of the top seven got to 20 and no one got past 31. Stuart Clark, who'd received his baggy green from big Merv in a short on-field ceremony among the team before the game, took five wickets for the innings, including three of the first four to fall, and was just magnificent. His first over was the 16th of the innings. He started with a maiden to Smith, Andrew Symonds bowled a maiden to Herschelle Gibbs, and then third ball of his second over in Test cricket, Sarfraz had the South African captain caught behind, prodding at one that moved away from him.

Our reaction to this dismissal was spontaneous, as we charged to Test cricket's newest wicket-taker to congratulate him on his instant success. It's almost a race to see who can get there first to slap him on the back and ruffle his hair. The energy that goes through the whole team in this situation is seductive, in part because we can all remember how nervous we were at the start of our careers, how much we wanted to succeed and how good it felt when we first tasted success. But Stuey had just started. With the fifth ball of his third over he had Jacques Kallis — who with his impeccable technique and unending patience was the sort of batsman who could grind out a big score on this wicket — slashing hard but straight to Matty Hayden in the gully. Then, with the third ball of his sixth over, he bowled Gibbs, whose confidence must have been sky high after his one-day fireworks in Jo'burg, with a beautiful leg-cutter that knocked over the off stump. At lunch, South Africa were 4–66, and Sarfraz's bowling figures were six overs, two maidens, three wickets for 13 runs. To think that 48 hours earlier he wasn't going to be selected!

We were 1–63 at stumps and in a good position, especially as we expected (or was that hoped?) the pitch might settle down. But it never did. The key partnership of the Test was the 154-run effort Haydos and I put together in our first innings, but though I was proud of the way we both battled through, we were also a bit lucky. You had to be to stay out there for that period of time on such an unpredictable surface. Still, I really felt I earned my success, which was a point that our assistant coach Dene Hills made in a team meeting straight after the game.

I had seen the ball seaming all over the place throughout the South African first innings. I'd seen Brett Lee get the ball moving sideways at pace, Clark and Michael Kasprowicz seam it from a fair height, and Andrew Symonds get some to jag as if he was a fast off-spinner. I knew the speedy Ntini, tall Andre Nel and the medium-paced seamers, Kallis and Andrew Hall, would do the same. So I resolved that whenever I went forward, which would be the case unless they pitched genuinely short, I'd go as far forward as I could. If that meant I wore some on the body (which I did), so be it. Ntini pinned me a few times — in the guts, on the back thigh, the bottom hand — but the stings of the blows just added to my motivation. The key was that I always watched the ball *really* closely. Provided my judgment was good then I was a chance.

Dene compared my approach with that of some of the South Africans, who were either pinned to the crease when they batted or stayed on the legside of the line of most deliveries. Gibbs' dismissal on the first day was a perfect example of that latter approach. It wasn't a question of superior physical courage on my part; our opponents are tough cricketers, and you can't play Test cricket for any length of time if you haven't got ticker. Rather — and this is what Dene emphasised to the lads — it was that I went out to bat with a logical plan that I had the courage to implement, even though there were times when it wasn't easy. At the other end, the taller, left-handed Haydos was content to let the bowlers come to him, letting plenty of balls go. He scored only 10 runs from the first 50 balls he faced, as the South Africans seemed slow to realise that this was a different batsman to the bold hitter they'd often seen in the past. For Matt to launch into an attacking shot here, a delivery had to be either pitched right up or be really short. I was very disappointed for him when he skied a pull shot to deep mid-wicket when he was on 94. On this wicket, that score was worth many more than a hundred.

I'm firmly of the view that Test-class batsmen do not need to be told how to bat. I'm not talking about technique, but about the process of making runs and building an innings. If a batsman wants to succeed consistently, he has to think about what he is going to do before he gets out to the middle. Matt and I both did this. Part of this process involves observing what has been happening and another part involves listening to coaches and talking with your team-mates to discover what they have learnt and maybe what they are going to do. I am always happy to talk batting with my team-mates, but they have to be the ones who work out how they are going to play. One of the strengths of our team is how well we communicate — both in the way we ask the right questions and the manner in which we are all keen and often able to provide answers. Lang, Haydos and I have been helping each other like this for years.

For all my planning, there were still a few moments during my innings when I tempted fate, notably when I top-edged a pull shot to fine leg, where Andre Nel spilt the chance. There was also one snick that went uninterrupted through the slips cordon, while a couple of edges fell short of the slips, which was going to happen from time to time, given the lack of pace in the wicket. After I was dismissed, Damien Martyn came in and almost immediately edged another one that fell short, which prompted Graeme Smith to shout out, obviously for the benefit of the stump microphone, 'Please make the ball carry!' It might have been better if the keeper and the slips had moved closer to the batsmen, rather than moan about the wicket.

During the game, it became clear to us that the relationship between the South African side and the cricket community of Cape Town isn't particularly close. The team hierarchy went out of their way to show their displeasure with the pitch (Smith was quoted as calling it 'horrible'), Nel bagged the crowd for not being loud enough, while I will never forget how, as we did our warm-ups before the start of the third day's play, a group of around 100 locals gathered to let us know how keen they were for us not just to win, but to thrash the home team.

IT IS INTERESTING THAT even though Matt Hayden and I batted relatively slowly during our long partnership, and despite the fact that the pitch was very slow, there was still more than 300 runs scored on the second day. A total of 315 runs were scored in the day, for the loss of 12 wickets, in 84.2 overs. Here was an indication of how cricket has changed over my lifetime — even during a 'war of attrition' in 21st-century cricket, the runs keep coming.

In the 1980s, 300 runs in a day of Test cricket was considered almost impossible, whereas today that's often almost a minimum requirement. In the 1990–91 Ashes series in Australia, the most runs scored on the first day of a Test was the 269 Australia scored on the opening day of the fourth Test, at Adelaide, when Mark Waugh made a hundred on debut. Around the same time, I was a wide-eyed kid at the Australian Cricket Academy listening to the boss, Rod Marsh, telling a group of us, 'If you blokes aren't good enough to score 300 runs in a day you can all pack your bags up and go home now.' That was the style of cricket he wanted us to embrace. Maybe Rod was smart enough to see where the game was going, and wanted us to be ready for it; every indication since then, with his work in Australia and England, is that when it comes to cricket thinking he is ahead of his time. Many future Australian players came into contact with him when he was at the Academy, and his influence on the way we went on to play our sport was profound.

However, some of our blokes might have been *too* aggressive on the second afternoon, when we lost our last nine wickets for 133, and in doing so gave South Africa a chance to get back in the game. Fortunately, Bing then stepped up to dismiss de Villiers and Gibbs in his third over, and Warney was too good for Smith with his first delivery of the innings, so we still went into day three with a considerable advantage. Everyone knew that the key wicket was Kallis, and who else would do the trick for us than Stuart Clark, in one of those special moments that makes being in the leadership group one of the better roles in the world.

The origins of this dismissal went right back to Sydney, my 100th Test, when Kallis scored a hundred in the first innings and a fifty in the second. We knew he had a bad elbow that had troubled him in Australia, and we thought the way he was hitting through the offside, maybe because he was compensating slightly for the injury, indicated that he might be vulnerable to a ball that pitched short of a length just outside the line of off stump. He was aiming to hit that ball a little too square, which meant there was a chance he might offer a catch to the keeper, the slips or maybe the gully. Ironically, we did get him in the gully in the first innings, but that ball had been too short. He actually cut it really well, but in the air and straight to the fieldsman.

With Kallis 31 not out at stumps on day two it was natural we'd talk some more about how we'd bowl to him, and Warney, Gilly and I were all firmly of the view that the plan could work. Bing bowled the opening over to him, and the first ball beat the outside edge, the second was played defensively off the back foot to cover, the third was leg-glanced for four and the fourth brought a single to mid-wicket. Next over, after a drive to mid-on and a delivery that was too wide of the off stump, Sarfraz's third ball was perfect; Kallis tried to drive off the back foot, but the ball climbed on him a little, took the outside edge and Gilly snared a brilliant one-gloved catch.

There's something exhilarating about plans that come true, especially when they involve dismissing the batsman we feared most in the opposition side. Stuey began the day with a spell of eight overs that not only featured five maidens, two wickets (Kallis and Ashwell Prince) and only nine runs, but also a short, sharp burst that we loved but Mark Boucher didn't enjoy one bit.

Second ball, Boucher was laid low with an off-cutter to the groin, and in the following Clark over we thought he might have had him lbw twice. Then, still in the same over, he was definitely thumped on the helmet. It took 25 minutes, but finally Kasper had the South African caught at short mid-wicket, after Boucher had scored just two runs from 21 balls. This left South Africa in desperate trouble at 6–108, a lead for them of just five runs, and we were enjoying one of those moments when the bowling was excellent, the fielding sharp and the energy on full throttle. Boucher might have annoyed us with his pre-tour comments, and he's a rival who often likes a chat on the field, but we respect him as a tough competitor and he is always capable of scoring runs from the No. 7 spot. So while having him ruffled like this might not have been a defining moment in the match, there was certainly a sense of symbolism in seeing him so ruffled and unable to get the ball off the square.

The biggest partnership of their innings — 50 runs between Jacques Rudolph and Andrew Hall for the seventh wicket — was broken by a big-spinning leg-break from Warney that nicked Rudolph's bat as he tried to withdraw it and then clipped the off stump. Everyone was making a contribution. Then Clark came back to take two more wickets, giving him nine for the Test. This is the most captured by an Australian bowler on debut since Terry Alderman took 9–130 against England in 1981. The victory came as the sun disappeared behind Table Mountain, and it was the most satisfying win I've been involved in so far this summer. Had we not lost three wickets in three overs near the end, it would have been an even more decisive triumph, but that didn't really matter — it was extremely satisfying to be back playing some outstanding cricket so soon after losing the one-day series. And there is always something gratifying about winning a Test in three days that has nothing to do with the fact that I might now have a chance to get on the golf course on what would have been days four and five.

NOT LONG AFTER HUSS had hit the winning runs, Stuart Clark was up on stage accepting the man-of-the match award, which led to a little cameo that was entertaining in itself. When his name was called out, he strode up to get his trophy and the cheque that goes with it, only this time — rather than the massive cardboard imitation cheque you often see in these situations — he was handed an envelope. As is customary, the person with the microphone stopped him to ask a couple of questions, which he dead-batted pretty well, and then the interviewer said, 'Congratulations, thank you very much.' And Stuey just stood there. He was having such a good time, he was more than happy for the chat to continue. When he finally realised the presentation was over, he walked over to me, showed me the cheque, and asked, 'Do I get to keep all this, or do I have to split it with the boys?' He just didn't know. This was a whole new world to him.

'No, mate,' I said. 'It all goes in the team kitty.'

A little later, someone asked me how Glenn McGrath would have bowled on that wicket. 'McGrath would have been scary, that's for sure,' I said, 'but so would Shaun Pollock.' Pollock missed the game because of injury, but knowing how good he is when fully fit, with his ability to hit the right spot consistently and seam it both ways, if he'd been available there's probably no way I could have scored as many as I did on that wicket. 'Can you compare Clark to McGrath?' was the next question.

'Stuart bowled just how Glenn would have bowled,' I replied.

That's probably the highest praise anyone could give Sarfraz Clark. He bowled beautifully. This was his Test match.

Thursday, March 23

THERE IS NO DOUBT the pitch in Cape Town was not perfect, and in the days following the first Test it seemed that the preparation of South African cricket pitches was a constant topic of discussion. 'Ultimately, it didn't play as we wanted,' said Mickey Arthur of the surface on which we took a 1–0 lead in the series.

'If they're telling groundsmen to water the pitch, then we've got a psychological advantage straight away before a ball is bowled,' offered Shane Warne. Jacques Kallis claimed that asking for a particular type of wicket is part of the home-ground advantage. 'I think everybody does it around the world,' he said.

With Stuart Clark's superb form, and with Stuey MacGill available if a wicket is going to be a turner, our attack now seems so well balanced I don't think South Africa can produce a wicket that will disadvantage us during the rest of this series. But what I think needs to be considered first in this debate is the potential damage to the game that can come from creating 'unnatural' wickets. I have already commented on the fear I have that Australian pitches are losing their variety in this era of 'drop-in' wickets, and I believe there is equal peril in getting curators to produce wickets that are anything other than typical of their venues. I think the Newlands groundsman should be asked to do no more than provide the best possible Newlands pitch in exactly the same way the Melbourne groundsman should be asked to do no more than provide the best possible MCG pitch. If all the wickets in a country are tailored to suit home teams or certain styles of cricket, Test series will become less of a true test. That is surely no good thing.

IF THE NUMBER OF questions I keep getting about next season is any indication, the 2006–07 Australia–England series is going to be bigger than the Olympics! On March 22 in Mumbai, England fought back to square their series with India by winning the third Test. They were without a number of their stars from 2005, including captain Michael Vaughan, vice captain Marcus Trescothick and pace bowlers Steve Harmison and Simon Jones, but with the inspiring Andrew Flintoff in charge and Andrew Strauss scoring another century (his eighth in 24 Tests) they prevailed by 212 runs. While the game was being played, I did an interview with the BBC's *Test Match Special* team, and not surprisingly the fate of the Ashes was all they seemed interested in. We have never been able to get right away from this topic this season, and nor have we sought to. After every Test win, when Lang (or Gilly for the Tests when Lang was injured) led us in our victory song, he has made reference to the rematch and how this success is just another step on the road to the ultimate goal: regaining that urn. When people describe the 2005 Ashes series as 'unforgettable' they are underlining how we feel about it. And the memories are definitely a spur for us now, not a bridle.

I sensed that my English interrogators were a little concerned about the way we have been winning Test matches this season. When they asked me about Stuart Clark, you could almost hear their disappointment that someone had stepped into Glenn McGrath's shoes so effectively. Of course, Pidge will always be our No. 1 quick while he is available, but it was still very nice to be able to inform them that we now have *two* tall guys who land the ball in the right locations most of the time and are good enough to hit the edge of the bat. 'All the bowlers did a terrific job in the last game,' I said, 'and we are hoping they can carry that on in the rest of the series.'

Was I confident this Australian team could beat England? 'We've pushed on,' I responded. 'There are other things we have had to focus on and to all of our credit we have managed to do that really well since we have been back from the Ashes.

'But when it does come around, I know we'll be up for it. I know we'll be ready.'

Wednesday, March 29

South Africa v Australia Test series

Second Test (March 24–28) at Durban: Australia 369 (RT Ponting 103, DR Martyn 57, MEK Hussey 75) and 4–307 declared (ML Hayden 102, RT Ponting 116) defeated South Africa 267 (AB de Villiers 50, JH Kallis 114; B Lee 5–69) and 297 (AB de Villiers 46, GC Smith 40, MV Boucher 51*, N Boje 48; SK Warne 6–86) by 112 runs

THE WORD GOING INTO this game was that the pitch would suit the seamers, but while it did have plenty of grass on it — prompting us to go in with an unchanged line-up and the South Africans to leave their medium-pacer, Andrew Hall, out to make room for the returning Shaun Pollock — it was another slow deck, which precluded aggressive batting and which ultimately led to one of Shane Warne's finest bowling efforts on the final day.

I was happy to bat first after winning the toss. We could see the beginnings of cracks forming underneath the grass on the pitch, which made the idea of Warney bowling in the fourth innings (something he is always keen on!) extremely appealing. However, Matthew Hayden was caught at third slip in the second over, which meant that I discovered first-hand very rapidly just how hard we would have to fight for our runs. That I managed to stay out there for most of the day was a source of great satisfaction.

My first-day hundred was my 29th in Tests, which took me level with Sir Donald Bradman on the all-time century-makers list, but when this fact was brought up in the media conference after the first day's play, I was quick to put things in perspective: The Don took 52 Tests to score his 29 hundreds, while I have played in almost double that to make mine. This knock was also one of the most drawn-out I have played. In all, I faced 225 deliveries to score

103, the 11th longest innings in terms of balls faced so far in my Test career. Of the 10 innings to involve more deliveries, the only one that featured less than 150 runs was the 104 I scored against the West Indies at Bridgetown in 1999, my third Test hundred.

The pitch was one of the reasons my run-scoring was so slow, but the South Africans' bowling tactics also played a part. I went out there assuming that Pollock would be very difficult to handle, but for most of the day, after just a few overs with the new ball, he seemed happy to aim half a metre outside the off stump. I could only assume that the South African leadership group had decided that the best way to win the game was to wear us down, give us nothing and hope we'd beat ourselves. It seemed such a negative approach, especially on a pitch that was a bit 'up and down', and it left us with little alternative other than to be patient. It would have been very romantic for us to hit out anyway and still prevail, but cricket rarely works that way. I resolved very early not to drive on the up at all, for fear of hitting a catch off a ball that 'stopped' on me, while the pull shot also had to stay in the locker unless the delivery was a rank long hop. So many 'dot' balls going through to the keeper made for a slow game, but we kept our discipline and when Mike Hussey played another terrific innings with the tail, adding 110 runs for the last three wickets with Warne, Kasprowicz and Clark, we were in the box seat. Then, after Jacques Kallis made a strange sort of century — very aggressive early, much more typically meticulous once he got to 50 — Brett Lee ran through South Africa's bottom order, bowling really quickly and taking his 200th Test-match wicket, and we were well on top.

I couldn't help but compare my innings with Kallis, not in terms of how we batted but how our team-mates responded to our efforts. It was all very well for me to battle through that first day, never feeling like I was truly 'in' but still fighting all the way, but if the tail had collapsed or the South African batsmen had come out on day two and blazed six runs an over from poor bowling, my innings wouldn't have counted for much. Instead, the guys were fantastic, and I could look back on my ton with enormous pride. On day two, after Stuart Clark had Kallis caught and bowled with his first delivery with the second new ball, the last four South African wickets fell for just 12 runs, giving us a first-innings lead of 102, and then Haydos and I went out and scored centuries against dispirited opponents. The contrast was stark. I decided to declare half an hour before tea on day four, when our lead had grown to 409 runs.

THE QUESTION OF WHETHER floodlights should be used to extend a day's play had been debated in Cape Town, when the lights were used every day during the evening session after the sun disappeared behind Table Mountain. I found batting late on the opening day there extremely awkward, when I had been worried that if either I or Matt Hayden had been dismissed in the final few overs, it might have triggered a collapse. Batting in the afternoon gloom was even trickier here, and we lost three wickets in the last nine overs of the first day, after two wickets had fallen in the first 79. I was actually dismissed by a good piece of bowling by Boje, who held one back and dropped it a little wider than I was expecting, and I hit a sharp chance to short cover. But in the gloom of the next half hour, Damien Martyn edged a catch to second slip, nightwatchman Brett Lee was caught behind off Makhaya Ntini and then Andrew Symonds wore one from Ntini on his helmet. Symmo ended up with a split, bloody lip, and we limped into stumps five down, having lost a slice of the advantage we'd earned through most of the day.

On day two, it got so dark that even with the lights we would have been forced off had I not kept the slow men on. It was a gamble to keep the faster bowlers out of the action, at a time when Kallis and AB de Villiers were looking reasonably comfortable, but there's never a really bad time for Shane to be bowling and it seemed much more assertive on our part to be out there trying to get a breakthrough rather than waiting until tomorrow. Unfortunately, the wicket we needed wouldn't come, and eventually I brought Clark on and after two balls the umpires got together and offered the South Africans the light. They were off in a flash. Ironically, Sarfraz promptly dismissed de Villiers in his first full over the following morning. It was typical of our new man that he forced the immediate breakthrough; we're calling him 'Golden Bullocks' because he's got that rare magic touch at the moment where he can get a wicket with almost anything. I remember Mark Waugh used to be like that — you'd bring him on and somehow the batsman would get himself out to a long hop or a full toss.

I'm dead against using floodlights in Test cricket. It's been known for years that the hardest time to bat in a day–night game is during the twilight, when the sun is all but gone but the lights don't have the same impact as they do at night. It is also recognised that it takes a while for the lights to reach full brightness, so if the officials decide to flick the lights switch on because they think that will help, there is still going to be a period before the lights make a difference when the batsmen are disadvantaged. If the people in charge want to use the lights in Tests, I think it should only happen if the batting team is happy for it to happen. But if the batsmen aren't keen, the players should come off.

Ironically, given my attitude, if the lights weren't used in Durban, this Test would have ended quite differently.

AFTER THE SECOND DAY'S play, Dene Hills had run into a former Australian Test batsman who I believe is over here with a tour group. 'When are you coaches going to do something about

Ponting's technique?' this bloke asked. 'He falls across his front foot and hits across the line too much.' During South Africa's first innings, I'd dropped Herschelle Gibbs at second slip, which only provided more ammunition. 'He can't catch,' was how my fielding was rated. 'He shouldn't be in the slips any more.' It's funny how the ex-players look at the modern game. Most of them are ultra-positive, but there are always a few who reckon they were better in their day. Dene recalled this rather one-sided conversation just as I was about to walk out to bat in our second innings, and while it didn't act as any extra motivation it still stuck in my mind as I scored a hundred in both innings of a Test for the third time in my career. I have no idea why this bloke was into me, but it was nice to maybe set him straight.

I'm fully aware that I've had an amazing run lately, and afterwards someone asked me if I was worried it might not last forever. But I've never thought about it ending, because it's not my way to overanalyse things, especially when things are going well. It's when things start going badly that people begin thinking about things too much, and in the past few years I've been extremely conscious of never letting self-doubt infiltrate my outlook. When I'm on strike, I don't want to be thinking about anything other than watching the ball. I say it to myself twice, every ball, once when the bowler is halfway through his run-up and again when he is in his delivery stride. 'Watch the ball ... Watch the ball.' This process reminds me of the most important thing I have to do and also keeps thoughts that don't matter from clouding my mind.

I'm not trying to sound cocky, but I can't think of any reason — other than injury or illness — why my good form shouldn't continue for a few more years. I know that preparing well, never setting limits on yourself and having the will to win are the most important keys to being successful. While I retain the desire to be the best player and best team-mate I can be, I believe I can keep improving and continue to try to get the maximum possible out of my game. An ambition I had when I came into the Australian team was to be a very successful part of a very successful team. I didn't know back then whether that meant I'd score five hundreds or 35, and really those type of numbers don't matter. If I continue to be a successful part of a very successful Aussie team then I'll be a satisfied man.

And, most importantly, it has to be fun. That sheer joy of being in the one-on-one battles I have with the bowlers — and at times with myself — out in the middle is one of the main reasons I play the game. It's never easy. Sometimes it hurts, physically and emotionally, but it's almost always fun, and the occasional bad times only serve to make the good times sweeter. At least this is how it is for me. The mateship that comes with being part of a team adds so much to this pleasure, and makes cricket the best game in the world. The competition and the camaraderie — and the fun that goes with them — are what I'll miss most when my career is over.

LANG, HAYDOS AND I all fought the temptation to go too hard in our second innings. There have been some occasions in the past where we have been in too much of a hurry to win Tests, and this impatience has come back to bite us. I remember against India in Adelaide in 2003–04, we scored 556 in our first innings and in the back of our minds we thought we were home. However, Rahul Dravid and VVS Laxman batted brilliantly to get India back into the game, and then we went and tried to re-establish our advantage as quickly as possible. No one seemed prepared to play the long, patient innings that was needed, we were bowled out for just 196, and Dravid contributed his second important knock of the Test to get his team home by four wickets. We didn't want to make the same mistake here in Durban; instead we batted South Africa out of the game. Back in Perth at the start of this long summer, they had survived for four sessions to save a Test, but you could tell from their body language that they didn't fancy having to do the same thing here.

Nothing captured their mental collapse more than the bizarre behaviour of Andre Nel in the minutes before we declared. Adam Gilchrist had just arrived at the crease, and he went from 0 to 22 in one over from Nel, five fours and a two, an assault that prompted the bowler to applaud sarcastically and growl abuse at the batsman, even though — given he'd just been smashed — this didn't seem like the most appropriate time to be mouthing off.

Nel has said a few things over the course of the summer, and though he always tries his heart out on the field, because he hasn't been able to follow through on his statements and antics he's ended up looking silly. This particularly embarrassing tirade underlined that fact, as did the comments of a couple of South African cricket commentators, who went out of their way to tell us how much they enjoyed Gilly's hitting. We've all reached the stage with Nel where we've just about had enough of him.

Graeme Smith was another South African not having a great Test. He'd lost the toss, I don't think his defensive tactics worked for him in the field and then he was dismissed by the first ball of South Africa's first innings. We have tried to keep him pinned down, on the basis that if we get on top of the opposing captain we damage the rest of his team at the same time, and on various occasions during the Tests in Australia and South Africa we have enjoyed reminding him that some of his big predictions have not come true. He knew he had to score some runs to back up his pronouncements, and we knew it too, and there didn't seem to be any harm in asking him when it was going to start happening. We did this knowing that he is a very good player with a history of making big scores if he gets past 50 (he has almost as many centuries as half-centuries in Test cricket), so there was pressure on us to dismiss him before he got going. That he has failed to do so in six Tests to date in 2005–06 (one for the World XI, five for South Africa) represents a major victory for us.

Smith's unfortunate series continued on day four of this Test. We had reached 1–125 at stumps the previous evening, a lead of 227, having spent a large part of the afternoon watching a crack turn into a crater in the area outside the left-hander's off stump at the end where Andre Nel had done most of his bowling. More than once on that third evening, I thought about how much fun Warney was going to have landing his spinners in that crevice when he was bowling to the South African left-handers — Smith, Ashwell Prince and Jacques Rudolph — on the final day. But when we arrived for the start of the fourth day's play, it was clear the damage had been fixed overnight, which is totally against the rules.

The match referee, Chris Broad, made some enquiries and then ordered that the repair work be undone at the first drinks break. Smith argued against this, and was clearly stewing as the groundsman came out to methodically chisel out the dirt that had been plugged into the damaged area. Nor did the South African captain like Haydos and me tapping at this region for the rest of our partnership. I think he thought we were doing this because we were trying to remind him that eventually he'd have to face Warney fizzing his leg breaks out of that broken surface. That's exactly what we were doing. Eventually, he cracked and for three overs, while I was the non-striker's end and he was fielding at mid-off, between deliveries we kept shouting at each other.

His view was that I wasn't 'playing the game fairly'.

'We get inside your head, don't we?' I kept replying.

THE TIMING OF THE declaration was awkward, simply because we didn't know how much time might be lost as the light deteriorated in the late afternoon. Back in 2002, the South Africans made 5–340 in the fourth innings to beat us here, on a track that got better as the game wore on. On this occasion, it had been murky for much of the day, and as the gloom really set in during the tea interval I started to realise that I'd made a mistake in assuming that the floodlights would ensure we'd get a reasonable number of overs in before stumps. Bing and Sarfraz sent down five overs before the break, and when play resumed I brought on Symmo, bowling medium-pace, and Warney, but after only 13 balls the umpires called a halt. We never got back on the field until the start of day five.

When I say 'we never got back on the field until the start of day five' I actually mean everyone else got back on the field. I never did, because I was laid very low by one of the worse cases of food poisoning I'll ever get in my life. For most of the night I was in the bathroom, with my belly in a constant state of rebellion, until around 4am I had to ring Alex Kountouris to see if he could save me. We knew that the Queensland Reds Super 14 rugby team, who are preparing for their game against the Sharks in Durban on Saturday night, were staying in our hotel, and while we don't have a doctor travelling with us, they do, so Alex's solution was wake their medico and ask for some help. Soon an injection was going into my arm, which at least stopped me vomiting all the time and got me a few scraps of sleep. However, I still felt worse than terrible in the morning, so I stayed behind to try to pinch some more kip while the rest of the team left for the ground for the warm-up. At this point, the plan was that I'd get there in time for the start of play.

And I actually did make it as far as the dressing-room, arriving around half an hour before the first ball was due to be bowled.

But I didn't even have the energy to get changed. Someone came up with the bright idea that because I'd lost a lot of fluid, I should get an energy drink into me, so I quickly downed one of those, and then, just as quickly, I lost a lot more fluid. I lay down in the physio's room, got up for a moment to tell the boys that there was no way I could go out there, and then I retreated to the darkness of my hotel room. I found a little sleep, watched a fair bit of cricket on the television, and then returned to the ground a little gingerly to witness the final stages of the match.

I'm glad I was there, not least because Warney was having one of his great days. The wicket-taking had started in his very first over, the 17th full over of the day, when de Villiers was stumped, breaking a 91-run opening partnership. By lunch, South Africa were 4–128, with Smith and Kallis also having fallen to the leg-spinner and Gibbs to a pearler from Stuart Clark. At tea, we needed three more wickets to win the Test, but the light was beginning to fade, which set up a dramatic final session. I think most people expected Boucher and Boje to defend grimly — after all, Boucher had faced 52 deliveries for just six runs to this point — but instead they came out and played some shots, especially Boje, who hit eight fours in less than an hour. Three of them came via hits through the covers in an over from Kasprowicz that also featured three no-balls (the third of which was caught off the edge by second slip), and the temptation must have been to make a bowling change. But Gilly had faith in Kasper and remained keen on the idea of getting Boje caught in the offside. He gave his man another over and after the first ball went for another boundary, Michael Clarke, fielding as my substitute, took an excellent catch at short cover.

Almost immediately, we took the new ball and for the next five overs the only addition to the total was a no-ball. An edge off Nel's bat didn't carry to Gilly, and then Bing almost had Boucher two balls in a row, first when the batsman let one go that shaved the stumps, and then when an inside edge thwarted an lbw shout. All the while, it seemed to be getting darker. We'd all been critical of Nel earlier in the game, but now he was very determined, and he broke the impasse when he edged Sarfraz through the slips to the third-man boundary. After six overs of great drama, the umpires conferred about the light, and Gilly quickly made a bowling change, bringing on Symmo and Warney. There'd be no more fast bowling for the remainder of the Test.

Symmo bowled an over to Boucher, who took a single off the fifth ball, and for the next four overs the South Africans appeared content with Boucher facing Warney and Nel opposed to Symmo. So Mike Hussey was brought on for one over to let our two spinners change ends. I'm not sure the batsmen had actually decided to keep to specific ends, but still the change proved a masterstroke, as Huss kept Boucher to just one four to third man, and then in his second over after the switch Warney had Nel caught off the glove by Matt Hayden at first slip. It was getting very gloomy, and we had gone off in similar conditions on day two (but only when I brought the quicks back on), so it was no surprise that the umpires kept conferring. Fortunately, they decided that the floodlights were doing enough to make conditions playable. Four overs later, to great jubilation among the fielding team and in the away dressing-room, Ntini padded up to a wrong 'un and was given out lbw, leaving Boucher marooned on a gallant 52 not out, having batted for more than three-and-a-half hours. It had been a close-run thing, but the series was won.

I MUST ADMIT THAT if a batsman scores a hundred in each innings of a Test, most times he should be man of the match, but on this occasion I'm sure the judges got it right by giving the award to Warney. Ntini was his sixth wicket of the day, the culmination of a superb exhibition of enormous skill and endurance. I don't know if he has ever bowled better than how he's bowling right now. He is an amazing man — in any Test, anywhere, he could bowl 30 overs straight and if his captain asked him if he wanted to keep going, I know exactly what the answer would be. He *always* wants to be in the contest, to the point that you've almost got to rip the ball out of his hand to make a bowling change. His competitive streak is one of the reasons he is such a legendary cricketer.

We know that our long season of cricket isn't over — there are still matches, one more here and a few in Bangladesh, to be won — but straight after this Test we still felt, in some ways at least, that the mission had been accomplished. Any series victory over a significant opponent, especially on their turf, is a major achievement. Inevitably then, the party afterwards was pretty big, but unfortunately I wasn't fit enough to have even one celebratory ale. I felt like a shadow, in more ways than one. I was able to meet the media after the game, but having explained to them how I spent most of the day, they soon realised that I couldn't offer all that much about what had happened on the field. So, of course, they switched to the Ashes …

I started my reply in pretty much the same way I've always responded to such questions since last October. 'We've looked at ourselves and looked at the team,' I said. 'We've identified areas where we can improve. We've got more coaching staff in place and we feel we're better prepared now for Test matches than we were before.'

However, now I could really take the conversation a step further. 'More importantly,' I continued, 'we've got players putting their hands up, which was maybe lacking a bit in the Ashes.'

I was thinking of how Warney had just won us this Test and how he's bowled in the past 12 months, of Haydos' run-scoring this summer, Bing's bowling, the emergence of Huss and Stuey Clark, Marto and Kasper are back, Pidge to come back ...

Our cricket has been excellent, hard-nosed and aggressive. It's hard not to be really happy with the way things are going.

Thursday, March 30

THE SECOND TEST FINISHED last Tuesday, and the third begins this Friday, which leaves us precious little time to recover from one game and prepare for the next. This timeframe is not unprecedented — we do it most years with the Melbourne Test starting on Boxing Day and then Sydney beginning a week later — but it's still a tough ask, and if they brought in a hard-and-fast rule saying there had to be a minimum three cricket-free days between the scheduled fifth day of one Test and the scheduled opening day of the next, I'd be supporting it.

When you have such little time between important Tests, usually the last thing you want to do is attend a major do on one of the nights in between, but last night in Johannesburg we made an exception. The function was organised by the television broadcaster SABC in association with Cricket South Africa, and it was because of CSA's involvement that we were invited and felt obliged to attend. I'm so glad we did. It was in part a charity dinner for the 'Desmond Tutu Diversity Trust', but also a celebration of Archbishop Tutu's 75th year (he was born on October 7, 1931) and life's work, with the feature being a wonderful speech by the Nobel Peace Prize winner. He was occasionally emotional, as he touched on the decades of racial discrimination, his rise to prominence in the Anglican Church and the peace movement, and the years since the historic 1993 elections that saw Nelson Mandela become South Africa's president. At other times he was extremely funny, and also occasionally — in part for the benefit of the members of the Australian and South African teams who were in the audience — something of a cricket analyst. Quite clearly, the Archbishop is a passionate cricket follower, but whether he was talking about our game or his experiences in more dangerous fields, there wasn't a moment when his words didn't have my full attention.

Though I have been to South Africa a number of times, I'm not sure I've ever fully stopped to realise how varied — in terms of language, culture and religion — this country is. A pamphlet on our table explained that the Desmond Tutu Diversity Trust wants to help celebrate and best manage this mix, rather than see it become a source of mistrust and prejudice. At one point, a film was shown that had been put together by SABC in which Archbishop Tutu was seen campaigning for the end of *apartheid*, often on the frontline encouraging peaceful protest while at the same time attempting to defuse some of the anger that might otherwise have led to violence. We often hear the word 'courage' used in cricket, but these examples of dignified and extreme bravery put things in perspective. I noticed that one of the South African players seemed to be shedding a tear.

A personal highlight came when Archbishop Tutu presented me with one of his books, *God Has a Dream: A Vision of Hope for Our Time*. He also asked me to pass on a message to Jane and Glenn McGrath: 'Please tell them we are thinking of them and miss Glenn not being here,' he said.

During the night, there was the inevitable auction, with the most popular memorabilia on offer inevitably being a product relating to the game five one-dayer. This was a framed collage that included a South African team shirt signed by their players, official scorecards from both innings, signed photographs of Herschelle Gibbs and myself that were taken during our centuries, and also autographed photos of Makhaya Ntini and Graeme Smith. From the moment the auctioneer got to work, the clamour for this piece was frenzied, with Shane Warne one of the keenest bidders. However, he was eventually outflanked by a local fan who went to 105,000 Rand (the equivalent of more than $A20,000) for the item. I never did get round to asking Warney where he was going to hang the thing if he'd come up with the top bid, and wondered whether he'd been cajoled into going so high by the very generous tribute Archbishop Tutu had paid him earlier in the evening.

'He is a genius,' the guest of honour told his audience as he waxed lyrical about our famous bowler. 'It is a privilege to watch someone like him.'

But then he added with mock indignation, in reference to Shane's match-winning spell the previous day, 'Why did you have to come and do it here?'

I must confess that before the night I knew very little about Archbishop Tutu's work. But he was so captivating, after we bid our farewells I promised myself that I would find out more about his inspirational life story. Considering all this remarkable man has achieved, the idea of having to play another Test match so soon after the last one suddenly didn't seem like such an exhausting task at all.

Wednesday, April 5

South Africa v Australia Test series
Third Test (March 31–April 4) at Johannesburg: South Africa 303 (AG Prince 93, N Boje 43) and 258 (HH Gibbs 53, SM Pollock 44, MV Boucher 63; SR Clark 4–64) lost to Australia 270 (MEK Hussey 73, B Lee 64; M Ntini 6–100) and 8–294 (MEK Hussey 89, DR Martyn 101; M Ntini 4–78) by two wickets

THERE HAS BEEN PLENTY of talk in recent years about the Australian team and the 'dead rubber syndrome' — about how we have often struggled to gain victories in Tests played at the end of a series that has already been won. But none of that talk has taken place in the Aussie dressing-room, at least not in my time as captain. We know there have been a number of instances of this occurring in the last decade — against the West Indies, South Africa and England in 1997, in South Africa in 2002, against England in 2002–03, in the Caribbean in 2003, in India in 2004 — but though these defeats have all occurred at the end of a rubber, we see that timing as more coincidence than anything. There have been reasons for all these losses, which have been varied (excellent play by our opponents, injuries, having to play back-to-back Tests in which we bowl a truckload of overs in the first match, a poor wicket) rather than a case of the same mistakes being repeated time and again. That is not to say we haven't learned from these defeats, but we do believe they are not indicative of a general malaise. Our focus leading up to the Test here in Johannesburg has been — as it is for every Test we play — to prepare in the right way and to make sure we are 'up' for the game, both mentally and physically.

In this case, we went into the game knowing that if we won we'd become the first Australian team to sweep a Test series in South Africa, and the first visiting team from any country to do so since 1896. We also wanted to help Justin Langer celebrate his 100th Test in style, and — having conquered our opponents home and away after a long and sometimes stressful summer — we didn't want to give South Africa anything positive to take out of the experience. We will play them again in the not too distant future, in one-day cricket perhaps as early as the Champions Trophy in October–November, and it would be nice for them to remember us as the team that didn't give them anything.

At the toss, I was greeted not by Graeme Smith, but by Jacques Kallis. Smith had damaged the ring finger on his right hand at practice the day before the Test, which meant he missed a Test for the first time since he made his debut against us in 2002 (when he started his career in Cape Town by being caught Ponting bowled McGrath for 3). Though he hadn't scored many runs against us in the Tests during the season, we were still a little relieved to see him out, not least because he's a good player who was due to make a score.

Further, the choice of his replacement as skipper seemed a little strange, because although there is no doubt that Kallis is one of the best batsmen in the game, he has never come across to us as a leader. He is a quiet bloke, off and on the field, who bowls his overs, makes all his runs, and otherwise just wanders around, never seeming to give too much of himself to his team or the game. When he comes out to bat, we often think we're a chance to get him out immediately purely because he looks as if he's half-asleep. We were all intrigued to see to how he would go as a Test captain.

And it seemed we weren't alone in thinking this way. 'It will be a challenge for him,' Mickey Arthur was quoted as saying when he was asked about Kallis' elevation to the top job. 'He's a quiet guy who gets in a bubble during Tests and sits on his own, but it might bring out the best in him.'

Kallis started well by winning the toss and electing to bat. As is customary, he then did a brief interview in which he was asked about how he felt being captain of his country. 'I've had a few opportunities to do it in the one-day games and enjoyed it,' he replied. 'But this is my first chance to captain the team in a four-day game.' I couldn't help laughing when I heard that. To me, though harmless in itself, this little gaffe summed him up.

THE WANDERERS WICKET WAS similar in many ways to the pitch we'd seen during the Test in Cape Town, in that it was almost impossible to bowl a straight ball on it. Consequently, only 238 runs were scored on the first day, as our quicks were very hard to get away. Ashwell Prince played an excellent defensive innings to reach 79 not out by the close, and the next day he went on to 93, after which we had just as much trouble against Shaun Pollock, Andre Nel and especially Makhaya Ntini, and were grateful for a 68-run seventh-wicket partnership between Mike Hussey and Brett Lee that allowed us to limit our first-innings deficit to 33 runs.

If one person was entitled to slow down because of all the work he'd done in the past six months it was Bing, but he was having a terrific game. At one point in South Africa's first innings, he said to me that he had 'never felt better', and I could tell that his rhythm was the best it has ever been. When I thought back to our conversation during the first Test against the West Indies in Brisbane, when he was struggling to understand his role, I couldn't help but feel good about the way he has evolved as a Test bowler. At the end of this Test — after matches against the World XI, West Indies, New Zealand, South Africa and Sri Lanka — Brett had taken 83 international wickets during the 2005–06 season, 50 of them in 10 Tests.

When Michael Kasprowicz broke down during South Africa's second innings, on this seaming wicket Bing and Stuart Clark had to do a lot of bowling, and they proved up to the task. Sarfraz's four wickets gave him 20 for the rubber, making him the first Australian bowler since Terry Alderman in 1981 to take 20 or more wickets in his maiden Test series, and he was later named player of the series. But Bing was man of the match, not least because he was there at the end, hitting the winning runs. He has become one of those rare cricketers you can never keep out of the game.

One of his victims during this Test was me. Late in South Africa's first innings, I dived full length to my left at second slip to try to catch the left-handed Nicky Boje, but the ball hit the tip of my left thumb in exactly the same place where I broke it during the semi-final of the 2004 Champions Trophy at Edgbaston. That injury cost me the first three Tests of the series against India that followed, meaning I missed out on being on the field when Australia won a series in India for the first time since 1969. This time, almost immediately, the end of my thumb went black, the throbbing was exactly the same as it had been in England, so I resigned myself to my fate. Instead of going off, I went to mope at cover and within a couple of balls Boje smashed a ball from Sarfraz straight past me, and I couldn't help thinking it was lucky I didn't have to try to stop it. I had to get it looked at, and while I was in the dressing-room Prince's long innings ended when he edged Bing straight to Lang, my replacement at second slip. Fortunately, Alex Kountouris was able to set my mind at rest, and I was back on the field within four overs, with the thumb strapped, still aching, but in one piece.

I'll never forget Bing's bowling at the start of day four. He had been running on empty the previous evening, when Mark Boucher and Andre Nel batted through the last hour and extended South Africa's lead towards 300. We all knew we had to bowl them out as quickly as possible the next morning, and Brett charged in at Boucher with what must have been one of the most thrilling and dangerous first overs of the day in Test history. First ball, the batsman was hit on the helmet. By the third ball, Bing was up over 150ks, and fourth ball we were sure Boucher was caught behind as he sparred at a riser. The fifth delivery was top-edged over Gilly for four, and then a desperate pull shot was late and miscued, with the skied ball landing halfway between the keeper and Stuey Clark at deep fine leg. Boucher took three from Shane Warne's opening over, and then he aimed a wild heave at the first ball of Bing's second over and was caught behind. A bouncer and a yorker aimed at Ntini's middle stump later, and the innings was over. We needed 292 to sweep the series.

DURING A SHORT TEAM meeting after our first innings, we had thought about the way we batted and come to the conclusion that a few of us had tried to score too quickly. South Africa had scored at a run-rate of just over three runs per over in their first innings, while we had gone at 4.3 runs per over in ours, with a few of us batting as if we had to score our runs as quickly as possible before we copped an unplayable delivery. Batting was awkward, we decided, but not so difficult that such radical measures were necessary.

With Justin Langer out of action, Gilly wanted to open the batting in our second innings, as he does in one-day cricket, his logic being that if our run-chase got off to a flying start we'd put the pressure back on the South Africans. There was some merit in his argument, not least because it would have meant that Mike Hussey could stay at No. 5, where he has been so successful. However, I believed that we could chase any total batting last as long as we approached the task in a measured, mature way. The key, I thought, was to get through the first 20 overs of our second innings; if we did that, I was confident batting would get easier as the ball grew older. Indeed, if we survived the first hour of our innings, my greatest fear was the second new ball.

Had this debate between Gilly and me occurred during the Ashes series in 2005, he might have talked me around. He was very keen on his plan, and, of course, it might have worked. But I was the captain and I wanted to do it my way. Hussey went out with Hayden, and though Haydos and I were dismissed in the first 14 overs, Huss played his second big innings of the game while Damien Martyn contributed his best Test knock in a year.

They added 165 for the third wicket, batting for 52.5 overs until Huss was trapped lbw by one from Boje that spun a long way.

Marto had been picked for this tour with one eye on the upcoming Ashes series, because the selectors and team hierarchy really believe he is still the best No. 4 batsman in Australia. The adaptability he showed here in batting for nearly five hours and the poise he provided as he pushed us close to the win was simply fantastic. Because of the state of the wicket, and because we were one specialist batsman down, I rate this effort as one of the best run-chases I've ever seen, and Marto was the glue who held it all together. It was especially gratifying to see our middle-order come through, because there have been question marks over them since the Ashes series. We reached the end of the fourth day needing 44 runs to win with four wickets in hand.

Or was that three wickets in hand, with Lang unable to bat?

IT WAS NICE TO win a close Test, not least because over the past few years we've lost a few, most notably that two-run loss at Edgbaston in 2005. The coincidence that Lee and Kasprowicz were the blokes in the middle when the winning runs were hit this time was not lost on anyone who'd been in England, or, I reckon, any cricket fan back in Australia who watched the two dramatic finishes on television. If you'd seen Bing and Kasper in the dressing-room at the end of the Edgbaston Test, just the shattered looks on their faces, you would realise just how much that loss stung them. This time, they shared their jubilation, first on the field, then in the dressing-room, then back on the ground for the post-game presentation. Later it was back in the rooms for a few beers, with our favourite music booming, and then Justin Langer called out, 'One more song and then it's time.' We all knew what that meant; we'd been looking forward to it for a while. Lang might not have been right to bat, but the doctor hadn't ruled him out of leading us in the team anthem, and after we linked arms and gathered in a circle around a massage bench, he stepped up and started an emotional introduction. Part of his spiel was a reminder of the Ashes loss and a look forward to 2006–07. Then he highlighted some of the great performances in this game and through the series, including those of Bing and Kasper, Huss, Warney, Marto, Sarfraz …

Most of it was about all we had achieved and how proud he was to be a part of this Australian team. We all had beers in our hands and Lang was concussed, so you could say we were all a little groggy, but it was terrific fun. And then we sang *Under the Southern Cross* as loudly and passionately as we have done in a long, long time.

LATER, I COULDN'T HELP thinking about something Graeme Smith had said to me at the Desmond Tutu Diversity Trust testimonial dinner. We had a good chat that night, during which he commented on how hard it was playing against Australia for so long during one extended summer. 'Six months' cricket against you blokes,' he said, 'it's just too hard.' I loved him saying that, because it highlighted what a tough, uncompromising side we've become.

Graeme autographed a South African team shirt and gave it to me at the end of this Jo'burg Test, and I signed an Aussie one for him. As we swapped them, I asked him if he was going to be fit to play against New Zealand, who are due to play three Tests in South Africa in April–May, the first of them starting on April 15.

'We'll see how things go,' he replied. 'I think I'll be right.'

'It's going to start all over again with you and "Flem", isn't it?' I asked. It's common knowledge that he and the Black Caps captain Stephen Fleming don't get on and have had some decent sledging battles on the field in the past.

Graeme looked at me and said quietly, 'No it won't happen. I've learnt my lesson.'

We had felt for a while that most of the South African captain's comments (and probably those from Mark Boucher, too) had been about trying to absorb all of the attention — from the media and from us — and in the process minimise the pressure on the rest of his team. I believe that was more misguided than admirable. It made life extremely hard for Graeme as a batsman, because he had so much on his plate, and it also gave some of the men in his side an out, as someone else was taking the heat when they were falling short. This latter situation contrasted totally with the players and support staff in the Aussie squad, who put their hands up after the 2005 series against England, recognised where they were falling short, and took full responsibility for their role in the team's revival. I learnt a lot from our Ashes defeat, and came out of the experience a better captain. Maybe the same will happen to Graeme Smith after his battles with my Australian team.

Part X

One Test After Another

Australia in Bangladesh
April 2006

Friday, April 7

BACK IN EARLY FEBRUARY, I did a short interview with the London *Telegraph*. The story that followed was hardly a serious exposé of me, the Australian team or the game of cricket, rather it was one of those 'five-minute' pieces that feature short, sharp answers on a broad range of topics. The intention, I think, was to capture the breadth of my interest in sport, so the story began with a question about what it was like sailing on ABN AMRO ONE, which I'd enjoyed a couple of days before. After that, there were also enquiries about my *first sporting memory* ('playing at school with all my friends, or in the backyard in Mowbray'), *most memorable sporting moment* ('being on the winning side at two of three World Cup finals'), *worst sporting moment* ('losing the Ashes last summer'), *which sporting event I would pay the most to see* ('the US Masters'), *and miss* ('French clay-court tennis; tennis is better on grass') and so on. I guess they were interested in me as part of Britain's ongoing enthusiasm for anything to do with Ashes cricket.

All was going well until I was asked, 'What is the greatest change you would like to see in the running of cricket?'

'I think the international schedule is about right, with 30 one-dayers and 15 Tests a year,' I replied. 'What I would not have is the minnow nations in the World Cup and the Champions

Trophy, and I would not have Bangladesh and Zimbabwe playing Tests at present.'

Soon, I was answering the last question — *Who would you like to invite to dinner, and why?* ('Tiger Woods. I would love to talk about the excellence of his game and book a few lessons with him. Nelson Mandela — he has an interesting life story to tell. Don Bradman would be good, as would Sir Anthony Hopkins, whose films I enjoy.') and then I was on my way. But after the piece was published on February 14 the comment about Bangladesh and Zimbabwe got plenty of attention, especially in Bangladesh, one example being a comment from Pakistan's former great fast bowler Wasim Akram, who wrote in a column in Dhaka's *Daily Star* newspaper: 'Mr Ponting, you must keep your mouth shut and look back to what they did against you in Cardiff last year.'

I'd made a mistake and both Cricket Australia and I felt obliged to make statements, with mine reading in part: 'If it takes teams like Australia playing teams like Bangladesh for the developing Test nations to improve their skills, then I'm all for it. I'm looking forward to the challenge of leading Australia in Bangladesh.' As we continued our tour of South Africa, the debate died down somewhat, but I knew I'd be asked to explain my remarks as soon as we landed in Bangladesh for the first-ever Test tour of that country by an Aussie team.

AT A MEDIA CONFERENCE this morning, 24 hours after we landed here in Dhaka after a 17-hour flight from Johannesburg, I clarified my position as soon as the subject came up, but not (as I'm sure some people believed) because I thought that was the politically correct thing to do. I wasn't taken out of context or misquoted back in February; what I said just wasn't thought through. I do believe that the ICC needs to think carefully about both the Champions Trophy and the World Cup, to make sure they remain elite competitions that are not clogged up by including too many teams that have no chance of winning. I also have grave concerns about the future of the Zimbabwean national team, which has declined significantly in recent years for reasons that are well beyond the control of their players, and I wonder if there needs to be a 'second-tier' grade of international cricket, where teams can learn the ropes before they progress to Test matches. Once teams *dominate* at that level, then maybe it'll be time for a promotion. But it was wrong for me to suggest that Bangladesh should be stripped of their Test status, to go backwards if you like. I shouldn't have denigrated them as I did.

When I made that comment to the *Telegraph*, I was thinking only about the ideal cricket world right now, without considering what needs to happen to best grow the game across the planet for the future. I am happy to concede that having teams such as Bangladesh in Test cricket at present is the best way forward, just as it was for Sri Lanka in the early 1980s, Pakistan in the 1950s, India, New Zealand and the West Indies between the wars. We have already seen Bangladesh improve as a one-day combination — they beat Sri Lanka in a game at Bogra in the country's north six weeks ago and then swept Kenya in a four-match series in March — and it could happen in Test cricket, too, if people (including me) are patient.

Later in the media conference, I was invited to compare the present Bangladesh team with the one we played in Darwin and Cairns in 2003.

'As we look at them now, there has been a lot of improvement, particularly in the one-day game,' I said. 'We just like to think that their cricket and infrastructure will keep improving. This will give them a chance to be a good international team in the future. They must have improved having had a lot of exposure against the better teams. The more exposure they get, the better they will be.'

WE KNOW THESE UPCOMING matches will be tricky for us. We've been playing cricket for a long, long time now, given that our last real break was July–August 2004, before the Champions Trophy in England. Since then we've played in India, Australia, New Zealand, Australia, New Zealand, England, Australia, New Zealand, Australia, South Africa and now here. The wickets will be drier and dustier than South Africa, and their attack is dominated by spinners. The desire is there in the Australian camp to win the matches on this tour, and to be honest we won't be happy unless we dominate them, but I am worried by just how tired I feel. It seems ridiculous to expect us to start a Test here in Dhaka just five days after I was contemplating having to prevent Justin Langer from batting at the end of the final Test in South Africa.

Saturday, April 8

FOR MOST CRICKET FOLLOWERS, I imagine Bangladesh is an almost unknown country — in the sense that they would know of it as a fledgling Test team, with some promising players who have achieved the occasional victory over more seasoned opponents, most notably when they beat us at Cardiff last June — but they might not know where it is, or what it is like. To get to the capital, Dhaka, from Johannesburg we had to fly to Dubai and then head east, across India, to land in one of the most densely populated countries in the world. (I actually looked this up on *Wikipedia*: Bangladesh has a population of 142 million people, eighth highest among the countries of the world, fitting into 143,998 km^2, which gives it a population density of 985 people per km^2; India's figures are 1103 million people, 3.3 million km^2, 336 people per km^2; Australia's are 20 million people, 7.7 million km^2, 2.6 people per km^2. Bangladesh ranks 11th in the list of most densely populated countries, behind Monaco, Macau, Hong Kong, Singapore, Gibraltar, Vatican City, Malta, Bermuda, Maldives and Bahrain, none of which has an area greater than 1100km^2. India ranks 31st and Australia 224th, out of 230 nations.)

When we landed in Dhaka, our greeting was less frenetic than it is when we arrive in India, in that there weren't many hundreds of people at the airport specifically there to see us. Similarly, we are not instantly recognised and then crowded at the hotel or on the street by hordes of friendly but pressing cricket-mad locals, but throughout the city there are just people everywhere. Space is always at a premium. Our security on this tour has been a concern for Cricket Australia, to the point that it wasn't until late January, when a four-man team from CA travelled to Bangladesh to inspect the venues and check out the security arrangements, that the tour was given the all clear. There is a sense here that the place is a little dangerous, and I expect we'll be spending all our spare time in or around our hotels, both here and in Chittagong, where we play the second Test and the first one-dayer.

The local cricket officials and the hotel staff have clearly done everything they can to ensure that our stay is as comfortable and enjoyable as possible. But the one thing they couldn't help us with was the lethargy we felt when we first arrived, a malady that has been accentuated by the long bus rides we're enduring to get to the ground at Fatullah, on the outskirts of Dhaka, where the first Test will be played. The regular international cricket venue, the Bangabandhu National Stadium, is currently being renovated, so our Test was switched to the Narayanganj Osmani Stadium, which only hosted its first ODI 16 days ago when the home side defeated Kenya. The ground itself looks fine, and the facilities are more than adequate, but unfortunately it is the best part of an hour's drive from our hotel. Measures have been put in place, with police positioned all along our route to try to clear the way, but in such a hot, stifling, crowded city it is still a slow, stop-start journey that leaves us all irritated and edgy by the time we return to our hotel after practice. All we can do is head straight for the pool on the roof of the hotel for a recovery session and to cool off in more ways than one.

Each day during the Test that starts tomorrow, we will be eating our breakfast while we make our way to the stadium. This will be a first for me — making sure I have my special breakfast box, packed by the hotel staff, with me as I climb on board the team bus. This way I can make the most of my time in the minutes before our 7am departure for a 10am start of play.

THE ORIGINAL INTENTION WAS that the Test squad for this tour would be the same 14 who were in South Africa, but Justin Langer, Michael Kasprowicz and Shaun Tait have dropped out, replaced by Phil Jaques, Mitchell Johnson and Jason Gillespie. My understanding is that none of the three guys who are out is seriously hurt, but the advice we received from the medicos was they would definitely not have been fit for the first Test, and would have struggled to make it for the second, so it seems sensible to bring the replacements in. Our biggest concern was with Lang, but all indications are that he'll be fine in a couple of weeks. I read that when he arrived home in Perth he compared how he was feeling to a 'massive hangover', but then said, 'There are definitely no worries about the future, none at all. This was a freak incident, and that was the thing about batting in the second innings [in Johannesburg]. The only danger was getting re-concussed in that short period of time.'

Lang also described the last morning of the Jo'burg Test as 'one of the great days of my Test career', which is incredible in a way when you think about the personal heartbreak he must have felt at not being able to contribute on the field. He's a tough bugger is Lang, and a great team man.

When it came to picking the Test XI for the first Test here, we went away from the team set-up that worked for us so well in South Africa. First, we decided to go into the game with five bowlers instead of four, on the basis that Shane Warne, Brett Lee and Stuart Clark have all worked hard over the past three weeks, so they will welcome the extra support. With the wicket sure to be dry and flat, Stuart MacGill has been brought back, and we've gone for Gillespie as the fifth bowler, because of both his experience and the fact that the 40 wickets at 21.28 he took in the 2005–06 Pura Cup suggest he's a man in good form. The selectors then brought Michael Clarke back into the middle-order, with Mike Hussey to open, instead of just bringing Phil Jaques in as the new opener. I know this was a very tight call, but Pup impressed us with the way he worked on his game in South Africa. The really unlucky bloke is Symmo, but the feeling was that with five bowlers already in the line-up he wasn't going to get many overs, and with that in mind the chance to give Pup another chance proved too tempting.

WHILE WE WERE IN South Africa, the Australian one-day squad for the three games that follow the Tests here was announced, with the one change from the group that played in South Africa being South Australian off-spinner Dan Cullen being selected instead of Mick Lewis. I don't think this is a knock on Mick so much as a reflection of two facts: one, the conditions here in Bangladesh will suit the spinners more than the seamers; and two, Dan is the sort of talented young cricketer we're keen to have a look at, and — as with Mitch Johnson in the Test squad — this seems an excellent opportunity to do just that.

Friday, April 14

Bangladesh v Australia Test series
First Test (April 9–13) at Fatullah: Bangladesh 427 (Shahriar Nafees 138, Habibul Bashar 76, Rajin Saleh 67; SR MacGill 8–108) and 148 lost to Australia 269 (AC Gilchrist 144; Mohammad Rafique 5–62) and 7–307 (ML Hayden 72, RT Ponting 118*; Mohammad Rafique 4–98) by three wickets

THE FIRST THING I have to say about this game is that Bangladesh played extremely well, and could have won if a few things had worked out differently. It is also true that we did not perform too brilliantly at all, yet we still found enough to get over the line. Stuart MacGill bowled well in their first innings, which stopped them achieving a huge total, Adam Gilchrist batted superbly to rescue us after our top-order collapsed on day two, and I was proud of the way I stuck at it in our second innings, but overall this effort was a long way from our best. The tiring schedule of late is something of an explanation, but only in the sense that we didn't recognise how much it had taken out of us until the game had almost slipped away. And maybe we were a fraction complacent, though only, I must stress, in our preparation — once we were on the field we were trying 100 per cent. I had told the guys in our pre-Test meetings to conserve their energy at training, on the basis that what we needed most was a freshen up. I wasn't worried about how hard we trained, I told them, but maybe we relaxed too much. A few days later, we had to dig deep to get ourselves back in the Test, and fortunately there is enough character and pride in our squad that we were able to recover.

It would have been handy if we'd won the toss, as that might have given the bowlers an extra day or two with their feet up. Instead, we found ourselves out on the field on a very hot day against a team that was a lot more ready than we were. At lunch, after just 25 overs, they were off and running at 1–144, with Shahriar Nafees batting excellently for 60 not out, having already given an indication that he was going to play Warney as well as anyone has done in a long time. Shane's bowling figures at this point were 0–38 from six overs, while Bing had also been harshly treated, going for 44 runs from eight, including a tremendous cover drive for four from their captain Habibul Bashar off the last ball before-lunch. We had to admire their spunk.

Our best two bowlers in that first innings turned out to be two blokes who hadn't played any Test cricket in a while — MacGill and Jason Gillespie — and I don't think there was any coincidence there. This was the first time Magilla had claimed eight victims in a Test innings, as he closes in on 200 career wickets (a remarkable achievement for a guy who, because his career has coincided with Warney's, has not played as much Test cricket as he deserves), while Dizzy kept things tight and steady on a wicket that offered him nothing. We actually did well to keep them to 427 after they were 4–351 just prior to stumps on day one, but then we undid all that good work by losing 6–93 before stumps on day two.

It looked like we were going to have to follow on. That we didn't was due entirely to Gilly, who came out when the fourth wicket fell with the score on 61 and was the last wicket to fall, for 144 from 212 balls (not that quick by his standards), when the innings total was 269. That means he scored almost 70 per cent of the runs scored after he arrived at the crease, having only batted with a specialist batsman for the first 18 of them, when he was batting with Pup. Had Gilly played this sort of knock against an established cricket nation, I'm sure it would have been described as one of the greatest Test innings of all time, but because it was Bangladesh putting the pressure on I bet it will be downgraded — which is unfair, because it was their turf, their tails were up and we were desperate. He came through for us again.

We were still facing a deficit of 158 when Bangladesh went back in, but this time our bowlers were excellent. Warney had hurt his shoulder on the opening day, and there was a time when we feared he might not be able to bowl at all in the second innings, but instead he kept things watertight on the third afternoon and then cleaned up the tail at the start of day four. Dizzy was also excellent, as the local batsman seemed to get very edgy as the thought of a historic victory drew closer. By stumps on day four we probably had our noses back in front, needing another 95 runs to win with six wickets in hand. I went to bed that night 72 not out, having set myself a personal mission of batting through to the end of the game.

The only time I thought we might lose on the final day came when I was 97 and we were seven wickets down and needing 24 more runs to win. Shahadat Hossain bowled a short delivery at me that I tried to pull but top-edged. For a moment, time stood still, as I knew the ball was flying in the air but I wasn't sure where. It could have gone straight up in the air, or more likely, I thought, the damn thing was going down deep fine leg's throat. Fortunately, it was halfway between, and though the man on the fence, Mashrafe Mortaza, tried his best to take the catch, it got away from him and Dizzy and I walked through for a single. I think we all sensed that was their last chance, and about 20 minutes after lunch the victory was achieved without us losing another wicket.

FOR ME, TWO THINGS came out of this match. One was the confirmation that no matter how good a team you are in modern Test cricket, if you play below your best you're going to get beaten. The Ashes in 2005 proved that. England were an excellent side and played very well, while we weren't at our best so we lost. It sounds simple, but it just underlines the fact that you've got to prepare right *every* time. In this game, against the lowest-ranked Test side, we did drop our standards a lot, at least in the lead-up and for the first two days when we were probably playing at around 30 or 40 per cent of our ability, and it nearly cost us. If we'd performed this way against one of the better Test sides, we would have been thrashed. Though we've been the dominant Test nation for the last few years, there is not necessarily as great a distance between us and our rivals as our recent results over the last few years suggest.

I sometimes wish that the people who want to downgrade our achievements by questioning the quality of our opponents would remember this fact more often. If winning was easy, everyone would do it.

The second thing is that, given the hole we dug for ourselves, this developed into one of our best-ever recoveries of recent times. It probably won't be classed as such, because of who our opponents were, but to fight back from our position at stumps on day two to win with a little in hand was quite an achievement. We had to a lot of things right — keeping the pressure on when they batted, digging in and being patient as we chased a difficult target (the pitch was spinning a fair bit), maintaining our desire for those three days and reminding ourselves and each other that the victory was worth the effort. It was also reassuring to take the Bangladeshis down a peg or two, because we felt they got just a little uppity when they held the whip hand for the first half of the game, and even when a couple of wickets fell on the fourth afternoon. We've certainly learnt some lessons from this game, and I hope they have too.

Saturday, April 15

> Mentally it's such a tough ask — to travel and just have a few days' break between that last Test in South Africa ... That was a really tough Test match. It usually takes a week to get over a game like that. Our guys just look tired. They weren't with it on the first day. It's the worst they've played in a long time ...

THESE WORDS CAME FROM a newspaper column written by Steve Waugh that was published in the News Limited papers in Australia yesterday. Stephen, of course, was speaking from vast experience, so I hope his opinion is respected. However, I sense there is not too much sympathy in other quarters for the argument that our schedule over the past few weeks has been too tight, even though we are now being asked to start another Test match just three days after the previous one has finished. I wish people would appreciate just how tough an ask that is.

We didn't make it known before the first Test, but if we'd been fair dinkum, there were a couple of blokes who shouldn't have played in Dhaka simply because they were too fatigued. But to have left them out would have gone against our philosophy that we should be playing our strongest side in every Test we play. With one-day cricket, because there are so many matches, you can and should rest guys occasionally, but never in a Test match unless it is absolutely necessary. I wish the authorities would give us a break, but at the same time I understand how difficult it must be to devise the international cricket program, so the last thing I want to be is militant about it. What should happen, then?

As a general rule, I would like to see a minimum three days off between Test matches. I'd also like some recognition from the itinerary makers that even with a three-day gap, the players will be mentally and physically tested by playing so much cricket in such a short space of time, so we can't keep going as we have in the past four weeks, playing one Test after another. The number of Tests is not the problem, and while I'd like to see a slight reduction in the amount of one-day cricket we play, that is not really the issue here either. It's just a situation where we need to recognise that playing Test cricket or a one-day series or tournament is tough work and that the participants need time to recover between games so they can keep playing to their full ability. International cricket should always be a test of skill and stamina, rather than just a matter of survival.

The fact that Cricket Australia chief executive James Sutherland and a few CA directors were in Dhaka at the start of the first Test was a good thing, I'm sure, because they could see for themselves how spent we were at the *start* of that game. My fear, though, is that the debate about the programming might spin out of control, and I can already sense the cynics lining up to ridicule our complaints. It is true that we are very well paid and that Cricket Australia looks after us with top-class accommodation and business-class travel, and it is also a fact that a number of members of the Australian squad will be heading off to England to play county cricket while the rest of us enjoy a four-month break. This is all good and we are grateful for it, but it doesn't change the fact that elite sports people need time to recover after a major performance; if we don't get that time then standards will suffer and careers will be shortened. I don't want to see either of those things happen, for the sake of the players themselves, the team and Australian cricket.

It is also true that CA presented the program for this tour to the Australian Cricketers' Association and that we approved it. However, we were only given two alternatives — the other being that we fly home from South Africa, stay in Australia for a few days, and then fly back to Bangladesh and start a Test two or three days later. We didn't like all those kilometres and the short pre-Test preparation that were part of that travel plan either, so we chose the lesser of two evils. For all this, I don't think CA and the players are actually all that far apart in what we both want and need, so hopefully we can get things right for the immediate future and beyond.

APART FROM THE SCHEDULING debate, there have also been a couple of selection decisions made during the past few days. First, during the first Test, news was released that Nathan Bracken and Dan Cullen had been called into the Test squad, a decision that reflected our general concerns about the fitness of a few guys in the squad. Two days later, Andrew Hilditch revealed that Shane Watson has not fully recovered from a calf injury he picked up during Queensland's big win in the Pura Cup final three weeks back (a match in which Watto scored 201 retired hurt, Brad Hodge scored a hundred in Victoria's first innings and Mitchell Johnson took 10 wickets). James Hopes will take Shane's place in our squad for the three one-dayers that follow the second Test.

Andrew was making these announcements as the new chairman of selectors, having taken over from Trevor Hohns, who stepped down on April 4 after 13 seasons as a selector, and nearly 10 years as chairman. While it's not for me as Australian captain to comment on selections, I can point out that in the time Trevor was in charge the Australian team won a lot more games than it lost. He must have been doing something right.

Another matter that got some coverage concerned Gilly's actions on the second day, when he gave a few sponsors a mention while he was encouraging team-mates out on the field. These free plugs were promptly picked up on the stump microphones and heard across the cricket world. We had been under the impression, both in South Africa and here, that the stump mikes would be turned off between deliveries (as occurs almost always in Australia), but too often this hasn't been the case. This has resulted in the occasional lively comment being heard by the public, and Gilly's lines were a response to that. Some critics reckon it would be easier if we just didn't say anything, but I think everyone has to accept that the atmosphere can get emotional at times and that there are certain things that should just stay on the field.

Friday, April 21

Bangladesh v Australia Test series
Second Test (April 16–20) at Chittagong: Bangladesh 197 (Rajin Saleh 71) and 304 (Shahriar Nafees 79, Habibul Bashar 49, Mohammad Rafique 65; SK Warne 5–113, SCG MacGill 4–95) lost to Australia 4–581 declared (PA Jaques 66, JN Gillespie 201*, RT Ponting 52, MEK Hussey 182) by an innings and 80 runs

THERE WAS A MOMENT in this Test when Adam Gilchrist wouldn't leave me alone. Jason Gillespie was 197 not out, on the verge of a Test double century, and Gilly wanted to make sure I was going to declare as soon as Dizzy reached 200. Mohammad

Rafique started a new over ... and there was no run from the first ball ... or the second. The third delivery was well flighted, pitching just outside the leg stump, the batsman tried to flick it away, and it sped down off the edge to fine leg for four. Our man had become the first nightwatchman to score 200 in a Test-match innings, and I was on my feet, with Gilly right behind me, applauding enthusiastically and at the same waving them straight in. By going to 201, Dizzy had passed Steve Waugh's highest Test score (200 against the West Indies at Kingston in 1995) and David Boon's highest Test score (200 against New Zealand at the WACA in 1989–90). But he was still short of the 204 not out Gilly scored against South Africa at Johannesburg in 2002, his highest Test score, and for our wicketkeeper that mattered. Knowing how Dizzy would go on about it, as he'd already done with some other players' highest scores he'd beaten, I understood where he was coming from.

Before this innings, Dizzy had reached 50 in a Test innings twice: 54 not out against New Zealand at the Gabba in 2004–05 and 50 not out against Pakistan at the MCG later that same season. This was his 92nd Test innings, breaking the record for the most Test innings before you make your first Test hundred. Along the way he beat the highest score in Tests of many great Australian players and a number of present or recent team-mates, including: Glenn McGrath (61), Brett Lee (64), Damien Fleming (71*), Andrew Symonds (72), Merv Hughes (72*), Dennis Lillee (73*), Paul Reiffel (79), Alan Davidson (80), Michael Bevan (91), Shane Warne (99), Tony Mann (105, the previous highest score by an Australian nightwatchman), Richie Benaud (122), Rod Marsh (132), Geoff Marsh (138), Keith Miller (147), Michael Clarke (151), Mark Waugh (153*), Ian Healy (161*), Damien Martyn (165), Charlie Macartney (170), Darren Lehmann (177), Clem Hill (191), Ian Chappell (196) and

Lindsay Hassett (198*). Dizzy didn't know all these scores, but he did know plenty of them and he loved it every time he conquered another one.

Obviously, this was an unexpected performance, but in another way it wasn't so surprising. Dizzy is a good, sensible defensive batsman, who has played some important hands supporting better-equipped players such as Steve Waugh, Adam Gilchrist, Simon Katich and Mike Hussey in important late-order partnerships. He'd been terrific at the end of the first Test in Dhaka, scoring 4 not out and staying with me while we achieved the 30 runs we needed to win the game. The circumstances here were perfect for him — a flat deck, average bowlers, plenty of time and, because Dizzy has been on the fringe of the team since the Ashes loss, plenty of motivation to take advantage of his recall in every way he could. All he needed was the guts and stamina to keep going and going, and he has plenty of that. About the only thing he did wrong through his entire knock was run his captain out, and I'm sure I'll forgive him one day for that. 'He called me through and I was in my own little fog,' was the surviving batsman's explanation when he talked about it later, after making his first hundred. 'I felt pretty ordinary for a while, I still do, but these things happen in cricket. It was my fault. I thought, "I better do all right here."'

We're all taught, when something like this happens, to not throw your own wicket away, but try to make up for it. Dizzy definitely did that here. Not bad for a bloke who later admitted he'd never even scored a hundred in the backyard before.

My co-author dug up a few stats about the innings, which underline what a rare diamond it was:

- It was the highest score by a nightwatchman in Test cricket, beating the previous record of 125 by Mark Boucher, for

South Africa against Zimbabwe in November 1999. Boucher was down to bat at No. 9 in that innings but came in at No. 6 late on day 2, so I guess it counts, though we've always considered him to be a good enough Test bat to go in at six or seven.

- Dizzy's effort was the sixth instance of a nightwatchman scoring a Test hundred, after Nasim-ul-Ghani (Pakistan versus England in 1962), Tony Mann (Australia versus India, 1977–78), Syed Kirmani (India versus Australia, 1979) and Boucher twice (South Africa versus Zimbabwe in 1999–2000 and versus England in 1999–2000).

- He took 390 minutes to reach his hundred, making it the slowest Test hundred (in terms of minutes batted) ever made by an Australian, breaking Justin Langer's old record of 388 minutes, versus Pakistan at Hobart in 1999–2000. It was funny how Dizzy kept feeding us stats about his innings, and whose highest score he was now passing. But never did he mention that fact about his knock being the slowest Test hundred ever made by an Australian.

- He became the seventh Australian to open the bowling and score a hundred in the same Test, after Charles Kelleway, Jack Gregory, Stan McCabe, Ray Lindwall, Keith Miller and Gary Gilmour. (Mark Waugh scored 99 and opened the bowling at Lord's in 1993.) He was the first Australian to open the bowling and score 200.

- The 320-run partnership for the fourth wicket between Dizzy and Mike Hussey was the 11th highest by Australians in Tests. Huss was dismissed for 182, his best effort in Test matches to date, when Dizzy was 174. When someone asked Mr Cricket what was his motivation for keeping on going, he replied, 'I didn't want to be outdone by Diz.' He batted beautifully, but on the day 182 wasn't enough.

One amusing aspect of Dizzy's dig centred on the fact that he had brought a brand new bat along with him for this tour. He used it in the first Test, when he hit the winning runs by cutting the second new ball out towards the backward-point boundary (the ball crossed the rope, but because we'd already completed a single before that happened, he was only credited with one run for the shot). It was a stroke that left a juicy red mark in the middle of the face. Now Dizzy is a bloke who over the years has made something of an art form out of finding other guys' new gear and signing his autograph all over that gear — you might proudly pull your new pads out of your kit and there's 'Jason Gillespie' penned in a prominent position. Apparently, Merv Hughes used to do this in his heyday, and Glenn McGrath's been known to do the same dastardly trick as well. This time, though, someone had taken Dizzy's new bat, and with a black Texta had drawn a circle all the way around that big red 'cherry', so when he went out to bat in Chittagong the cherry *and* the black circle highlighting it were on display every time he acknowledged the applause for his fifty ... his hundred ... the 150 ... and the unbeaten 201!

THERE WERE A LOT of excellent Australian performances in this Test, but unfortunately many of them were lost in the excitement of Dizzy's remarkable achievement. Shane Warne and Stuart MacGill both bowled beautifully, taking 15 of the 20 Bangladesh wickets to fall, while Huss took his Test career batting average back over 75 and Phil Jaques (in for Damien Martyn, who hurt his elbow) played his first substantial Test innings, looking right at home until he top-edged a sweep to square leg. That was the only wicket to fall on day two, a day in which a lot of time was lost because of a spectacular thunderstorm, while I was the only man dismissed on day three. The game ended when the last six Bangladeshi wickets fell before the scheduled lunch break on the final day, all to spin, completing our 11th Test-match win of the long season, from 12 games. This was a solid, professional performance on our part, and I think the Bangladesh team got a truer appreciation of our ability from this game than they did in Fatullah.

We'd gone into the game with a point to prove after the first Test, which was why we played it as hard as we could. Actually, I don't know any other way to play, and the rest of the guys in the team are the same, but I have been told a couple of people outside the squad had a problem with us playing it hard. Our ambition to win well was the reason we used a nightwatchman at the end of day one, and why Warne and MacGill bowled so many overs while Dan Cullen delivered only a few. We had brought in Dan for Stuey Clark because it was obvious the Chittagong wicket was going to suit the slow men, and also because we felt that Sarfraz had looked a little flat in Dhaka after his fantastic performances in South Africa, but even though he only bowled seven overs in each innings of this Test, I'm still glad we picked him. It gave us a chance to have a look at him and I like what we saw.

If I did make a mistake with the spinners in this series, it was with Shane on the first day of the series, when he was getting hammered by Shahriar Nafees and Habibul Bashar. But he's such a great bowler, and has done the job for us so often, I think you've got to show faith in him. Same with Glenn McGrath. There will be rare occasions when such a policy doesn't work, but there'll be plenty more times when the champions come through for you. Once these blokes get on a roll, they win you games and series.

As for the nightwatchman, our only concern at the time was that using one might hold us up on the following day. Because Dizzy is a slow run-scorer he can clog an end up if he bats for a while, which can lead to the pressure building up on the other batsman as the game slows to a walk. That's why Brett Lee is a good nightwatchman, because if he does stay awhile, the next morning he'll get the scoreboard ticking over and infuriate the bowlers. But I'd already asked a lot of Bing this summer, while Dizzy was reasonably fresh, having bowled only five overs for the day, so he got the opportunity and boy did he take it. Our next Test match will be the first Ashes Test at the Gabba next November, and there will probably be eight fast bowlers trying to get into the side: Bracken, Clark, Gillespie, Johnson, Kasprowicz, Lee, McGrath and Tait. Dizzy had to so something to keep his name firmly in the selectors' minds, and his man-of-the-series performance here in Bangladesh, bowling nicely and batting as he did, definitely did that.

THE ONLY DOWNER TO come out of the game for me was the fine I copped (25 per cent of my match fee) after being found guilty of dissent over an incident on the first day. I will always maintain I was unlucky on this occasion, and I must admit to being a little confused by the way the match referee, Jeff Crowe of New Zealand, handled the matter.

Aftab Ahmed, the Bangladesh No. 6, had tried to whip a full toss through mid-wicket, but only succeeded in getting an inside edge onto his boot, the ball spun up into the air, and Gilly completed the catch. To me, it looked a fairly obvious out, but the umpires decided to go to the TV umpire, to make sure the ball had not touched the ground at the same time it hit the batsman's boot. We had no problem with that; it was good adjudicating. While we were waiting, I checked with the umps to confirm what they were checking, and was told that in their minds there was no doubt that Aftab had hit the ball.

'Okay, no worries,' I said.

Unfortunately, there was a breakdown in communication between the ground and the TV umpire, and after a long delay it was the green (not out) light, rather the red (out) one we'd all been expecting that started flashing. I was incredulous, not least because we had heard from our dressing-room that the replay proved beyond doubt that the batsman was out. We'd had a bad experience with the TV umpire in Dhaka, when Matthew Hayden was given out run out on what we thought was dubious video evidence, but this time we just couldn't believe what had happened.

I went over to the umpires and said, 'Hang on a minute. Did the third umpire know what he was supposed to look at?' It seemed the 'man upstairs' had ruled that there was doubt as to whether the batsman had actually hit the ball. I'm not sure if what I said made any difference, but the umpires did go back to the third umpire, who informed them that the replay clearly showed that there was no contact between ball and pitch. So, finally, they gave Aftab out.

Jeff Crowe fronted a media conference that night, but not to discuss that dismissal. There had been a major incident at the ground earlier in the day, after a local press photographer's taxi was refused entry to the ground and then the photographer was allegedly treated roughly by security when he complained. The start of play was delayed when local photographers and reporters staged a protest next to the pitch, but though they eventually moved on when they were asked to, there was another protest during the lunch break, which led to some nasty incidents on the field when the police moved in. At one point, the protesters seemed to be running for their lives and desperately looking for an escape route, trying to avoid the police who were swinging their guns like baseball bats. Eventually, they tried to get into the dressing-room area. We could tell they were terrified, and we were a little apprehensive, too, because just for a moment we didn't know how it was going to turn out. Eventually, things seemed to return to normal, though from what I understand, the press box was pretty empty for the rest of the day. After stumps, Jeff decided to make a public call for better security at the ground.

Before that media conference concluded, Jeff was asked about my 'incident'. I was told that he replied, 'No, I've had no report from the umpires. As far as I'm concerned nothing is going to happen.'

However, the following morning I was surprised to discover that I had been reported, and that night I attended a hearing with Jeff, the umpires, our manager Steve Bernard, coach John Buchanan and myself. I explained what happened, the umpires backed me up, and I really didn't think I was in any bother until Jeff handed down his verdict. 'Although I have sympathy for Ricky, I cannot accept his move towards the on-field umpires as they made a move towards resuming play,' he explained later. 'He did not ask for the third umpire to be consulted, but when he made that move and spoke to the officials, I believe his involvement played a part in prompting the referral. That is a breach of the ICC's Test-match playing conditions, which states that players may not appeal to the umpire to use the replay system.'

Earlier, Jeff had admitted to the media that there had been a communication problem between the umpires on the field and the TV umpire, whose English is apparently not that good. I'm sure I was very unlucky, but I guess I have to cop it sweet.

THE NIGHT OF OUR second Test win, we adjourned to the rooftop area of the hotel, where we ordered some pizzas from the Pizza Hut across the road, formed a big circle of chairs next to the pool, had a few beers and just reminisced about all we've been through. We also talked about what's ahead, cricket-wise, after the break that's coming up once we complete the one-dayers here. There's the Champions Trophy in India in October–November, the Ashes Tests and a number of one-dayers during the Australian home season, and then the World Cup in the Caribbean in March–April. It will be a huge seven months, and there isn't an Australian cricketer who was in that circle who doesn't keenly want to be a part of it.

Monday, May 1

One-day Series

Game One at Chittagong (April 23): Bangladesh 195 (47 overs: Habibul Bashar 52; GB Hogg 3–37) lost to Australia 6–196 (44 overs: AC Gilchrist 76; Abdur Razzak 3–36) by four wickets

Game Two at Fatullah (April 26): Australia 5–250 (50 overs: MJ Clarke 54, A Symonds 103*; Mashrafe Mortaza 3–54) defeated Bangladesh 183 (48 overs: Habibul Bashar 70; GB Hogg 3–34) by 67 runs

Game Three at Fatullah (April 28): Bangladesh 124 (42.3 overs: GB Hogg 3–17) lost to Australia 1–127 (22.4 overs: MJ Cosgrove 74, SM Katich 42*) by nine wickets

THE CROWDS WERE NOISY and vibrant, and for the first game and a bit the home team was very competitive, but in the end we drew away to win this one-day series decisively.

We didn't change our approach to the series because of who our opponents were or because we were at the end of a long campaign. There was no lust for revenge because of what happened in England last year, nor a temptation to relax because Bangladesh is ranked so far below us. I simply reminded the guys before we began that our objective should always be to go out and try to win our games as decisively as we can. If that means we win in 30 overs, then terrific; if we sneak home off the last ball of the 50th over, that's fine, too, as long as our attitude is right. The conditions were pretty tough — we lost the toss two times out of three, which meant we were chasing runs on slow wickets that suited their bowlers more than ours — but we came through with a bit of style. And given that we had a number of our top players out, I thought that was terrific.

That we were not at full strength was reflected by the eight blokes who bowled our overs during the final game of this long summer. Mitchell Johnson, Brett Dorey, James Hopes, Mike Hussey, Dan Cullen, Mark Cosgrove, Michael Clarke and Brad Hogg all had a turn at the bowling crease. None of them bowled even one over in the Super Series last October.

Pup was actually lucky to be playing at all in this series, after he split his head open in an accident on the pool deck of our Chittagong hotel the day before the opening game. As we'd done every day after training, we had headed straight for the roof area to try to dilute the afternoon heat, and this time Pup and I were among the first to arrive. I had vivid memories of he and Symmo running around the slippery tiled surrounds of the pool the first time we went there, a couple of days before the second Test. They were trying to outbomb each other, and it was a miracle at least one of them didn't lose his balance and do himself some damage. I remember saying to them, like a nagging father rousing on his kids, 'You blokes are going to slip over one day, and then you'll know about it.'

Sure enough, I had my back to Pup and the pool when I heard him commence his run-up, and I only had time to turn around and yell, 'No! Don't do it!' Moments later, he got it all wrong as his feet went from under him at precisely the wrong moment ...

his body was almost parallel to the water, feet first, when ... THUMP! ... the back of his melon collided with the edge of the pool. It would have been funny if it hadn't been so horribly serious.

Pup went straight down and I dived in with visions of him being out cold at the bottom of the pool. Fortunately, he wasn't unconscious, but as he came to the surface he was holding his head and there was blood everywhere. I got him out, laid him down and could see a massive cut across the back of his skull that eventually needed more than a dozen stitches. For the game the next day, he needed a lot of tape around his head and he had to be very careful when he put his helmet on, because the wound was precisely where the helmet sits. But he could hardly complain. He was a very lucky boy.

Fortunately, the knock didn't seem to hurt his cricket at all. A number of our 'established' players did well in these games, and he was one of those. Adam Gilchrist was at his dynamic best in the opening game of the series, slamming 76 from 46 deliveries, which proved very handy given that the rest of the batsmen struggled against some very tight bowling and we got home with only four wickets and six overs to spare. Three days later, Andrew Symonds scored his third ODI century of the season, but this was not your typical Symmo slugfest; instead he hit only two sixes and six fours as he and Pup adapted cleverly to the conditions to give us a total that was well beyond the locals. Brett Lee and Nathan Bracken bowled well in game one, while throughout the three matches, Brad Hogg's bowling was excellent and he was justly named player of the series.

But as good as these guys were, what I was most taken with was the form of some of our new guys, especially Mitchell Johnson, Dan Cullen and Mark Cosgrove. I am always keen to expose the 'fringe' players to the highest level, and with a number of established players unavailable this was an excellent time to do that. These three guys were the ones who really took advantage of their opportunity.

Dan had to work hard to get his first wicket, which didn't come until his second spell in game three, but his economy rate through the series was first-class. He finished with 2–25 from 7.3 overs in that game, on a pitch that we were able to score at nearly a run a ball, and afterwards some observers were suggesting he might be our No. 1 one-day spinner by the time the World Cup arrives. Mitch had played two one-dayers for Australia previously this summer, one in New Zealand and one in South Africa, without much success, but he responded fantastically here, when picked for all three matches. He improved every time, and was particularly impressive when he took the new ball in the final match. It's been hard to hide the fact that we're keen on his potential, and I think we're just starting to see some of that enormous talent come out now. Cosgrove, who came into the team to replace Damien Martyn, played beautifully in the final game, winning his first man-of-the-match award in ODI cricket at the earliest opportunity. The fact that he is just 21 years old, Dan is 22 and Mitch 24, is also an encouraging sign. As I've said many times, I don't think age is an issue in terms of the make-up of the Australian team — I'm all about picking the best group of players available, however old they may be. But having been a young bloke when I made my debut, I know there is a place for tyros in the Australian set-up, as long as they are good enough. To see gifted young players coming through is surely no bad thing.

AND THEN, FINALLY, WE were home. Back last September, the atmosphere was a bit chaotic as the media pack at Sydney Airport sought my reaction to the Ashes loss and Dennis Lillee's comments that I had to be sacked. This time, the mood was much more sedate. Just enough questions for the evening news bulletins and the following day's sports pages, and then I was in the car with Rianna for the drive home. I was worn out more mentally than physically, but I had a grin from ear to ear, in part because I was back with the woman I love, but also because this time the cricket adventure had gone so well.

I'm not one for looking back too much, and to be honest, so much has happened in the past seven months that a lot of it is now a blur. If you asked me now what stands out it would be simply how tough the South Africa and Bangladesh tours were, one on top of the other. At times, that was just hard work. We've played a lot of games since last October and battled unbelievably hard, but the wins have made it worthwhile, as has the fun, the joy and the mateship that have come with our success. I feel like the long break I'll now enjoy has been well earned. I won't think about cricket much, not until late August when we go into camp; until then I'm going to stick to simple things — I'll revel in waking up in my own bed, walking down to the local newsagent to grab a paper and a coffee, working out which Kangaroos games I can go to, planning my next 18 holes . . .

The golf might be my biggest worry. We landed in Sydney early yesterday morning, and once I got home I spent the day doing as little as possible. Twenty-four hours later, you'd probably have expected me to sleep in and do about as much as I'd done the day before. You'd be wrong! An invitation to play at The Lakes, the famous championship layout located near the airport, was too good to pass up, and I was on the first tee at 7am. Of course, my playing partners wanted to talk about the cricket, while I preferred to yarn about anything but, and I think they understood. It was a lot cooler than Dhaka, and the fairways were green with grass. The only spin was the backspin

I managed with some of my approach shots (or the unlucky bounces that left my ball in the rough). No one reacted like Andre Nel if things didn't go their way. There was no backchat, no pressure at all except from that competitive edge that gets in my head every time I'm involved in sport, no media at the end of each hole, looking for a comment. Occasionally, I'd look over and see another plane taking off, and just for a second I'd be thinking about the passengers locked in the aircraft or maybe those back in the departure lounge, bidding their friends and family goodbye. I wasn't envious at all. I was just glad to be home.

Epilogue

No Limits

The Fight for the Ashes
2006–07

BACK ON NOVEMBER 9, 2005, I predicted that some good might come out of England regaining the Ashes. That comment didn't mean we were happy we'd lost, or that we hadn't tried our hardest to win, but if this Australian side was going to get back to its best or even exceed the standards set by great Aussie teams of the recent past, then maybe we did need that special kind of kick up the backside that only comes with a serious setback.

In my opinion, it wasn't hard to work out what went wrong during that fateful Ashes series. There were too many batting failures by our side, too many times when our bowlers — Shane Warne and Glenn McGrath apart — lacked penetration and control, too many dropped catches, too many no-balls. It was significant how few major partnerships there were by Australians in those Tests, whether we were batting or bowling, which meant we could never exploit small advantages or dig ourselves out of holes. Losing Pidge for two Tests out of five also hurt us, but we should have been good enough to overcome even that.

Identifying what went wrong was easy. Finding the remedy was harder, until I looked at the way we were preparing ourselves and decided that we just weren't getting the type of practice we needed. In the nets, we weren't preparing with our opponents in mind. This was especially true of the batsmen — in the nets, it was too much about just getting the feel of bat on ball, or about getting your feet moving, rather than deliberately rehearsing for what we would be facing in the middle. Our practices weren't competitive enough; it was as if we wanted to avoid rather than recreate the intensity of game day. As I've documented in this book, we set out to fix this problem from the first training session of the new season.

I have always been an advocate of training competitively, so with hindsight I'm dirty as the captain that I allowed us to slip away from that philosophy when we were in the UK in 2005. As an example, I have also always said that all the fielding practice we do in preparation for a game should be done in a group, as a team, but that stopped happening consistently. I always wanted to be the finest fielder in my group, and as a young member of the Australian team that meant my aim was to be the best fielder in the world. At training, I always sought to be better than Mark Waugh, who in my eyes was the best we had. I think the more you challenge yourself in a group, with other eyes and other pressures on you, the better you will be. Further, the energy that comes with the competition lifts the whole team.

I knew we had to get our training back to that level, but it was all very well for me to say that — unless everyone in the squad made the same commitment and had the same belief in the value of competitive practice as I did, it wasn't going to work. But the bowlers started charging at the nets from day one of our preparation for the Super Series, and the batsmen stood up to them. Eleven Test wins out of 12 is testament to how unconditionally everyone responded and how good our method of preparation now is. It is because the response of the guys was so total that I can guarantee that the mistakes we made in the last Ashes series won't be repeated this time.

IT'S IMPOSSIBLE TO DOWNPLAY how passionate and important Ashes cricket can be. A bloke like Mike Hussey is going to absolutely love it! We shouldn't have been caught short in 2005, but we were, even though the first time we were challenged we responded well. The opening day of the series, at Lord's, was an unbelievable day of Test cricket — Australia all out for 190; England 7 for 92 — as intense a period of play as I have ever experienced. It was my first Ashes Test as captain, which was a buzz in itself, and the build-up to the game had been littered with plenty of hopeful comments from the home camp and pages and hours of media hype. England thought they were a chance to beat us; we were very keen to put them back in their box. They were happy to bowl first, we liked the idea of batting so we could take on their fast bowlers and also give Warney a chance to bowl at them when they had to bat last. The queues outside the ground were long, when the Test finally started there wasn't a spare seat in the house, and Justin Langer was hit smack on the elbow by Steve Harmison from the second ball of the series. It was a while before some feeling came back into Lang's hands so he could grip his bat. Four overs later, Matthew Hayden was clunked on the helmet as he tried to pull a Harmison riser through the legside. Still in the first hour, another bouncer from Harmison clipped my helmet grille and I felt blood seeping out of my face and down onto my shirt. Later, England captain Michael Vaughan and I had a bit of a barney about the English fielders throwing the ball in our general direction when we were batting.

Glenn McGrath began the series with 499 Test-match wickets, and first ball after tea, at the start of the seventh over of the Poms' reply, he had Marcus Trescothick caught by Lang in the slips to go to 500. By stumps, our great fast man had taken 5–21 from 13 overs, one of the great spells of cricket history, and we had our noses back in front. I think everyone — players, fans and

Four images from what South Africans now call 'the greatest one-day game ever played'. Above left: One of my nine sixes. Above: This was one record that didn't last for long. Below right: Herschelle Gibbs during the innings of his life. Below left: Graeme Smith batted nearly as well as Gibbs, which is high praise.

One of debutant Stuart Clark's five wickets in his first Test innings — in the first Test at Cape Town — was Herschelle Gibbs.

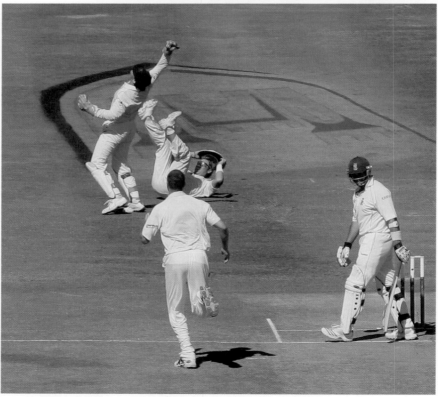

Our dismissal of Jacques Kallis (right) in the second innings of the first Test, caught behind off Stuart Clark, came about just the way we'd planned.

Above: Two more South African wickets, this time from the second Test, at Durban: Graeme Smith (left) is caught by Justin Langer for a first-ball duck and Mark Boucher (right) is bowled comprehensively by Brett Lee.

While Michael Clarke and Shaun Tait bring Matt Hayden and me some refreshments during our long second-innings partnership, the Durban groundstaff try to return the pitch to the condition it had been at stumps the previous day.

Above: Adam Gilchrist
introduces himself to Andre Nel
at Durban.

Right: Andrew Symonds, Stuart
Clark and Brett Lee mob Shane
Warne after the great leg-spinner
had bowled us to victory late on
the final day of the second Test.

Australian and South African cricketers with the remarkable Archbishop Desmond Tutu
in Johannesburg: (from left) Justin Langer, me, Michael Kasprowicz (obscured),
Archbishop Tutu, Herschelle Gibbs (obscured), Jacques Kallis and Shaun Pollock.

Left: Justin Langer's first ball of his 100th Test ends in disaster when he is crunched on the head by a delivery from Makhaya Ntini.

Below left: Damien Martyn celebrates his superb second-innings century that took Australia to the brink of a famous victory.

Below: Brett Lee (in the foreground) has just hit the winning runs at Jo'burg, and neither his nor his partner Michael Kasprowicz's feet can touch the ground.

Above: Stuart MacGill has just taken the first 8-for of his international career, during the first Test in Bangladesh.

Right: Adam Gilchrist hits us back into the game at Fatullah.

Leaving the field with Jason Gillespie at the end of the first Test, after we'd completed one of Australia's best comeback victories of recent times.

Shane Warne with Dan Cullen after the South Australian offie had been presented with his first baggy green cap.

Next to being out in the middle, this is where Phil Jaques most wants to be — in the nets with a bat in his hands (this time in Fatullah).

Mike Hussey and Jason Gillespie after their colossal stand at Chittagong. Note the black Texta circle on Dizzy's bat.

Mark Cosgrove (above) and Mitchell Johnson (right) were two of nine Aussies who made their international debut in 2005–06. The other seven were Cameron White, Stuart Clark, Brad Hodge, Mick Lewis, Phil Jaques, Brett Dorey and Dan Cullen.

The Aussie team after the final ODI in Bangladesh. Back (from left): Brett Lee (in green-and-gold cap), Nathan Bracken, Brett Dorey, Mike Hussey (in green-and-gold cap), James Hopes, Mitchell Johnson, Simon Katich; Front: Andrew Symonds, Brad Hogg, Adam Gilchrist, me, Dan Cullen, Michael Clarke, Mark Cosgrove.

commentators — was exhausted by the end it, purely because of all the adrenalin that had been generated. The crazy part is, while we went on to win that Test decisively, our play never reached that fever pitch again throughout the English summer. I want our guys to remember that intensity and recapture that passion for the *entire* 2006–07 Ashes series.

The one thing we have to guard against is getting too wound up. We talked so often about the Ashes throughout the days covered in this book — whenever we were analysing the way we were training, whenever we recalled the temporary decline in our fielding standards, whenever we sang the team song after an important win, often when we talked to reporters, usually when we spoke to our fans — that everyone in the squad knows how important this series is going to be for us. I believe this is where our experience can work in our favour.

Most of the guys in our squad have played plenty of Test cricket (and relative newcomers like Huss and Stuart Clark are mature cricketers and sensible men), we've all just enjoyed a season of much success, so we know that what we are doing is working, that we're now heading in the right direction. We know that if each of us gets his preparation right and stays committed to the sense of team we've built up, then everything else should look after itself.

Still, the expectations will be colossal — with plenty of people telling us that we *have* to regain the Ashes — and for this reason, I believe we have to make an effort to stay away from the pre-series bustle and build-up as much as we can. I remember in the lead-up to the 2003 World Cup, we were based at Potchefstroom, two hours from Johannesburg and away from everybody and everything. The chance that move gave us to work together, steer clear of any pre-tournament hysteria, focus on our preparation and bond as a group, was priceless, and I believe was one of the key factors in our ultimate victory in that trophy.

IN AN IDEAL WORLD, I'd love our line-up from 2005 to play their line-up from 2005, just to prove that the result then was an aberration. It's not going to happen, of course, with injuries likely to keep a couple of guys out while some new blood in both camps has come through, but the way things are shaping, the composition of the two sides won't be that different. But while our personnel might be similar, I can assure you we are no longer the same team. We are better players because we have learnt there is no end to how far you can improve, provided you keep on working. It's that reality that John Buchanan has always emphasised: there are no limits.

Our players are better because we're preparing better. I'm a better captain because I am now more decisive. That's the biggest change for me from 2005. Nowadays, if I recognise a problem, I'll address it immediately rather than hope it might fix itself or just go away. I've learnt that you can have too much faith in the players under you, that sometimes things won't change unless you make them change. She'll be right might be a great old Australian attitude, but it doesn't always win you Test series. A good example is a poor training session — you can't just hope it's going to improve or afterwards shrug shoulders and say, 'We'll get it right next time.' It has to get better now.

England will have to lift their game if they are going to have any chance of beating us, but they are still an excellent team, so we have to be on guard. In the same period that we have won 11 of 12 Tests, they have won four of 12 (not including the controversial Test against Pakistan at The Oval that ended in a forfeit), but the gap between the sides is definitely not as big as that. In my view, the biggest danger man could be Kevin Pietersen, who might even develop into the next superstar of world cricket. Potentially, he's that good, and with Andrew Flintoff he gives their middle-order a touch of the dynamic. As I'm sure every Australian cricket fan remembers, Flintoff had a fantastic series against us last time, and if he's fit and firing he'll also be very important for the tourists.

Of our guys, there are many I could nominate as potentially our key men. But the two Aussies I will most enjoy watching as we go into this Ashes battle are our opening bats. Before the last Ashes series, Lang and Haydos were averaging more than 55 runs per partnership, but in the first four Tests in England they averaged only 31, mainly, it must be said, because Matty was struggling. Lang's return for the series was fractionally down on his Test career numbers, but he still topped the Australian averages. As the No. 3, I appreciated more than most what a difference this drop in production from our openers made. We need their runs, to go with their desire and commitment. Of course, Matty rebounded in spectacular style in 2005–06, playing as well as he's ever played, but Justin had a mediocre season by his standards, in part because he never had a chance to get going, missing three Tests in Australia, not batting in his 100th Test and then not touring Bangladesh. I want both guys to have big Ashes series and I'm confident they will.

The way Lang trains, the manner in which he works on his game, his total sense of team, how he talks about what it means to play a Test match — these characteristics all play a part in shaping the team psyche. He's a bloke who has experienced plenty of ups and downs during his career, but he's *always* fought back. His work ethic and commitment to excellence have never been an issue. I love playing with all my team-mates, but there's something special about playing with Justin Langer. So much of what he does captures what the spirit of the baggy green means to me. As a team, we got that spirit back in 2005–06. That's why we're going to be terribly hard to beat when the Englishmen confront us on our home turf, when the fight for the Ashes resumes.

Scores and Averages

2005–06

Series	Page
ICC Super Series One-Day Internationals	286
ICC Super Series Test Match	291
West Indies in Australia Test Matches	294
Chappell–Hadlee Trophy One-Day Internationals	302
South Africa in Australia Test Matches	307
South Africa in Australia Twenty20 International	315
VB Series One-Day Internationals (Australia, South Africa, Sri Lanka)	316
Australia in South Africa Twenty20 International	334
Australia in South Africa One-Day Internationals	335
Australia in South Africa Test Matches	342
Australia in Bangladesh Test Matches	350
Australia in Bangladesh One-Day Internationals	356
Australian Team Averages 2005–06	361

AUSTRALIA V ICC WORLD XI, FIRST ODI
Telstra Dome, Melbourne • October 5, 2005 (50-over match)
Result: Australia won by 93 runs • Toss: Australia
Umpires: Aleem Dar (Pak) and SJA Taufel (Aus) • TV Umpire: RE Koertzen (SA)
Match Referee: RS Madugalle (SL) • Player of the Match: SR Watson

Australia innings		R	M	B	4	6
+AC Gilchrist	b Kallis	45	76	48	7	0
SM Katich	c & b Muralitharan	58	133	78	4	0
*RT Ponting	c Lara b Pollock	23	33	27	1	1
DR Martyn	c Vettori b Muralitharan	0	5	3	0	0
A Symonds	c Flintoff b Vettori	36	73	54	1	1
MJ Clarke	c & b Vettori	6	20	16	0	0
MEK Hussey	c Pietersen b Vettori	32	61	44	1	0
SR Watson	c Lara b Vettori	8	15	15	0	0
B Lee	not out	26	22	17	1	1
NW Bracken	not out	2	12	3	0	0
Extras	(b 2, lb 6, w 6, nb 5)	19				
Total	(8 wkts, 50 ov, 229 mins)	255				

DNB: GD McGrath.

FALL: 1–80 (Gilchrist, 14.1 ov), 2–128 (Ponting, 22.2 ov),3–128 (Martyn, 23.3 ov), 4–142 (Katich, 27.2 ov), 5–154 (Clarke, 31.5 ov), 6–206 (Symonds, 41.4 ov), 7–223 (Watson, 45.5 ov), 8–231 (Hussey, 47.5 ov).

BOWLING: Shoaib Akhtar 9–1–49–0; Pollock 8–1–32–1; Flintoff 9–1–66–0; Kallis 4–0–26–1; Muralitharan 10–0–41–2; Vettori 10–1–33–4

ICC World XI innings		R	M	B	4	6
+KC Sangakkara	c Ponting b Watson	64	126	94	7	0
V Sehwag	c Hussey b McGrath	6	22	10	0	0
JH Kallis	lbw McGrath	8	28	23	1	0
BC Lara	c Symonds b Bracken	0	3	2	0	0
R Dravid	c Ponting b Lee	4	30	14	0	0
KP Pietersen	lbw Watson	2	12	6	0	0
A Flintoff	c McGrath b Watson	38	71	52	2	1
Shahid Afridi	lbw Symonds	2	4	4	0	0
*SM Pollock	run out (Watson)	5	14	12	0	0
DL Vettori	c Ponting b Lee	15	34	28	0	0
Shoaib Akhtar	not out	10	9	5	1	1
Extras	(lb 1, w 6, nb 1)	8				
Total	(all out, 41.3 ov, 181 mins)	162				

FALL: 1–18 (Sehwag, 5.1 ov), 2–45 (Kallis, 11.6 ov), 3–50 (Lara, 12.5 ov), 4–75 (Dravid, 18.6 ov), 5–82 (Pietersen, 21.4 ov), 6–101 (Sangakkara, 27.5 ov), 7–104 (Shahid Afridi, 28.6 ov), 8–118 (Pollock, 32.4 ov), 9–150 (Flintoff, 39.3 ov), 10–162 (Vettori, 41.3 ov).

BOWLING: Lee 7.3–2–31–2; McGrath 7–1–13–2; Bracken 8–0–36–1; Watson 10–0–43–3; Symonds 9–0–38–1

Australia substitute: CL White (for DR Martyn, ICC World XI innings, 16.0 ov); ICC World XI substitute: Shahid Afridi (for M Muralitharan, Australia innings, 43.0 ov).

AUSTRALIA V ICC WORLD XI, SECOND ODI
Telstra Dome, Melbourne • October 7, 2005 (50-over match)
Result: Australia won by 55 runs • Toss: Australia
Umpires: DB Hair (Aus) and RE Koertzen (SA) • TV Umpire: Aleem Dar (Pak)
Match Referee: RS Madugalle (SL) • Player of the Match: AC Gilchrist

Australia innings		R	M	B	4	6
+AC Gilchrist	b Sehwag	103	129	79	8	4
SM Katich	b Muralitharan	47	87	71	3	0
*RT Ponting	run out	66	105	72	4	0
DR Martyn	b Flintoff	54	66	54	5	0
A Symonds	not out	31	27	14	1	2
MJ Clarke	not out	17	24	15	1	0
Extras	(lb 4, w 1, nb 5)	10				
Total	(4 wkts, 50 ov, 221 mins)	328				

DNB: MEK Hussey, SR Watson, B Lee, NW Bracken, SR Clark.

FALL: 1–110 (Katich, 19.3 ov), 2–173 (Gilchrist, 28.3 ov), 3–276 (Ponting, 45.2 ov), 4–276 (Martyn, 45.3 ov).

Bowling: Shoaib Akhtar 8–1–61–0; Pollock 8–0–49–0; Flintoff 8–0–64–1; Muralitharan 10–0–43–1; Vettori 10–0–54–0; Kallis 3–0–33–0; Sehwag 3–0–20–1

ICC World XI innings		R	M	B	4	6
CH Gayle	c Gilchrist b Watson	54	82	48	8	1
V Sehwag	c Ponting b Lee	21	17	15	4	0
+KC Sangakkara	run out	61	84	44	9	1
JH Kallis	run out	11	38	25	0	0
BC Lara	c Symonds b Bracken	5	15	10	0	0
R Dravid	b Symonds	26	67	35	2	0
A Flintoff	c Symonds b Bracken	42	48	50	3	0
KP Pietersen	c Watson b Clark	16	26	22	0	1
*SM Pollock	c White b Clark	15	21	16	0	0
DL Vettori	not out	10	15	8	0	0
Shoaib Akhtar	c Watson b Bracken	2	4	3	0	0
Extras	(lb 1, w 6, nb 3)	10				
Total	(all out, 45.3 ov, 213 mins)	273				

FALL: 1–27 (Sehwag, 4.1 ov), 2–125 (Gayle, 16.1 ov), 3–151 (Sangakkara, 19.6 ov), 4–157 (Lara, 23.1 ov), 5–157 (Kallis, 23.2 ov), 6–220 (Flintoff, 36.1 ov), 7–235 (Dravid, 39.2 ov), 8–250 (Pietersen, 42.1 ov), 9–267 (Pollock, 44.3 ov), 10–273 (Shoaib Akhtar, 45.3 ov).

Bowling: Lee 8–1–47–1; Bracken 7.3–0–43–3; Clark 9–0–55–2; Watson 10–1–56–1; Symonds 8–0–49–1; White 3–0–22–0

Australia substitute: CL White (for SM Katich, ICC World XI innings, 0.0 ov); ICC World XI substitute: CH Gayle (for M Muralitharan, Australia innings, 47.0 ov).

AUSTRALIA V ICC WORLD XI, THIRD ODI
Telstra Dome, Melbourne • October 9, 2005 (50-over match)
Result: Australia won by 156 runs • Toss: Australia
Umpires: Aleem Dar (Pak) and DB Hair (Aus) • TV Umpire: SJA Taufel (Aus)
Match Referee: RS Madugalle (SL) • Player of the Match: SR Watson
Player of the Series: AC Gilchrist

Australia innings		R	M	B	4	6
+AC Gilchrist	c & b Pollock	32	39	31	2	1
MJ Clarke	lbw Ntini	3	9	3	0	0
*RT Ponting	c Lara b Muralitharan	68	99	84	8	1
DR Martyn	lbw Vettori	33	85	44	3	0
A Symonds	c Sangakkara b Muralitharan	1	8	5	0	0
MEK Hussey	not out	75	93	74	5	1
SR Watson	not out	66	88	66	4	0
Extras	(lb 7, w 1, nb 7)	15				
Total	(5 wkts, 50 ov, 212 mins)	293				

DNB: CL White, B Lee, NW Bracken, GD McGrath.

FALL: 1–15 (Clarke, 1.4 ov), 2–58 (Gilchrist, 8.5 ov), 3–143 (Ponting, 24.5 ov), 4–146 (Symonds, 26.3 ov), 5–148 (Martyn, 27.5 ov).

Bowling: Pollock 9–0–67–1; Ntini 7–0–58–1; Flintoff 4.2–0–23–0; Muralitharan 10–1–38–2; Kallis 1.4–0–11–0; Vettori 10–0–34–1; Gayle 6–0–42–0; Sehwag 2–0–13–0

ICC World XI innings		R	M	B	4	6
CH Gayle	b Lee	0	1	2	0	0
V Sehwag	run out	37	89	40	4	1
+KC Sangakkara	c Martyn b McGrath	13	15	15	2	0
JH Kallis	c Hussey b Lee	2	12	10	0	0
BC Lara	c Gilchrist b Lee	0	1	1	0	0
A Flintoff	b Watson	21	34	25	4	0
R Dravid	c Martyn b Lee	16	50	38	1	0
*SM Pollock	c White b Watson	8	44	27	1	0
DL Vettori	c Clarke b Watson	0	5	5	0	0
Shahid Afridi	c McGrath b Watson	16	12	8	2	1
M Ntini	not out	0	2	0	0	0
Extras	(lb 6, w 14, nb 4)	24				
Total	(all out, 27.5 ov, 137 mins)	137				

FALL: 1–0 (Gayle, 0.2 ov), 2–20 (Sangakkara, 3.4 ov), 3–27 (Kallis, 6.3 ov), 4–27 (Lara, 6.4 ov), 5–87 (Flintoff, 13.5 ov), 6–99 (Sehwag, 17.5 ov), 7–119 (Dravid, 24.3 ov), 8–120 (Vettori, 25.3 ov), 9–137 (Pollock, 27.3 ov), 10–137 (Shahid Afridi, 27.5 ov).

Bowling: Lee 9–2–30–4; McGrath 6–0–26–1; Bracken 5–0–36–0; Watson 7.5–0–39–4

Australia substitute: JR Hopes (not used); ICC World XI substitute: Shahid Afridi (for M Muralitharan, ICC World XI innings, 0.0 ov).

ICC SUPER SERIES ONE-DAY INTERNATIONAL AVERAGES

AUSTRALIA BATTING AND FIELDING

Name	ODIs	Inn	NO	Runs	HS	Ave	SR	100	50	Ct	St
MEK Hussey	3	2	1	107	75*	107.00	90.68	–	1	2	–
SR Watson	3	2	1	74	66*	74.00	91.36	–	1	2	–
AC Gilchrist	3	3	0	180	103	60.00	113.92	1	–	2	–
SM Katich	2	2	0	105	58	52.50	70.47	–	1	–	–
RT Ponting	3	3	0	157	68	52.33	85.79	–	2	4	–
A Symonds	3	3	1	68	36	34.00	93.15	–	–	3	–
DR Martyn	3	3	0	87	54	29.00	86.14	–	1	2	–
MJ Clarke	3	3	1	26	17*	13.00	76.47	–	–	1	–
B Lee	3	1	1	26	26*	–	152.94	–	–	–	–
NW Bracken	3	1	1	2	2*	–	66.67	–	–	–	–
CL White	3	0	–	–	–	–	–	–	–	2	–
GD McGrath	2	0	–	–	–	–	–	–	–	2	–
SR Clark	1	0	–	–	–	–	–	–	–	–	–

AUSTRALIA BOWLING

Name	ODIs	O	M	R	W	Ave	Best	4w	SR	Econ
GD McGrath	2	13	1	39	3	13.00	2–13	–	26.00	3.00
B Lee	3	24.3	5	108	7	15.43	4–30	1	21.00	4.41
SR Watson	3	27.5	1	138	8	17.25	4–39	1	20.88	4.96
SR Clark	1	9	0	55	2	27.50	2–55	–	27.00	6.11
NW Bracken	3	20.3	0	115	4	28.75	3–43	–	30.75	5.61
A Symonds	3	17	0	87	2	43.50	1–38	–	51.00	5.12
CL White	3	3	0	22	0	–	–	–	–	7.33

ICC WORLD XI BATTING AND FIELDING

Name	ODIs	Inn	NO	Runs	HS	Ave	SR	100	50	Ct	St
KC Sangakkara	3	3	0	138	64	46.00	90.20	–	2	1	–
A Flintoff	3	3	0	101	42	33.67	79.53	–	–	1	–
CH Gayle	2	2	0	54	54	27.00	108.00	–	1	–	–
V Sehwag	3	3	0	64	37	21.33	98.46	–	–	–	–
R Dravid	3	3	0	46	26	15.33	52.87	–	–	–	–
DL Vettori	3	3	1	25	15	12.50	60.98	–	–	2	–
Shoaib Akhtar	2	2	1	12	10*	12.00	150.00	–	–	–	–
SM Pollock	3	3	0	28	15	9.33	50.91	–	–	1	–
KP Pietersen	2	2	0	18	16	9.00	64.29	–	–	1	–
Shahid Afridi	2	2	0	18	16	9.00	150.00	–	–	–	–
JH Kallis	3	3	0	21	11	7.00	36.21	–	–	–	–
BC Lara	3	3	0	5	5	1.66	38.46	–	–	3	–
M Ntini	1	1	1	0	0*	–	–	–	–	–	–
M Muralitharan	3	0	–	–	–	–	–	–	–	1	–

ICC WORLD XI BOWLING

Name	ODIs	O	M	R	W	Ave	Best	4w	SR	Econ
DL Vettori	3	30	1	121	5	24.20	4–33	1	36.00	4.03
M Muralitharan	3	30	1	122	5	24.40	2–38	–	36.00	4.07
V Sehwag	3	5	0	33	1	33.00	1–20	–	30.00	6.60
M Ntini	1	7	0	58	1	58.00	1–58	–	42.00	8.29
JH Kallis	3	8.4	0	70	1	70.00	1–26	–	52.00	8.07
SM Pollock	3	25	1	148	2	74.00	1–32	–	75.00	5.92
A Flintoff	3	21.2	1	153	1	153.00	1–64	–	128.00	7.17
Shoaib Akhtar	2	17	2	110	0	–	–	–	–	6.47
CH Gayle	2	6	0	42	0	–	–	–	–	7.00

ICC SUPER SERIES

Matches in the Super Series were given full international status. The only previous match involving a ' World XI' to be given full Test or ODI status was the 'Tsunami Appeal' one-dayer played between a World XI and an Asia XI at the MCG on January 10, 2005. A three-game series between an Africa XI and an Asia XI staged in South Africa in August 2005 was also given ODI status.

The most notable previous example of a World XI playing in a high-profile series of matches occurred in 1970, after South Africa's scheduled tour of England for that season was cancelled due to protests over the South African government's policy of apartheid. In its place, a series of five five-day 'Tests' was played between England and a high-class Rest of the World side. In Australia in 1971–72, again after a South African tour was cancelled because of apartheid, a similar five-match series was staged. Between 1977 and 1979, a World XI competed in five-day and one-day games against Australian and West Indian sides in World Series Cricket. The runs scored and wickets taken in these instances are not included in official Test or ODI career records.

ICC SUPER SERIES ONE-DAY INTERNATIONALS

Debuts
Cameron White (game one) was the 152nd Australian to play ODI cricket
Stuart Clark (game two) was the 153rd Australian to play ODI cricket

Hundreds
Adam Gilchrist (103 for Australia in game two) scored his 12th ODI century, in his 221st match.

Four wickets in an innings
Daniel Vettori (4–33 for World XI in game one) took four or more wickets in an ODI for the fifth time, in his 155th match.
Brett Lee (4–30 for Australia in game three) took four or more wickets in an ODI for the 12th time, in his 115th match.
Shane Watson (4–39 for Australia in game three) took four or more wickets in an ODI for the first time, in his 40th match.

ICC SUPER SERIES TEST MATCH

Hundreds
Matthew Hayden (111 for Australia) scored his 22nd Test century in his 73rd match.

Five wickets in an innings
Stuart MacGill (5–43 for Australia) took five or more wickets in a Test innings for the 11th time, in his 34th match.

AUSTRALIA V ICC WORLD XI, ONLY TEST
Sydney Cricket Ground • October 14–17, 2005 (six-day match)
Result: Australia won by 210 runs • Toss: Australia
Umpires: RE Koertzen (SA) and SJA Taufel (Aus) • TV Umpire: DB Hair (Aus)
Match Referee: RS Madugalle (SL) • Player of the Match: ML Hayden
Player of the Series: AC Gilchrist

Stumps Scores
Day 1: Australia 6–331 (Gilchrist 94, Warne 1; 85.0 ov)
Day 2: Australia 345, ICC World XI 190, Australia 1–66 (Hayden 27, Ponting 17; 20.0 ov)
Day 3: Australia 199, ICC World XI 2–25 (Dravid 17, Lara 0; 8 ov)

Australia innings		R	M	B	4	6
JL Langer	b Harmison	0	1	3	0	0
ML Hayden	c Kallis b Muralitharan	111	277	180	12	0
*RT Ponting	c Kallis b Flintoff	46	96	76	6	1
MJ Clarke	c Sehwag b Vettori	39	87	68	4	0
SM Katich	run out	0	9	9	0	0
+AC Gilchrist	lbw Flintoff	94	161	111	8	4
SR Watson	lbw Muralitharan	24	65	60	1	0
SK Warne	c Kallis b Flintoff	5	31	20	0	0
B Lee	c Smith b Flintoff	1	21	10	0	0
GD McGrath	run out	0	10	5	0	0
SCG MacGill	not out	0	3	5	0	0
Extras	(b 5, lb 11, w 3, nb 6)	25				
Total	(all out, 90 ov, 386 mins)	345				

FALL: 1–0 (Langer, 0.3 ov), 2–73 (Ponting, 22.5 ov), 3–154 (Clarke, 43.6 ov), 4–163 (Katich, 46.2 ov), 5–260 (Hayden, 65.6 ov), 6–323 (Watson, 82.3 ov), 7–331 (Gilchrist, 85.2 ov), 8–339 (Warne, 87.6 ov), 9–344 (Lee, 89.2 ov), 10–345 (McGrath, 89.6 ov).

Bowling: Harmison 18–3–60–1; Flintoff 18–3–59–4; Kallis 7–1–35–0; Muralitharan 30–3–102–2; Vettori 17–3–73–1

ICC World XI first innings		R	M	B	4	6
*GC Smith	c Gilchrist b Lee	12	33	25	1	0
V Sehwag	c Katich b Warne	76	148	82	14	0
R Dravid	c Gilchrist b McGrath	0	5	6	0	0
BC Lara	lbw McGrath	5	9	8	1	0
JH Kallis	c Hayden b Warne	44	125	94	8	0
Inzamam-ul-Haq	st Gilchrist b MacGill	1	5	5	0	0
A Flintoff	c Lee b MacGill	35	44	36	0	4
+MV Boucher	c Gilchrist b Warne	0	2	2	0	0
DL Vettori	not out	8	33	16	0	0
SJ Harmison	c Clarke b MacGill	1	7	8	0	0
M Muralitharan	c Langer b MacGill	2	7	4	0	0
Extras	(b 1, lb 1, w 1, nb 3)	6				
Total	(all out, 47.1 ov, 214 mins)	190				

FALL: 1–27 (Smith, 7.4 ov), 2–31 (Dravid, 8.6 ov), 3–43 (Lara, 10.4 ov), 4–134 (Sehwag, 30.3 ov), 5–135 (Inzamam-ul-Haq, 31.2 ov), 6–147 (Kallis, 38.2 ov), 7–151 (Boucher, 38.5 ov), 8–183 (Flintoff, 43.4 ov), 9–184 (Harmison, 45.3 ov), 10–190 (Muralitharan, 47.1 ov).

Bowling: McGrath 12–4–34–2; Lee 8–1–54–1; Watson 6–0–38–0; Warne 12–3–23–3; MacGill 9.1–0–39–4

Australia second innings		R	M	B	4	6
JL Langer	c Smith b Kallis	22	40	33	2	0
ML Hayden	b Harmison	77	203	120	9	0
*RT Ponting	c Boucher b Flintoff	54	189	111	4	0
MJ Clarke	b Harmison	5	6	8	1	0
SM Katich	c & b Muralitharan	2	19	22	0	0
+AC Gilchrist	c Kallis b Muralitharan	1	10	3	0	0
SR Watson	c Boucher b Flintoff	10	59	37	1	0
SK Warne	c Dravid b Flintoff	7	24	19	0	0
B Lee	c Muralitharan b Harmison	3	48	28	0	0
GD McGrath	c Smith b Muralitharan	2	13	9	0	0
SCG MacGill	not out	0	5	5	0	0
Extras	(b 7, lb 7, nb 2)	16				
Total	(all out, 65.3 ov, 303 mins)	199				

FALL: 1–30 (Langer, 8.4 ov), 2–152 (Hayden, 41.5 ov), 3–160 (Clarke, 43.4 ov), 4–167 (Ponting, 47.6 ov), 5–167 (Katich, 48.4 ov), 6–170 (Gilchrist, 50.1 ov), 7–177 (Warne, 55.4 ov), 8–192 (Watson, 61.3 ov), 9–195 (McGrath, 64.1 ov), 10–199 (Lee, 65.3 ov).

Bowling: Harmison 12.3–2–41–3; Flintoff 16–2–48–3; Kallis 3–1–3–1; Muralitharan 24–4–55–3; Vettori 10–0–38–0

ICC World XI second innings (target: 355 runs)		R	M	B	4	6
*GC Smith	b McGrath	0	2	5	0	0
V Sehwag	c Gilchrist b MacGill	7	24	13	0	1
R Dravid	c Hayden b Warne	23	110	68	3	0
BC Lara	c Gilchrist b Warne	36	96	51	7	0
JH Kallis	not out	39	109	85	3	1
Inzamam-ul-Haq	lbw Lee	0	4	2	0	0
A Flintoff	c sub (BJ Hodge) b MacGill	15	40	27	2	0
+MV Boucher	c Hayden b Warne	17	36	43	1	0
DL Vettori	c Ponting b MacGill	0	6	5	0	0
SJ Harmison	lbw MacGill	0	2	1	0	0
M Muralitharan	st Gilchrist b MacGill	0	2	3	0	0
Extras	(b 1, lb 2, nb 4)	7				
Total	(all out, 50 ov, 204 mins)	144				

FALL: 1–0 (Smith, 0.5 ov), 2–18 (Sehwag, 5.6 ov), 3–56 (Dravid, 20.5 ov), 4–69 (Lara, 22.6 ov), 5–70 (Inzamam-ul-Haq, 23.5 ov), 6–122 (Flintoff, 35.2 ov), 7–143 (Boucher, 46.6 ov), 8–144 (Vettori, 49.2 ov), 9–144 (Harmison, 49.3 ov), 10–144 (Muralitharan, 49.6 ov).

Bowling: McGrath 6–3–8–1; Lee 10–2–42–1; Warne 19–4–48–3; MacGill 15–4–43–5

MOST SUCCESSFUL BOWLERS AT THE SYDNEY CRICKET GROUND

Following this Test, Shane Warne and Stuart MacGill were entrenched as the two leading wicket-takers in Tests at the SCG. Warne had taken 60 Test wickets in 12 Tests at the famous ground, while MacGill had 49 wickets from seven games. Next best is Charlie Turner, one of the great bowlers of the 19th century, who took 45 wickets at the SCG in six Tests.

At the conclusion of this Test, the only other bowlers with 40 or more Test wickets at the SCG were Dennis Lillee (43), Ray Lindwall (42) and Glenn McGrath (41 wickets). Warne (two wickets), MacGill (four) and McGrath (three) would add to their tallies later in 2005–06, during the third Test of the series against South Africa.

ICC SUPER SERIES TEST AVERAGES

AUSTRALIA BATTING AND FIELDING

Name	Tests	Inn	NO	Runs	HS	Ave	SR	100	50	Ct	St
ML Hayden	1	2	0	188	111	94.00	62.67	1	1	3	–
RT Ponting	1	2	0	100	54	50.00	53.48	–	1	1	–
AC Gilchrist	1	2	0	95	94	47.50	83.33	–	1	5	2
MJ Clarke	1	2	0	44	39	22.00	57.89	–	–	1	–
SR Watson	1	2	0	34	24	17.00	35.05	–	–	–	–
JL Langer	1	2	0	22	22	11.00	61.11	–	–	1	–
SK Warne	1	2	0	12	7	6.00	30.77	–	–	–	–
B Lee	1	2	0	4	3	2.00	10.53	–	–	1	–
SM Katich	1	2	0	2	2	1.00	6.45	–	–	1	–
GD McGrath	1	2	0	2	2	1.00	14.29	–	–	–	–
SCG MacGill	1	2	2	0	0*	–	0.00	–	–	–	–

AUSTRALIA BOWLING

Name	Tests	O	M	R	W	Ave	Best	5w	10w	SR	Econ
SCG MacGill	1	24.1	4	82	9	9.11	5–43	1	–	16.11	3.39
SK Warne	1	31	7	71	6	11.83	3–23	–	–	31.00	2.29
GD McGrath	1	18	7	42	3	14.00	2–34	–	–	36.00	2.33
B Lee	1	18	3	96	2	48.00	1–42	–	–	54.00	5.33
SR Watson	1	6	0	38	0	–	–	–	–	–	6.33

ICC WORLD XI BATTING AND FIELDING

Name	Tests	Inn	NO	Runs	HS	Ave	SR	100	50	Ct	St
JH Kallis	1	2	1	83	44	83.00	46.37	–	–	4	–
V Sehwag	1	2	0	83	76	41.50	87.37	–	1	1	–
A Flintoff	1	2	0	50	35	25.00	79.37	–	–	–	–
BC Lara	1	2	0	41	36	20.50	69.49	–	–	–	–
R Dravid	1	2	0	23	23	11.50	31.08	–	–	1	–
MV Boucher	1	2	0	17	17	8.50	37.78	–	–	2	–
DL Vettori	1	2	1	8	8*	8.00	38.09	–	–	–	–
GC Smith	1	2	0	12	12	6.00	40.00	–	–	3	–
M Muralitharan	1	2	0	2	2	1.00	28.57	–	–	2	–
SJ Harmison	1	2	0	1	1	0.50	11.11	–	–	–	–
Inzamam–ul–Haq	1	2	0	1	1	0.50	14.29	–	–	–	–

ICC WORLD XI BOWLING

Name	Tests	O	M	R	W	Ave	Best	5w	10w	SR	Econ
A Flintoff	1	34	5	107	7	15.29	4–59	–	–	29.14	3.15
SJ Harmison	1	30.3	5	101	4	25.25	3–41	–	–	45.75	3.31
M Muralitharan	1	54	7	157	5	31.40	3–55	–	–	64.80	2.91
JH Kallis	1	10	2	38	1	38.00	1–3	–	–	60.00	3.80
DL Vettori	1	27	3	111	1	111.00	1–73	–	–	162.00	4.11

AUSTRALIA V WEST INDIES, FIRST TEST
The Gabba, Brisbane • November 3–6, 2005 (five-day match)

Result: Australia won by 379 runs • Toss: West Indies
Umpires: IL Howell (SA) and RE Koertzen (SA) • TV Umpire: PD Parker (Aus)
Match Referee: MJ Procter (SA) • Player of the Match: RT Ponting

Stumps Scores
Day 1: Australia 7–340 (Warne 31, Lee 19; 85 ov)
Day 2: Australia 435, West Indies 6–182 (Ramdin 12, Powell 4; 62 ov)
Day 3: West Indies 210, Australia 2–283 (Ponting 104, Clarke 14; 66 ov)

Australia innings		R	M	B	4	6
ML Hayden	lbw Collymore	37	129	80	4	0
MEK Hussey	c Ramdin b Powell	1	26	14	0	0
*RT Ponting	c Sarwan b Lawson	149	316	213	15	0
MJ Clarke	c Ramdin b Collymore	5	11	13	1	0
SM Katich	c Gayle b Collymore	0	9	3	0	0
+AC Gilchrist	lbw Collymore	44	92	64	5	0
SR Watson	lbw Edwards	16	71	53	2	0
SK Warne	c Ramdin b Powell	47	110	73	4	0
B Lee	c Collymore b Powell	47	127	82	6	1
NW Bracken	c Sarwan b Edwards	37	61	51	4	0
GD McGrath	not out	6	17	8	0	0
Extras	(b 5, lb 13, w 6, nb 22)	46				
Total	(all out, 105.3 ov, 489 mins)	435				

FALL: 1–9 (Hussey, 5.1 ov), 2–101 (Hayden, 26.4 ov), 3–108 (Clarke, 28.5 ov), 4–111 (Katich, 30.2 ov), 5–215 (Gilchrist, 49.6 ov), 6–273 (Watson, 67.6 ov), 7–294 (Ponting, 73.4 ov), 8–369 (Warne, 93.1 ov), 9–417 (Lee, 101.6 ov), 10–435 (Bracken, 105.3 ov).

Bowling: Edwards 21.3–1–94–2; Powell 20–1–100–3; Collymore 26–4–72–4; Lawson 14–0–73–1; Samuels 4–0–29–0; Gayle 20–3–49–0

West Indies first innings		R	M	B	4	6
CH Gayle	c Gilchrist b McGrath	10	21	18	2	0
DS Smith	b McGrath	88	249	175	10	0
RR Sarwan	c Gilchrist b McGrath	21	47	26	4	0
BC Lara	lbw Lee	30	101	71	3	1
*S Chanderpaul	c Bracken b Warne	2	45	32	0	0
MN Samuels	c Gilchrist b McGrath	5	12	9	1	0
+D Ramdin	not out	37	100	76	6	0
DB Powell	c Gilchrist b Warne	4	26	25	1	0
FH Edwards	b Warne	2	40	26	0	0
CD Collymore	c Clarke b Warne	0	7	2	0	0
JJC Lawson	lbw Warne	0	5	5	0	0
Extras	(lb 7, w 1, nb 3)	11				
Total	(all out, 77 ov, 331 mins)	210				

FALL: 1–20 (Gayle, 4.5 ov), 2–74 (Sarwan, 14.4 ov), 3–134 (Lara, 39.3 ov), 4–149 (Chanderpaul, 50.3 ov), 5–161 (Samuels, 53.1 ov), 6–174 (Smith, 57.2 ov), 7–187 (Powell, 64.4 ov), 8–204 (Edwards, 74.5 ov), 9–210 (Collymore, 76.1 ov), 10–210 (Lawson, 76.6 ov).

Bowling: McGrath 22–3–72–4; Lee 15–4–59–1; Bracken 10–4–23–0; Warne 28–9–48–5; Clarke 2–1–1–0

Australia second innings

		R	M	B	4	6
MEK Hussey	c Collymore b Gayle	29	75	65	2	0
ML Hayden	c Sarwan b Gayle	118	233	163	10	2
*RT Ponting	not out	104	182	158	8	0
MJ Clarke	not out	14	24	18	1	0
Extras	(b 6, lb 3, w 1, nb 8)	18				
Total	(2 wkts dec, 66 ov, 258 mins)	283				

FALL: 1–71 (Hussey, 16.1 ov), 2–258 (Hayden, 60.3 ov).

Bowling: Edwards 5–0–27–0; Powell 5–1–24–0; Lawson 6–0–47–0; Collymore 11–0–56–0; Gayle 27–4–74–2; Samuels 12–1–46–0

West Indies second innings (target: 509 runs)

		R	M	B	4	6
CH Gayle	c Warne b Watson	33	87	57	2	2
DS Smith	c Warne b Lee	3	31	22	0	0
RR Sarwan	c Gilchrist b Lee	31	159	92	5	0
BC Lara	c Hayden b Bracken	14	69	51	2	0
*S Chanderpaul	lbw Bracken	7	31	25	1	0
MN Samuels	not out	17	52	20	3	0
+D Ramdin	c Gilchrist b Lee	6	12	16	0	0
DB Powell	lbw Bracken	0	14	4	0	0
FH Edwards	b Bracken	0	1	1	0	0
CD Collymore	lbw Lee	4	7	6	1	0
JJC Lawson	b Lee	1	12	9	0	0
Extras	(lb 3, nb 10)	13				
Total	(all out, 49 ov, 242 mins)	129				

FALL: 1–11 (Smith, 7.2 ov), 2–53 (Gayle, 17.4 ov), 3–85 (Lara, 33.5 ov), 4–99 (Chanderpaul, 39.6 ov), 5–99 (Sarwan, 40.1 ov), 6–105 (Ramdin, 42.5 ov), 7–106 (Powell, 45.3 ov), 8–106 (Edwards, 45.4 ov), 9–114 (Collymore, 46.6 ov), 10–129 (Lawson, 48.6 ov).

Bowling: McGrath 11–3–22–0; Lee 14–4–30–5; Watson 6–0–25–1; Bracken 16–3–48–4; Warne 2–1–1–0

A GAME OF HUNDREDS

This first Test was the 100th Test match staged between Australia and the West Indies, and Australia's win was their 46th in these games. By series end, Australia had won 48 Tests, lost 32, drawn 21 and tied one against the Windies.

Glenn McGrath became the first bowler in Test history to take 100 wickets against the West Indies when he dismissed Marlon Samuels at the Gabba. As he also had 136 wickets against England, he became the second Australian and fifth bowler to take 100 wickets against two Test-playing teams. The West Indies' Lance Gibbs, Courtney Walsh and Curtly Ambrose each took 100 wickets against England and Australia. Shane Warne has taken 100 wickets against England, New Zealand and South Africa.

McGrath would finish this series with 110 career wickets against the West Indies. At September 6, 2006, he had 542 Test wickets, third on the all-time list behind Warne (685 wickets) and Sri Lanka's Muttiah Muralitharan (657).

AUSTRALIA V WEST INDIES, SECOND TEST

Bellerive Oval, Hobart • November 17–21, 2005 (five-day match)

Result: Australia won by nine wickets • Toss: West Indies
Umpires: Aleem Dar (Pak) and RE Koertzen (SA) • TV Umpire: SJ Davis (Aus)
Match Referee: MJ Procter (SA) • Player of the Match: MEK Hussey

Stumps Scores

Day 1: West Indies 149, Australia 0–60 (Hayden 31, Hussey 26, 18 ov)
Day 2: Australia 1–256 (Hussey 116, Ponting 17, 66 ov)
Day 3: Australia 406, West Indies 4–82 (Lara 18, Samuels 2, 24 ov)
Day 4: West Indies 334

West Indies first innings

		R	M	B	4	6
CH Gayle	lbw McGrath	56	153	116	7	2
DS Smith	b Lee	4	36	16	0	0
RR Sarwan	c Gilchrist b McGrath	2	40	23	0	0
BC Lara	lbw Lee	13	68	46	1	0
*S Chanderpaul	c Hodge b MacGill	39	140	102	3	0
MN Samuels	c Gilchrist b McGrath	5	37	22	1	0
DJJ Bravo	c Hodge b MacGill	3	17	17	0	0
+D Ramdin	c Warne b MacGill	2	8	7	0	0
DB Powell	c Gilchrist b Lee	15	42	40	1	0
FH Edwards	c Symonds b McGrath	0	22	16	0	0
CD Collymore	not out	3	13	9	0	0
Extras	(lb 3, w 1, nb 3)	7				
Total	(all out, 68.3 ov, 293 mins)	149				

FALL: 1–15 (Smith, 7.3 ov), 2–26 (Sarwan, 14.5 ov), 3–60 (Lara, 27.2 ov), 4–119 (Chanderpaul, 49.4 ov), 5–119 (Gayle, 50.3 ov), 6–124 (Bravo, 55.1 ov), 7–126 (Ramdin, 57.2 ov), 8–130 (Samuels, 58.3 ov), 9–141 (Edwards, 64.6 ov), 10–149 (Powell, 68.3 ov).

Bowling: McGrath 23–9–31–4; Lee 13.3–6–32–3; Symonds 10–4–17–0; Warne 11–2–48–0; MacGill 11–3–18–3

Australia innings

		R	M	B	4	6
ML Hayden	c Bravo b Collymore	110	265	169	11	1
MEK Hussey	c Sarwan b Bravo	137	388	234	19	0
*RT Ponting	b Edwards	17	43	40	2	0
MJ Clarke	c sub (DR Smith) b Edwards	5	29	23	0	0
BJ Hodge	lbw Collymore	60	153	108	9	0
A Symonds	run out	1	13	8	0	0
+AC Gilchrist	c sub (DR Smith) b Bravo	2	7	4	0	0
SK Warne	c Sarwan b Powell	1	12	7	0	0
B Lee	c Ramdin b Edwards	18	46	27	0	0
SCG MacGill	not out	20	54	26	2	0
GD McGrath	run out	14	31	24	1	0
Extras	(lb 6, w 3, nb 12)	21				
Total	(all out, 109.4 ov, 525 mins)	406				

FALL: 1–231 (Hayden, 56.2 ov), 2–257 (Ponting, 66.2 ov), 3–271 (Clarke, 72.3 ov), 4–306 (Hussey, 81.3 ov), 5–315 (Symonds, 84.3 ov), 6–317 (Gilchrist, 85.4 ov), 7–324 (Warne, 88.4 ov), 8–362 (Lee, 98.3 ov), 9–377 (Hodge, 103.2 ov), 10–406 (McGrath, 109.4 ov).

Bowling: Edwards 27.4–2–116–3; Powell 24–2–117–1; Collymore 28–11–54–2; Bravo 23–2–96–2; Gayle 7–0–17–0

West Indies second innings		R	M	B	4	6
CH Gayle	b McGrath	4	2	4	1	0
DS Smith	c Ponting b McGrath	8	37	21	1	0
RR Sarwan	c Gilchrist b Lee	32	75	58	6	0
BC Lara	c Gilchrist b Warne	45	171	119	5	0
*S Chanderpaul	c Gilchrist b Lee	10	23	12	2	0
MN Samuels	c Hodge b Warne	29	120	87	2	0
DJJ Bravo	b Warne	113	281	202	15	0
+D Ramdin	c Warne b MacGill	71	225	190	6	0
DB Powell	lbw MacGill	0	26	19	0	0
FH Edwards	not out	2	22	15	0	0
CD Collymore	c Gilchrist b Warne	0	7	8	0	0
Extras	(b 4, lb 12, w 1, nb 3)	20				
Total	(all out, 122 ov, 499 mins)	334				

FALL: 1–4 (Gayle, 0.4 ov), 2–27 (Smith, 7.3 ov), 3–62 (Sarwan, 16.6 ov), 4–76 (Chanderpaul, 22.3 ov), 5–133 (Lara, 47.5 ov), 6–140 (Samuels, 51.1 ov), 7–322 (Ramdin, 108.3 ov), 8–326 (Powell, 116.2 ov), 9–332 (Bravo, 119.6 ov), 10–334 (Collymore, 121.6 ov).

Bowling: McGrath 25–13–29–2; Lee 27–4–99–2; Symonds 5–1–9–0; Warne 39–4–112–4; MacGill 26–4–69–2

Australia second innings (target: 78 runs)		R	M	B	4	6
MEK Hussey	not out	31	96	82	3	0
ML Hayden	c Smith b Gayle	46	93	73	6	0
*RT Ponting	not out	0	2	3	0	0
Extras	(nb 1)	1				
Total	(1 wkt, 26.1 ov, 96 mins)	78				

FALL: 1–77 (Hayden, 25.3 ov).

Bowling: Edwards 5–1–16–0–(1nb); Powell 7–1–21–0; Bravo 7–1–21–0; Gayle 6–2–16–1; Sarwan 1.1–0–4–0

HUNDREDS IN CONSECUTIVE TESTS

By scoring centuries in the fifth Ashes Test at The Oval in 2005, the Super Series Test in Sydney, and the first two Tests of this series, Matthew Hayden became the third batsman — after Sir Donald Bradman (who did it three times) and England's Ken Barrington — to twice score a hundred in four consecutive Tests. Hayden had previously achieved this in Tests against South Africa in 2001–02.

Bradman actually scored hundreds in a record six straight Tests between 1936–37 and 1938. He was injured and did not bat in his next Test, Australia's last before World War II, and then scored centuries in his first two Tests after the war. South Africa's Jacques Kallis scored centuries in five consecutive Tests in 2003–04. Nine men — Bradman, Barrington, Hayden, Australia's Jack Fingleton and Neil Harvey, West Indies' Everton Weekes and Clyde Walcott, and India's Sunil Gavaskar and Rahul Dravid — have scored centuries in four consecutive Tests.

AUSTRALIA V WEST INDIES, THIRD TEST

Adelaide Oval • November 25–29, 2005 (five-day match)

Result: Australia won by seven wickets • Toss: West Indies
Umpires: Aleem Dar (Pak) and BF Bowden (NZ) • TV Umpire: SJ Davis (Aus)
Match Referee: MJ Procter (SA) • Player of the Match: BC Lara • Player of the Series: ML Hayden

Stumps Scores

Day 1: West Indies 7–352 (Lara 202, Powell 7; 90 ov)
Day 2: West Indies 405, Australia 3–229 (Hodge 13, Hussey 0; 61 ov)
Day 3: Australia 428, West Indies 2–68 (Sarwan 53, Powell 0; 21 ov)
Day 4: West Indies 204, Australia 2–76 (Hayden 38, Hodge 10, 28 ov)

West Indies first innings		R	M	B	4	6
WW Hinds	c Hayden b Lee	10	23	19	2	0
DS Smith	c Hayden b Lee	7	28	15	1	0
RR Sarwan	c Symonds b Lee	16	60	34	1	0
BC Lara	b McGrath	226	405	298	22	0
*S Chanderpaul	c Gilchrist b Symonds	25	97	77	0	0
DJJ Bravo	c Ponting b MacGill	34	95	59	2	0
DR Smith	c Symonds b MacGill	14	26	20	1	1
+D Ramdin	lbw McGrath	27	69	44	4	0
DB Powell	lbw McGrath	14	77	50	2	0
FH Edwards	c Hayden b Warne	10	53	36	1	0
CD Collymore	not out	5	34	23	0	0
Extras	(b 2, lb 5, w 1, nb 9)	17				
Total	(all out, 111.2 ov, 488 mins)	405				

FALL: 1–16 (Hinds, 5.1 ov), 2–19 (DS Smith, 5.5 ov), 3–53 (Sarwan, 18.2 ov), 4–121
(Chanderpaul, 42.4 ov), 5–237 (Bravo, 64.2 ov), 6–263 (DR Smith, 69.4 ov), 7–333 (Ramdin,
86.5 ov), 8–381 (Lara, 98.6 ov), 9–388 (Powell, 102.4 ov), 10–405 (Edwards, 111.2 ov).

Bowling: McGrath 36–3–106–3; Lee 28–3–111–3; Symonds 16–5–44–1; Warne
19.2–2–77–1; MacGill 18–3–60–2

Australia innings		R	M	B	4	6
JL Langer	c Ramdin b Edwards	99	279	174	10	0
ML Hayden	c Chanderpaul b Bravo	47	82	58	6	0
*RT Ponting	lbw Bravo	56	168	122	6	0
BJ Hodge	lbw Edwards	18	54	35	2	0
MEK Hussey	not out	133	293	215	13	3
A Symonds	b Bravo	9	69	51	1	0
+AC Gilchrist	c Chanderpaul b Bravo	6	20	18	0	0
SK Warne	c & b Bravo	0	3	3	0	0
B Lee	c Ramdin b Bravo	9	15	9	0	0
SCG MacGill	b Edwards	22	116	51	2	0
GD McGrath	b DR Smith	5	39	17	0	0
Extras	(lb 7, w 2, nb 15)	24				
Total	(all out, 123.3 ov, 573 mins)	428				

FALL: 1–97 (Hayden, 17.3 ov), 2–211 (Ponting, 54.3 ov), 3–228 (Langer, 60.3 ov), 4–238
(Hodge, 66.1 ov), 5–271 (Symonds, 81.3 ov), 6–277 (Gilchrist, 87.1 ov), 7–277 (Warne,
87.4 ov), 8–295 (Lee, 91.1 ov), 9–388 (MacGill, 114.6 ov), 10–428 (McGrath, 123.3 ov).

Bowling: Edwards 23–4–114–3; Powell 24–6–80–0; Collymore 23–1–59–0; Bravo
27–7–84–6; DR Smith 17.3–3–59–1; Hinds 9–1–25–0

West Indies second innings

		R	M	B	4	6
WW Hinds	st Gilchrist b Warne	15	70	50	2	0
DS Smith	c Ponting b Lee	0	20	11	0	0
RR Sarwan	lbw Lee	62	141	109	6	0
DB Powell	b Warne	2	37	24	0	0
BC Lara	c Hayden b Warne	17	37	27	1	0
*S Chanderpaul	c Hodge b Warne	4	46	31	0	0
DJJ Bravo	b Lee	64	175	126	10	0
DR Smith	lbw Warne	0	2	2	0	0
+D Ramdin	c Gilchrist b Warne	28	59	50	4	0
FH Edwards	c Warne b Lee	9	73	53	1	0
CD Collymore	not out	1	5	3	0	0
Extras	(lb 2)	2				
Total	(all out, 81 ov, 339 mins)	204				

FALL: 1–2 (DS Smith, 5.2 ov), 2–60 (Hinds, 18.5 ov), 3–72 (Powell, 28.4 ov), 4–96 (Lara, 36.4 ov), 5–96 (Sarwan, 37.1 ov), 6–106 (Chanderpaul, 46.4 ov), 7–106 (DR Smith, 46.6 ov), 8–160 (Ramdin, 62.5 ov), 9–203 (Bravo, 80.1 ov), 10–204 (Edwards, 80.6 ov).

Bowling: McGrath 18–8–25–0; Lee 17–5–46–4; Symonds 2–0–9–0; Warne 33–9–80–6; MacGill 11–2–42–0

Australia second innings (target: 182 runs)

		R	M	B	4	6
JL Langer	c DR Smith b Collymore	20	72	43	1	0
ML Hayden	not out	87	261	174	12	0
*RT Ponting	c Sarwan b Collymore	3	20	17	0	0
BJ Hodge	c DR Smith b Powell	23	85	65	3	0
MEK Hussey	not out	30	81	61	3	0
Extras	(lb 3, w 1, nb 15)	19				
Total	(3 wkts, 58 ov, 261 mins)	182				

FALL: 1–51 (Langer, 14.4 ov), 2–55 (Ponting, 20.2 ov), 3–110 (Hodge, 39.4 ov).

Bowling: Edwards 11–1–52–0–(7nb, 1w); Powell 14–2–40–1; Collymore 20–6–51–2–(6nb); Sarwan 12–2–35–0; DR Smith 1–0–1–0

LEADING RUN-SCORERS IN TEST CRICKET

When he reached 214 in the West Indies' first innings, Brian Lara became the new leading run-scorer in Test cricket, surpassing Allan Border's old mark of 11,174. By September 6, 2006, the top 10 run-getters list looked this way:

Player	Team	Tests	Inn	NO	Runs	HS	Ave	100	50
Brian Lara	WI	128	227	6	11505	400*	52.06	32	47
Allan Border	Aus	156	265	44	11174	205	50.56	27	63
Steve Waugh	Aus	168	260	46	10927	200	51.06	32	50
Sachin Tendulkar	Ind	132	211	22	10469	248*	55.39	35	41
Sunil Gavaskar	Ind	125	214	16	10122	236*	51.12	34	45
Rahul Dravid	Ind	104	176	22	9049	270	58.76	23	46
Graham Gooch	Eng	118	215	6	8900	333	42.58	20	46
Javed Miandad	Pak	124	189	21	8832	280*	52.57	23	43
Ricky Ponting	Aus	105	175	24	8792	257	58.23	31	34
Viv Richards	WI	121	182	12	8540	291	50.24	24	45

WEST INDIES IN AUSTRALIA TEST AVERAGES

AUSTRALIA BATTING AND FIELDING

Name	Tests	Inn	NO	Runs	HS	Ave	SR	100	50	Ct	St
MEK Hussey	3	6	3	361	137	120.33	53.80	2	–	–	–
ML Hayden	3	6	1	445	118	89.00	62.06	2	1	5	–
RT Ponting	3	6	2	329	149	82.25	59.49	2	1	3	–
JL Langer	1	2	0	119	99	59.50	54.84	–	1	–	–
SCG MacGill	2	2	1	42	22	42.00	54.55	–	–	–	–
NW Bracken	1	1	0	37	37	37.00	72.55	–	–	1	–
BJ Hodge	2	3	0	101	60	33.67	48.56	–	1	4	–
B Lee	3	3	0	74	47	24.67	62.71	–	–	–	–
AC Gilchrist	3	3	0	52	44	17.33	60.47	–	–	15	1
SK Warne	3	3	0	48	47	16.00	57.83	–	–	5	–
SR Watson	1	1	0	16	16	16.00	30.19	–	–	–	–
GD McGrath	3	3	1	25	14	12.50	51.02	–	–	–	–
MJ Clarke	2	3	1	24	14*	12.00	44.44	–	–	1	–
A Symonds	2	2	0	10	9	5.00	16.95	–	–	3	–
SM Katich	1	1	0	0	0	0.00	0.00	–	–	–	–

AUSTRALIA BOWLING

Name	Tests	O	M	R	W	Ave	Best	5w	10w	SR	Econ
NW Bracken	1	26	7	71	4	17.75	4–48	–	–	39.00	2.73
B Lee	3	114.3	26	377	18	20.94	5–30	1	–	38.17	3.29
GD McGrath	3	129	39	285	13	21.92	4–31	–	–	59.54	2.21
SK Warne	3	132.2	27	366	16	22.88	6–80	2	–	49.63	2.77
SR Watson	1	6	0	25	1	25.00	1–25	–	–	36.00	4.17
SCG MacGill	2	66	12	189	7	27.00	3–18	–	–	56.57	2.86
A Symonds	2	33	10	79	1	79.00	1–44	–	–	198.00	2.39
MJ Clarke	2	2	1	1	0	–	–	–	–	–	0.50

WEST INDIES BATTING AND FIELDING

Name	Tests	Inn	NO	Runs	HS	Ave	SR	100	50	Ct	St
BC Lara	3	6	0	345	226	57.50	56.37	1	–	–	–
DJJ Bravo	2	4	0	214	113	53.50	52.97	1	1	2	–
D Ramdin	3	6	1	171	71	34.20	44.65	–	1	6	–
RR Sarwan	3	6	0	164	62	27.33	47.95	–	1	6	–
CH Gayle	2	4	0	103	56	25.75	52.82	–	1	1	–
MN Samuels	2	4	1	56	29	18.67	40.58	–	–	–	–
DS Smith	3	6	0	110	88	18.33	42.31	–	1	1	–
S Chanderpaul	3	6	0	87	39	14.50	31.18	–	–	2	–
WW Hinds	1	2	0	25	15	12.50	36.23	–	–	–	–
DR Smith	1	2	0	14	14	7.00	63.64	–	–	2	–
DB Powell	3	6	0	35	15	5.83	21.60	–	–	–	–
FH Edwards	3	6	1	23	10	4.60	15.65	–	–	–	–
CD Collymore	3	6	3	13	5*	4.33	25.49	–	–	2	–
JJC Lawson	1	2	0	1	1	0.50	7.14	–	–	–	–

WEST INDIES BOWLING

Name	Tests	O	M	R	W	Ave	Best	5w	10w	SR	Econ
DJJ Bravo	2	57	10	201	8	25.13	6–84	1	–	42.75	3.53
CD Collymore	3	108	22	292	8	36.50	4–72	–	–	81.00	2.70
CH Gayle	2	60	9	156	3	52.00	2–74	–	–	120.00	2.60
FH Edwards	3	93.1	9	419	8	52.38	3–114	–	–	69.88	4.50
DR Smith	1	18.3	3	60	1	60.00	1–59	–	–	111.00	3.24
DB Powell	3	94	13	382	5	76.40	3–100	–	–	112.80	4.06
JJC Lawson	1	20	0	120	1	120.00	1–73	–	–	120.00	6.00
WW Hinds	1	9	1	25	0	–	–	–	–	–	2.78
RR Sarwan	3	13.1	2	39	0	–	–	–	–	–	2.96
MN Samuels	2	16	1	75	0	–	–	–	–	–	4.69

AUSTRALIA V WEST INDIES TEST SERIES

Debuts

Mike Hussey (first Test) was the 393rd Australian to play Test cricket.
Brad Hodge (second Test) was the 394th Australian to play Test cricket.

Hundreds

Ricky Ponting (149 and 104 for Australia in the first Test) scored his 24th and 25th Test centuries, in his 95th match.
Matthew Hayden (118 for Australia in the first Test) scored his 23rd Test century, in his 74th match.
Matthew Hayden (110 for Australia in the second Test) scored his 24th Test century, in his 75th match.
Mike Hussey (137 for Australia in the second Test) scored his first Test century, in his second match.
Dwayne Bravo (113 for the West Indies in the second Test) scored his second Test century, in his eighth Test.
Brian Lara (226 for the West Indies in the third Test) scored his 31st Test century, in his 121st Test.
Mike Hussey (133* for Australia in the third Test) scored his second Test century, in his third match.

Five wickets in an innings

Shane Warne (5–48 for Australia in the first Test) took five or more wickets in a Test innings for the 33rd time, in his 130th match.
Brett Lee (5–30 for Australia in the first Test) took five or more wickets in a Test innings for the fifth time, in his 44th match.
Dwayne Bravo (6–84 for the West Indies in the third Test) took five or more wickets in a Test innings for the second time, in his ninth match.
Shane Warne (6–80 for Australia in the third Test) took five or more wickets in a Test innings for the 34th time, in his 132nd match.

NEW ZEALAND V AUSTRALIA, FIRST ODI

Eden Park, Auckland • December 3, 2005 (50-over match)

Result: Australia won by 147 runs • Toss: New Zealand
Umpires: Aleem Dar (Pak) and AL Hill (NZ) • TV Umpire: BF Bowden (NZ)
Match Referee: RS Madugalle (SL) • Player of the Match: B Lee

Australia innings		R	M	B	4	6
+AC Gilchrist	c Astle b Franklin	3	8	13	0	0
SM Katich	c Vettori b Styris	54	94	65	6	1
*RT Ponting	lbw Vettori	63	97	64	5	3
BJ Hodge	b Styris	13	26	24	1	0
A Symonds	b Vettori	44	65	59	5	0
MJ Clarke	c Franklin b Cairns	31	67	49	2	1
MEK Hussey	not out	21	33	20	1	1
B Lee	b Cairns	0	1	2	0	0
GB Hogg	c Vettori b Mills	4	9	5	0	0
NW Bracken	not out	1	3	2	0	0
Extras	(lb 6, w 9, nb 3)	18				
Total	(8 wkts, 50 ov, 208 mins)	252				

DNB: SR Clark.

Fall: 1–3 (Gilchrist, 1.6 ov), 2–121 (Katich, 21.4 ov), 3–136 (Ponting, 24.4 ov), 4–148 (Hodge, 29.2 ov), 5–207 (Symonds, 42.6 ov), 6–230 (Clarke, 46.3 ov), 7–231 (Lee, 46.6 ov), 8–249 (Hogg, 49.1 ov).

Bowling: Mills 10–1–35–1; Franklin 4–0–29–1; Oram 7–0–54–0; Cairns 9–0–54–2; Styris 10–0–45–2; Vettori 10–1–29–2

New Zealand innings		R	M	B	4	6
L Vincent	b Bracken	4	7	9	1	0
NJ Astle	c Clarke b Clark	14	64	27	1	0
HJH Marshall	b Lee	5	13	6	0	0
SB Styris	c Clarke b Bracken	1	13	16	0	0
JAH Marshall	lbw Lee	1	5	5	0	0
CD McMillan	c Hussey b Lee	0	13	9	0	0
CL Cairns	not out	37	81	32	4	1
JDP Oram	b Clark	23	36	34	1	1
+BB McCullum	c White b Clark	2	10	10	0	0
*DL Vettori	c Ponting b Symonds	8	20	15	1	0
JEC Franklin	c Gilchrist b Symonds	0	3	3	0	0
Extras	(b 4, lb 1, w 5)	10				
Total	(all out, 27.4 ov, 137 mins)	105				

Fall: 1–5 (Vincent, 1.5 ov), 2–16 (HJH Marshall, 4.2 ov), 3–19 (Styris, 7.3 ov), 4–20 (JAH Marshall, 8.3 ov), 5–28 (McMillan, 10.6 ov), 6–33 (Astle, 12.3 ov), 7–74 (Oram, 20.5 ov), 8–82 (McCullum, 22.5 ov), 9–105 (Vettori, 27.1 ov), 10–105 (Franklin, 27.4 ov).

Bowling: Lee 6–4–5–3; Bracken 8–0–40–2; Clark 7–1–19–3; Symonds 5.4–1–32–2; White 1–0–4–0

Australia substitute: CL White (SM Katich, New Zealand innings, 0.0 ov) ; New Zealand substitute: JAH Marshall (KD Mills, New Zealand innings, 7.3 ov).

NEW ZEALAND V AUSTRALIA, SECOND ODI
Westpac Stadium, Wellington • December 7, 2005 (50-over match)

Result: Australia won by 2 runs • Toss: Australia
Umpires: Aleem Dar (Pak) and BF Bowden (NZ) • TV Umpire: AL Hill (NZ)
Match Referee: RS Madugalle (SL) • Player of the Match: A Symonds

Australia innings		R	M	B	4	6
+AC Gilchrist	c Cairns b Mills	8	11	9	1	0
SM Katich	run out	36	94	50	3	0
*RT Ponting	c McCullum b Mills	28	29	32	5	0
BJ Hodge	c HJH Marshall b Cairns	0	11	8	0	0
A Symonds	b Vettori	156	149	127	12	8
MJ Clarke	not out	82	110	77	9	0
MEK Hussey	not out	1	1	1	0	0
Extras	(lb 4, w 3, nb 4)	11				
Total	(5 wkts, 50 ov, 205 mins)	322				

DNB: B Lee, GB Hogg, NW Bracken, SR Clark.

Fall: 1–10 (Gilchrist, 2.2 ov), 2–47 (Ponting, 8.5 ov), 3–50 (Hodge, 11.4 ov), 4–101 (Katich, 21.2 ov), 5–321 (Symonds, 49.4 ov).

Bowling: Mills 10–0–60–2; Franklin 4–0–36–0; Cairns 9–0–66–1; Oram 5–0–39–0; Styris 10–0–46–0–(1w); Vettori 10–0–51–1; Astle 2–0–20–0.

New Zealand innings		R	M	B	4	6
L Vincent	c Gilchrist b Lewis	71	67	49	9	2
NJ Astle	c Clark b Lewis	22	77	43	2	0
CD McMillan	c Hussey b Clark	9	23	19	0	0
HJH Marshall	lbw Hogg	10	37	19	0	0
SB Styris	c & b Hogg	25	40	32	1	0
CL Cairns	c Lee b Lewis	60	61	52	4	3
JDP Oram	c Clark b Lee	41	64	40	5	0
+BB McCullum	run out	48	54	33	5	0
JAH Marshall	run out	6	15	7	0	0
*DL Vettori	not out	8	21	6	1	0
KD Mills	run out	0	2	1	0	0
Extras	(lb 10, w 8, nb 2)	20				
Total	(all out, 49.5 ov, 234 mins)	320				

Fall: 1–93 (Vincent, 14.1 ov), 2–98 (Astle, 16.1 ov), 3–109 (McMillan, 19.1 ov), 4–134 (HJH Marshall, 24.1 ov), 5–156 (Styris, 30.4 ov), 6–237 (Cairns, 40.6 ov), 7–271 (Oram, 44.3 ov), 8–295 (JAH Marshall, 47.2 ov), 9–319 (McCullum, 49.3 ov), 10–320 (Mills, 49.5 ov).

Bowling: Lee 10–0–85–1; Bracken 7–0–49–0; Lewis 9.5–0–56–3; Clark 10–0–49–1; Hogg 7–0–34–2; Symonds 6–0–37–0

Australia substitute: ML Lewis (SM Katich, New Zealand innings, 8.0 ov); New Zealand substitute: JAH Marshall (JEC Franklin, New Zealand innings, 43.2 ov).

NEW ZEALAND V AUSTRALIA, THIRD ODI
Jade Stadium, Christchurch
December 10, 2005 (50-over match)

Result: New Zealand won by two wickets • Toss: New Zealand
Umpires: Aleem Dar (Pak) and GA Baxter (NZ) • TV Umpire: EA Watkin (NZ)
Match Referee: RS Madugalle (SL) • Player of the Match: SB Styris

Australia innings		R	M	B	4	6
+AC Gilchrist	lbw Mills	0	2	3	0	0
SM Katich	c Styris b Martin	2	16	4	0	0
*RT Ponting	lbw Vettori	75	88	67	10	2
BJ Hodge	c Mills b Styris	59	118	83	8	0
A Symonds	c Mills b Vettori	1	3	2	0	0
MJ Clarke	c Mills b Martin	71	97	74	9	1
MEK Hussey	not out	88	80	56	7	5
CL White	c Vettori b Martin	0	2	1	0	0
NW Bracken	not out	21	20	12	0	2
Extras	(lb 4, w 8, nb 2)	14				
Total	(7 wkts, 50 ov, 210 mins)	331				

DNB: ML Lewis, SR Clark.

Fall: 1–0 (Gilchrist, 0.3 ov), 2–7 (Katich, 3.1 ov), 3–122 (Ponting, 20.1 ov), 4–124 (Symonds, 20.6 ov), 5–177 (Hodge, 31.3 ov), 6–259 (Clarke, 45.1 ov), 7–259 (White, 45.2 ov).

Bowling: Mills 10–1–64–1; Martin 9–0–65–3; Cairns 6–0–61–0; Oram 8–0–69–0; Vettori 10–1–37–2; Styris 7–0–31–1

New Zealand innings		R	M	B	4	6
L Vincent	c Hussey b Clark	39	48	33	6	1
SP Fleming	c Gilchrist b Bracken	0	14	9	0	0
NJ Astle	c White b Clark	14	24	22	2	0
HJH Marshall	b White	27	67	31	2	1
SB Styris	c Symonds b Clark	101	142	96	12	2
CD McMillan	c Gilchrist b Symonds	11	21	18	1	0
CL Cairns	c Gilchrist b Lewis	6	15	11	0	0
JDP Oram	b Clark	42	43	37	3	2
+BB McCullum	not out	50	32	25	3	4
*DL Vettori	not out	23	30	12	2	1
Extras	(lb 9, w 10)	19				
Total	(8 wkts, 49 ov, 220 mins)	332				

DNB: KD Mills.

Fall: 1–12 (Fleming, 3.3 ov), 2–50 (Astle, 8.6 ov), 3–61 (Vincent, 10.5 ov), 4–149 (Marshall, 24.3 ov), 5–179 (McMillan, 29.1 ov), 6–194 (Cairns, 32.5 ov), 7–257 (Oram, 42.4 ov), 8–258 (Styris, 42.6 ov).

Bowling: Lewis 9–0–77–1; Bracken 9–1–41–1; Clark 10–1–55–4; Johnson 9–0–64–0; White 4–0–34–1; Symonds 8–0–52–1

Australia substitute: MG Johnson (SM Katich, New Zealand innings, 8.0 ov); New Zealand substitute: SP Fleming (CS Martin, New Zealand innings, 0.0 ov).

CHAPPELL–HADLEE TROPHY AVERAGES

AUSTRALIA BATTING AND FIELDING

Name	ODIs	Inn	NO	Runs	HS	Ave	SR	100	50	Ct	St
MJ Clarke	3	3	1	184	82*	92.00	92.00	–	2	2	–
A Symonds	3	3	0	201	156	67.00	106.91	1	–	1	–
RT Ponting	3	3	0	166	75	55.33	101.84	–	2	1	–
SM Katich	3	3	0	92	54	30.67	77.31	–	1	–	–
BJ Hodge	3	3	0	72	59	24.00	62.61	–	1	–	–
GB Hogg	2	1	0	4	4	4.00	80.00	–	–	1	–
AC Gilchrist	3	3	0	11	8	3.67	44.00	–	–	5	–
B Lee	2	1	0	0	0	0.00	0.00	–	–	1	–
CL White	2	1	0	0	0	0.00	0.00	–	–	2	–
MEK Hussey	3	3	3	110	88*	–	142.86	–	1	3	–
NW Bracken	3	2	2	22	21*	–	157.14	–	–	–	–
SR Clark	3	0	–	–	–	–	–	–	–	2	–
ML Lewis	2	0	–	–	–	–	–	–	–	–	–
MG Johnson	1	0	–	–	–	–	–	–	–	–	–

AUSTRALIA BOWLING

Name	ODIs	O	M	R	W	Ave	Best	4w	SR	Econ
SR Clark	3	27	2	123	8	15.38	4–55	1	20.25	4.56
GB Hogg	2	7	0	34	2	17.00	2–34	–	21.00	4.86
B Lee	2	16	4	90	4	22.50	3–5	–	24.00	5.63
ML Lewis	2	18.5	0	133	4	33.25	3–56	–	28.25	7.06
CL White	2	5	0	38	1	38.00	1–34	–	30.00	7.60
A Symonds	3	19.4	1	121	3	40.33	2–32	–	39.33	6.15
NW Bracken	3	24	1	130	3	43.33	2–40	–	48.00	5.42
MG Johnson	1	9	0	64	0	–	–	–	–	7.11

NEW ZEALAND BATTING AND FIELDING

Name	ODIs	Inn	NO	Runs	HS	Ave	SR	100	50	Ct	St
CL Cairns	3	3	1	103	60	51.50	108.42	–	1	1	–
BB McCullum	3	3	1	100	50*	50.00	147.06	–	1	1	–
SB Styris	3	3	0	127	101	42.33	88.19	1	–	1	–
DL Vettori	3	3	2	39	23*	39.00	118.18	–	–	3	–
L Vincent	3	3	0	114	71	38.00	125.27	–	1	–	–
JDP Oram	3	3	0	106	42	35.33	95.50	–	–	–	–
NJ Astle	3	3	0	50	22	16.67	54.35	–	–	1	–
HJH Marshall	3	3	0	42	27	14.00	75.00	–	–	1	–
CD McMillan	3	3	0	20	11	6.67	43.48	–	–	–	–
JAH Marshall	2	2	0	7	6	3.50	58.33	–	–	–	–
KD Mills	3	1	0	0	0	0.00	0.00	–	–	3	–
JEC Franklin	2	1	0	0	0	0.00	0.00	–	–	1	–
SP Fleming	1	1	0	0	0	0.00	0.00	–	–	–	–
CS Martin	1	0	–	–	–	–	–	–	–	–	–

NEW ZEALAND BOWLING

Name	ODIs	O	M	R	W	Ave	Best	4w	SR	Econ
CS Martin	1	9	0	65	3	21.67	3–65	–	18.00	7.22
DL Vettori	3	30	2	117	5	23.40	2–29	–	36.00	3.90
KD Mills	3	30	2	159	4	39.75	2–60	–	45.00	5.30
SB Styris	3	27	0	122	3	40.67	2–45	–	54.00	4.52
CL Cairns	3	24	0	181	3	60.33	2–54	–	48.00	7.54
JEC Franklin	2	8	0	65	1	65.00	1–29	–	48.00	8.13
JDP Oram	3	20	0	162	0	–	–	–	–	8.10
NJ Astle	3	2	0	20	0	–	–	–	–	10.00

CHAPPELL–HADLEE TROPHY SERIES

The inaugural Chappell–Hadlee Trophy series was staged in 2004–05 in Australia. New Zealand won the opening game, at the Telstra Dome, by four wickets, and the home side levelled the series with a 17-run win at the SCG. The scheduled third game at the Gabba was abandoned without a ball being bowled.

Debuts
Brad Hodge (game one) was the 154th Australian to play ODI cricket
Mick Lewis (game two) was the 155th Australian to play ODI cricket
Mitchell Johnson (game three) was the 156th Australian to play ODI cricket

Note: This was the first instance of three Australians making their ODI debuts in the same series or tournament since Nathan Bracken, Simon Katich and Brad Haddin gained their first caps during the 2000–01 Carlton Series (now the VB Series). It was the first instance of three Australians making their ODI debuts in three consecutive matches since Greg Ritchie (game one) and Wayne Phillips (game two) made their first appearances in a two-game series in Pakistan in 1982 and Carl Rackemann and Kepler Wessels then debuted in Australia's next ODI, the opening World Series Cup encounter of 1982–83.

Hundreds
Andrew Symonds (156 for Australia in game two) scored his third ODI century, in his 129th match.
Scott Styris (101 for New Zealand in game three) scored his third ODI century, in his 108th match.

Four wickets in an innings
Stuart Clark (4–55 for Australia in game three) took four or more wickets in an ODI for the first time, in his fourth match.

AUSTRALIA V SOUTH AFRICA, FIRST TEST

WACA Ground, Perth • December 16–20, 2005 (five-day match)

Result: Match Drawn • Toss: Australia

Umpires: SA Bucknor (WI) and BR Doctrove (WI) • TV Umpire: DJ Harper (Aus)

Match Referee: BC Broad (Eng) • Player of the Match: BJ Hodge

Stumps Scores

Day 1: Australia 258, South Africa 0–38 (de Villiers 14, Smith 18; 7 ov)

Day 2: South Africa 296, Australia 1–38 (Langer 15, Lee 0; 11 ov)

Day 3: Australia 4–310 (Hodge 91, Hussey 54; 99 ov)

Day 4: Australia 8–528 dec, South Africa 2–85 (Gibbs 17, Rudolph 18; 36 ov)

Australia innings		R	M	B	4	6
JL Langer	c Smith b Ntini	37	136	89	6	0
ML Hayden	c Rudolph b Ntini	0	5	2	0	0
*RT Ponting	lbw Pollock	71	155	107	12	0
BJ Hodge	c Boucher b Ntini	41	121	96	4	0
MEK Hussey	c Langeveldt b Ntini	23	84	51	3	0
A Symonds	b Nel	13	48	29	2	0
+AC Gilchrist	c Gibbs b Ntini	6	18	13	1	0
SK Warne	lbw Langeveldt	24	51	30	3	0
B Lee	not out	19	48	29	4	0
NW Bracken	c Boucher b Nel	10	11	11	2	0
GD McGrath	c Boucher b Nel	0	1	1	0	0
Extras	(b 4, lb 2, w 2, nb 6)	14				
Total	(all out, 75.2 ov, 348 mins)	258				

Fall: 1–0 (Hayden, 1.2 ov), 2–111 (Langer, 29.6 ov), 3–117 (Ponting, 36.2 ov), 4–180 (Hussey, 55.2 ov), 5–185 (Hodge, 57.5 ov), 6–199 (Gilchrist, 61.5 ov), 7–210 (Symonds, 65.6 ov), 8–243 (Warne, 72.4 ov), 9–258 (Bracken, 75.1 ov), 10–258 (McGrath, 75.2 ov).

Bowling: Pollock 19–6–46–1; Ntini 19–3–64–5; Langeveldt 17–1–100–1; Nel 17.2–3–29–3; Kemp 3–0–13–0

South Africa first innings		R	M	B	4	6
AB de Villiers	b Warne	68	166	109	10	0
*GC Smith	c Ponting b Bracken	34	91	65	5	0
HH Gibbs	b Lee	21	58	43	4	0
JA Rudolph	c Langer b Lee	8	35	28	1	0
AG Prince	lbw Warne	28	102	79	2	0
JM Kemp	c Hodge b McGrath	7	44	29	1	0
+MV Boucher	c Hayden b Warne	62	115	77	7	0
SM Pollock	b Lee	34	52	35	6	0
A Nel	not out	4	38	20	0	0
CK Langeveldt	lbw Lee	0	1	1	0	0
M Ntini	c Hodge b Lee	12	8	10	2	0
Extras	(b 4, lb 2, nb 12)	18				
Total	(all out, 81.2 ov, 364 mins)	296				

Fall: 1–83 (Smith, 19.4 ov), 2–127 (Gibbs, 33.4 ov), 3–135 (de Villiers, 36.6 ov), 4–145 (Rudolph, 41.5 ov), 5–167 (Kemp, 51.6 ov), 6–187 (Prince, 60.4 ov), 7–264 (Pollock, 73.3 ov), 8–282 (Boucher, 78.6 ov), 9–283 (Langeveldt, 79.3 ov), 10–296 (Ntini, 81.2 ov).

Bowling: McGrath 18–3–59–1; Lee 22.2–1–93–5; Bracken 12–3–46–1; Warne 29–4–92–3

Australia second innings		R	M	B	4	6
JL Langer	b Pollock	47	180	114	8	0
ML Hayden	c Boucher b Langeveldt	20	43	33	5	0
B Lee	lbw Langeveldt	32	62	53	4	0
*RT Ponting	c Boucher b Ntini	53	161	106	4	0
BJ Hodge	not out	203	469	332	22	0
MEK Hussey	c Boucher b Pollock	58	172	121	8	0
A Symonds	c Gibbs b Langeveldt	25	79	49	4	0
+AC Gilchrist	c Rudolph b Nel	44	68	58	4	0
SK Warne	lbw Kemp	5	6	7	1	0
NW Bracken	not out	14	46	24	1	0
Extras	(b 5, lb 4, w 1, nb 17)	27				
Total	(8 wkts dec, 146.4 ov, 651 ms) 528					

Fall: 1–37 (Hayden, 10.3 ov), 2–86 (Lee, 24.4 ov), 3–129 (Langer, 40.2 ov), 4–184 (Ponting, 61.1 ov), 5–316 (Hussey, 100.4 ov), 6–377 (Symonds, 118.2 ov), 7–444 (Gilchrist, 134.2 ov), 8–451 (Warne, 135.6 ov).

Bowling: Pollock 36–6–98–2; Ntini 34–8–113–1; Langeveldt 31–3–117–3; Nel 28–2–104–1; Rudolph 6.4–1–29–0; Kemp 11–0–58–1

South Africa second innings (target: 491 runs)		R	M	B	4	6
*GC Smith	lbw Bracken	30	100	65	4	0
AB de Villiers	c Hodge b Warne	12	76	57	2	0
HH Gibbs	c Warne b Lee	33	129	104	5	0
JA Rudolph	not out	102	431	283	13	0
AG Prince	lbw Warne	8	55	45	1	0
JM Kemp	c Ponting b Warne	55	213	166	9	0
+MV Boucher	not out	13	52	39	2	0
Extras	(b 18, lb 13, nb 3)	34				
Total	(5 wkts, 126 ov, 533 mins)	287				

Fall: 1–35 (de Villiers, 17.3 ov), 2–55 (Smith, 22.4 ov), 3–109 (Gibbs, 48.3 ov), 4–138 (Prince, 61.5 ov), 5–250 (Kemp, 113.4 ov).

Bowling: McGrath 24–11–39–0–(1nb); Lee 31–9–83–1–(2nb); Warne 47–21–83–3; Bracken 19–5–37–1; Symonds 3–0–6–0; Hodge 2–0–8–0

DOUBLE CENTURIES AS MAIDEN HUNDREDS

In scoring 203 not out, Brad Hodge became the seventh Australian to score a double century against South Africa. His score was the fourth highest maiden century by an Australian in Test cricket — behind only Bob Simpson's 311 against England at Old Trafford in 1964, Sid Barnes' 234 in the second Ashes Test of 1946–47, and the 210 scored by Dean Jones in cricket second Tied Test, at Madras in 1986. (Like Hodge, Jones was playing his third Test when he completed that famous innings.) The only other Australian to turn his first Test century into a double ton was Syd Gregory, who scored 201 against England at the SCG in 1894–95.

Hodge also became only the second Australian to score a double century in the third innings of a Test match. Sir Donald Bradman did this twice, in consecutive Ashes Tests at Melbourne and Adelaide in 1936–37.

AUSTRALIA V SOUTH AFRICA, SECOND TEST

Melbourne Cricket Ground • December 26–30, 2005 (five-day match)

Result: Australia won by 184 runs • Toss: Australia
Umpires: Asad Rauf (Pak) and SA Bucknor (WI) • TV Umpire: RL Parry (Aus)
Match Referee: BC Broad (Eng) • Player of the Match: MEK Hussey

Stumps Scores
Day 1: Australia 8–239 (Hussey 23; 89.1 ov)
Day 2: Australia 355, South Africa 2–169 (Gibbs 54, Kallis 17; 58 ov)
Day 3: South Africa 311, Australia 2–110 (Hayden 45, Hodge 17; 37 ov)
Day 4: Australia 7–321 dec, South Africa 6–99 (Prince 16, Pollock 13; 42 ov)

Australia innings		R	M	B	4	6
PA Jaques	c Rudolph b Pollock	2	12	12	0	0
ML Hayden	c Smith b Pollock	65	228	177	9	0
*RT Ponting	c Gibbs b Nel	117	298	198	13	0
BJ Hodge	c Smith b Pollock	7	30	26	1	0
MEK Hussey	b Ntini	122	247	203	14	4
A Symonds	c Boucher b Nel	0	1	1	0	0
+AC Gilchrist	c Gibbs b Nel	2	14	7	0	0
SK Warne	c Boje b Nel	9	18	14	1	0
B Lee	lbw Ntini	4	26	16	0	0
SCG MacGill	b Ntini	4	13	11	1	0
GD McGrath	not out	11	120	56	0	0
Extras	(b 2, lb 4, w 2, nb 4)	12				
Total	(all out, 119.3 ov, 506 mins)	355				

Fall: 1–2 (Jaques, 2.6 ov), 2–154 (Hayden, 54.4 ov), 3–176 (Hodge, 62.2 ov), 4–207 (Ponting, 74.4 ov), 5–207 (Symonds, 74.5 ov), 6–213 (Gilchrist, 78.2 ov), 7–227 (Warne, 82.4 ov), 8–239 (Lee, 89.1 ov), 9–248 (MacGill, 91.6 ov), 10–355 (Hussey, 119.3 ov).

Bowling: Pollock 26–5–67–3; Ntini 22.3–3–70–3; Kallis 21.5–4–69–0; Nel 31–6–84–4; Boje 18.1–3–59–0

South Africa first innings		R	M	B	4	6
AB de Villiers	lbw McGrath	61	178	141	9	0
*GC Smith	lbw Lee	22	62	42	2	0
HH Gibbs	b Symonds	94	347	234	15	0
JH Kallis	b Lee	23	108	91	2	0
AG Prince	c Ponting b Warne	6	22	19	0	0
JA Rudolph	b Lee	13	40	36	2	0
+MV Boucher	lbw Symonds	23	48	40	4	0
SM Pollock	lbw Symonds	9	37	21	1	0
N Boje	b Warne	12	43	27	2	0
A Nel	c Hussey b MacGill	14	28	21	3	0
M Ntini	not out	10	12	10	2	0
Extras	(b 2, lb 7, nb 15)	24				
Total	(all out, 111 ov, 467 mins)	311				

Fall: 1–36 (Smith, 14.1 ov), 2–122 (de Villiers, 42.1 ov), 3–184 (Kallis, 69.2 ov), 4–192 (Prince, 73.5 ov), 5–214 (Rudolph, 85.1 ov), 6–260 (Boucher, 96.4 ov), 7–265 (Gibbs, 98.4 ov), 8–281 (Pollock, 104.1 ov), 9–291 (Boje, 107.4 ov), 10–311 (Nel, 110.6 ov).

Bowling: McGrath 27–13–57–1; Lee 28–5–92–3; Symonds 20–6–50–3; Warne 21–7–62–2; MacGill 15–3–41–1

Australia second innings		R	M	B	4	6
ML Hayden	c Boucher b Kallis	137	356	242	17	2
PA Jaques	lbw Nel	28	64	44	3	0
*RT Ponting	lbw Pollock	11	48	29	0	0
BJ Hodge	c Boucher b Nel	24	80	63	3	0
MEK Hussey	c Kallis b Smith	31	94	74	2	0
A Symonds	c Nel b Kallis	72	69	54	5	6
+AC Gilchrist	c Prince b Kallis	0	4	1	0	0
SK Warne	not out	0	1	0	0	0
Extras	(b 6, lb 3, nb 9)	18				
Total	(7 wkts dec, 83 ov, 361 mins)	321				

Fall: 1–53 (Jaques, 14.1 ov), 2–82 (Ponting, 25.2 ov), 3–131 (Hodge, 44.1 ov), 4–193 (Hussey, 67.2 ov), 5–317 (Hayden, 82.3 ov), 6–321 (Symonds, 82.5 ov), 7–321 (Gilchrist, 82.6 ov).

Bowling: Pollock 23–5–60–1; Ntini 8–2–17–0; Kallis 11–0–58–3; Nel 20–3–71–2; Boje 14–1–65–0; Smith 7–0–41–1

South Africa second innings (target: 366 runs)		R	M	B	4	6
*GC Smith	c Gilchrist b McGrath	25	70	52	3	0
AB de Villiers	st Gilchrist b Warne	8	64	44	1	0
HH Gibbs	b Warne	9	18	11	2	0
JH Kallis	c Gilchrist b Symonds	9	39	26	2	0
AG Prince	c Hayden b Warne	26	147	120	2	0
JA Rudolph	b Symonds	4	8	5	1	0
+MV Boucher	c Ponting b Warne	5	30	18	0	0
SM Pollock	not out	67	156	120	8	1
N Boje	b McGrath	13	58	38	0	1
A Nel	c Gilchrist b McGrath	2	10	7	0	0
M Ntini	b MacGill	2	5	6	0	0
Extras	(lb 6, w 1, nb 4)	11				
Total	(all out, 74 ov, 307 mins)	181				

Fall: 1–39 (de Villiers, 15.2 ov), 2–45 (Smith, 16.3 ov), 3–58 (Gibbs, 19.1 ov), 4–64 (Kallis, 24.4 ov), 5–72 (Rudolph, 26.3 ov), 6–82 (Boucher, 33.1 ov), 7–130 (Prince, 55.3 ov), 8–166 (Boje, 70.1 ov), 9–178 (Nel, 72.2 ov), 10–181 (Ntini, 73.6 ov).

Bowling: McGrath 15–3–44–3; Lee 11–4–23–0; Warne 28–7–74–4; Symonds 4–2–6–2; MacGill 16–7–28–1

MOST TEST WICKETS IN A CALENDAR YEAR

When he dismissed South Africa's Ashwell Prince in Perth, Shane Warne broke Dennis Lillee's record for the most Test wickets in a calendar year. Lillee took 85 wickets in 13 Tests in 1981. Following this Boxing Day Test, Warne finished 2005 with 96 wickets in 15 Tests.

This was the fourth occasion that Warne has taken 70 or more wickets in a calendar year (a feat achieved 15 times in Test history, by nine bowlers). He took 72 wickets in 1993, 70 in 1994 and 70 in 2004. On four other occasions (52 wickets in 1995, 68 in 1997, 58 in 2001 and 67 in 2002) he has taken more than 50 wickets in one year.

AUSTRALIA V SOUTH AFRICA, THIRD TEST
Sydney Cricket Ground • January 2–6, 2006 (five-day match)

Result: Australia won by eight wickets • Toss: South Africa
Umpires: Aleem Dar (Pak) and BF Bowden (NZ) • TV Umpire: RL Parry (Aus)
Match Referee: BC Broad (Eng) • Player of the Match: RT Ponting • Player of the Series: RT Ponting

Stumps Scores
Day 1: South Africa 3–230 (Kallis 80, Prince 62; 74 ov)
Day 2: South Africa 9–451 dec, Australia 3–54 (Ponting 13; 14.2 ov)
Day 3: Australia 359, South Africa 1–4 (Smith 3; 1.3 ov)
Day 4: South Africa 3–94 (Kallis 14, Prince 0; 22 ov)

South Africa first innings		R	M	B	4	6
AB de Villiers	c Gilchrist b Lee	2	25	18	0	0
*GC Smith	lbw Lee	39	125	77	6	0
HH Gibbs	b McGrath	27	64	49	5	0
JH Kallis	c McGrath b Symonds	111	361	275	17	0
AG Prince	lbw Warne	119	395	271	13	0
JA Rudolph	c Gilchrist b McGrath	38	138	110	5	0
+MV Boucher	c Gilchrist b MacGill	5	29	23	0	0
SM Pollock	c Hodge b Lee	46	86	64	3	0
J Botha	not out	20	62	46	2	0
A Nel	c Hodge b Warne	12	10	8	2	0
CK Langeveldt	not out	1	4	3	0	0
Extras	(b 9, lb 6, nb 16)	31				
Total	(9 wkts dec, 154.4 ov, 660 mins)	451				

Fall: 1–16 (de Villiers, 5.6 ov), 2–69 (Gibbs, 20.3 ov), 3–86 (Smith, 28.1 ov), 4–305 (Kallis, 104.3 ov), 5–344 (Prince, 121.5 ov), 6–355 (Boucher, 128.4 ov), 7–394 (Rudolph, 140.5 ov), 8–433 (Pollock, 152.1 ov), 9–449 (Nel, 153.5 ov).

Bowling: McGrath 34–17–65–2; Lee 30.4–7–82–3; Symonds 23–4–69–1; Warne 36–5–106–2; Hussey 2–0–12–0; MacGill 29–5–102–1

Australia innings		R	M	B	4	6
JL Langer	b Langeveldt	25	23	20	3	0
ML Hayden	b Langeveldt	4	15	11	0	0
*RT Ponting	lbw Kallis	120	257	174	12	1
BJ Hodge	c Rudolph b Nel	6	33	23	0	0
MEK Hussey	c Boucher b Botha	45	149	111	8	0
A Symonds	lbw Nel	12	77	51	1	0
+AC Gilchrist	c Boucher b Nel	86	156	109	10	2
SK Warne	c Boucher b Nel	0	1	1	0	0
B Lee	c Smith b Kallis	17	49	40	3	0
SCG MacGill	c Nel b Pollock	29	52	21	5	0
GD McGrath	not out	1	33	12	0	0
Extras	(lb 10, w 2, nb 2)	14				
Total	(all out, 95.1 ov, 431 mins)	359				

Fall: 1–22 (Hayden, 3.5 ov), 2–35 (Langer, 5.4 ov), 3–54 (Hodge, 14.2 ov), 4–184 (Hussey, 49.6 ov), 5–222 (Ponting, 63.2 ov), 6–226 (Symonds, 66.5 ov), 7–226 (Warne, 66.6 ov), 8–263 (Lee, 77.5 ov), 9–322 (MacGill, 88.3 ov), 10–359 (Gilchrist, 95.1 ov).

Bowling: Pollock 25–3–109–1; Langeveldt 24–4–108–2; Nel 24.1–3–81–4; Kallis 15–4–25–2; Botha 7–2–26–1

South Africa second innings		R	M	B	4	6
*GC Smith	lbw McGrath	5	12	9	0	0
AB de Villiers	lbw Lee	1	7	4	0	0
HH Gibbs	run out	67	99	74	11	0
JH Kallis	not out	50	180	96	3	0
AG Prince	c Ponting b MacGill	18	39	30	2	0
JA Rudolph	c McGrath b MacGill	4	5	7	0	0
+MV Boucher	st Gilchrist b MacGill	11	14	13	2	0
SM Pollock	not out	26	24	21	2	1
Extras	(b 3, lb 4, w 3, nb 2)	12				
Total	(6 wkts dec, 42 ov, 200 mins)	194				

Fall: 1–4 (de Villiers, 1.3 ov), 2–6 (Smith, 2.4 ov), 3–92 (Gibbs, 21.4 ov), 4–123 (Prince, 30.6 ov), 5–129 (Rudolph, 32.3 ov), 6–152 (Boucher, 36.3 ov).

Bowling: McGrath 15–2–61–1; Lee 10–3–48–1; Warne 11–1–45–0; MacGill 6–1–33–3

Australia second innings (target: 287 runs)		R	M	B	4	6
JL Langer	b Langeveldt	20	49	32	5	0
ML Hayden	c Smith b Botha	90	197	134	11	0
*RT Ponting	not out	143	202	159	16	0
BJ Hodge	not out	27	51	42	3	0
Extras	(lb 1, w 3, nb 4)	8				
Total	(2 wkts, 60.3 ov, 258 mins)	288				

Fall: 1–30 (Langer, 11.2 ov), 2–212 (Hayden, 44.4 ov).

Bowling: Pollock 14–2–55–0; Langeveldt 14–1–52–1; Nel 7–0–46–0; Botha 12.3–0–77–1; Kallis 2–0–8–0; Rudolph 11–0–49–0

RICKY PONTING'S 100TH TEST

Ricky Ponting became the ninth Australian and the 35th cricketer to play 100 Tests. By scoring 120 in the first innings, he became the six man, third captain and first Australian to score a century in his 100th Test. In making 143 not out on the final day, he became the first man to score a century in each innings of his 100th Test. The previous examples of a batsman hitting a hundred in his 100th Test were:

Centurion	Score	Team	Opponent	Venue	Season
Colin Cowdrey	104	England	Australia	Birmingham	1968
Javed Miandad	145	Pakistan	India	Lahore	1989–90
Gordon Greenidge	149	West Indies	England	St John's	1989–90
Alec Stewart	105	England	India	Manchester	2000
Inzamam-ul-Haq	184	Pakistan	India	Bangalore	2004–05

Cowdrey and Inzamam led their teams during their 100th Test. Before the end of April 2006, a further six cricketers — Muttiah Muralitharan (Sri Lanka), Rahul Dravid (India), Justin Langer (Australia, in the third Test against South Africa at Johannesburg), Stephen Fleming (New Zealand), Jacques Kallis (South Africa) and Shaun Pollock (South Africa) — each played in their 100th Test.

In the Test at Sydney, South Africa became the second team in cricket history to lose a Test after declaring in both innings (West Indies did so against England at Port-of-Spain in 1968). Australia's successful run-chase of 2–288 was an SCG record, surpassing the 4–276 that Harry Trott's Australian team achieved in the fifth Ashes Test of 1897–98.

SOUTH AFRICA IN AUSTRALIA TEST AVERAGES

AUSTRALIA BATTING AND FIELDING

Name	Tests	Inn	NO	Runs	HS	Ave	SR	100	50	Ct	St
RT Ponting	3	6	1	515	143*	103.00	66.62	3	2	5	–
BJ Hodge	3	6	2	308	203*	77.00	52.92	1	–	5	–
MEK Hussey	3	5	0	279	122	55.80	49.82	1	1	1	–
ML Hayden	3	6	0	316	137	52.67	52.75	1	2	2	–
JL Langer	2	4	0	129	47	32.25	50.59	–	–	1	–
AC Gilchrist	3	5	0	138	86	27.60	73.40	–	1	6	2
A Symonds	3	5	0	122	72	24.40	66.30	–	1	–	–
B Lee	3	4	1	72	32	24.00	52.17	–	–	–	–
NW Bracken	1	2	1	24	14*	24.00	68.57	–	–	–	–
SCG MacGill	2	2	0	33	29	16.50	103.13	–	–	–	–
PA Jaques	1	2	0	30	28	15.00	53.57	–	–	–	–
GD McGrath	3	3	2	12	11*	12.00	17.39	–	–	2	–
SK Warne	3	5	1	38	24	9.50	73.08	–	–	1	–

AUSTRALIA BOWLING

Name	Tests	O	M	R	W	Ave	Best	5w	10w	SR	Econ
A Symonds	3	50	12	131	6	21.83	3–50	–	–	50.00	2.62
B Lee	3	133	29	421	13	32.38	5–93	1	–	61.38	3.17
SK Warne	3	172	45	462	14	33.00	4–74	–	–	73.71	2.69
SCG MacGill	2	66	16	204	6	34.00	3–33	–	–	66.00	3.09
GD McGrath	3	133	49	325	8	40.63	3–44	–	–	99.75	2.44
NW Bracken	1	31	8	83	2	41.50	1–37	–	–	93.00	2.68
BJ Hodge	3	2	0	8	0	–	–	–	–	–	4.00
MEK Hussey	3	2	0	12	0	–	–	–	–	–	6.00

SOUTH AFRICA BATTING AND FIELDING

Name	Tests	Inn	NO	Runs	HS	Ave	SR	100	50	Ct	St
JH Kallis	2	4	1	193	111	64.33	39.63	1	1	1	–
SM Pollock	3	5	2	182	67*	60.67	69.73	–	1	–	–
HH Gibbs	3	6	0	251	94	41.83	48.74	–	2	4	–
AG Prince	3	6	0	205	119	34.17	36.35	1	–	1	–
JA Rudolph	3	6	1	169	102*	33.80	36.03	1	–	4	–
JM Kemp	1	2	0	62	55	31.00	31.79	–	1	–	–
GC Smith	3	6	0	155	39	25.83	50.00	–	–	5	–
AB de Villiers	3	6	0	152	68	25.33	40.75	–	2	–	–
MV Boucher	3	6	1	119	62	23.80	56.67	–	1	12	–
N Boje	1	2	0	25	13	12.50	38.46	–	–	1	–
M Ntini	2	3	1	24	12	12.00	92.31	–	–	–	–
A Nel	3	4	1	32	14	10.67	57.14	–	–	2	–
CK Langeveldt	2	2	1	1	1*	1.00	25.00	–	–	1	–
J Botha	1	1	1	20	20*	–	43.48	–	–	–	–

SOUTH AFRICA BOWLING

Name	Tests	O	M	R	W	Ave	Best	5w	10w	SR	Econ
M Ntini	2	83.3	16	264	9	29.33	5–64	1	–	55.67	3.16
A Nel	3	127.3	17	415	14	29.64	4–81	–	–	54.64	3.25
JH Kallis	2	49.5	8	160	5	32.00	3–58	–	–	59.80	3.21
GC Smith	3	7	0	41	1	41.00	1–41	–	–	42.00	5.86
J Botha	1	19.3	2	103	2	51.50	1–26	–	–	58.50	5.28
CK Langeveldt	2	86	9	377	7	53.85	3–117	–	–	73.71	4.38
SM Pollock	3	143	27	435	8	54.38	3–67	–	–	107.25	3.04
JM Kemp	1	14	0	71	1	71.00	1–58	–	–	84.00	5.07
JA Rudolph	3	17.4	1	78	0	–	–	–	–	–	4.41
N Boje	1	32.1	4	124	0	–	–	–	–	–	3.85

AUSTRALIA V SOUTH AFRICA TEST SERIES

Debuts

Phil Jaques (second Test) was the 395th Australian to play Test cricket.

Johan Botha (third Test) was the 299th South African to play Test cricket.

Hundreds

Brad Hodge (203* for Australia in the first Test) scored his first Test century, in his third match.

Jacques Rudolph (102* for South Africa in the first Test) scored his fifth Test century, in his 28th match.

Ricky Ponting (117 for Australia in the second Test) scored his 26th Test century, in his 99th match

Mike Hussey (122 for Australia in the second Test) scored his third Test century, in his fifth match.

Matthew Hayden (137 for Australia in the second Test) scored his 25th Test century, in his 78th match.

Jacques Kallis (111 for South Africa in the third Test) scored his 23rd Test century, in his 96th match.

Ashwell Prince (119 for South Africa in the third Test) scored his third Test century, in his 15th match.

Ricky Ponting (120 and 143* for Australia in the third Test) scored his 27th and 28th Test centuries, in his 100th match.

Five wickets in an innings

Brett Lee (5–93 for Australia in the first Test) took five or more wickets in a Test innings for the sixth time, in his 47th match.

Makhaya Ntini (5–64 for South Africa in the first Test) took five or more wickets in a Test innings for the 10th time, in his 60th match.

AUSTRALIA V SOUTH AFRICA
The Gabba, Brisbane • 9 January 2006 (20-over match)

Result: Australia won by 95 runs • Toss: Australia

Umpires: BNJ Oxenford (Aus) and RL Parry (Aus) • TV Umpire: NS McNamara (Aus)

Match Referee: RG Archer (Aus) • Player of the Match: DR Martyn

Australia innings		R	M	B	4	6
JR Hopes	c Kallis b Pollock	17	25	20	2	0
DR Martyn	c Gibbs b Zondeki	96	79	56	7	5
*RT Ponting	c Pollock b Botha	27	22	18	2	2
A Symonds	not out	54	32	26	6	2
MJ Clarke	not out	0	3	0	0	0
Extras	(b 4, lb 3, w 8)	15				
Total	(3 wkts, 20 ov, 82 mins)	209				

DNB: MEK Hussey, +BJ Haddin, SM Katich, NW Bracken, SR Clark, ML Lewis.

Fall: 1–57 (Hopes, 6.4 ov), 2–103 (Ponting, 11.2 ov), 3–187 (Martyn, 19.1 ov).

Bowling: Pollock 4–0–34–1; Kruger 4–0–29–0; Zondeki 3–0–41–1; Hall 4–0–38–0; Botha 4–0–43–1; Kallis 1–0–17–0

South Africa innings		R	M	B	4	6
*GC Smith	b Hopes	22	32	26	3	0
HH Dippenaar	c Haddin b Bracken	1	7	5	0	0
HH Gibbs	c Clark b Bracken	0	1	2	0	0
+MV Boucher	c Haddin b Clark	29	30	21	5	0
SM Pollock	c Lewis b Symonds	24	21	17	2	1
JH Kallis	run out	15	12	13	1	1
JA Rudolph	not out	6	19	7	0	0
AJ Hall	c Hussey b Hopes	11	6	10	1	0
J Botha	c Katich b Symonds	2	3	4	0	0
GJP Kruger	c Martyn b Lewis	3	3	5	0	0
M Zondeki	b Lewis	0	1	1	0	0
Extras	(w 1)	1				
Total	(all out, 18.3 ov, 78 mins)	114				

Fall: 1–7 (Dippenaar, 2.2 ov), 2–7 (Gibbs, 2.4 ov), 3–38 (Smith, 7.5 ov), 4–56 (Boucher, 10.2 ov), 5–92 (Pollock, 13.2 ov), 6–92 (Kallis, 13.6 ov), 7–106 (Hall, 16.2 ov), 8–109 (Botha, 17.1 ov), 9–114 (Kruger, 18.2 ov), 10–114 (Zondeki, 18.3 ov).

Bowling: Bracken 3–0–9–2; Lewis 3.3–0–18–2; Clark 4–0–35–1; Hopes 4–0–26–2; Symonds 4–0–26–2

AUSTRALIA V SRI LANKA (GAME ONE)

Telstra Dome, Melbourne • January 13, 2006 (50-over match)

Result: Australia won by 116 runs • Points: Australia 5, Sri Lanka 0 • Toss: Sri Lanka
Umpires: MR Benson (Eng) and SJA Taufel (Aus) • TV Umpire: RL Parry (Aus)
Match Referee: JJ Crowe (NZ) • Player of the Match: A Symonds

Australia innings		R	M	B	4	6
+AC Gilchrist	lbw Perera	13	21	14	2	0
SM Katich	run out	60	110	78	5	0
*RT Ponting	b Perera	13	33	18	0	1
DR Martyn	b Fernando	70	110	64	5	2
A Symonds	c Dilshan b Mubarak	66	63	61	5	4
MJ Clarke	not out	45	47	39	3	1
MEK Hussey	not out	34	42	29	3	0
Extras	(lb 8, w 6, nb 3)	17				
Total	(5 wkts, 50 ov, 220 mins)	318				

DNB: JR Hopes, B Lee, NW Bracken, GD McGrath.

Fall: 1–25 (Gilchrist, 5.1 ov), 2–58 (Ponting, 11.6 ov), 3–132 (Katich, 23.4 ov), 4–238 (Martyn, 38.2 ov), 5–238 (Symonds, 39.2 ov).

Bowling: Vaas 10–0–73–0; Perera 10–0–45–2; Fernando 10–0–60–1; Muralitharan 10–1–67–0; Dilshan 8–0–55–0Mubarak 2–0–10–1

Sri Lanka innings		R	M	B	4	6
WU Tharanga	b Lee	2	2	2	0	0
J Mubarak	c Ponting b Lee	1	14	4	0	0
MG Vandort	run out	48	146	117	3	0
+KC Sangakkara	c Martyn b Bracken	16	34	31	2	0
TM Dilshan	b Bracken	29	64	37	3	0
DPMD Jayawardene	c & b Hopes	50	59	47	4	0
*MS Atapattu	c Katich b Hogg	9	8	11	0	0
RP Arnold	not out	28	37	36	1	0
WPUJC Vaas	not out	7	17	15	0	0
Extras	(b 1, lb 3, w 8)	12				
Total	(7 wkts, 50 ov, 190 mins)	202				

DNB: PDRL Perera, CRD Fernando.

Fall: 1–2 (Tharanga, 0.2 ov), 2–11 (Mubarak, 2.4 ov), 3–32 (Sangakkara, 10.6 ov), 4–93 (Dilshan, 27.1 ov), 5–118 (Vandort, 35.1 ov), 6–137 (Atapattu, 38.1 ov), 7–176 (Jayawardene, 44.2 ov).

Bowling: Lee 7–0–29–2; McGrath 9–1–30–0; Bracken 8–2–11–2; Hopes 9–1–35–1; Hogg 10–0–57–1; Symonds 4–0–20–0; Clarke 3–0–16–0

Australia substitute: GB Hogg (DR Martyn, Sri Lanka innings, 24.0 ov) ; Sri Lanka substitute: MG Vandort (M Muralitharan, Sri Lanka innings, 0.2 ov).

AUSTRALIA V SOUTH AFRICA (GAME TWO)

The Gabba, Brisbane • January 15, 2006 (50-over match)

Result: South Africa won by five wickets • Points: South Africa 4, Australia 0
Toss: Australia • Umpires: Aleem Dar (Pak) and SJA Taufel (Aus)
TV Umpire: DJ Harper (Aus) • Match Referee: JJ Crowe (NZ) • Player of the Match: SM Pollock

Australia innings		R	M	B	4	6
+AC Gilchrist	b Pollock	0	1	1	0	0
SM Katich	c Smith b Pollock	0	12	7	0	0
*RT Ponting	c & b Zondeki	33	61	47	6	0
DR Martyn	b Pollock	12	23	18	2	0
A Symonds	c Boucher b Hall	9	35	16	1	0
MJ Clarke	c Boucher b Hall	8	18	14	1	0
MEK Hussey	b Kruger	73	125	107	5	0
B Lee	run out	57	130	70	1	3
NW Bracken	not out	7	26	12	0	0
SR Clark	b Hall	15	9	10	1	1
GD McGrath	run out	0	1	1	0	0
Extras	(b 3, lb 3, w 4, nb 4)	14				
Total	(all out, 49.5 ov, 225 mins)	228				

Fall: 1–0 (Gilchrist, 0.1 ov), 2–4 (Katich, 2.4 ov), 3–29 (Martyn, 8.1 ov), 4–60 (Ponting, 14.1 ov), 5–64 (Symonds, 15.4 ov), 6–71 (Clarke, 17.6 ov), 7–194 (Hussey, 44.5 ov), 8–207 (Lee, 47.4 ov), 9–228 (Clark, 49.4 ov), 10–228 (McGrath, 49.5 ov).

Bowling: Pollock 10–2–30–3; Kruger 9–1–43–1; Hall 9.5–1–43–3; Zondeki 10–2–64–1; Kallis 6–0–23–0; Smith 5–0–19–0

South Africa innings		R	M	B	4	6
*GC Smith	c Katich b McGrath	12	35	26	1	0
HH Dippenaar	run out	74	184	115	8	0
JH Kallis	run out	0	3	1	0	0
HH Gibbs	c Martyn b Bracken	16	26	27	2	0
AG Prince	c Hussey b McGrath	19	74	41	1	0
+MV Boucher	not out	63	81	62	6	1
JM Kemp	not out	29	38	21	3	1
Extras	(b 4, lb 9, w 5)	18				
Total	(5 wkts, 48.5 ov, 223 mins)	231				

DNB: SM Pollock, AJ Hall, M Zondeki, GJP Kruger.

Fall: 1–27 (Smith, 7.5 ov), 2–27 (Kallis, 8.3 ov), 3–55 (Gibbs, 14.4 ov), 4–125 (Prince, 31.6 ov), 5–162 (Dippenaar, 40.5 ov).

Bowling: Lee 10–1–47–0; McGrath 9–0–35–2; Bracken 8.5–1–37–1; Clark 10–0–41–0; Hopes 8–0–44–0; Symonds 3–0–14–0

Australia substitute: JR Hopes (DR Martyn, South Africa innings, 18.0 ov); South Africa substitute: J Botha (not used).

SOUTH AFRICA V SRI LANKA (GAME THREE)

The Gabba, Brisbane • January 17, 2006 (50-over match)

Result: Sri Lanka won by 94 runs • Points: Sri Lanka 5, South Africa 0
Toss: South Africa • Umpires: Aleem Dar (Pak) and DJ Harper (Aus)
TV Umpire: PD Parker (Aus) • Match Referee: JJ Crowe (NZ)• Player of the Match: KC Sangakkara

Sri Lanka innings		R	M	B	4	6
WU Tharanga	c Boucher b Kruger	16	23	18	2	0
J Mubarak	lbw Botha	61	112	69	9	0
+KC Sangakkara	c Smith b Pollock	88	145	109	10	0
TM Dilshan	c Gibbs b Zondeki	15	27	20	0	0
*MS Atapattu	run out	33	62	43	2	0
DPMD Jayawardene	c Prince b Botha	14	21	15	1	1
RP Arnold	not out	15	23	17	1	0
WPUJC Vaas	not out	14	13	14	1	0
Extras	(lb 12, w 9, nb 5)	26				
Total	(6 wkts, 50 ov, 217 mins)	282				

DNB: KMDN Kulasekara, PDRL Perera, M Muralitharan.

Fall: 1–33 (Tharanga, 5.3 ov), 2–145 (Mubarak, 23.5 ov), 3–172 (Dilshan, 30.4 ov), 4–211 (Sangakkara, 38.1 ov), 5–244 (Jayawardene, 43.4 ov), 6–259 (Atapattu, 45.6 ov).

Bowling: Pollock 10–1–39–1; Kruger 8–0–61–1; Hall 10–0–58–0; Zondeki 9–0–49–1; Botha 10–0–49–2; Smith 3–0–14–0

South Africa innings		R	M	B	4	6
*GC Smith	lbw Vaas	3	11	10	0	0
HH Dippenaar	b Kulasekara	10	28	12	2	0
JA Rudolph	run out	53	80	63	8	0
HH Gibbs	run out	7	32	16	0	0
AG Prince	c Kulasekara b Bandara	29	65	44	2	0
+MV Boucher	c Dilshan b Bandara	62	96	71	3	2
JM Kemp	b Bandara	10	24	21	0	0
SM Pollock	c Atapattu b Vaas	4	16	9	0	0
AJ Hall	b Muralitharan	4	6	9	0	0
J Botha	lbw Muralitharan	2	7	8	0	0
GJP Kruger	not out	0	4	3	0	0
Extras	(lb 1, w 3)	4				
Total	(all out, 44.2 ov, 189 mins)	188				

Fall: 1–8 (Smith, 2.3 ov), 2–30 (Dippenaar, 5.6 ov), 3–57 (Gibbs, 13.3 ov), 4–93 (Rudolph, 20.4 ov), 5–127 (Prince, 29.2 ov), 6–152 (Kemp, 35.6 ov), 7–179 (Pollock, 40.1 ov), 8–184 (Hall, 41.5 ov), 9–188 (Botha, 43.3 ov), 10–188 (Boucher, 44.2 ov).

Bowling: Vaas–8–2–21–2; Perera 6–0–38–0; Kulasekara 6–0–24–1; Dilshan 6–0–29–0; Muralitharan 9–1–34–2; Bandara 8.2–0–31–3; Mubarak 1–0–10–0

Sri Lanka substitute: CM Bandara (WU Tharanga, South Africa innings, 0.0 ov); South Africa substitute: JA Rudolph (M Zondeki, Sri Lanka innings, 46.0 ov).

AUSTRALIA V SOUTH AFRICA (GAME FOUR)

Telstra Dome, Melbourne • January 20, 2006 (50-over match)

Result: Australia won by 59 runs • Points: Australia 5, South Africa 0
Toss: Australia • Umpires: MR Benson (Eng) and DJ Harper (Aus)
TV Umpire: PD Parker (Aus) • Match Referee: JJ Crowe (NZ) • Player of the Match: B Lee

Australia innings		R	M	B	4	6
DR Martyn	b Pollock	11	9	9	2	0
PA Jaques	c Boucher b van der Wath	94	145	112	14	0
*RT Ponting	c Smith b Hall	9	30	19	1	0
A Symonds	c Prince b Steyn	7	22	14	1	0
MJ Clarke	c Boucher b van der Wath	34	65	44	4	0
MEK Hussey	c Kruger b Hall	18	37	31	0	0
+BJ Haddin	b Pollock	1	3	4	0	0
JR Hopes	c Botha b Hall	38	56	47	1	0
B Lee	b Smith	6	9	9	0	0
BR Dorey	c Kemp b Hall	2	13	8	0	0
GD McGrath	not out	2	7	6	0	0
Extras	(lb 3, w 13, nb 7)	23				
Total	(all out, 49.2 ov, 210 mins)	245				

Fall: 1–17 (Martyn, 2.4 ov), 2–55 (Ponting, 9.6 ov), 3–85 (Symonds, 14.5 ov), 4–172 (Clarke, 30.3 ov), 5–177 (Jaques, 32.5 ov), 6–181 (Haddin, 34.1 ov), 7–208 (Hussey, 40.3 ov), 8–221 (Lee, 43.4 ov), 9–238 (Dorey, 47.1 ov), 10–245 (Hopes, 49.2 ov).

Bowling: Pollock 10–2–31–2; Steyn 5–0–58–1; Hall 9.2–0–35–4; Kruger 6–0–35–0; Botha 10–0–47–0; van der Wath 5–0–21–2; Smith 4–0–15–1

South Africa innings		R	M	B	4	6
*GC Smith	c Haddin b Lee	9	19	17	1	0
HH Dippenaar	b Lee	41	130	93	3	0
AJ Hall	b Lee	1	7	4	0	0
HH Gibbs	lbw Hogg	39	70	53	4	1
AG Prince	b Lee	21	35	27	1	1
+MV Boucher	lbw Hogg	5	21	12	0	0
JM Kemp	b Lee	3	6	8	0	0
JJ van der Wath	c Haddin b Hogg	0	7	6	0	0
SM Pollock	c Haddin b Dorey	46	36	31	1	4
J Botha	not out	15	40	25	1	0
GJP Kruger	c Symonds b McGrath	0	5	7	0	0
Extras	(b 1, lb 2, w 2, nb 1)	6				
Total	(all out, 47 ov, 200 mins)	186				

Fall: 1–12 (Smith, 4.3 ov), 2–16 (Hall, 6.2 ov), 3–84 (Gibbs, 24.5 ov), 4–114 (Dippenaar, 31.5 ov), 5–119 (Prince, 33.3 ov), 6–123 (Kemp, 35.2 ov), 7–123 (Boucher, 36.2 ov), 8–124 (van der Wath, 36.6 ov), 9–185 (Pollock, 45.3 ov), 10–186 (Kruger, 46.6 ov).

Bowling: Lee 10–1–22–5; McGrath 9–2–35–1; Dorey 9–1–51–1; Hopes 7–1–28–0; Hogg 10–0–32–3; Symonds 2–0–15–0

Australia substitute: GB Hogg (PA Jaques, South Africa innings, 20.0 ov); South Africa substitute: JJ van der Wath (DW Steyn, Australia innings, 18.0 ov).

AUSTRALIA V SRI LANKA (GAME FIVE)

Sydney Cricket Ground • January 22, 2006 (50-over match)

Result: Sri Lanka won by 51 runs • Points: Sri Lanka 4, Australia 0
Toss: Sri Lanka • Umpires: MR Benson (Eng) and SJ Davis (Aus)
TV Umpire: RL Parry (Aus) • Match Referee: JJ Crowe (NZ) • Player of the Match: ST Jayasuriya

Sri Lanka innings		R	M	B	4	6
J Mubarak	c Haddin b Lee	2	28	19	0	0
ST Jayasuriya	st Haddin b Hogg	114	132	96	10	4
+KC Sangakkara	c & b Symonds	78	132	95	7	0
DPMD Jayawardene	b Bracken	56	61	48	4	0
*MS Atapattu	not out	31	54	27	2	0
TM Dilshan	c & b Clarke	6	5	6	0	0
RP Arnold	run out	6	7	7	1	0
WPUJC Vaas	c Hussey b Bracken	2	7	4	0	0
Extras	(b 2, lb 8, w 2, nb 2)	14				
Total	(7 wkts, 50 ov, 216 mins)	309				

DNB: KMDN Kulasekara, PDRL Perera, M Muralitharan.

Fall: 1–24 (Mubarak, 6.2 ov), 2–187 (Jayasuriya, 31.1 ov), 3–227 (Sangakkara, 38.3 ov), 4–280 (Jayawardene, 45.3 ov), 5–289 (Dilshan, 46.6 ov), 6–297 (Arnold, 48.3 ov), 7–309 (Vaas, 49.6 ov).

Bowling: Lee 10–1–50–1; Bracken 9–1–40–2; Dorey 4–0–35–0; Hopes 6–0–65–0; Symonds 10–0–44–1; Hogg 6–0–31–1; Clarke 5–0–34–1

Australia innings		R	M	B	4	6
DR Martyn	c Kulasekara b Vaas	8	19	18	1	0
SM Katich	c Mubarak b Perera	19	59	29	3	0
*RT Ponting	c Muralitharan b Perera	13	28	24	2	0
MJ Clarke	c Muralitharan b Bandara	67	110	70	5	0
+BJ Haddin	b Muralitharan	41	50	44	6	0
MEK Hussey	run out (Vaas)	0	4	1	0	0
A Symonds	run out (Dilshan/Sangakkara)	31	39	32	2	1
JR Hopes	c Vaas b Bandara	43	58	46	3	0
B Lee	c Dilshan b Bandara	3	9	5	0	0
GB Hogg	not out	22	47	30	1	0
NW Bracken	c Atapattu b Bandara	0	2	2	0	0
Extras	(lb 5, w 5, nb 1)	11				
Total	(all out, 50 ov, 217 mins)	258				

Fall: 1–16 (Martyn, 4.5 ov), 2–36 (Ponting, 10.3 ov), 3–41 (Katich, 12.6 ov), 4–110 (Haddin, 24.5 ov), 5–111 (Hussey, 25.2 ov), 6–184 (Symonds, 35.4 ov), 7–188 (Clarke, 36.3 ov), 8–197 (Lee, 38.3 ov), 9–257 (Hopes, 49.3 ov), 10–258 (Bracken, 49.6 ov).

Bowling: Vaas 9–2–32–1; Perera 9–2–37–2; Kulasekara 4–0–22–0; Muralitharan 10–0–54–1; Bandara 10–0–58–4; Jayasuriya 8–0–50–0

Sri Lanka substitute: CM Bandara (RP Arnold, Australia innings, 0.0 ov); Australia substitute: GB Hogg (BR Dorey, Sri Lanka innings, 19.0 ov).

SOUTH AFRICA V SRI LANKA (GAME SIX)
Adelaide Oval • January 24, 2006 (50-over match)

Result: South Africa won by 9 runs • Points: South Africa 4, Sri Lanka 0
Toss: South Africa • Umpires: Aleem Dar (Pak) and DJ Harper (Aus)
TV Umpire: SJ Davis (Aus) • Match Referee: JJ Crowe (NZ) • Player of the Match: HH Dippenaar

South Africa innings		R	M	B	4	6
*GC Smith	st Sangakkara b Muralitharan	28	87	50	2	0
HH Dippenaar	not out	125	209	145	7	0
JJ van der Wath	c Arnold b Muralitharan	0	2	1	0	0
JA Rudolph	c & b Dilshan	11	26	27	0	0
HH Gibbs	b Perera	68	64	65	4	3
SM Pollock	c Atapattu b Kulasekara	8	15	8	0	0
JM Kemp	not out	6	5	4	1	0
Extras	(b 2, lb 11, w 4)	17				
Total	(5 wkts, 50 ov, 209 mins)	263				

DNB: +MV Boucher, AJ Hall, AG Prince, CK Langeveldt.

Fall: 1–72 (Smith, 18.2 ov), 2–72 (van der Wath, 18.3 ov), 3–101 (Rudolph, 25.5 ov), 4–220 (Gibbs, 45.3 ov), 5–249 (Pollock, 48.4 ov).

Bowling: Vaas 10–1–55–0; Perera 7–0–45–1; Kulasekara 9–1–35–1; Muralitharan 10–0–45–2; Dilshan 8–0–43–1; Jayasuriya 6–0–27–0

Sri Lanka innings		R	M	B	4	6
J Mubarak	c Prince b Pollock	4	17	19	0	0
ST Jayasuriya	st Boucher b Hall	37	55	30	4	2
+KC Sangakkara	c & b van der Wath	23	41	31	4	0
TM Dilshan	not out	82	162	108	3	0
*MS Atapattu	run out (Boucher)	23	48	40	0	0
DPMD Jayawardene	b van der Wath	52	72	52	4	0
RP Arnold	b Hall	11	14	11	1	0
CM Bandara	run out (Hall)	0	2	1	0	0
WPUJC Vaas	c Botha b Pollock	9	7	7	0	0
M Muralitharan	not out	0	3	3	0	0
Extras	(lb 6, w 5, nb 2)	13				
Total	(8 wkts, 50 ov, 221 mins)	254				

DNB: KMDN Kulasekara.

Fall: 1–11 (Mubarak, 4.5 ov), 2–68 (Jayasuriya, 12.6 ov), 3–68 (Sangakkara, 14.1 ov), 4–117 (Atapattu, 26.2 ov), 5–224 (Jayawardene, 44.1 ov), 6–242 (Arnold, 47.2 ov), 7–242 (Bandara, 47.3 ov), 8–253 (Vaas, 48.6 ov).

Bowling: Pollock 10–1–51–2; Langeveldt 10–0–62–0; van der Wath 10–1–37–2; Hall 10–1–38–2; Botha 9–0–53–0; Smith 1–0–7–0

South Africa substitute: J Botha (JM Kemp, Sri Lanka innings, 11.0 ov); Sri Lanka substitute: CM Bandara (PDRL Perera, Sri Lanka innings, 47.2 ov).

AUSTRALIA V SRI LANKA (GAME SEVEN)
Adelaide Oval • January 26, 2006 (50-over match)

Result: Australia won by five wickets • Points: Australia 4, Sri Lanka 0
Toss: Sri Lanka • Umpires: Aleem Dar (Pak) and SJ Davis (Aus)
TV Umpire: RL Parry (Aus) • Match Referee: JJ Crowe (NZ) • Player of the Match: A Symonds

Sri Lanka innings		R	M	B	4	6
J Mubarak	c Lee b Symonds	34	59	47	3	2
WU Tharanga	c Martyn b McGrath	31	100	66	2	0
+KC Sangakkara	b Hogg	25	46	37	1	1
DPMD Jayawardene	c Symonds b Bracken	25	58	36	0	0
*MS Atapattu	c Martyn b Bracken	32	44	48	1	0
TM Dilshan	b Hogg	1	11	9	0	0
RP Arnold	not out	27	47	28	2	0
WPUJC Vaas	c Hogg b Symonds	15	23	20	0	0
WCA Ganegama	b Symonds	7	8	8	1	0
KMDN Kulasekara	not out	2	5	4	0	0
Extras	(b 4, lb 4, w 8, nb 3)	19				
Total	(8 wkts, 50 ov, 212 mins)	218				

DNB: M Muralitharan.

Fall: 1–53 (Mubarak, 13.3 ov), 2–96 (Tharanga, 23.3 ov), 3–100 (Sangakkara, 24.5 ov), 4–155 (Atapattu, 37.5 ov), 5–161 (Jayawardene, 39.1 ov), 6–167 (Dilshan, 40.2 ov), 7–196 (Vaas, 46.5 ov), 8–207 (Ganegama, 48.5 ov).

Bowling: Lee 10–0–40–0; McGrath 8–1–26–1; Bracken 10–1–45–2; Symonds 9–1–48–3; Hogg 10–0–35–2; Hodge 3–0–16–0

Australia innings		R	M	B	4	6
*+AC Gilchrist	c Ganegama b Kulasekara	34	40	33	5	1
SM Katich	c Sangakkara b Dilshan	52	123	89	5	0
BJ Hodge	b Kulasekara	5	35	16	0	0
DR Martyn	b Muralitharan	46	93	72	1	0
A Symonds	c Tharanga b Muralitharan	32	44	33	2	0
MJ Clarke	not out	16	40	18	1	0
MEK Hussey	not out	25	36	30	2	0
Extras	(lb 2, w 7)	9				
Total	(5 wkts, 48.3 ov, 214 mins)	219				

DNB: GB Hogg, B Lee, NW Bracken, GD McGrath.

Fall: 1–47 (Gilchrist, 9.3 ov), 2–73 (Hodge, 17.1 ov), 3–115 (Katich, 28.6 ov), 4–175 (Symonds, 40.1 ov), 5–177 (Martyn, 40.3 ov).

Bowling: Vaas 8.3–0–41–0; Ganegama 6–0–41–0; Kulasekara 9–0–32–2; Muralitharan 10–0–35–2; Bandara 10–0–44–0; Dilshan 5–0–24–1

Sri Lanka substitute: CM Bandara (MS Atapattu, Australia innings, 21.0 ov); Australia substitute: SR Clark (not used).

AUSTRALIA V SRI LANKA (GAME EIGHT)

WACA Ground, Perth • January 29, 2006 (50-over match)

Result: Australia won by six wickets • Points: Australia 4, Sri Lanka 0
Toss: Sri Lanka • Umpires: MR Benson (Eng) and PD Parker (Aus)
TV Umpire: RL Parry (Aus) • Match Referee: JJ Crowe (NZ)
ODI Debut: CK Kapugedera (SL). • Player of the Match: AC Gilchrist

Sri Lanka innings		R	M	B	4	6
J Mubarak	c Hodge b Clark	15	52	34	1	0
ST Jayasuriya	c Gilchrist b Lee	0	11	7	0	0
+KC Sangakkara	run out	6	19	11	0	0
DPMD Jayawardene	c McGrath b Symonds	69	144	93	4	0
RP Arnold	c Clarke b Clark	56	107	87	1	0
TM Dilshan	run out	35	47	33	3	0
CK Kapugedera	c Hogg b Lee	22	33	25	2	0
*WPUJC Vaas	not out	6	9	7	0	0
KMDN Kulasekara	run out	0	2	1	0	0
M Muralitharan	not out	3	2	2	0	0
Extras	(lb 12, w 9)	21				
Total	(8 wkts, 50 ov, 225 mins)	233				

DNB: CRD Fernando.

Fall: 1–6 (Jayasuriya, 2.5 ov), 2–16 (Sangakkara, 7.1 ov), 3–27 (Mubarak, 10.3 ov), 4–148 (Arnold, 36.3 ov), 5–170 (Jayawardene, 40.4 ov), 6–224 (Dilshan, 47.6 ov), 7–225 (Kapugedera, 48.4 ov), 8–227 (Kulasekara, 49.1 ov).

Bowling: Lee 10–0–42–2; McGrath 10–2–35–0; Clark 10–0–40–2; Symonds 10–0–54–1; Hogg 10–0–50–0

Australia innings		R	M	B	4	6
*+AC Gilchrist	c & b Muralitharan	116	131	105	11	4
SM Katich	b Vaas	82	154	110	7	0
BJ Hodge	c Sangakkara b Fernando	2	6	5	0	0
DR Martyn	not out	13	34	20	1	0
A Symonds	c Jayawardene b Vaas	5	6	3	1	0
MJ Clarke	not out	9	10	8	1	0
Extras	(lb 1, w 4, nb 5)	10				
Total	(4 wkts, 41 ov, 176 mins)	237				

DNB: MEK Hussey, GB Hogg, B Lee, GD McGrath, SR Clark.

Fall: 1–191 (Gilchrist, 32.2 ov), 2–200 (Hodge, 33.5 ov), 3–209 (Katich, 36.3 ov), 4–221 (Symonds, 38.2 ov).

Bowling: Vaas 8–1–39–2; Fernando 9–0–52–1; Kulasekara 8–1–37–0; Ganegama 1–0–20–0; Muralitharan 10–0–53–1; Dilshan 3–0–24–0; Jayasuriya 2–0–11–0

Sri Lanka substitute: WCA Ganegama (RP Arnold, Australia innings, 11.0 ov); Australia substitute: BR Dorey (not used).

SOUTH AFRICA V SRI LANKA (GAME NINE)

WACA Ground, Perth • January 31, 2006 (50-over match)

Result: South Africa won by five wickets • Points: South Africa 4, Sri Lanka 0
Toss: Sri Lanka • Umpires: MR Benson (Eng) and PD Parker (Aus)
TV Umpire: RL Parry (Aus) • Match Referee: JJ Crowe (NZ) • Player of the Match: GC Smith

Sri Lanka innings		R	M	B	4	6
J Mubarak	b Smith	31	65	50	5	0
ST Jayasuriya	c Prince b Smith	86	96	65	9	3
+KC Sangakkara	c Kemp b Langeveldt	16	40	24	1	0
DPMD Jayawardene	lbw Smith	1	7	8	0	0
*MS Atapattu	c Rudolph b van der Wath	7	23	17	0	0
RP Arnold	c Kemp b Pollock	15	44	46	1	0
TM Dilshan	run out	37	74	42	3	0
WPUJC Vaas	run out	0	1	2	0	0
KMDN Kulasekara	c Kemp b Pollock	1	4	6	0	0
CM Bandara	run out	11	30	22	0	1
M Muralitharan	not out	1	8	6	0	0
Extras	(lb 10, w 3, nb 2)	15				
Total	(all out, 47.4 ov, 205 mins)	221				

Fall: 1–94 (Mubarak, 15.6 ov), 2–137 (Jayasuriya, 21.5 ov), 3–142 (Jayawardene, 23.5 ov), 4–144 (Sangakkara, 24.3 ov), 5–159 (Atapattu, 30.3 ov), 6–179 (Arnold, 36.4 ov), 7–179 (Vaas, 37.1 ov), 8–182 (Kulasekara, 38.4 ov), 9–216 (Bandara, 45.4 ov), 10–221 (Dilshan, 47.4 ov).

Bowling: Pollock 10–3–17–2; Langeveldt 10–0–50–1; Hall 9–0–48–0; van der Wath 8.4–0–66–1; Smith 10–0–30–3

South Africa innings		R	M	B	4	6
*GC Smith	c Sangakkara b Muralitharan	41	70	52	4	1
HH Dippenaar	c Sangakkara b Muralitharan	87	139	94	7	3
JA Rudolph	st Sangakkara b Bandara	25	62	48	0	0
HH Gibbs	b Muralitharan	4	10	8	0	0
+MV Boucher	not out	30	50	33	1	0
JM Kemp	st Sangakkara b Bandara	6	11	12	0	0
AG Prince	not out	20	27	25	3	0
Extras	(b 4, w 6, nb 1)	11				
Total	(5 wkts, 45.1 ov, 193 mins)	224				

DNB: SM Pollock, JJ van der Wath, AJ Hall, J Botha.

Fall: 1–84 (Smith, 16.4 ov), 2–164 (Rudolph, 31.6 ov), 3–164 (Dippenaar, 32.1 ov), 4–175 (Gibbs, 34.4 ov), 5–190 (Kemp, 37.6 ov).

Bowling: Vaas 9–1–39–0; Arnold 1–0–11–0; Kulasekara 5.1–0–22–0; Muralitharan 10–0–44–3; Dilshan 7–0–44–0; Bandara 10–0–47–2; Jayasuriya 3–0–13–0

Sri Lanka substitute: CM Bandara (CRD Fernando, Sri Lanka innings, 38.4 ov); South Africa substitute: J Botha (CK Langeveldt, Sri Lanka innings, 45.4 ov).

AUSTRALIA V SOUTH AFRICA (GAME 10)

Telstra Dome, Melbourne • February 3, 2006 (50-over match)

Result: Australia won by 80 runs • Points: Australia 5, South Africa 0
Toss: Australia • Umpires: Aleem Dar (Pak) and PD Parker (Aus)
TV Umpire: RL Parry (Aus) • Match Referee: JJ Crowe (NZ) • Player of the Match: MEK Hussey

Australia innings		R	M	B	4	6
+AC Gilchrist	b Hall	33	41	43	4	0
SM Katich	c Pollock b van der Wath	25	70	43	2	0
*RT Ponting	c van der Wath b Botha	53	102	63	2	1
DR Martyn	c Botha b Smith	34	55	46	2	0
A Symonds	run out	65	84	60	5	1
MJ Clarke	run out	1	3	2	0	0
MEK Hussey	b van der Wath	62	58	44	9	0
B Lee	not out	0	2	1	0	0
Extras	(b 1, lb 1, w 4, nb 2)	8				
Total	(7 wkts, 50 ov, 215 mins)	281				

DNB: BR Dorey, SR Clark, GB Hogg.

Fall: 1–45 (Gilchrist, 9.6 ov), 2–71 (Katich, 16.2 ov), 3–145 (Martyn, 30.5 ov), 4–163 (Ponting, 35.5 ov), 5–167 (Clarke, 36.5 ov), 6–276 (Hussey, 49.3 ov), 7–281 (Symonds, 49.6 ov).

Bowling: Pollock 10–2–20–0; Langeveldt 6–0–50–0; Hall 10–0–56–1; van der Wath 10–0–82–2; Smith 10–0–59–1; Botha 4–0–12–1

South Africa innings		R	M	B	4	6
*GC Smith	lbw Lee	0	2	2	0	0
HH Dippenaar	c Gilchrist b Clark	9	31	23	0	0
JA Rudolph	run out	19	57	39	1	0
HH Gibbs	b Hopes	33	52	40	5	0
J Botha	c Gilchrist b Lee	46	107	61	4	0
AG Prince	run out	24	46	39	2	0
JM Kemp	c Hopes b Lee	20	27	30	1	0
+MV Boucher	c Ponting b Lee	0	2	1	0	0
SM Pollock	c sub (DR Martyn) b Symonds	16	22	17	1	0
AJ Hall	not out	19	36	35	0	0
JJ van der Wath	not out	8	13	14	0	1
Extras	(w 6, nb 1)	7				
Total	(9 wkts, 50 ov, 209 mins)	201				

Fall: 1–0 (Smith, 0.2 ov), 2–13 (Dippenaar, 7.1 ov), 3–48 (Rudolph, 13.5 ov), 4–69 (Gibbs, 19.2 ov), 5–117 (Prince, 30.6 ov), 6–155 (Kemp, 38.1 ov), 7–156 (Boucher, 38.4 ov), 8–156 (Botha, 38.6 ov), 9–183 (Pollock, 45.1 ov).

Bowling: Lee 10–2–30–4; Clark 8–1–34–1; Dorey 10–0–48–0; Hopes 6–1–16–1; Hogg 7–0–32–0; Symonds 9–0–41–1

Australia substitute: JR Hopes (DR Martyn, South Africa innings, 12.0 ov); South Africa substitute: J Botha (CK Langeveldt, Australia innings, 25.0 ov).

AUSTRALIA V SOUTH AFRICA (GAME 11)

Sydney Cricket Ground • February 5, 2006 (50-over match)

Result: Australia won by 57 runs • Points: Australia 4, South Africa 0
Toss: Australia • Umpires: Aleem Dar (Pak) and PD Parker (Aus)
TV Umpire: RL Parry (Aus) • Match Referee: JJ Crowe (NZ) • Player of the Match: AC Gilchrist

Australia innings		R	B	4	6
+AC Gilchrist	c Boucher b Langeveldt	88	66	14	0
SM Katich	c Kemp b van der Wath	11	17	1	0
*RT Ponting	c Gibbs b Botha	72	61	8	0
A Symonds	c Hall b Smith	7	12	1	0
DR Martyn	run out	79	75	5	0
MJ Clarke	c Rudolph b Hall	27	37	0	0
MEK Hussey	not out	47	33	4	1
Extras	(lb 4, w 8, nb 1)	13			
Total	(6 wkts, 50 ov)	344			

DNB: B Lee, NW Bracken, SR Clark, GB Hogg.

Fall: 1–65 (Katich, 8.1 ov), 2–138 (Gilchrist, 17.1 ov), 3–168 (Symonds, 22.1 ov), 4–203 (Ponting, 29.3 ov), 5–263 (Clarke, 40.5 ov), 6–344 (Martyn, 49.6 ov).

Bowling: van der Wath 10–0–76–1; Zondeki 4–0–42–0; Hall 10–0–69–1; Langeveldt 6–0–49–1; Smith 10–0–52–1; Botha 10–0–52–1

South Africa innings		R	B	4	6
*GC Smith	c Gilchrist b Lee	6	8	1	0
HH Dippenaar	c Hussey b Clark	27	29	4	0
HH Gibbs	c Gilchrist b Symonds	46	54	6	0
+MV Boucher	c Hopes b Symonds	76	83	3	2
JM Kemp	c Bracken b Hogg	28	36	3	0
AG Prince	run out	25	37	0	0
JA Rudolph	not out	31	39	2	0
JJ van der Wath	not out	37	16	2	4
Extras	(lb 7, w 2, nb 2)	11			
Total	(6 wkts, 50 ov)	287			

DNB: AJ Hall, J Botha, CK Langeveldt.

Fall: 1–7 (Smith, 2.1 ov), 2–52 (Dippenaar, 10.3 ov), 3–105 (Gibbs, 19.2 ov), 4–172 (Kemp, 31.6 ov), 5–199 (Boucher, 36.3 ov), 6–236 (Prince, 44.4 ov).

Bowling: Lee 6–0–31–1; Bracken 9–0–51–0; Clark 10–0–70–1; Hopes 5–0–35–0; Symonds 10–0–42–2; Hogg 10–0–51–1

Australia substitute: JR Hopes (SM Katich, South Africa innings, 10.3 ov); South Africa substitute: CK Langeveldt (M Zondeki, Australia innings, 14.0 ov).

SOUTH AFRICA V SRI LANKA (GAME 12)

Bellerive Oval, Hobart • February 7, 2006 (50-over match)

Result: Sri Lanka won by 76 runs • Points: Sri Lanka 5, South Africa 0
Toss: Sri Lanka • Umpires: MR Benson (Eng) and DJ Harper (Aus)
TV Umpire: RL Parry (Aus) • Match Referee: JJ Crowe (NZ)
Player of the Match: CM Bandara

Sri Lanka innings		R	M	B	4	6
*MS Atapattu	c Hall b van der Wath	80	165	122	5	0
ST Jayasuriya	b Pollock	25	38	26	2	1
+KC Sangakkara	c Dippenaar b van der Wath	62	113	77	5	0
DPMD Jayawardene	lbw Hall	11	28	17	1	0
J Mubarak	c Prince b Hall	14	25	19	1	0
TM Dilshan	b Hall	30	37	24	2	1
CK Kapugedera	b Botha	3	5	6	0	0
WPUJC Vaas	c Botha b Langeveldt	5	7	5	0	0
M Muralitharan	c Botha b Langeveldt	1	6	5	0	0
CRD Fernando	not out	1	6	2	0	0
PDRL Perera	not out	1	2	1	0	0
Extras	(b 3, lb 5, w 12, nb 4)	24				
Total	(9 wkts, 50 ov, 226 mins)	257				

Fall: 1–52 (Jayasuriya, 8.5 ov), 2–175 (Sangakkara, 35.2 ov), 3–190 (Atapattu, 37.5 ov), 4–207 (Jayawardene, 41.5 ov), 5–212 (Mubarak, 43.2 ov), 6–220 (Kapugedera, 45.1 ov), 7–229 (Vaas, 46.4 ov), 8–241 (Muralitharan, 48.3 ov), 9–254 (Dilshan, 49.4 ov).

Bowling: Pollock 10–0–35–1; Steyn 3–0–32–0; Hall 10–0–50–3; Langeveldt 10–0–47–2; van der Wath 9–1–41–2; Smith 3–0–19–0; Botha 5–0–25–1

South Africa innings		R	M	B	4	6
*GC Smith	c Muralitharan b Bandara	67	124	76	5	0
HH Dippenaar	lbw Vaas	9	26	21	1	0
HH Gibbs	c & b Vaas	0	2	3	0	0
+MV Boucher	b Fernando	24	53	36	3	0
AG Prince	c & b Bandara	22	63	41	0	0
JM Kemp	lbw Bandara	0	2	1	0	0
SM Pollock	c Sangakkara b Bandara	15	30	26	0	0
AJ Hall	not out	18	38	30	0	0
JJ van der Wath	b Muralitharan	0	2	2	0	0
J Botha	c sub (CK Kapugedera) b Jayasuriya	17	21	22	1	0
CK Langeveldt	c Mubarak b Dilshan	1	2	5	0	0
Extras	(lb 3, w 4, nb 1)	8				
Total	(all out, 43.4 ov, 191 mins)	181				

Fall: 1–19 (Dippenaar, 6.2 ov), 2–19 (Gibbs, 6.5 ov), 3–77 (Boucher, 17.4 ov), 4–113 (Smith, 26.1 ov), 5–114 (Kemp, 26.4 ov), 6–137 (Prince, 32.4 ov), 7–146 (Pollock, 34.5 ov), 8–147 (van der Wath, 35.2 ov), 9–178 (Botha, 42.3 ov), 10–181 (Langeveldt, 43.4 ov).

Bowling: Vaas 7–3–17–2; Perera 6–0–40–0; Fernando 7–1–32–1; Muralitharan 8–0–28–1; Dilshan 4.4–0–23–1; Bandara 9–0–31–4; Jayasuriya 2–0–7–1

Sri Lanka substitute: CM Bandara (CK Kapugedera, South Africa innings, 20.0 ov); South Africa substitute: J Botha (DW Steyn, Sri Lanka innings, 18.0 ov).

AUSTRALIA V SRI LANKA (FIRST FINAL)
Adelaide Oval • February 10, 2006 (50-over match)

Result: Sri Lanka won by 22 runs • Toss: Sri Lanka

Umpires: Aleem Dar (Pak) and DJ Harper (Aus) • TV Umpire: RL Parry (Aus)

Match Referee: JJ Crowe (NZ) • Player of the Match: KC Sangakkara

Sri Lanka innings		R	M	B	4	6
*MS Atapattu	b Hogg	53	103	77	6	0
ST Jayasuriya	c Hogg b Clark	25	41	22	1	1
+KC Sangakkara	c & b Symonds	83	146	106	3	1
DPMD Jayawardene	c & b Clark	11	25	20	0	0
RP Arnold	c Symonds b Bracken	24	48	34	0	0
TM Dilshan	not out	26	36	20	0	2
CK Kapugedera	c Symonds b Bracken	38	21	21	2	3
WPUJC Vaas	run out	1	2	1	0	0
M Muralitharan	c Symonds b Bracken	0	2	1	0	0
KMDN Kulasekara	not out	0	2	0	0	0
Extras	(lb 4, w 7, nb 2)	13				
Total	(8 wkts, 50 ov, 222 mins)	274				

DNB: PDRL Perera.

Fall: 1–44 (Jayasuriya, 9.1 ov), 2–109 (Atapattu, 23.4 ov), 3–133 (Jayawardene, 30.1 ov), 4–200 (Arnold, 41.6 ov), 5–212 (Sangakkara, 44.1 ov), 6–270 (Kapugedera, 49.2 ov), 7–272 (Vaas, 49.4 ov), 8–272 (Muralitharan, 49.5 ov).

Bowling: Lee 10–1–48–0; Bracken 10–0–61–3; Clark 10–1–48–2; Symonds 10–0–66–1; Hogg 10–0–47–1

Australia innings		R	M	B	4	6
+AC Gilchrist	c Arnold b Kulasekara	26	46	27	2	1
SM Katich	run out	56	121	81	6	0
*RT Ponting	run out	0	4	0	0	0
DR Martyn	run out	1	15	7	0	0
A Symonds	st Sangakkara b Muralitharan	16	25	18	0	1
MJ Clarke	run out	80	127	83	4	0
MEK Hussey	run out	16	24	21	1	0
JR Hopes	c Dilshan b Muralitharan	3	8	3	0	0
GB Hogg	c Jayasuriya b Bandara	1	3	5	0	0
B Lee	b Muralitharan	19	37	34	0	0
NW Bracken	not out	13	21	16	0	0
Extras	(b 2, lb 12, w 7)	21				
Total	(all out, 49.1 ov, 218 mins)	252				

Fall: 1–51 (Gilchrist, 10.1 ov), 2–52 (Ponting, 11.1 ov), 3–64 (Martyn, 14.3 ov), 4–94 (Symonds, 19.4 ov), 5–122 (Katich, 24.6 ov), 6–156 (Hussey, 30.6 ov), 7–165 (Hopes, 33.2 ov), 8–166 (Hogg, 34.1 ov), 9–213 (Lee, 43.6 ov), 10–252 (Clarke, 49.1 ov).

Bowling: Vaas 10–0–60–0; Perera 7–0–28–0; Kulasekara 9–0–47–1; Muralitharan 10–0–40–3; Bandara 10–0–51–1; Dilshan 2–0–7–0; Jayasuriya 1.1–0–5–0

Sri Lanka substitute: CM Bandara (CK Kapugedera, Australia innings, 21.0 ov); Australia substitute: JR Hopes (SR Clark, Australia innings, 31.0 ov).

AUSTRALIA V SRI LANKA (SECOND FINAL)

Sydney Cricket Ground • February 12, 2006 (50-over match)

Result: Australia won by 167 runs • Toss: Australia
Umpires: MR Benson (Eng) and PD Parker (Aus) • TV Umpire: DJ Harper (Aus)
Match Referee: JJ Crowe (NZ) • Player of the Match: A Symonds

Australia innings		R	M	B	4	6
+AC Gilchrist	c Dilshan b Vaas	0	1	2	0	0
SM Katich	lbw Vaas	1	10	5	0	0
*RT Ponting	c Vaas b Perera	124	178	127	9	3
DR Martyn	c Jayawardene b Vaas	8	4	5	2	0
A Symonds	lbw Vaas	151	194	127	13	3
MJ Clarke	not out	54	46	28	6	0
MEK Hussey	not out	23	15	8	3	1
Extras	(lb 1, w 4, nb 2)	7				
Total	(5 wkts, 50 ov, 227 mins)	368				

DNB: GB Hogg, B Lee, SR Clark, NW Bracken.

Fall: 1–0 (Gilchrist, 0.2 ov), 2–2 (Katich, 2.1 ov), 3–10 (Martyn, 2.6 ov), 4–247 (Ponting, 40.4 ov), 5–320 (Symonds, 47.1 ov).

Bowling: Vaas 10–0–56–4; Perera 10–1–72–1; Kulasekara 5–0–41–0; Muralitharan 10–0–99–0; Dilshan 2–0–10–0; Jayasuriya 8–0–52–0; Bandara 5–0–37–0

Sri Lanka innings		R	M	B	4	6
*MS Atapattu	c Gilchrist b Clark	24	63	35	2	0
ST Jayasuriya	c Lee b Bracken	0	7	6	0	0
+KC Sangakkara	b Bracken	13	18	13	3	0
DPMD Jayawardene	b Hogg	50	67	48	8	0
RP Arnold	not out	64	102	62	6	1
TM Dilshan	c Ponting b Symonds	13	12	14	2	0
CK Kapugedera	run out	1	5	3	0	0
WPUJC Vaas	c Clarke b Hogg	0	3	6	0	0
CM Bandara	c Clark b Symonds	0	5	6	0	0
M Muralitharan	c Lewis b Bracken	27	38	24	2	2
PDRL Perera	c Ponting b Bracken	0	3	2	0	0
Extras	(lb 4, w 2, nb 3)	9				
Total	(all out, 36 ov, 166 mins)	201				

Fall: 1–4 (Jayasuriya, 1.4 ov), 2–26 (Sangakkara, 5.3 ov), 3–74 (Atapattu, 13.5 ov), 4–116 (Jayawardene, 20.1 ov), 5–139 (Dilshan, 23.6 ov), 6–145 (Kapugedera, 25.1 ov), 7–146 (Vaas, 26.2 ov), 8–147 (Bandara, 27.4 ov), 9–200 (Muralitharan, 35.2 ov), 10–201 (Perera, 35.6 ov).

Bowling: Lee 8–0–42–0; Bracken 6–0–30–4; Clark 5–0–28–1; Lewis 5–0–30–0; Symonds 5–1–32–2; Hogg 7–0–35–2

Australia substitute: ML Lewis (DR Martyn, Sri Lanka innings, 8.0 ov); Sri Lanka substitute: CM Bandara (KMDN Kulasekara, Australia innings, 24.0 ov).

AUSTRALIA V SRI LANKA (THIRD FINAL)

The Gabba, Brisbane • February 14, 2006 (50-over match)

Result: Australia won by nine wickets • Toss: Sri Lanka

Umpires: Aleem Dar (Pak) and DJ Harper (Aus) • TV Umpire: PD Parker (Aus)

Match Referee: JJ Crowe (NZ) • Player of the Match: AC Gilchrist • Player of the Series: A Symonds

Sri Lanka innings		R	B	4	6
*MS Atapattu	c Symonds b Bracken	7	16	1	0
ST Jayasuriya	c Symonds b Bracken	6	12	1	0
+KC Sangakkara	lbw Clarke	59	85	5	0
DPMD Jayawardene	c Katich b Clark	86	91	8	0
RP Arnold	c Ponting b Bracken	76	71	4	0
TM Dilshan	c Hussey b Clark	3	4	0	0
CK Kapugedera	c Symonds b Lewis	9	6	0	1
WPUJC Vaas	run out	11	12	0	0
M Muralitharan	run out	3	3	0	0
CRD Fernando	not out	1	1	0	0
Extras	(lb 2, w 2, nb 1)	5			
Total	(9 wkts, 50 ov)	266			

DNB: PDRL Perera.

Fall: 1–7 (Jayasuriya, 3.1 ov), 2–28 (Atapattu, 7.5 ov), 3–128 (Sangakkara, 28.2 ov), 4–204 (Jayawardene, 40.6 ov), 5–213 (Dilshan, 42.2 ov), 6–238 (Kapugedera, 45.2 ov), 7–259 (Arnold, 48.5 ov), 8–265 (Muralitharan, 49.5 ov), 9–266 (Vaas, 49.6 ov).

Bowling: Lee 10–0–58–0; Bracken 10–1–44–3; Lewis 10–1–52–1; Clark 10–0–45–2; Symonds 5–0–39–0; Clarke 5–0–26–1

Australia innings		R	B	4	6
+AC Gilchrist	b Muralitharan	122	91	13	4
SM Katich	not out	107	142	9	0
*RT Ponting	not out	28	41	1	0
Extras	(lb 5, w 4, nb 1)	10			
Total	(1 wkt, 45.3 ov)	267			

DNB: DR Martyn, A Symonds, MJ Clarke, MEK Hussey, B Lee,ML Lewis, SR Clark, NW Bracken.

Fall: 1–196 (Gilchrist, 32.2 ov).

Bowling: Vaas 10–0–45–0; Perera 8–1–50–0; Fernando 6–0–45–0; Dilshan 3.3–0–21–0; Muralitharan 10–1–50–1; Bandara 6–0–36–0; Jayawardene 2–0–15–0

Sri Lanka substitute: CM Bandara (CK Kapugedera, Australia innings, 24.1 ov); Australia substitute: GB Hogg (not used).

FINAL VB SERIES POINTS TABLE

Team	Played	Won	Lost	NR	Tie	BP	Points
Australia	8	6	2	–	–	3	27
Sri Lanka	8	3	5	–	–	2	14
South Africa	8	3	5	–	–	–	12

Notes

1. NR indicates 'No Result'; BP indicates 'Bonus Points'.
2. Four points were awarded for a win; two points for a tie or no result. A team that achieved a run rate of
   1.25 times that of their opponents in a game was awarded one bonus point. A team's run rate was
   calculated by dividing the runs scored in an innings by the number of overs faced.

VB SERIES AVERAGES

AUSTRALIA BATTING AND FIELDING

Name	ODIs	Inn	NO	Runs	HS	Ave	SR	100	50	Ct	St
PA Jaques	1	1	0	94	94	94.00	83.93	–	1	–	–
MEK Hussey	11	9	4	298	73	59.60	98.03	–	2	4	–
MJ Clarke	11	10	4	341	80	56.83	99.42	–	3	3	–
AC Gilchrist	9	9	0	432	122	48.00	113.09	2	1	6	–
SM Katich	10	10	1	413	107*	45.89	68.72	1	4	3	–
RT Ponting	9	9	1	345	124	43.13	86.25	1	2	5	–
A Symonds	11	10	0	389	151	38.90	103.46	1	2	10	–
DR Martyn	11	10	1	282	79	31.33	84.43	–	2	4	–
JR Hopes	7	3	0	84	43	28.00	87.50	–	–	3	–
GB Hogg	9	2	1	23	22*	23.00	65.71	–	–	3	–
B Lee	11	5	1	85	57	21.25	71.43	–	1	2	–
BJ Haddin	2	2	0	42	41	21.00	87.50	–	–	4	1
NW Bracken	8	3	2	20	13*	20.00	66.67	–	–	1	–
SR Clark	7	1	0	15	15	15.00	150.00	–	–	2	–
BJ Hodge	2	2	0	7	5	3.50	33.33	–	–	1	–
BR Dorey	3	1	0	2	2	2.00	25.00	–	–	–	–
GD McGrath	5	2	1	2	2*	2.00	28.57	–	–	1	–
ML Lewis	2	0	–	–	–	–	–	–	–	1	–

AUSTRALIA BOWLING

Name	ODIs	O	M	R	W	Ave	Best	4w	SR	Econ
NW Bracken	8	70.5	6	319	17	18.76	4–30	1	25.00	4.50
B Lee	11	101	6	439	15	29.27	5–22	2	40.40	4.35
GB Hogg	9	80	0	370	11	33.64	3–32	–	43.64	4.63
SR Clark	7	63	2	306	9	34.00	2–40	–	42.00	4.86
A Symonds	11	77	2	415	11	37.73	3–48	–	42.00	5.39
MJ Clarke	11	13	0	76	2	38.00	1–26	–	39.00	5.85
GD McGrath	5	45	6	161	4	40.25	2–35	–	67.50	3.58
ML Lewis	2	15	1	82	1	82.00	1–52	–	90.00	5.47
JR Hopes	7	41	3	223	2	111.50	1–16	–	123.00	5.44
BR Dorey	3	23	1	134	1	134.00	1–51	–	138.00	5.83
BJ Hodge	2	3	0	16	0	–	–	–	–	5.33

SRI LANKA BATTING AND FIELDING

Name	ODIs	Inn	NO	Runs	HS	Ave	SR	100	50	Ct	St
RP Arnold	10	10	4	322	76	53.67	80.70	–	3	2	–
MG Vandort	1	1	0	48	48	48.00	41.02	–	–	–	–
KC Sangakkara	11	11	0	469	88	42.64	75.77	–	5	5	4
DPMD Jayawardene	11	11	0	425	86	38.64	89.47	–	6	2	–
ST Jayasuriya	8	8	0	293	114	36.63	110.98	1	1	1	–
MS Atapattu	10	10	1	299	80	33.22	68.58	–	2	3	–
TM Dilshan	11	11	2	277	82*	30.78	87.38	–	1	6	–
J Mubarak	8	8	0	162	61	20.25	62.07	–	1	2	–
WU Tharanga	3	3	0	49	31	16.33	56.98	–	–	1	–
CK Kapugedera	5	5	0	73	38	14.60	119.67	–	–	–	–
M Muralitharan	11	7	3	35	27	8.75	79.55	–	–	4	–
WPUJC Vaas	11	11	3	70	15	8.75	75.27	–	–	3	–
WCA Ganegama	2	1	0	7	7	7.00	87.50	–	–	1	–
CM Bandara	9	3	0	11	11	3.67	37.93	–	–	1	–
KMDN Kulasekara	8	4	2	3	2*	1.50	27.27	–	–	2	–
PDRL Perera	8	2	1	1	1*	1.00	33.33	–	–	–	–
CRD Fernando	5	2	2	2	1*	–	66.67	–	–	–	–

SRI LANKA BOWLING

Name	ODIs	O	M	R	W	Ave	Best	4w	SR	Econ
J Mubarak	8	3	0	20	1	20.00	1–10	–	18.00	6.67
CM Bandara	9	68.2	0	335	14	23.93	4–31	2	29.29	4.90
M Muralitharan	11	107	3	549	16	34.31	3–40	–	40.13	5.13
WPUJC Vaas	11	99.3	10	478	11	43.45	4–56	1	54.27	4.80
KMDN Kulasekara	8	55.1	2	260	5	52.00	2–32	–	66.20	4.71
PDRL Perera	8	63	4	355	6	59.17	2–37	–	63.00	5.63
CRD Fernando	5	32	1	189	3	63.00	1–32	–	64.00	5.91
TM Dilshan	11	49.1	0	280	3	93.33	1–23	–	98.33	5.69
ST Jayasuriya	8	30.1	0	165	1	165.00	1–7	–	181.00	5.47
WCA Ganegama	2	7	0	61	0		–	–	–	8.71
DPMD Jayawardene	11	2	0	15	0		–	–	–	7.50
RP Arnold	10	1	0	11	0		–	–	–	11.00

SOUTH AFRICA BATTING AND FIELDING

Name	ODIs	Inn	NO	Runs	HS	Ave	SR	100	50	Ct	St
HH Dippenaar	8	8	1	382	125*	54.57	71.80	1	2	1	–
MV Boucher	8	7	2	260	76	52.00	87.25	–	3	6	1
JA Rudolph	5	5	1	139	53	34.75	64.35	–	1	2	–
AG Prince	8	7	1	160	29	26.67	62.99	–	–	5	–
J Botha	7	4	1	80	46	26.67	68.97	–	–	5	–
HH Gibbs	8	8	0	213	68	26.63	80.08	–	1	2	–
AJ Hall	8	4	2	42	19*	21.00	53.85	–	–	2	–
GC Smith	8	8	0	166	67	20.75	68.88	–	1	3	–
SM Pollock	7	5	0	89	46	17.80	97.80	–	–	1	–
JM Kemp	8	8	2	102	29*	17.00	76.69	–	–	5	–
JJ van der Wath	6	5	2	45	37*	15.00	115.38	–	–	2	–
CK Langeveldt	5	1	0	1	1	1.00	20.00	–	–	–	–
GJP Kruger	3	2	1	0	0*	0.00	0.00	–	–	1	–
JH Kallis	1	1	0	0	0	0.00	0.00	–	–	–	–
M Zondeki	3	0	–	–	–	–	–	–	–	1	–
DW Steyn	2	0	–	–	–	–	–	–	–	–	–

SOUTH AFRICA BOWLING

Name	ODIs	O	M	R	W	Ave	Best	4w	SR	Econ
SM Pollock	7	70	11	223	11	20.27	3–30	–	38.18	3.19
AJ Hall	8	78.1	2	397	14	28.36	4–35	1	33.50	5.08
JJ van der Wath	6	52.4	2	323	10	32.30	2–21	–	31.60	6.13
GC Smith	8	46	0	215	6	35.83	3–30	–	46.00	4.67
J Botha	7	48	0	238	5	47.60	2–49	–	57.60	4.96
CK Langeveldt	5	42	0	258	4	64.50	2–47	–	63.00	6.14
GJP Kruger	3	23	1	139	2	69.50	1–43	–	69.00	6.04
M Zondeki	3	23	2	155	2	77.50	1–49	–	69.00	6.74
DW Steyn	2	8	0	90	1	90.00	1–58	–	48.00	11.25
JH Kallis	1	6	0	23	0	–	–	–	–	3.83

VB SERIES

Debuts

Michael Vandort (game one) was the 128th Sri Lankan to play ODI cricket.

Garnett Kruger (game two) was the 82nd South African to play ODI cricket.

Brett Dorey and Phil Jaques (game four) were the 156th and 157th Australians to play ODI cricket.

Johan van der Wath (game four) was the 83rd South African to play ODI cricket.

Chamara Kapugedera (game eight) was the 129th Sri Lankan to play ODI cricket

Hundreds

Sanath Jayasuriya (114 for Sri Lanka in game five) scored his 19th ODI century, in his 347th match.

Boeta Dippenaar (125* for South Africa in game six) scored his third ODI century, in his 90th match.

Adam Gilchrist (116 for Australia in game eight) scored his 13th ODI century, in his 229th match.

Ricky Ponting (124 for Australia in the second final) scored his 19th ODI century, in his 246th match.

Andrew Symonds (151 for Australia in the second final) scored his fourth ODI century, in his 140th match.

Adam Gilchrist (122 for Australia in the third final) scored his 14th ODI century, in his 234th match.

Simon Katich (107* for Australia in the third final) scored his first ODI century, in his 33rd match.

Four wickets in an innings

Andrew Hall (4–35 for South Africa in game four) took four or more wickets in an ODI for the second time, in his 58th match.

Brett Lee (5–22 for Australia in game four) took four or more wickets in an ODI for the 13th time, in his 120th match.

Malinga Bandara (4–58 for Sri Lanka in game five) took four or more wickets in an ODI for the first time, in his fourth match.

Brett Lee (4–30 for Australia in game 10) took four or more wickets in an ODI for the 14th time, in his 124th match.

Malinga Bandara (4–31 for Sri Lanka in game 12) took four or more wickets in an ODI for the second time, in his eighth match.

Chaminda Vaas (4–56 for Sri Lanka in the second final) took four or more wickets in an ODI for the 13th time, in his 274th match.

Nathan Bracken (4–30 in the second final) took four or more wickets in an ODI for the second time, in his 30th match.

SOUTH AFRICA V AUSTRALIA

New Wanderers Stadium, Johannesburg • February 24, 2006 (20-over match)
Result: South Africa won by 2 runs • Toss: South Africa
Umpires: M Erasmus (SA) and KH Hurter (SA) • TV Umpire: BG Jerling (SA)
Match Referee: BC Broad (Eng) • Player of the Match: GC Smith

South Africa innings		R	M	B	4	6
*GC Smith	not out	89	89	58	11	1
LL Bosman	b Lewis	23	26	18	3	1
HH Gibbs	lbw Lewis	56	46	34	4	4
SM Pollock	c Clark b Watson	2	4	3	0	0
JJ van der Wath	c Clarke b Bracken	14	10	7	1	1
+AB de Villiers	not out	0	3	0	0	0
Extras	(b 3, lb 10, w 4)	17				
Total	(4 wkts, 20 ov, 89 mins)	201				

DNB: ND McKenzie, AJ Hall, RJ Peterson, R Telemachus, M Ntini.

Fall: 1–48 (Bosman, 5.4 ov), 2–159 (Gibbs, 16.1 ov), 3–170 (Pollock, 17.1 ov), 4–191 (van der Wath, 19.3 ov).

Bowling: Lee 3–0–15–0; Bracken 4–0–44–1; Lewis 4–0–31–2; Clark 4–0–25–0; Watson 3–0–35–1; Hogg 2–0–38–0

Australia innings		R	M	B	4	6
+AC Gilchrist	lbw Hall	1	6	2	0	0
SM Katich	c Smith b Telemachus	39	42	22	6	1
*RT Ponting	lbw Hall	6	11	8	1	0
DR Martyn	c de Villiers b van der Wath	17	11	9	3	0
MJ Clarke	st de Villiers b Peterson	37	33	24	0	3
SR Watson	b Peterson	4	9	6	0	0
GB Hogg	c Smith b Hall	41	35	25	2	3
B Lee	not out	43	36	21	4	2
NW Bracken	not out	3	8	3	0	0
Extras	(lb 3, w 5)	8				
Total	(7 wkts, 20 ov, 95 mins)	199				

DNB: ML Lewis, SR Clark.

Fall: 1–16 (Gilchrist, 1.1 ov), 2–34 (Ponting, 3.3 ov), 3–53 (Martyn, 5.3 ov), 4–78 (Katich, 8.2 ov), 5–93 (Watson, 10.5 ov), 6–124 (Clarke, 12.6 ov), 7–181 (Hogg, 18.4 ov).

Bowling: Ntini 3–0–44–0; Hall 4–0–22–3; Telemachus 4–0–40–1; van der Wath 4–0–40–1; Smith 2–0–21–0; Peterson 3–0–29–2

SOUTH AFRICA V AUSTRALIA, FIRST ODI

SuperSport Park, Centurion • February 26, 2006 (50-over match*)

Result: South Africa won by six wickets (Duckworth/Lewis Method) • Toss: Australia
Umpires: BG Jerling (SA) and JW Lloyds (Eng) • TV Umpire: KH Hurter (SA)
Match Referee: BC Broad (Eng) • Player of the Match: GC Smith

Australia innings		R	M	B	4	6
*+AC Gilchrist	c Nel b Ntini	14	35	19	3	0
SM Katich	b Ntini	2	14	16	0	0
DR Martyn	lbw Pollock	1	4	3	0	0
MJ Clarke	c de Villiers b Pollock	53	109	82	6	0
MEK Hussey	c Dippenaar b Pollock	56	102	73	4	1
SR Watson	b Hall	22	64	38	1	0
GB Hogg	run out	13	21	16	1	0
B Lee	not out	38	41	28	1	2
NW Bracken	run out	16	8	7	0	2
MG Johnson	not out	0	3	0	0	0
Extras	(b 1, lb 5, w 8)	14				
Total	(8 wkts, 47 ov, 202 mins)	229				

DNB: ML Lewis.

Fall: 1–4 (Katich, 3.4 ov), 2–5 (Martyn, 4.1 ov), 3–25 (Gilchrist, 7.5 ov), 4–125 (Clarke, 31.2 ov), 5–132 (Hussey, 33.4 ov), 6–157 (Hogg, 38.6 ov), 7–208 (Watson, 45.2 ov), 8–227 (Bracken, 46.4 ov).

Bowling: Pollock 10–1–23–3; Ntini 9–3–42–2; Nel 10–0–62–0; Hall 8–0–36–1; Peterson 7–0–36–0; Smith 3–0–24–0

South Africa innings		R	M	B	4	6
*GC Smith	not out	119	172	124	12	1
HH Dippenaar	b Bracken	10	26	16	2	0
HH Gibbs	run out	0	5	1	0	0
AB de Villiers	c Gilchrist b Hogg	43	51	30	7	1
+MV Boucher	run out	4	29	17	0	0
JM Kemp	not out	24	59	38	2	0
Extras	(lb 1, w 5, nb 1)	7				
Total	(4 wkts, 37.3 ov, 172 mins)	207				

DNB: SM Pollock, RJ Peterson, AJ Hall, M Ntini, A Nel.

Fall: 1–24 (Dippenaar, 5.5 ov), 2–28 (Gibbs, 6.5 ov), 3–111 (de Villiers, 17.1 ov), 4–134 (Boucher, 22.6 ov).

Bowling: Lee 10–0–59–0; Bracken 8–1–27–1; Johnson 3–0–28–0; Lewis 3–0–25–0; Hogg 8–1–30–1; Clarke 3.3–0–19–0; Watson 2–0–18–0

Australia substitute: SR Clark (not used); South Africa substitute: AG Prince (not used).

* Match initially reduced to 47 overs per side because of rain. After a further delay, South Africa were set 204 to win in 41 overs.

SOUTH AFRICA V AUSTRALIA, SECOND ODI

Newlands, Cape Town • March 3, 2006 (50-over match)

Result: South Africa won by 196 runs • Toss: South Africa
Umpires: KH Hurter (SA) and JW Lloyds (Eng) • TV Umpire: BG Jerling (SA)
Match Referee: BC Broad (Eng) • Player of the Match: M Ntini

South Africa innings		R	M	B	4	6
*GC Smith	b Clark	24	36	29	3	0
HH Dippenaar	b Watson	31	60	43	6	0
HH Gibbs	c & b Hogg	66	105	71	8	0
AB de Villiers	b Watson	18	33	23	3	0
+MV Boucher	lbw Hogg	42	67	59	1	3
JM Kemp	not out	51	73	41	1	4
SM Pollock	c Clarke b Lee	38	36	27	3	2
RJ Peterson	c Martyn b Clark	4	6	3	1	0
AJ Hall	not out	4	14	4	0	0
Extras	(b 1, lb 5, w 5)	11				
Total	(7 wkts, 50 ov, 215 mins)	289				

DNB: A Nel, M Ntini.

Fall: 1–45 (Smith, 8.3 ov), 2–57 (Dippenaar, 13.5 ov), 3–95 (de Villiers, 21.3 ov), 4–175 (Gibbs, 34.4 ov), 5–192 (Boucher, 38.5 ov), 6–254 (Pollock, 46.3 ov), 7–262 (Peterson, 47.3 ov).

Bowling: Lee 8–0–51–1; Bracken 10–0–45–0; Clark 10–2–69–2; Watson 10–0–46–2; Hogg 9–1–48–2; Clarke 3–0–24–0

Australia innings		R	M	B	4	6
*+AC Gilchrist	c Boucher b Ntini	1	5	7	0	0
SM Katich	c de Villiers b Nel	16	79	48	3	0
PA Jaques	c Kemp b Ntini	0	3	4	0	0
DR Martyn	c Dippenaar b Ntini	4	13	9	0	0
MJ Clarke	c Boucher b Ntini	1	17	15	0	0
MEK Hussey	c Kemp b Nel	22	69	48	2	1
SR Watson	c Boucher b Ntini	27	70	39	3	0
GB Hogg	c Pollock b Peterson	6	12	8	1	0
B Lee	c Dippenaar b Nel	1	4	4	0	0
NW Bracken	c Boucher b Ntini	10	18	20	1	0
SR Clark	not out	2	7	5	0	0
Extras	(lb 1, w 2)	3				
Total	(all out, 34.3 ov, 150 mins)	93				

Fall: 1–1 (Gilchrist, 1.1 ov), 2–1 (Jaques, 1.5 ov), 3–5 (Martyn, 5.2 ov), 4–7 (Clarke, 9.3 ov), 5–33 (Katich, 18.2 ov), 6–57 (Hussey, 24.5 ov), 7–70 (Hogg, 27.2 ov), 8–71 (Lee, 28.1 ov), 9–86 (Bracken, 32.6 ov), 10–93 (Watson, 34.3 ov).

Bowling: Pollock 7–4–9–0; Ntini 9.3–4–22–6; Nel 8–2–30–3; Hall 5–1–15–0; Peterson 5–1–16–1

South Africa substitute: AG Prince (not used); Australia substitute: MG Johnson (not used).

SOUTH AFRICA V AUSTRALIA, THIRD ODI
St George's Park, Port Elizabeth • March 5, 2006 (50-over match)

Result: Australia won by 24 runs
Toss: South Africa • Umpires: BG Jerling (SA) and JW Lloyds (Eng)
TV Umpire: KH Hurter (SA) • Match Referee: BC Broad (Eng) • Player of the Match: B Lee

Australia innings		R	M	B	4	6
+AC Gilchrist	c Boucher b Pollock	25	35	33	3	0
SM Katich	run out	49	103	80	4	1
*RT Ponting	c Peterson b Pollock	62	123	82	5	0
DR Martyn	c Telemachus b Ntini	51	79	69	1	1
MJ Clarke	run out	25	42	23	0	1
MEK Hussey	c Gibbs b Hall	22	16	10	1	2
B Lee	not out	6	7	3	1	0
SR Watson	not out	4	5	3	0	0
Extras	(lb 1, w 6, nb 3)	10				
Total	(6 wkts, 50 ov, 208 mins)	254				

DNB: GB Hogg, NW Bracken, SR Clark.

Fall: 1–36 (Gilchrist, 8.5 ov), 2–99 (Katich, 24.3 ov), 3–173 (Ponting, 40.5 ov), 4–214 (Martyn, 45.5 ov), 5–243 (Hussey, 48.6 ov), 6–244 (Clarke, 49.0 ov).

Bowling: Pollock 10–1–45–2; Ntini 9–0–56–1; Telemachus 8–0–59–0; Hall 9–1–39–1; Peterson 10–1–39–0; Smith 4–0–15–0

South Africa innings		R	M	B	4	6
*GC Smith	c Gilchrist b Lee	10	13	12	2	0
HH Dippenaar	lbw Watson	16	75	35	2	0
HH Gibbs	run out	16	38	30	2	0
AB de Villiers	c Hogg b Clarke	68	134	92	6	1
+MV Boucher	c Gilchrist b Lee	5	18	11	1	0
JM Kemp	c Bracken b Clark	0	5	5	0	0
SM Pollock	b Watson	69	80	74	7	1
AJ Hall	c Gilchrist b Lee	5	12	6	0	0
RJ Peterson	c Gilchrist b Lee	3	9	5	0	0
R Telemachus	lbw Bracken	29	17	13	0	3
M Ntini	not out	1	14	4	0	0
Extras	(lb 3, w 2, nb 3)	8				
Total	(all out, 47.2 ov, 211 mins)	230				

Fall: 1–15 (Smith, 2.2 ov), 2–43 (Gibbs, 10.5 ov), 3–60 (Dippenaar, 15.1 ov), 4–68 (Boucher, 19.3 ov), 5–69 (Kemp, 20.3 ov), 6–188 (Pollock, 42.2 ov), 7–192 (de Villiers, 43.1 ov), 8–197 (Hall, 44.2 ov), 9–199 (Peterson, 44.5 ov), 10–230 (Telemachus, 47.2 ov).

Bowling: Lee 9–2–48–4; Bracken 8.2–1–40–1; Clark 9–0–32–1; Watson 10–0–49–2; Clarke 9–0–46–1; Hogg 2–0–12–0

Australia substitute: MG Johnson (not used); South Africa substitute: AG Prince (not used).

SOUTH AFRICA V AUSTRALIA, FOURTH ODI
Kingsmead, Durban • March 10, 2006 (50-over match)

Result: Australia won by one wicket • Toss: South Africa
Umpires: KH Hurter (SA) and JW Lloyds (Eng) • TV Umpire: BG Jerling (SA)
Match Referee: BC Broad (Eng) • Player of the Match: HH Dippenaar

South Africa innings		R	M	B	4	6
*GC Smith	c Gilchrist b Bracken	1	6	3	0	0
HH Dippenaar	c Clarke b Lee	101	220	145	9	0
HH Gibbs	c Gilchrist b Bracken	1	18	10	0	0
AB de Villiers	lbw Lewis	38	63	45	4	2
JH Kallis	c Hussey b Symonds	21	34	27	1	1
+MV Boucher	c Gilchrist b Lewis	19	42	27	1	0
JM Kemp	lbw Clark	1	10	9	0	0
SM Pollock	not out	53	45	33	8	0
R Telemachus	run out	0	1	1	0	0
AJ Hall	run out	0	1	0	0	0
Extras	(b 1, lb 3, w 2, pen 5)	11				
Total	(9 wkts, 50 ov, 224 mins)	246				

DNB: M Ntini.

Fall: 1–1 (Smith, 1.2 ov), 2–9 (Gibbs, 5.4 ov), 3–81 (de Villiers, 19.5 ov), 4–118 (Kallis, 28.2 ov), 5–170 (Boucher, 37.4 ov), 6–173 (Kemp, 40.2 ov), 7–245 (Dippenaar, 49.3 ov), 8–246 (Telemachus, 49.5 ov), 9–246 (Hall, 49.6 ov).

Bowling: Lee 10–0–55–1; Bracken 10–2–36–2; Clark 10–1–49–1; Lewis 10–0–38–2; Symonds 6–0–31–1; Hussey 2–0–15–0; Clarke 2–0–13–0

Australia innings		R	M	B	4	6
+AC Gilchrist	c de Villiers b Kallis	45	93	44	8	1
SM Katich	c Kallis b Hall	46	75	68	5	0
*RT Ponting	c Boucher b Telemachus	7	26	17	1	0
DR Martyn	c Boucher b Telemachus	1	5	7	0	0
A Symonds	b Telemachus	76	96	71	9	2
MJ Clarke	c Boucher b Kallis	7	42	23	1	0
MEK Hussey	run out	19	34	24	2	0
B Lee	c Boucher b Ntini	6	18	8	1	0
NW Bracken	b Hall	7	23	14	1	0
SR Clark	not out	16	28	18	2	0
ML Lewis	not out	4	7	4	0	0
Extras	(b 1, lb 2, w 7, nb 3)	13				
Total	(9 wkts, 49.1 ov, 228 mins)	247				

Fall: 1–87 (Katich, 17.5 ov), 2–99 (Gilchrist, 21.1 ov), 3–100 (Martyn, 22.2 ov), 4–101 (Ponting, 22.4 ov), 5–140 (Clarke, 31.3 ov), 6–192 (Hussey, 39.5 ov), 7–218 (Symonds, 42.6 ov), 8–218 (Lee, 43.1 ov), 9–241 (Bracken, 47.6 ov).

Bowling: Pollock 5–2–22–0; Ntini 10–1–50–1; Hall 9.1–1–52–2; Telemachus 10–1–34–3; Kallis 9–0–46–2; Kemp 4–0–17–0; Smith 2–0–23–0

South Africa substitute: RJ Peterson (not used); Australia substitute: GB Hogg (not used).

SOUTH AFRICA V AUSTRALIA, FIFTH ODI

New Wanderers Stadium, Johannesburg • March 12, 2006 (50-over match)

Result: South Africa won by one wicket • Toss: Australia

Umpires: Aleem Dar (Pak) and BG Jerling (SA) • TV Umpire: KH Hurter (SA)

Match Referee: BC Broad (Eng) • Joint Player of the Match: HH Gibbs and RT Ponting

Player of the Series: SM Pollock (SA)

Australia innings		R	M	B	4	6
+AC Gilchrist	c Hall b Telemachus	55	68	44	9	0
SM Katich	c Telemachus b Ntini	79	138	90	9	1
*RT Ponting	c Dippenaar b Telemachus	164	154	105	13	9
MEK Hussey	c Ntini b Hall	81	75	51	9	3
A Symonds	not out	27	23	13	3	1
B Lee	not out	9	13	7	0	0
Extras	(lb 4, w 5, nb 10)	19				
Total	(4 wkts, 50 ov, 234 mins)	434				

DNB: DR Martyn, MJ Clarke, NW Bracken, SR Clark, ML Lewis.

Fall: 1–97 (Gilchrist, 15.2 ov), 2–216 (Katich, 30.3 ov), 3–374 (Hussey, 46.1 ov), 4–407 (Ponting, 47.4 ov).

Bowling: Ntini 9–0–80–1; Hall 10–0–80–1; van der Wath 10–0–76–0; Telemachus 10–1–87–2; Smith 4–0–29–0; Kallis 6–0–70–0; Kemp 1–0–8–0

South Africa innings		R	M	B	4	6
*GC Smith	c Hussey b Clarke	90	100	55	13	2
HH Dippenaar	b Bracken	1	6	7	0	0
HH Gibbs	c Lee b Symonds	175	142	111	21	7
AB de Villiers	c Clarke b Bracken	14	43	20	1	0
JH Kallis	c & b Symonds	20	22	21	1	0
+MV Boucher	not out	50	79	43	4	0
JM Kemp	c Martyn b Bracken	13	20	17	0	0
JJ van der Wath	c Ponting b Bracken	35	20	18	1	3
R Telemachus	c Hussey b Bracken	12	10	6	2	0
AJ Hall	c Clarke b Lee	7	9	4	1	0
M Ntini	not out	1	3	1	0	0
Extras	(b 4, lb 8, w 4, nb 4)	20				
Total	(9 wkts, 49.5 ov, 228 mins)	438				

Fall: 1–3 (Dippenaar, 1.2 ov), 2–190 (Smith, 22.1 ov), 3–284 (de Villiers, 30.5 ov), 4–299 (Gibbs, 31.5 ov), 5–327 (Kallis, 37.4 ov), 6–355 (Kemp, 42.1 ov), 7–399 (van der Wath, 46.3 ov), 8–423 (Telemachus, 48.2 ov), 9–433 (Hall, 49.3 ov).

Bowling: Lee 7.5–0–68–1; Bracken 10–0–67–5; Clark 6–0–54–0; Lewis 10–0–113–0; Symonds 9–0–75–2; Clarke 7–0–49–1

Australia substitute: GB Hogg (not used); South Africa substitute: RJ Peterson (not used).

AUSTRALIA IN SOUTH AFRICA ONE-DAY INTERNATIONAL AVERAGES

AUSTRALIA BATTING AND FIELDING

Name	ODIs	Inn	NO	Runs	HS	Ave	SR	100	50	Ct	St
A Symonds	2	2	1	103	76	103.00	122.62	–	1	1	–
RT Ponting	3	3	0	233	164	77.67	114.22	1	1	1	–
MEK Hussey	5	5	0	200	81	40.00	97.09	–	2	3	–
SM Katich	5	5	0	192	79	38.40	63.58	–	1	–	–
B Lee	5	5	3	60	38*	30.00	120.00	–	–	1	–
AC Gilchrist	5	5	0	140	55	28.00	95.24	–	1	8	–
SR Watson	3	3	1	53	27	26.50	66.25	–	–	–	–
MJ Clarke	5	4	0	86	53	21.50	60.14	–	1	4	–
DR Martyn	5	4	0	57	51	14.25	64.78	–	1	2	–
NW Bracken	5	3	0	33	16	11.00	80.49	–	–	1	–
GB Hogg	3	2	0	19	13	9.50	79.17	–	–	2	–
PA Jaques	1	1	0	0	0	0.00	0.00	–	–	–	–
SR Clark	4	2	2	18	16*	–	78.26	–	–	–	–
ML Lewis	3	1	1	4	4*	–	100.00	–	–	–	–
MG Johnson	1	1	1	0	0*	–	–	–	–	–	–

AUSTRALIA BOWLING

Name	ODIs	O	M	R	W	Ave	Best	4w	SR	Econ
NW Bracken	5	46.2	4	215	9	23.89	5–67	1	30.89	4.64
SR Watson	3	22	0	113	4	28.25	2–46	–	33.00	5.14
GB Hogg	3	19	2	90	3	30.00	2–48	–	38.00	4.74
A Symonds	2	15	0	106	3	35.33	2–75	–	30.00	7.07
B Lee	5	44.5	2	281	7	40.14	4–48	1	38.43	6.27
SR Clark	4	35	3	204	4	51.00	2–69	–	52.50	5.83
MJ Clarke	5	24.3	0	151	2	75.50	1–46	–	73.50	6.16
ML Lewis	3	23	0	176	2	88.00	2–38	–	69.00	7.65
MG Johnson	1	3	0	28	0	–	–	–	–	9.33
MEK Hussey	5	2	0	15	0	–	–	–	–	7.50

SOUTH AFRICA BATTING AND FIELDING

Name	ODIs	Inn	NO	Runs	HS	Ave	SR	100	50	Ct	St
SM Pollock	4	3	1	160	69	80.00	119.40	–	2	1	–
GC Smith	5	5	1	244	119*	61.00	109.42	1	1	–	–
HH Gibbs	5	5	0	258	175	51.60	115.70	1	1	1	–
AB de Villiers	5	5	0	181	68	36.20	86.19	–	1	3	–
JJ van der Wath	1	1	0	35	35	35.00	194.44	–	–	–	–
HH Dippenaar	5	5	0	159	101	31.80	64.63	1	–	4	–
MV Boucher	5	5	1	120	50*	30.00	76.43	–	1	9	–
JM Kemp	5	5	2	89	51*	29.67	80.90	–	1	2	–
JH Kallis	2	2	0	41	21	20.50	85.42	–	–	1	–
R Telemachus	3	3	0	41	29	13.67	205.00	–	–	2	–
AJ Hall	5	4	1	16	7	5.33	114.29	–	–	1	–
RJ Peterson	3	2	0	7	4	3.50	87.50	–	–	1	–
M Ntini	5	2	2	2	1*	–	40.00	–	–	1	–
A Nel	2	0	–	–	–	–	–	–	–	1	–

SOUTH AFRICA BOWLING

Name	ODIs	O	M	R	W	Ave	Best	4w	SR	Econ
SM Pollock	4	32	8	99	5	19.80	3–23	–	38.40	3.09
M Ntini	5	46.3	8	250	11	22.73	6–22	1	25.36	5.38
A Nel	2	18	2	92	3	30.67	3–30	–	36.00	5.11
R Telemachus	3	28	2	180	5	36.00	3–34	–	33.60	6.43
AJ Hall	5	41.1	3	222	5	44.40	2–52	–	49.40	5.39
JH Kallis	2	15	0	116	2	58.00	2–46	–	45.00	7.73
RJ Peterson	3	22	2	91	1	91.00	1–16	–	132.00	4.14
GC Smith	5	13	0	91	0	–	–	–	–	7.00
JJ van der Wath	1	10	0	76	0	–	–	–	–	7.60
JM Kemp	5	5	0	25	0	–	–	–	–	5.00

SOUTH AFRICA V AUSTRALIA ONE-DAY INTERNATIONALS

Hundreds

Graeme Smith (119* for South Africa in game one) scored his sixth ODI century, in his 87th match.

Boeta Dippenaar (101 for South Africa in game four) scored his fourth ODI century, in his 98th match.

Ricky Ponting (164 for Australia in game five) scored his 20th ODI century, in his 250th match.

Herschelle Gibbs (175 for South Africa in game five) scored his 16th ODI century, in his 185th match.

Four wickets in an innings

Makhaya Ntini (6–22 for South Africa in game two) took four or more wickets in an ODI for the ninth time, in his 126th match.

Brett Lee (4–48 for Australia in game three) took four or more wickets in an ODI for the 15th time, in his 131st match.

Nathan Bracken (5–67 in game five) took four or more wickets in an ODI for the third time, in his 36th match.

Game Five

South Africa's winning score of 9–438 established a new record innings total in an ODI, beating the score hit by Australia (4–434) when Ricky Ponting's team batted first in this same match. A total of more than 390 had previously been achieved three times in a ODI innings: 5–398 by Sri Lanka against Kenya at Kandy in 1995–96; 5–397 (in 44 overs) by New Zealand against Zimbabwe at Bulawayo in August 2005; and 4–391 by England against Bangladesh at Trent Bridge in June 2005. (In July 2006, Sri Lanka set a new mark by smashing 9–443 in an ODI against Holland at Amstelveen.)

South Africa's successful run-chase was the highest in ODIs, beating the 8–332 New Zealand had achieved against Australia in the third Chappell–Hadlee Trophy game at Christchurch the previous December. The 872 runs scored in this game five is easily the highest aggregate for an ODI, destroying the previous record of 693 made by India and Pakistan at Karachi in 2004.

SOUTH AFRICA V AUSTRALIA, FIRST TEST

Newlands, Cape Town • March 16–18, 2006 (five-day match)

Result: Australia won by seven wickets • Toss: South Africa
Umpires: Aleem Dar (Pak) and BR Doctrove (WI) • TV Umpire: KH Hurter (SA)
Match Referee: BC Broad (Eng) • Player of the Match: SR Clark

Stumps Scores
Day 1: South Africa 205, Australia 1–63 (Hayden 22, Ponting 20; 23 ov)
Day 2: Australia 308, South Africa 3–70 (Kallis 31, Prince 14; 20 ov)

South Africa first innings		R	M	B	4	6
*GC Smith	c Gilchrist b Clark	19	75	58	2	0
AB de Villiers	b Kasprowicz	8	39	29	1	0
HH Gibbs	b Clark	18	71	46	3	0
JH Kallis	c Hayden b Clark	6	10	12	0	0
AG Prince	c Hayden b Lee	17	105	67	1	0
JA Rudolph	c Gilchrist b Kasprowicz	10	15	14	2	0
+MV Boucher	c Gilchrist b Clark	16	29	23	3	0
AJ Hall	c Hayden b Lee	24	73	55	3	0
N Boje	lbw Clark	31	60	48	5	0
A Nel	lbw Lee	18	50	31	1	1
M Ntini	not out	17	25	15	1	1
Extras	(lb 6, nb 15)	21				
Total	(all out, 63.5 ov, 280 mins)	205				

Fall: 1–24 (de Villiers, 9.3 ov), 2–42 (Smith, 17.3 ov), 3–48 (Kallis, 19.5 ov), 4–61 (Gibbs, 25.3 ov), 5–76 (Rudolph, 28.2 ov), 6–104 (Boucher, 35.2 ov), 7–124 (Prince, 43.3 ov), 8–148 (Hall, 51.6 ov), 9–173 (Boje, 57.5 ov), 10–205 (Nel, 63.5 ov).

Bowling: Lee 14.5–2–37–3; Kasprowicz 13–0–44–2; Symonds 10–2–22–0; Clark 17–3–55–5; Warne 9–0–41–0

Australia innings		R	M	B	4	6
JL Langer	lbw Nel	16	40	31	3	0
ML Hayden	c Rudolph b Ntini	94	236	173	14	1
*RT Ponting	c Hall b Kallis	74	178	112	8	1
DR Martyn	c Boucher b Kallis	22	81	59	3	0
MEK Hussey	c Boucher b Hall	6	32	23	0	0
A Symonds	c Nel b Boje	55	82	47	3	4
+AC Gilchrist	c Smith b Kallis	12	20	19	1	0
SK Warne	c de Villiers b Boje	7	30	18	1	0
B Lee	c Gibbs b Ntini	0	6	3	0	0
MS Kasprowicz	not out	6	28	20	0	0
SR Clark	c Gibbs b Nel	8	23	19	0	0
Extras	(lb 7, w 1)	8				
Total	(all out, 87.2 ov, 389 mins)	308				

Fall: 1–21 (Langer, 9.5 ov), 2–175 (Ponting, 50.3 ov), 3–192 (Hayden, 54.5 ov), 4–214 (Hussey, 61.6 ov), 5–236 (Martyn, 70.2 ov), 6–272 (Gilchrist, 74.6 ov), 7–294 (Symonds, 79.3 ov), 8–294 (Lee, 80.3 ov), 9–296 (Warne, 81.2 ov), 10–308 (Clark, 87.2 ov).

Bowling: Ntini 21–2–76–2; Nel 22.2–6–45–2; Hall 16–2–66–1; Boje 16–4–63–2; Kallis 12–0–51–3

South Africa second innings		R	M	B	4	6
AB de Villiers	c Gilchrist b Lee	7	18	12	1	0
*GC Smith	lbw Warne	16	63	34	2	0
HH Gibbs	b Lee	0	2	2	0	0
JH Kallis	c Gilchrist b Clark	36	86	50	5	0
AG Prince	c Gilchrist b Clark	27	89	64	3	0
JA Rudolph	b Warne	41	146	112	6	0
+MV Boucher	c Langer b Kasprowicz	2	33	21	0	0
AJ Hall	not out	34	105	69	4	0
N Boje	c & b Clark	14	18	15	3	0
A Nel	b Clark	4	4	5	1	0
M Ntini	c Kasprowicz b Warne	6	13	6	1	0
Extras	(w 3, nb 7)	10				
Total	(all out, 63.5 ov, 291 mins)	197				

Fall: 1–20 (de Villiers, 4.2 ov), 2–20 (Gibbs, 4.4 ov), 3–37 (Smith, 11.3 ov), 4–75 (Kallis, 21.3 ov), 5–92 (Prince, 31.4 ov), 6–108 (Boucher, 38.5 ov), 7–158 (Rudolph, 55.6 ov), 8–179 (Boje, 60.1 ov), 9–183 (Nel, 60.6 ov), 10–197 (Ntini, 63.5 ov).

Bowling: Lee 17–5–47–2; Kasprowicz 12–0–39–1; Clark 16–7–34–4; Warne 18.5–1–77–3

Australia second innings (target: 95 runs)		R	M	B	4	6
JL Langer	b Ntini	34	91	56	4	0
ML Hayden	c Gibbs b Ntini	32	87	70	4	0
*RT Ponting	lbw Ntini	1	13	4	0	0
DR Martyn	not out	9	30	13	0	0
MEK Hussey	not out	14	23	20	1	0
Extras	(lb 5)	5				
Total	(3 wkts, 27.1 ov, 125 mins)	95				

Fall: 1–71 (Hayden, 20.3 ov), 2–71 (Langer, 20.6 ov), 3–76 (Ponting, 22.1 ov).

Bowling: Nel 7–1–25–0; Ntini 10–3–28–3; Hall 5–1–16–0; Boje 5.1–1–21–0

NINE WICKETS ON DEBUT

Stuart Clark's match analysis of 9–88 in this game was the third best achieved by an Australian on his Test debut, behind only Bob Massie's 16–137 at Lord's in 1972 and Clarrie Grimmett's 11–82 in the fifth Ashes Test of 1924–25. Four other Australians have taken nine wickets on debut: William Cooper, 9–200 v England in 1881–82; Jack Ferris, 9–103 v England in 1886–87; Jack Saunders, 9–162 v England in 1901–02; Terry Alderman, 9–130 v England in 1981.

Clark became the 12th Australian to take five wickets in a Test innings at the first opportunity. Only Massie (8–84), Charlie Turner (6–15), Rodney Hogg (6–74), Peter Taylor (6–78), Grimmett (5–45), Brett Lee (5–47) and Bob McLeod (5–53) have returned better figures on debut than Clark's 5–55.

SOUTH AFRICA V AUSTRALIA, SECOND TEST

Kingsmead, Durban • March 24–28, 2006 (five-day match)

Result: Australia won by 112 runs • Toss: Australia

Umpires: SA Bucknor (WI) and BR Doctrove (WI) • TV Umpire: BG Jerling (SA)

Match Referee: BC Broad (Eng) • Player of the Match: SK Warne

Stumps Scores

Day 1: Australia 5–228 (Hussey 10, Symonds 4; 88 ov)

Day 2: Australia 369, South Africa 2–140 (de Villiers 48, Kallis 72; 39.2 ov)

Day 3: South Africa 267, Australia 1–125 (Hayden 36, Ponting 48; 36 ov)

Day 4: Australia 4–307 dec, South Africa 0–29 (de Villiers 17, Smith 10; 7.1 ov)

Australia first innings		R	M	B	4	6
JL Langer	c Boucher b Kallis	35	167	125	5	0
ML Hayden	c de Villiers b Ntini	0	5	2	0	0
*RT Ponting	c Gibbs b Boje	103	320	225	11	0
DR Martyn	c Kallis b Ntini	57	171	134	10	0
MEK Hussey	lbw Kallis	75	228	155	10	1
B Lee	c Boucher b Ntini	0	11	7	0	0
A Symonds	lbw Nel	13	83	53	1	0
+AC Gilchrist	c Boucher b Nel	2	11	10	0	0
SK Warne	c de Villiers b Pollock	36	56	31	6	1
MS Kasprowicz	c de Villiers b Nel	7	15	13	0	0
SR Clark	not out	13	34	15	2	0
Extras	(b 9, lb 10, w 2, nb 7)	28				
Total	(all out, 127.1 ov, 555 mins)	369				

Fall: 1–0 (Hayden, 1.2 ov), 2–97 (Langer, 39.1 ov), 3–198 (Ponting, 79.3 ov), 4–218 (Martyn, 82.2 ov), 5–219 (Lee, 84.3 ov), 6–253 (Symonds, 102.1 ov), 7–259 (Gilchrist, 104.5 ov), 8–315 (Warne, 117.1 ov), 9–327 (Kasprowicz, 120.1 ov), 10–369 (Hussey, 127.1 ov).

Bowling: Pollock 32–11–73–1; Ntini 24–4–81–3; Nel 31–8–83–3; Kallis 21.1–8–52–2; Boje 19–1–61–1

South Africa first innings		R	M	B	4	6
*GC Smith	c Langer b Lee	0	1	1	0	0
AB de Villiers	c Hayden b Clark	50	175	137	4	0
HH Gibbs	b Kasprowicz	9	15	14	2	0
JH Kallis	c & b Clark	114	344	223	17	0
AG Prince	c Symonds b Warne	33	86	61	4	0
JA Rudolph	c Hussey b Warne	13	43	41	2	0
+MV Boucher	b Lee	19	74	43	3	0
SM Pollock	c Gilchrist b Lee	1	6	4	0	0
N Boje	not out	6	24	14	1	0
A Nel	c Hayden b Lee	5	9	7	1	0
M Ntini	c Ponting b Lee	0	2	1	0	0
Extras	(lb 3, nb 14)	17				
Total	(all out, 88.4 ov, 394 mins)	267				

Fall: 1–0 (Smith, 0.1 ov), 2–10 (Gibbs, 3.5 ov), 3–144 (de Villiers, 41.3 ov), 4–200 (Prince, 59.6 ov), 5–226 (Rudolph, 71.1 ov), 6–255 (Kallis, 83.1 ov), 7–256 (Pollock, 84.2 ov), 8–257 (Boucher, 86.4 ov), 9–267 (Nel, 88.3 ov), 10–267 (Ntini, 88.4 ov).

Bowling: Lee 19.4–5–69–5; Kasprowicz 14–0–60–1; Warne 25–2–80–2; Symonds 11–3–16–0; Hussey 1–0–2–0; Clark 18–4–37–2

Australia second innings		**R**	**M**	**B**	**4**	**6**
JL Langer	c Pollock b Boje	37	73	53	6	0
ML Hayden	c Boucher b Ntini	102	309	217	12	0
*RT Ponting	c Boje b Pollock	116	273	187	12	2
DR Martyn	not out	15	51	37	2	0
+AC Gilchrist	c Nel b Boje	24	13	9	5	0
Extras	(lb 5, w 1, nb 7)	13			
Total	(4 wkts dec, 82.4 ov, 361 mins)	307			

Fall: 1–49 (Langer, 16.2 ov), 2–250 (Hayden, 71.5 ov), 3–278 (Ponting, 80.1 ov), 4–307 (Gilchrist, 82.4 ov).

Bowling: Pollock 19–4–55–1; Ntini 15–2–62–1; Boje 26.4–4–87–2; Nel 14–3–58–0; Kallis 8–0–40–0

South Africa second innings (target: 410 runs)		**R**	**M**	**B**	**4**	**6**
AB de Villiers	st Gilchrist b Warne	46	117	80	7	0
*GC Smith	c Langer b Warne	40	133	75	5	0
HH Gibbs	c Warne b Clark	17	55	44	2	0
JH Kallis	lbw Warne	7	32	32	1	0
AG Prince	c Hussey b Clark	7	49	37	1	0
JA Rudolph	c Langer b Warne	36	81	52	7	0
+MV Boucher	not out	51	221	156	9	0
SM Pollock	b Lee	4	15	14	1	0
N Boje	c sub (MJ Clarke) b Kasprowicz	48	82	64	9	0
A Nel	c Hayden b Warne	14	68	46	3	0
M Ntini	lbw Warne	0	14	13	0	0
Extras	(b 5, lb 8, nb 14)	27			
Total	(all out, 99.5 ov, 438 mins)	297			

Fall: 1–91 (de Villiers, 24.4 ov), 2–98 (Smith, 28.1 ov), 3–122 (Kallis, 36.5 ov), 4–122 (Gibbs, 37.5 ov), 5–146 (Prince, 47.6 ov), 6–170 (Rudolph, 56.1 ov), 7–181 (Pollock, 59.4 ov), 8–253 (Boje, 79.2 ov), 9–292 (Nel, 95.4 ov), 10–297 (Ntini, 99.5 ov).

Bowling: Lee 22–6–65–1; Clark 21–6–46–2; Symonds 8–0–32–0; Warne 35.5–9–86–6; Kasprowicz 12–2–51–1; Hussey 1–0–4–0

HUNDREDS IN BOTH INNINGS AND 200 TEST WICKETS

By scoring 143 not out in Australia's second innings of his 100th Test, Ricky Ponting had become the 10th batsman, fourth Australian (after Allan Border, Greg Chappell and Matthew Hayden) and first captain to score a century in each innings of a Test twice. Now, he became the second batsman, after India's Sunil Gavaskar, to score a hundred in both innings of a Test three times, the first captain to do so and the first to do so in a single season.

When he bowled Mark Boucher in the first innings of this second Test, Brett Lee became the 12th Australian to take 200 Test wickets. This exclusive club is made up of Shane Warne (685 wickets as at September 6, 2006), Glenn McGrath (542), Dennis Lillee (355), Craig McDermott (291), Jason Gillespie (259), Richie Benaud (248), Graham McKenzie (246), Ray Lindwall (228), Clarrie Grimmett (216), Merv Hughes (212), Lee (211) and Jeff Thomson (200).

SOUTH AFRICA V AUSTRALIA. THIRD TEST

New Wanderers Stadium, Johannesburg • March 31–April 4, 2006 (five-day match)

Result: Australia won by two wickets • Toss: South Africa

Umpires: SA Bucknor (WI) and AL Hill (NZ) • TV Umpire: KH Hurter (SA)

Match Referee: BC Broad (Eng) • Player of the Match: B Lee • Player of the Series: SR Clark

Stumps Scores

Day 1: South Africa 6–238 (Prince 79, Pollock 4; 79 ov)
Day 2: South Africa 303, Australia 7–246 (Lee 42, Kasprowicz 0; 58.2 ov)
Day 3: Australia 270, South Africa 8–250 (Boucher 55, Nel 18; 69 ov)
Day 4: South Africa 258, Australia 6–248 (Martyn 93, Lee 5; 78.3 ov)

South Africa first innings		R	M	B	4	6
AB de Villiers	c Martyn b Clark	12	60	45	1	0
HH Gibbs	b Kasprowicz	16	76	44	2	0
HH Dippenaar	c Gilchrist b Clark	32	101	69	7	0
*JH Kallis	b Lee	37	123	92	6	0
AG Prince	c Langer b Lee	93	248	170	11	0
JA Rudolph	c Hayden b Warne	25	63	44	4	0
+MV Boucher	lbw Symonds	24	73	53	2	0
SM Pollock	c Ponting b Clark	8	25	17	2	0
N Boje	c Langer b Kasprowicz	43	71	46	9	0
A Nel	c Martyn b Lee	0	17	8	0	0
M Ntini	not out	0	7	5	0	0
Extras	(lb 4, nb 9)	13				
Total	(all out, 97.2 ov, 434 mins)	303				

Fall: 1–26 (de Villiers, 13.3 ov), 2–38 (Gibbs, 16.4 ov), 3–97 (Dippenaar, 36.3 ov), 4–106 (Kallis, 44.5 ov), 5–161 (Rudolph, 60.1 ov), 6–233 (Boucher, 77.3 ov), 7–251 (Pollock, 83.1 ov), 8–285 (Prince, 92.6 ov), 9–303 (Nel, 96.1 ov), 10–303 (Boje, 97.2 ov).

Bowling: Lee 24–8–5-3; Clark 28–8–81–3; Kasprowicz 24.2–4–86–2; Warne 13–2–49–1; Symonds 8–2–26–1

Australia innings		R	M	B	4	6
JL Langer	retired hurt	0	3	1	0	0
ML Hayden	c Gibbs b Ntini	3	15	7	0	0
*RT Ponting	c de Villiers b Ntini	34	62	40	5	1
DR Martyn	c Nel b Ntini	21	34	23	2	1
MEK Hussey	lbw Boje	73	202	153	11	0
A Symonds	lbw Ntini	4	13	11	0	0
+AC Gilchrist	c Rudolph b Nel	12	37	24	3	0
SK Warne	c Pollock b Ntini	36	61	33	7	0
B Lee	c Boje b Ntini	64	106	68	6	2
MS Kasprowicz	c Gibbs b Pollock	2	28	17	0	0
SR Clark	not out	0	5	0	0	0
Extras	(b 5, lb 14, w 2)	21				
Total	(all out, 62.5 ov, 286 mins)	270				

Fall: 1–12 (Hayden, 2.1 ov), 2–68 (Martyn, 10.2 ov), 3–73 (Ponting, 14.1 ov), 4–89 (Symonds, 16.6 ov), 5–106 (Gilchrist, 24.6 ov), 6–174 (Warne, 38.6 ov), 7–242 (Hussey, 55.3 ov), 8–260 (Kasprowicz, 61.6 ov), 9–270 (Lee, 62.5 ov).

Bowling: Ntini 18.5–2–100–6; Nel 15–2–42–1; Pollock 15–2–56–1; Kallis 10–2–43–0; Boje 4–1–10–1

South Africa second innings		R	M	B	4	6
AB de Villiers	b Clark	4	17	15	0	0
HH Gibbs	c Martyn b Warne	53	125	87	6	1
HH Dippenaar	c Hayden b Clark	20	40	21	4	0
*JH Kallis	lbw Clark	27	125	82	4	0
AG Prince	c Symonds b Warne	9	42	30	1	0
SM Pollock	c Gilchrist b Lee	44	77	47	6	0
JA Rudolph	c Gilchrist b Clark	0	9	3	0	0
+MV Boucher	c Gilchrist b Lee	63	138	92	9	0
N Boje	c Symonds b Warne	4	17	14	1	0
A Nel	not out	18	72	41	3	0
M Ntini	b Lee	0	3	2	0	0
Extras	(b 6, lb 4, w 1, nb 5)	16				
Total	(all out, 71.3 ov, 334 mins)	258				

Fall: 1–9 (de Villiers, 3.4 ov), 2–55 (Dippenaar, 11.3 ov), 3–100 (Gibbs, 28.1 ov), 4–120 (Prince, 36.6 ov), 5–130 (Kallis, 39.5 ov), 6–140 (Rudolph, 41.5 ov), 7–186 (Pollock, 53.2 ov), 8–194 (Boje, 56.5 ov), 9–258 (Boucher, 71.1 ov), 10–258 (Ntini, 71.3 ov).

Bowling: Lee 18.3–3–57–3; Clark 18–4–64–4; Kasprowicz 2–0–12–0; Symonds 5–0–18–0; Ponting 2–1–7–0; Warne 26–5–90–3

Australia second innings (target: 292 runs)		R	M	B	4	6
ML Hayden	c de Villiers b Ntini	0	9	7	0	0
MEK Hussey	lbw Boje	89	263	197	12	0
*RT Ponting	c Boucher b Kallis	20	51	32	1	1
DR Martyn	lbw Pollock	101	286	208	13	0
A Symonds	c Boucher b Kallis	29	21	26	4	1
+AC Gilchrist	c Boucher b Ntini	0	5	1	0	0
SK Warne	c Boucher b Ntini	3	11	8	0	0
B Lee	not out	24	86	46	4	0
SR Clark	c Boucher b Ntini	10	22	13	2	0
MS Kasprowicz	not out	7	17	13	1	0
Extras	(b 1, lb 9, nb 1)	11				
Total	(8 wkts, 91.4 ov, 388 mins)	294				

Fall: 1–0 (Hayden, 2.1 ov), 2–33 (Ponting, 13.2 ov), 3–198 (Hussey, 66.1 ov), 4–228 (Symonds, 70.6 ov), 5–229 (Gilchrist, 71.2 ov), 6–237 (Warne, 73.3 ov), 7–258 (Martyn, 83.6 ov), 8–275 (Clark, 88.5 ov).

Bowling: Ntini 26–4–78–4; Nel 2–1–4–0; Pollock 25.4–3–81–1; Kallis 18–6–44–2; Boje 19–5–65–1; de Villiers 1–0–12–0

CLEAN SWEEPS

Australia's 3–0 sweep of a three-Test series was the 16th instance of an Australian team sweeping a series of three or more matches, but only the fourth instance of this occurring in a series played outside Australia. The previous times this had happened overseas were in New Zealand in early 2000 (3–0), against Pakistan in Sri Lanka and Sharjah in 2002 (3–0), and in Sri Lanka in early 2004 (3–0).

South Africa had previously been swept in a series involving three or more matches on four occasions: twice by England (3–0 in 1895–96, 3–0 in 1912) and twice by Australia (5–0 in 1931–32, 3–0 in 2001–02). Only the sweep of 1895–96 occurred in South Africa.

AUSTRALIA IN SOUTH AFRICA TEST AVERAGES

AUSTRALIA BATTING AND FIELDING

Name	Tests	Inn	NO	Runs	HS	Ave	SR	100	50	Ct	St
MEK Hussey	3	5	1	257	89	64.25	46.90	–	3	2	–
RT Ponting	3	6	0	348	116	58.00	58.00	2	1	2	–
DR Martyn	3	6	2	225	101	56.25	47.47	1	1	3	–
ML Hayden	3	6	0	231	102	38.50	48.52	1	1	8	–
JL Langer	3	5	1	122	37	30.50	45.86	–	–	6	–
B Lee	3	4	1	88	64	29.33	70.97	–	1	–	–
A Symonds	3	4	0	101	55	25.25	73.72	–	1	3	–
SK Warne	3	4	0	82	36	20.50	91.11	–	–	1	–
SR Clark	3	4	2	31	13*	15.50	65.96	–	–	2	–
MS Kasprowicz	3	4	2	22	7*	11.00	34.92	–	–	1	–
AC Gilchrist	3	5	0	50	24	10.00	79.37	–	–	11	1

AUSTRALIA BOWLING

Name	Tests	O	M	R	W	Ave	Best	5w	10w	SR	Econ
SR Clark	3	118	32	317	20	15.85	5–55	1	–	35.40	2.69
B Lee	3	116	29	332	17	19.53	5–69	1	–	40.94	2.86
SK Warne	3	127.4	19	423	15	28.20	6–86	1	–	51.07	3.31
MS Kasprowicz	3	77.2	6	292	7	41.71	2–44	–	–	66.29	3.78
A Symonds	3	42	7	114	1	114.00	1–26	–	–	252.00	2.71
MEK Hussey	3	2	0	6	0	–	–	–	–	–	3.00
RT Ponting	3	2	1	7	0	–	–	–	–	–	3.50

SOUTH AFRICA BATTING AND FIELDING

Name	Tests	Inn	NO	Runs	HS	Ave	SR	100	50	Ct	St
AJ Hall	1	2	1	58	34*	58.00	46.78	–	–	1	–
JH Kallis	3	6	0	227	114	37.83	46.23	1	–	1	–
MV Boucher	3	6	1	175	63	35.00	45.10	–	2	11	–
AG Prince	3	6	0	186	93	31.00	43.36	–	1	–	–
N Boje	3	6	1	146	48	29.20	72.64	–	–	2	–
HH Dippenaar	1	2	0	52	32	26.00	57.78	–	–	–	–
AB de Villiers	3	6	0	127	50	21.17	39.94	–	1	6	–
JA Rudolph	3	6	0	125	41	20.83	46.99	–	–	2	–
HH Gibbs	3	6	0	113	53	18.83	47.68	–	1	6	–
GC Smith	2	4	0	75	40	18.75	44.64	–	–	1	–
SM Pollock	2	4	0	57	44	14.25	69.51	–	–	2	–
A Nel	3	6	1	59	18*	11.80	42.75	–	–	3	–
M Ntini	3	6	2	23	17*	5.75	54.76	–	–	–	–

SOUTH AFRICA BOWLING

Name	Tests	O	M	R	W	Ave	Best	5w	10w	SR	Econ
M Ntini	3	114.5	17	425	19	22.37	6–100	1	1	36.26	3.70
JH Kallis	3	69.1	16	230	7	32.86	3–51	–	–	59.29	3.33
A Nel	3	91.2	21	257	6	42.83	3–83	–	–	91.33	2.81
N Boje	3	89.5	16	307	7	43.86	2–63	–	–	77.00	3.42
SM Pollock	2	91.4	20	265	4	66.25	1–55	–	–	137.50	2.89
AJ Hall	1	21	3	82	1	82.00	1–66	–	–	126.00	3.90
AB de Villiers	3	1	0	12	0	–	–	–	–	–	12.00

SOUTH AFRICA V AUSTRALIA TEST SERIES

Debuts

Stuart Clark (first Test) was the 396th Australian to play Test cricket.

Hundreds

Ricky Ponting (103 and 116 for Australia in the second Test) scored his 29th and 30th Test centuries, in his 102nd match.

Jacques Kallis (114 for South Africa in the second Test) scored his 24th Test century, in his 98th match.

Matthew Hayden (102 for Australia in the second Test) scored his 26th Test century, in his 81st match.

Damien Martyn (101 for Australia in the third Test) scored his 13 Test century, in his 64th match.

Five wickets in an innings

Brett Lee (5–69 for Australia in the second Test) took five or more wickets in a Test innings for the seventh time, in his 51st match.

Shane Warne (6–86 for Australia in the second Test) took five or more wickets in a Test innings for the 35th time, in his 137th match.

Makhaya Ntini (6–100 for South Africa in the third Test) took five or more wickets in a Test innings for the 11th time, in his 64th match.

10 wickets in a Test

Makhaya Ntini (10–178 for South Africa in the third Test) took 10 or more wickets in a Test for the third time, in his 64th match.

BANGLADESH V AUSTRALIA, FIRST TEST

Narayanganj Osmani Stadium, Fatullah • April 9–13, 2006 (five-day match)

Result: Australia won by three wickets • Toss: Bangladesh

Umpires: Aleem Dar (Pak) and Nadeem Ghauri (Pak) • TV Umpire: AFM Akhtaruddin (Ban)

Match Referee: JJ Crowe (NZ) • Player of the Match: AC Gilchrist

Stumps Scores

Day 1: Bangladesh 5–355 (Rajin Saleh 35, Khaled Mashud 2; 88 ov)
Day 2: Bangladesh 427, Australia 6–145 (Gilchrist 51, Lee 13; 52 ov)
Day 3: Australia 269, Bangladesh 5–124 (Rajin Saleh 29, Khaled Mashud 0; 41 ov)
Day 4: Bangladesh 148, Australia 4–212 (Ponting 72, Gilchrist 6; 74 ov)

Bangladesh first innings		R	M	B	4	6
Javed Omar	lbw Gillespie	27	52	40	6	0
Shahriar Nafees	b MacGill	138	274	189	19	0
*Habibul Bashar	c Lee b MacGill	76	187	113	11	0
Rajin Saleh	c sub (A Symonds) b MacGill	67	284	203	6	0
Mohammad Ashraful	lbw Gillespie	29	28	28	4	0
Aftab Ahmed	c Hayden b MacGill	29	73	54	3	0
+Khaled Mashud	st Gilchrist b MacGill	17	105	63	0	0
Mohammad Rafique	b MacGill	6	37	25	0	0
Mashrafe Mortaza	lbw MacGill	6	18	23	0	0
Shahadat Hossain	not out	3	23	9	0	0
Enamul Haque	c Hayden b MacGill	0	1	5	0	0
Extras	(lb 16, w 2, nb 11)	29				
Total	(all out, 123.3 ov)	427				

Fall: 1–51 (Javed Omar, 10.5 ov), 2–238 (Habibul Bashar, 50.4 ov), 3–265 (Shahriar Nafees, 60.2 ov), 4–295 (Mohammad Ashraful, 66.3 ov), 5–351 (Aftab Ahmed, 85.2 ov), 6–398 (Khaled Mashud, 107.5 ov), 7–416 (Mohammad Rafique, 117.2 ov), 8–417 (Rajin Saleh, 117.6 ov), 9–424 (Mashrafe Mortaza, 121.6 ov), 10–427 (Enamul Haque, 123.3 ov).

Bowling: Lee 19–5–68–0; Clark 25–4–69–0; Gillespie 23–7–47–2; Warne 20–1–112–0; MacGill 33.3–2–108–8; Clarke 3–0–7–0

Australia innings		R	M	B	4	6
ML Hayden	lbw Mashrafe Mortaza	6	11	12	0	0
MEK Hussey	b Mohammad Rafique	23	110	65	2	0
*RT Ponting	lbw Shahadat Hossain	21	40	32	3	0
DR Martyn	b Mohammad Rafique	4	17	11	1	0
MJ Clarke	b Enamul Haque	19	70	50	2	0
+AC Gilchrist	c Shahadat b M. Rafique	144	294	212	15	6
SK Warne	c Khaled b Enamul Haque	6	21	29	0	0
B Lee	lbw Mashrafe Mortaza	15	75	50	2	0
JN Gillespie	b Mohammad Rafique	26	113	88	1	0
SR Clark	lbw Mohammad Rafique	0	39	20	0	0
SCG MacGill	not out	0	12	5	0	0
Extras	(lb 4, nb 1)	5				
Total	(all out, 95.2 ov)	269				

Fall: 1–6 (Hayden, 2.2 ov), 2–43 (Ponting, 11.3 ov), 3–50 (Martyn, 14.4 ov), 4–61 (Hussey, 24.2 ov), 5–79 (Clarke, 31.2 ov), 6–93 (Warne, 37.6 ov), 7–156 (Lee, 56.3 ov), 8–229 (Gillespie, 83.2 ov), 9–268 (Clark, 93.3 ov), 10–269 (Gilchrist, 95.2 ov).

Bowling: Mashrafe Mortaza 22–3–56–2; Shahadat Hossain 14–2–48–1; Mohammad Rafique 32.2–9–62–5; Enamul Haque 25–4–83–2; Mohammad Ashraful 1–0–11–0; Rajin Saleh 1–0–5–0

Bangladesh second innings		R	M	B	4	6
Javed Omar	c Gilchrist b Gillespie	18	60	21	2	0
Shahriar Nafees	b Lee	33	49	38	7	0
*Habibul Bashar	run out	7	31	17	1	0
Rajin Saleh	c Hayden b Gillespie	33	166	118	2	0
Mohammad Ashraful	lbw Clark	4	21	14	0	0
Aftab Ahmed	lbw MacGill	17	73	56	2	0
+Khaled Mashud	b Gillespie	0	18	11	0	0
Mohammad Rafique	lbw Warne	14	21	18	3	0
Mashrafe Mortaza	b Warne	0	1	1	0	0
Shahadat Hossain	not out	1	12	8	0	0
Enamul Haque jnr	lbw Warne	0	3	3	0	0
Extras	(b 10, lb 7, nb 4)	21				
Total	(all out, 50 ov)	148				

Fall: 1–48 (Shahriar Nafees, 8.6 ov), 2–58 (Javed Omar, 11.1 ov), 3–66 (Habibul Bashar, 14.2 ov), 4–77 (Mohammad Ashraful, 18.6 ov), 5–124 (Aftab Ahmed, 38.2 ov), 6–128 (Khaled Mashud, 42.1 ov), 7–147 (Mohammad Rafique, 47.2 ov), 8–147 (Mashrafe Mortaza, 47.3 ov), 9–147 (Rajin Saleh, 48.4 ov), 10–148 (Enamul Haque, 49.6 ov).

Bowling: Lee 8–0–47–1–(2nb); Gillespie 11–4–18–3–(1nb); MacGill 13–4–30–1; Clark 4–2–8–1–(1nb); Warne 13–4–28–3; Clarke 1–1–0–0

Australia second innings (target: 307 runs)		R	M	B	4	6
ML Hayden	run out	72	273	152	8	1
MEK Hussey	b Enamul Haque	37	107	79	4	0
*RT Ponting	not out	118	367	253	13	0
DR Martyn	b Mohammad Rafique	7	30	19	0	0
MJ Clarke	c Khaled b M. Rafique	9	21	17	2	0
+AC Gilchrist	b Mohammad Rafique	12	27	18	1	0
SK Warne	lbw Mohammad Rafique	5	14	14	0	0
B Lee	c Khaled b Mashrafe Mortaza	29	79	74	3	1
JN Gillespie	not out	4	29	18	1	0
Extras	(b 4, lb 7, w 1, nb 2)	14				
Total	(7 wkts, 107 ov)	307				

Fall: 1–64 (Hussey, 25.1 ov), 2–173 (Hayden, 58.5 ov), 3–183 (Martyn, 65.5 ov), 4–205 (Clarke, 71.4 ov), 5–225 (Gilchrist, 77.5 ov), 6–231 (Warne, 81.2 ov), 7–277 (Lee, 99.6 ov).

Bowling: Mashrafe Mortaza 22–7–51–1; Shahadat Hossain 20–5–67–0; Mohammad Rafique 38–6–98–4; Enamul Haque 27–5–80–1

MOST RUNS BY A WICKETKEEPER AND EIGHT WICKETS IN A TEST INNINGS

During his first-innings century, Adam Gilchrist scored his 5000th Test-match run, becoming the first wicketkeeper to pass this landmark. (England's Alec Stewart did score 8463 runs during his career, but only 4540 of those runs came in Tests when he was England's designated keeper.) Gilchrist has been Australia's keeper in all of his 85 Tests to the end of the 2005–06 season, which is in itself a record — no other Australian has played so many Tests from his debut without missing at least one match.

Stuart MacGill's 8–108 in the first innings of this Test was the 16th instance of an Australian bowler taking eight or more wickets in a Test innings, and the first time eight wickets in an innings had been achieved by an Australian bowler in a Test played outside of Australia or England.

BANGLADESH V AUSTRALIA, SECOND TEST

Chittagong Divisional Stadium • April 16–20, 2006 (five-day match)

Result: Australia won by an innings and 80 runs • Toss: Bangladesh
Umpires: Aleem Dar (Pak) and IL Howell (SA) • TV Umpire: Mahbubur Rahman (Ban)
Match Referee: JJ Crowe (NZ) • Player of the Match: JN Gillespie • Player of the Series: JN Gillespie

Stumps Scores

Day 1: Bangladesh 197, Australia 1–76 (Jaques 38, Gillespie 5, 24 ov)
Day 2: Australia 2–151 (Gillespie 28, Ponting 19, 46.4 ov)
Day 3: Australia 3–364 (Gillespie 102, Hussey 93; 111 ov)
Day 4: Australia 4–581 dec, Bangladesh 4–195 (Shahriar Nafees 75, Aftab Ahmed 1, 54 ov)

Bangladesh first innings		R	M	B	4	6
Javed Omar	lbw Gillespie	2	40	22	0	0
Shahriar Nafees	c Lee b Gillespie	0	7	3	0	0
*Habibul Bashar	c Jaques b Gillespie	9	8	8	2	0
Rajin Saleh	b MacGill	71	181	126	9	0
Mohammad Ashraful	c Hayden b Warne	6	32	16	0	0
Aftab Ahmed	c Gilchrist b Warne	18	85	40	2	1
+Khaled Mashud	not out	34	126	102	2	0
Mohammad Rafique	c Hayden b MacGill	19	15	14	3	1
Mashrafe Mortaza	c Gilchrist b Cullen	4	13	9	1	0
Abdur Razzak	c Lee b MacGill	15	36	25	2	0
Shahadat Hossain	c Gillespie b Warne	0	11	9	0	0
Extras	(lb 10, w 3, nb 6)	19				
Total	(all out, 61.2 ov, 278 mins)	197				

Fall: 1–0 (Shahriar Nafees, 1.3 ov), 2–11 (Habibul Bashar, 3.3 ov), 3–17 (Javed Omar, 7.2 ov), 4–41 (Mohammad Ashraful, 13.5 ov), 5–102 (Aftab Ahmed, 31.1 ov), 6–130 (Rajin Saleh, 40.3 ov), 7–152 (Mohammad Rafique, 44.5 ov), 8–157 (Mashrafe Mortaza, 47.5 ov), 9–193 (Abdur Razzak, 58.5 ov), 10–197 (Shahadat Hossain, 61.2 ov).

Bowling: Lee 9–2–36–0; Gillespie 5–2–11–3; Warne 18.2–3–47–3; MacGill 22–4–68–3; Cullen 7–0–25–1

Australia innings		R	M	B	4	6
ML Hayden	c sub b Mohammad Rafique	29	83	56	5	0
PA Jaques	c Shahriar b M. Rafique	66	163	98	8	1
JN Gillespie	not out	201	574	425	26	2
*RT Ponting	run out	52	128	94	4	1
MEK Hussey	c Shahadat b Aftab Ahmed	182	309	203	21	1
MJ Clarke	not out	23	55	42	1	0
Extras	(b 10, lb 10, w 5, nb 3)	28				
Total	(4 wkts dec, 152.3 ov, 647 ms)	581				

DNB: SK Warne, B Lee, +AC Gilchrist, DJ Cullen, SCG MacGill.

Fall: 1–67 (Hayden, 17.2 ov), 2–120 (Jaques, 35.5 ov), 3–210 (Ponting, 67.2 ov), 4–530 (Hussey, 138.5 ov).

Bowling: Mashrafe Mortaza 26–3–114–0; Shahadat Hossain 33–3–143–0; Mohammad Rafique 48.3–11–145–2; Abdur Razzak 30–5–99–0; Rajin Saleh 8–0–32–0; Aftab Ahmed 7–1–28–1

Bangladesh second innings

Bangladesh second innings		R	M	B	4	6
Javed Omar	lbw Lee	19	22	19	3	0
Shahriar Nafees	c Gilchrist b Warne	79	264	180	9	0
*Habibul Bashar	c Hayden b Warne	49	117	78	8	0
Rajin Saleh	c Ponting b Warne	5	18	15	0	0
Mohammad Ashraful	b Warne	29	53	42	5	0
Aftab Ahmed	c Gilchrist b MacGill	18	79	44	3	0
+Khaled Mashud	lbw MacGill	11	44	32	2	0
Mohammad Rafique	c Warne b MacGill	65	57	53	2	6
Mashrafe Mortaza	c Gillespie b Warne	1	4	4	0	0
Abdur Razzak	c Ponting b MacGill	0	4	1	0	0
Shahadat Hossain	not out	3	36	19	0	0
Extras	(b 7, lb 11, w 2, nb 5)	25				
Total	(all out, 80.2 ov, 353 mins)	304				

Fall: 1–25 (Javed Omar, 4.4 ov), 2–127 (Habibul Bashar, 31.2 ov), 3–137 (Rajin Saleh, 35.6 ov), 4–187 (Mohammad Ashraful, 49.6 ov), 5–201 (Shahriar Nafees, 59.2 ov), 6–229 (Aftab Ahmed, 66.1 ov), 7–230 (Khaled Mashud, 68.3 ov), 8–233 (Mashrafe Mortaza, 69.4 ov), 9–235 (Abdur Razzak, 70.2 ov), 10–304 (Mohammad Rafique, 80.2 ov).

Bowling: Lee 11–3–35–1; Gillespie 4–0–14–0; Warne 36–4–113–5; MacGill 22.2–3–95–4; Cullen 7–0–29–0

FASTEST TO 1000 TEST RUNS

During his long partnership with Jason Gillespie (see pages 264–65 for some statistics on Gillespie's double century), Mike Hussey scored his 1000th run in Test cricket. He did so during his 11th Test and 19th Test innings. The table of fastest Australians to 1000 Test runs — based on number of innings — looks this way (statistics are as at the completion of the innings in which the 1000th run was scored):

Rank	Batsman	Tests	Inn	NO	HS	Avge	100s	50s
1.	Don Bradman	7	13	1	254	99.67	5	2
2.	Neil Harvey	10	14	4	178	103.30	6	2
3.	Sid Barnes	11	17	1	234	63.13	3	4
4=.	Herbert Collins	12	18	1	203	63.65	4	4
4=.	Doug Walters	11	18	3	155	66.73	2	7
4=.	Mark Taylor	10	18	1	219	64.00	3	5
7.	Arthur Morris	12	19	3	155	64.00	5	4
7=.	Mike Hussey	11	19	4	182	75.93	4	4
9=.	Jack Fingleton	12	20	1	136	54.05	5	3
9=.	Norm O'Neill	14	20	5	181	70.47	4	3
9=.	Brian Booth	11	20	3	169	62.41	4	5

Hussey reached 1000 runs in 167 days, from the first day of his first Test to the third day of this Test. The previous quickest Australian to score 1000 runs in terms of time was Michael Slater, who took 292 days from his debut in the first Ashes Test of 1993 to reach four figures. The only other Australian batsmen to score their first 1000 Test runs in less than one year are Mark Taylor and Allan Border.

AUSTRALIA IN BANGLADESH TEST AVERAGES

AUSTRALIA BATTING AND FIELDING

Name	Tests	Inn	NO	Runs	HS	Ave	SR	100	50	Ct	St
JN Gillespie	2	3	2	231	201*	231.00	43.50	1	–	2	–
RT Ponting	2	3	1	191	118*	95.50	50.40	1	1	2	–
MEK Hussey	2	3	0	242	182	80.67	69.74	1	–	–	–
AC Gilchrist	2	2	0	156	144	78.00	67.83	1	–	5	1
PA Jaques	1	1	0	66	66	66.00	67.35	–	1	1	–
ML Hayden	2	3	0	107	72	35.67	48.64	–	1	6	–
MJ Clarke	2	3	1	51	23*	25.50	46.79	–	–	–	–
B Lee	2	2	0	44	29	22.00	35.48	–	–	3	–
SK Warne	2	2	0	11	6	5.50	25.58	–	–	1	–
DR Martyn	1	2	0	11	7	5.50	36.67	–	–	–	–
SR Clark	1	1	0	0	0	0.00	0.00	–	–	–	–
SCG MacGill	2	1	1	0	0*	–	0.00	–	–	–	–
DJ Cullen	1	0	–	–	–	–	–	–	–	–	–

AUSTRALIA BOWLING

Name	Tests	O	M	R	W	Ave	Best	5w	10w	SR	Econ
JN Gillespie	2	43	13	90	8	11.25	3–11	–	–	32.25	2.09
SCG MacGill	2	90.5	13	301	16	18.81	8–108	1	–	34.06	3.31
SK Warne	2	87.2	12	300	11	27.27	5–113	1	–	47.64	3.44
DJ Cullen	1	14	0	54	1	54.00	1–25	–	–	84.00	3.86
SR Clark	1	29	6	77	1	77.00	1–8	–	–	174.00	2.66
B Lee	2	47	10	186	2	93.00	1–35	–	–	141.00	3.96
MJ Clarke	2	4	1	7	0	–	–	–	–	–	1.75

BANGLADESH BATTING AND FIELDING

Name	Tests	Inn	NO	Runs	HS	Ave	SR	100	50	Ct	St
Shahriar Nafees	2	4	0	250	138	62.50	60.98	1	1	1	–
Rajin Saleh	2	4	0	176	71	44.00	38.10	–	2	–	–
Habibul Bashar	2	4	0	141	76	35.25	65.28	–	1	–	–
Mohammad Rafique	2	4	0	104	65	26.00	94.55	–	1	–	–
Khaled Mashud	2	4	1	62	34*	20.67	29.81	–	–	3	–
Aftab Ahmed	2	4	0	82	29	20.50	42.27	–	–	–	–
Mohammad Ashraful	2	4	0	68	29	17.00	68.00	–	–	–	–
Javed Omar	2	4	0	66	27	16.50	64.71	–	–	–	–
Abdur Razzak	1	2	0	15	15	7.50	57.69	–	–	–	–
Shahadat Hossain	2	4	3	7	3*	7.00	15.56	–	–	2	–
Mashrafe Mortaza	2	4	0	11	6	2.75	29.73	–	–	–	–
Enamul Haque	1	2	0	0	0	0.00	0.00	–	–	–	–

BANGLADESH BOWLING

Name	Tests	O	M	R	W	Ave	Best	5w	10w	SR	Econ
Mohammad Rafique	2	118.5	26	305	11	27.73	5–62	1	–	64.82	2.57
Aftab Ahmed	2	7	1	28	1	28.00	1–28	–	–	42.00	4.00
Enamul Haque jnr	1	52	9	163	3	54.33	2–83	–	–	104.00	3.13
Mashrafe Mortaza	2	70	13	221	3	73.67	2–56	–	–	140.00	3.16
Shahadat Hossain	2	67	10	258	1	258.00	1–48	–	–	402.00	3.85
Mohammad Ashraful	2	1	0	11	0	–	–	–	–	–	11.00
Rajin Saleh	2	9	0	37	0	–	–	–	–	–	4.11
Abdur Razzak	1	30	5	99	0	–	–	–	–	–	3.30

BANGLADESH V AUSTRALIA TEST SERIES

These were the first Tests played by Australia in Bangladesh. The two countries had played two Tests — one each in Darwin and Cairns — in Australia in 2003. Adam Gilchrist, Jason Gillespie, Matthew Hayden, Brett Lee, Stuart MacGill and Ricky Ponting are the Australians to have played in all four of these matches.

Debuts
Dan Cullen (second Test) was the 397th Australian to play Test cricket.
Abdur Razzak (second Test) was the 45th Bangladeshi to play Test cricket.

Hundreds
Shahriar Nafees (138 for Bangladesh in the first Test) scored his first Test century, in his fifth match.
Adam Gilchrist (144 for Australia in the first Test) scored his 16th Test century, in his 84th match.
Ricky Ponting (118* for Australia in the first Test) scored his 31st Test century, in his 104th match.
Jason Gillespie (201* for Australia in the second Test) scored his first Test century, in his 71st match.
Mike Hussey (182 for Australia in the second Test) scored his fourth Test century, in his 11th match.

Five wickets in an innings
Stuart MacGill (8–108 for Australia in the first Test) took five or more wickets in a Test innings for the 12th time, in his 39th match.
Mohammad Rafique (5–62 for Bangladesh in the first Test) took five or more wickets in a Test innings for the seventh time, in his 25th match.
Shane Warne (5–113 for Australia in the second Test) took five or more wickets in a Test innings for the 36th time, in his 140th match.

BANGLADESH V AUSTRALIA, FIRST ODI

Chittagong Divisional Stadium • April 23, 2006 (50-over match)

Result: Australia won by four wickets • Toss: Bangladesh
Umpires: IL Howell (SA) and Mahbubur Rahman (Ban) • TV Umpire: Nadir Shah (Ban)
Match Referee: JJ Crowe (NZ) • Player of the Match: AC Gilchrist

Bangladesh innings		R	M	B	4	6
Shahriar Nafees	c Gilchrist b Lee	16	34	19	2	0
Rajin Saleh	c Lee b Bracken	7	21	13	1	0
Aftab Ahmed	c Clarke b Lee	30	73	45	4	1
Mohammad Ashraful	c Cullen b Bracken	5	29	23	0	0
*Habibul Bashar	st Gilchrist b Hogg	52	117	93	3	1
Tushar Imran	c Gilchrist b Hogg	20	43	40	1	0
+Khaled Mashud	b Johnson	27	52	35	2	0
Mohammad Rafique	c Hogg b Symonds	8	20	11	0	0
Mashrafe Mortaza	c Gilchrist b Hogg	1	2	3	0	0
Abdur Razzak	not out	2	12	5	0	0
Syed Rasel	c Gilchrist b Symonds	0	3	4	0	0
Extras	(lb 5, w 13, nb 9)	27				
Total	(all out, 47 ov)	195				

Fall: 1–26 (Rajin Saleh, 3.5 ov), 2–33 (Shahriar Nafees, 6.2 ov), 3–52 (Mohammad Ashraful, 11.5 ov), 4–79 (Aftab Ahmed, 18.3 ov), 5–117 (Tushar Imran, 30.6 ov), 6–171 (Habibul Bashar, 42.2 ov), 7–182 (Khaled Mashud, 43.6 ov), 8–185 (Mashrafe Mortaza, 44.5 ov), 9–194 (Mohammad Rafique, 46.1 ov), 10–195 (Syed Rasel, 46.6 ov).

Bowling: Lee 8–0–34–2; Bracken 8–2–30–2; Johnson 7–0–34–1; Hussey 3–0–13–0; Cullen 10–2–36–0; Hogg 10–1–37–3; Symonds 1–0–6–2

Australia innings		R	M	B	4	6
+AC Gilchrist	lbw Abdur Razzak	76	50	46	9	5
SM Katich	c Habibul b Mashrafe Mortaza	18	57	28	2	0
MJ Clarke	run out	16	77	49	1	0
A Symonds	lbw Abdur Razzak	0	10	6	0	0
*RT Ponting	lbw Abdur Razzak	14	26	31	2	0
MEK Hussey	not out	36	82	61	0	1
GB Hogg	c Syed Rasel b Tushar Imran	7	20	17	0	0
B Lee	not out	12	33	30	1	0
Extras	(b 1, lb 7, w 6, nb 3)	17				
Total	(6 wkts, 44 ov)	196				

DNB: NW Bracken, DJ Cullen, MG Johnson.

Fall: 1–96 (Gilchrist, 10.5 ov), 2–101 (Katich, 11.5 ov), 3–109 (Symonds, 14.4 ov), 4–133 (Ponting, 22.4 ov), 5–155 (Clarke, 30.3 ov), 6–174 (Hogg, 36.4 ov).

Bowling: Syed Rasel 4–0–35–0; Mashrafe Mortaza 7–0–58–1; Abdur Razzak 10–1–36–3; Mohammad Rafique 10–1–14–0; Tushar Imran 8–0–24–1; Rajin Saleh 5–0–21–0

BANGLADESH V AUSTRALIA, SECOND ODI

Narayanganj Osmani Stadium, Fatullah • April 26, 2006 (50-over match)

Result: Australia won by 67 runs • Toss: Australia

Umpires: IL Howell (SA) and AFM Akhtaruddin (Ban) • TV Umpire: Nadir Shah (Ban)

Match Referee: JJ Crowe (NZ) • Player of the Match: A Symonds

Australia innings		R	M	B	4	6
+AC Gilchrist	lbw Mashrafe Mortaza	32	42	30	4	1
SM Katich	c Shahriar b Mashrafe Mortaza	26	62	36	3	0
*RT Ponting	b Mashrafe Mortaza	5	9	6	1	0
MJ Clarke	c Alok Kapali b Mohammad Rafique	54	121	90	2	0
A Symonds	not out	103	143	125	6	2
MEK Hussey	b Abdur Razzak	18	29	15	3	0
Extras	(b 1, lb 2, w 7, nb 2)	12				
Total	(5 wkts, 50 ov)	250				

DNB: GB Hogg, B Lee, NW Bracken, DJ Cullen, MG Johnson.

Fall: 1–55 (Gilchrist, 8.6 ov), 2–64 (Ponting, 10.5 ov), 3–65 (Katich, 12.3 ov), 4–205 (Clarke, 44.6 ov), 5–250 (Hussey, 49.6 ov).

Bowling: Mashrafe Mortaza 9.1–0–54–3; Shahadat Hossain 10–0–50–0; Abdur Razzak 7.5–0–34–1; Mohammad Rafique 10–0–39–1; Alok Kapali 4–0–23–0; Tushar Imran 4–0–16–0; Rajin Saleh 5–0–31–0

Bangladesh innings		R	M	B	4	6
Shahriar Nafees	lbw Lee	0	2	2	0	0
Rajin Saleh	c Gilchrist b Bracken	0	9	1	0	0
Javed Omar	c Lee b Hussey	34	86	56	5	0
Tushar Imran	b Bracken	2	9	11	0	0
*Habibul Bashar	c Hussey b Clarke	70	153	114	6	0
+Khaled Mashud	b Clarke	36	75	62	1	0
Alok Kapali	c Hussey b Hogg	10	27	16	0	0
Mohammad Rafique	c & b Lee	0	3	1	0	0
Mashrafe Mortaza	c Clarke b Hogg	15	23	19	1	0
Abdur Razzak	b Hogg	3	10	6	0	0
Shahadat Hossain	not out	1	3	2	0	0
Extras	(b 2, lb 3, w 5, nb 2)	12				
Total	(all out, 48 ov)	183				

Fall: 1–0 (Shahriar Nafees, 0.2 ov), 2–4 (Rajin Saleh, 1.1 ov), 3–8 (Tushar Imran, 3.3 ov), 4–70 (Javed Omar, 19.6 ov), 5–146 (Khaled Mashud, 39.5 ov), 6–157 (Habibul Bashar, 41.3 ov), 7–159 (Mohammad Rafique, 42.1 ov), 8–168 (Alok Kapali, 45.3 ov), 9–182 (Mashrafe Mortaza, 47.2 ov), 10–183 (Abdur Razzak, 47.6 ov).

Bowling: Lee 8–2–29–2; Bracken 6–1–16–2; Johnson 6–0–24–0; Hussey 5–0–22–1; Cullen 10–0–37–0; Hogg 9–0–34–3; Clarke 4–0–16–2

BANGLADESH V AUSTRALIA, THIRD ODI

Narayanganj Osmani Stadium, Fatullah • April 28, 2006 (50-over match)

Result: Australia won by nine wickets • Toss: Bangladesh
Umpires: IL Howell (SA) and Nadir Shah (Ban) • TV Umpire: AFM Akhtaruddin (Ban)
Match Referee: JJ Crowe (NZ) • Player of the Match: MJ Cosgrove • Player of the Series: GB Hogg

Bangladesh innings		R	M	B	4	6
Shahriar Nafees	lbw Johnson	0	2	3	0	0
Rajin Saleh	b Clarke	37	122	102	5	0
Aftab Ahmed	c Gilchrist b Dorey	1	14	8	0	0
Mohammad Ashraful	c Cullen b Hopes	13	46	32	1	0
*Habibul Bashar	st Gilchrist b Hogg	33	85	50	3	0
Alok Kapali	c Katich b Hogg	5	11	9	0	0
+Khaled Mashud	st Gilchrist b Cullen	11	44	30	0	0
Mohammad Rafique	b Johnson	0	18	11	0	0
Mashrafe Mortaza	c Symonds b Cullen	2	15	8	0	0
Abdur Razzak	c Symonds b Hogg	1	3	3	0	0
Shahadat Hossain	not out	2	4	4	0	0
Extras	(w 14, nb 5)	19				
Total	(all out, 42.3 ov)	124				

Fall: 1–0 (Shahriar Nafees, 0.3 ov), 2–8 (Aftab Ahmed, 3.1 ov), 3–41 (Mohammad Ashraful, 13.4 ov), 4–80 (Rajin Saleh, 28.4 ov), 5–92 (Alok Kapali, 31.1 ov), 6–107 (Habibul Bashar, 35.2 ov), 7–117 (Mohammad Rafique, 38.6 ov), 8–118 (Khaled Mashud, 40.2 ov), 9–122 (Abdur Razzak, 41.2 ov), 10–124 (Mashrafe Mortaza, 42.3 ov).

Bowling: Johnson 8–1–24–2; Dorey 4–1–12–1; Hopes 5–3–8–1; Hussey 5–1–13–0; Cullen 7.3–1–25–2; Cosgrove 4–0–12–0; Clarke 3–0–13–1; Hogg 6–0–17–3.

Australia innings		R	M	B	4	6
MJ Cosgrove	b Abdur Razzak	74	94	69	7	2
SM Katich	not out	42	96	69	5	0
GB Hogg	not out	4	1	1	1	0
Extras	(w 4, nb 3)	7				
Total	(1 wkt, 22.4 ov, 96 mins)	127				

DNB: MJ Clarke, A Symonds, MEK Hussey, JR Hopes, *+AC Gilchrist,BR Dorey, DJ Cullen, MG Johnson.

Fall: 1–123 (Cosgrove, 22.3 ov).

Bowling: Mashrafe Mortaza 4–1–17–0; Shahadat Hossain 5–0–32–0; Abdur Razzak 6.4–1–35–1; Mohammad Rafique 6–1–28–0; Rajin Saleh 1–0–15–0

AUSTRALIA IN BANGLADESH ONE-DAY INTERNATIONAL AVERAGES

AUSTRALIA BATTING AND FIELDING

Name	ODIs	Inn	NO	Runs	HS	Ave	SR	100	50	Ct	St
A Symonds	3	2	1	103	103*	103.00	78.63	1	–	2	–
MJ Cosgrove	1	1	0	74	74	74.00	107.25	–	1	–	–
AC Gilchrist	3	2	0	108	76	54.00	142.11	–	1	6	3
MEK Hussey	3	2	1	54	36*	54.00	71.05	–	–	2	–
SM Katich	3	3	1	86	42*	43.00	64.67	–	–	1	–
MJ Clarke	3	2	0	70	54	35.00	50.36	–	1	2	–
GB Hogg	3	2	1	11	7	11.00	61.11	–	–	1	–
RT Ponting	2	2	0	19	14	9.50	51.35	–	–	–	–
B Lee	2	1	1	12	12*	–	40.00	–	–	3	–
DJ Cullen	3	0	–	–	–	–	–	–	–	2	–
MG Johnson	3	0	–	–	–	–	–	–	–	–	–
NW Bracken	2	0	–	–	–	–	–	–	–	–	–
BR Dorey	1	0	–	–	–	–	–	–	–	–	–
JR Hopes	1	0	–	–	–	–	–	–	–	–	–

AUSTRALIA BOWLING

Name	ODIs	O	M	R	W	Ave	Best	4w	SR	Econ
A Symonds	3	1	0	6	2	3.00	2–6	–	3.00	6.00
JR Hopes	1	5	3	8	1	8.00	1–8	–	30.00	1.60
MJ Clarke	3	7	0	29	3	9.67	2–16	–	14.00	4.14
GB Hogg	3	25	1	88	9	9.77	3–17	–	16.67	3.52
NW Bracken	2	14	3	46	4	11.50	2–16	–	21.00	3.29
BR Dorey	1	4	1	12	1	12.00	1–12	–	24.00	3.00
B Lee	2	16	2	63	4	15.75	2–29	–	24.00	3.94
MG Johnson	3	21	1	82	3	27.33	2–24	–	42.00	3.90
MEK Hussey	3	13	2	48	1	48.00	1–22	–	78.00	3.69
DJ Cullen	3	27.3	3	98	2	49.00	2–25	–	82.50	3.56
MJ Cosgrove	1	4	0	12	0	–	–	–	–	3.00

BANGLADESH BATTING AND FIELDING

Name	ODIs	Inn	NO	Runs	HS	Ave	SR	100	50	Ct	St
Habibul Bashar	3	3	0	155	70	51.67	60.31	–	2	1	–
Javed Omar	1	1	0	34	34	34.00	60.71	–	–	–	–
Khaled Mashud	3	3	0	74	36	24.67	58.27	–	–	–	–
Aftab Ahmed	2	2	0	31	30	15.50	58.49	–	–	–	–
Rajin Saleh	3	3	0	44	37	14.67	37.93	–	–	–	–
Tushar Imran	2	2	0	22	20	11.00	43.14	–	–	–	–
Mohammad Ashraful	2	2	0	18	13	9.00	32.73	–	–	–	–
Alok Kapali	2	2	0	15	10	7.50	60.00	–	–	1	–
Mashrafe Mortaza	3	3	0	18	15	6.00	60.00	–	–	–	–
Shahriar Nafees	3	3	0	16	16	5.33	66.67	–	–	1	–
Abdur Razzak	3	3	1	6	3	3.00	42.86	–	–	–	–
Mohammad Rafique	3	3	0	8	8	2.67	34.78	–	–	–	–
Syed Rasel	1	1	0	0	0	0.00	0.00	–	–	1	–
Shahadat Hossain	2	2	2	3	2*	–	50.00	–	–	–	–

BANGLADESH BOWLING

Name	ODIs	O	M	R	W	Ave	Best	4w	SR	Econ
Abdur Razzak	3	24.3	2	105	5	21.00	3–36	–	29.40	4.29
Mashrafe Mortaza	3	20.1	1	129	4	32.25	3–54	–	30.25	6.40
Tushar Imran	2	12	0	40	1	40.00	1–24	–	72.00	3.33
Mohammad Rafique	3	26	2	81	1	81.00	1–39	–	156.00	3.12
Shahadat Hossain	2	15	0	82	0	–	–	–	–	5.47
Rajin Saleh	3	11	0	67	0	–	–	–	–	6.09
Alok Kapali	2	4	0	23	0	–	–	–	–	5.75
Syed Rasel	1	4	0	35	0	–	–	–	–	8.75

BANGLADESH V AUSTRALIA ONE-DAY INTERNATIONALS

Debuts
Dan Cullen (game one) was the 158th Australian to play ODI cricket.
Mark Cosgrove (game three) was the 159th Australian to play ODI cricket.

Hundreds
Andrew Symonds (103* for Australia in game two) scored his fifth ODI century, in his 145th match.

AUSTRALIA'S ODI RECORD FOR 2005–06

Opponent	Played	Won	Lost	NR	Tied
ICC World XI	3	3	–	–	–
New Zealand	3	2	1	–	–
South Africa	9	5	4	–	–
Sri Lanka	7	5	2	–	–
Bangladesh	3	3	–	–	–
Total	25	18	7	–	–

AUSTRALIA'S TEST RECORD FOR 2005–06

Opponent	Played	Won	Lost	Drawn	Tied
ICC World XI	1	1	–	–	–
West Indies	3	3	–	–	–
South Africa	6	5	–	1	–
Bangladesh	2	2	–	–	–
Total	12	11	–	1	–

AUSTRALIAN TEAM AVERAGES 2005–06
TEST CRICKET

BATTING AND FIELDING

Name	Tests	Inn	NO	Runs	HS	Ave	SR	100	50	Ct	St
JN Gillespie	2	3	2	231	201*	231.00	43.50	1	–	2	–
RT Ponting	12	23	4	1483	149	78.05	59.51	8	6	13	–
MEK Hussey	11	19	4	1139	182	75.93	53.57	4	4	3	–
ML Hayden	12	23	1	1287	137	58.50	55.67	5	6	24	–
BJ Hodge	5	9	2	409	203*	58.43	51.77	1	1	9	–
DR Martyn	4	8	2	236	101	39.33	46.83	1	1	3	–
JL Langer	7	13	0	392	99	32.67	50.65	–	1	8	–
PA Jaques	2	3	0	96	66	32.00	62.34	–	1	1	–
NW Bracken	2	3	1	61	37	30.50	70.93	–	–	1	–
AC Gilchrist	12	17	0	491	144	28.88	72.10	1	2	42	7
SCG MacGill	7	7	4	75	29	25.00	60.48	–	–	–	–
B Lee	12	15	2	282	64	21.69	52.03	–	1	4	–
A Symonds	8	11	0	233	72	21.18	61.32	–	2	6	–
MJ Clarke	5	8	2	119	39	19.83	49.79	–	–	2	–
SR Watson	2	3	0	50	24	16.67	33.33	–	–	–	–
SK Warne	12	16	1	191	47	12.73	62.21	–	–	8	–
MS Kasprowicz	3	4	2	22	7*	11.00	34.92	–	–	1	–
SR Clark	4	5	2	31	13*	10.33	46.27	–	–	2	–
GD McGrath	7	8	3	39	14	7.80	29.55	–	–	2	–
SM Katich	2	3	0	2	2	0.67	5.88	–	–	1	–
DJ Cullen	1	0	–	–	–	–	–	–	–	–	–

BOWLING

Name	O	M	R	W	Ave	Best	5w	10w	SR	Econ
JN Gillespie	43	13	90	8	11.25	3–11	–	–	32.25	2.09
SR Clark	147	38	394	21	18.76	5–55	1	–	42.00	2.68
SCG MacGill	247	45	776	38	20.42	8–108	2	–	39.00	3.14
NW Bracken	57	15	154	6	25.67	4–48	–	–	57.00	2.70
SK Warne	550.2	110	1622	62	26.16	6–80	4	–	53.26	2.95
B Lee	428.3	97	1412	52	27.15	5–30	3	–	49.44	3.30
GD McGrath	280	95	652	24	27.17	4–31	–	–	70.00	2.33
A Symonds	125	29	324	8	40.50	3–50	–	–	93.75	2.59
MS Kasprowicz	77.2	6	292	7	41.71	2–44	–	–	66.29	3.78
DJ Cullen	14	0	54	1	54.00	1–25	–	–	84.00	3.86
SR Watson	12	0	63	1	63.00	1–25	–	–	72.00	5.25
MJ Clarke	6	2	8	0	–	–	–	–	–	1.33
MEK Hussey	4	0	18	0	–	–	–	–	–	4.50
RT Ponting	2	1	7	0	–	–	–	–	–	3.50
BJ Hodge	2	0	8	0	–	–	–	–	–	4.00

ONE-DAY INTERNATIONAL CRICKET

BATTING AND FIELDING

Name	ODIs	Inn	NO	Runs	HS	Ave	SR	100	50	Ct	St
MJ Cosgrove	1	1	0	74	74	74.00	107.25	–	1	–	–
MEK Hussey	25	21	9	769	88*	64.08	98.46	–	6	14	–
A Symonds	22	20	3	864	156	50.82	101.41	3	3	17	–
RT Ponting	20	20	1	920	164	48.42	93.21	2	7	11	–
PA Jaques	2	2	0	94	94	47.00	81.03	–	1	–	–
MJ Clarke	25	22	6	707	82*	44.19	82.31	–	7	12	–
SR Watson	6	5	2	127	66*	42.33	78.88	–	1	2	–
SM Katich	23	23	2	888	107*	42.29	68.10	1	7	4	–
AC Gilchrist	23	22	0	871	122	39.59	110.53	3	3	27	3
SR Clark	15	3	2	33	16*	33.00	100.00	–	–	2	–
JR Hopes	8	3	0	84	43	28.00	87.50	–	–	3	–
DR Martyn	19	17	1	426	79	26.63	81.45	–	4	8	–
B Lee	23	13	6	183	57	26.14	83.94	–	1	7	–
BJ Haddin	2	2	0	42	41	21.00	87.50	–	–	4	1
NW Bracken	21	9	5	77	21*	19.25	66.67	–	–	2	–
BJ Hodge	5	5	0	79	59	15.80	58.09	–	1	1	–
GB Hogg	17	7	2	57	22*	11.40	69.51	–	–	7	–
GD McGrath	7	2	1	2	2*	2.00	28.57	–	–	3	–
BR Dorey	4	1	0	2	2	2.00	25.00	–	–	–	–
CL White	5	1	0	0	0	0.00	0.00	–	–	4	–
ML Lewis	7	1	1	4	4*	–	100.00	–	–	1	–
MG Johnson	5	1	1	0	0*	–	–	–	–	–	–
DJ Cullen	3	0	–	–	–	–	–	–	–	2	–

BOWLING

Name	O	M	R	W	Ave	Best	4w	SR	Econ
SR Watson	49.5	1	251	12	20.92	4–39	1	24.92	5.04
NW Bracken	175.4	14	825	37	22.30	5–67	2	28.49	4.70
GB Hogg	131	3	582	25	23.28	3–17	–	31.44	4.44
B Lee	202.2	19	981	37	26.51	5–22	4	32.81	4.85
GD McGrath	58	7	200	7	28.57	2–13	–	49.71	3.45
SR Clark	134	7	688	23	29.91	4–55	1	34.96	5.13
A Symonds	129.4	3	735	21	35.00	3–48	–	37.05	5.67
MJ Clarke	44.3	0	256	7	36.57	2–16	–	38.14	5.75
DJ Cullen	27.3	3	98	2	49.00	2–25	–	82.50	3.56
ML Lewis	56.5	1	391	7	55.86	3–56	–	48.71	6.88
MG Johnson	33	1	174	3	58.00	2–24	–	66.00	5.27
CL White	8	0	60	1	60.00	1–34	–	48.00	7.50
MEK Hussey	15	2	63	1	63.00	1–22	–	90.00	4.20
BR Dorey	27	2	146	2	73.00	1–12	–	81.00	5.41
JR Hopes	46	6	231	3	77.00	1–8	–	92.00	5.02
MJ Cosgrove	4	0	12	0	–	–	–	–	3.00
BJ Hodge	3	0	16	0	–	–	–	–	5.33

Index

A

Abdur Razzak 271
ABN AMRO ONE 150–151, 248
ABN AMRO TWO 151
Aftab Ahmed 268–269
Alcott, Errol 13, 54, 99, 123, 211;
    value to Australian team
    185–187
Alderman, Terry 219, 240
Aleem Dar 26, 32, 139
Allan Border Medal 154–157
Armstrong, Geoff 7, 264
Arnold, Russel 157, 165
Arthur, Mickey 111, 210, 221, 239
Asad Rauf 111
The Ashes (general) 15, 68, 86,
    280
The Ashes (2005)
  age of Australian team 19–20
  Australian team line-up 57
  Cricket Australia review
    committee 12–13, 37, 82–83
  criticism of Australian team 7,
    10–12, 17, 19, 20, 24, 25
  England coaching set-up 13–14,
    82
  England team line-up 19
  fifth Test 39, 56
  first Test 38, 91, 280–281
  fourth Test 46–47
  interest in Australia 25
  mistakes by Australia 12, 32, 47,
    155, 174, 242, 245, 258, 278
  rumours of fight between RP and
    Warne 102
  second Test 4, 102, 243
  Warne's performance 20, 156
The Ashes (2006–07) 17, 76,
    221–222, 234–235, 243, 244,
    248, 268, 271, 278–283
Atapattu, Marvan 35, 136–137,
    153, 154, 157, 163, 165
Atherton, Mike 110

Australia in Bangladesh 2005–06
  Australian one-day squad named
    254–255
  Australian team's exhaustion
    252–253, 259–260
  Australian Test squad named
    253
  controversy over RP's pre–tour
    comments 249–251
  first Test 254, 255–259, 264
  one-day series 271–274
  second Test 262–271
Australia in South Africa 2005–06
  Australian Test players arrive 204
  Australian Test squad named
    193–194
  fifth ODI 197–204, 208
  first ODI 183, 188–189
  first Test 210–220
  flight to South Africa 168–169
  fourth ODI 195–197
  one-day team selection 170
  pitches 181, 193, 210, 220–221,
    223, 230
  second ODI 183, 188–189
  second Test 223–235
  South African crowds 168, 174,
    175, 180–181, 216
  South African negativity 224
  teams compared 244–245
  third ODI 190–192
  third Test 2–7, 237–244
  twenty20 international 175–176,
    179–181, 184
  use of floodlights 225, 226
Australian Cricket Academy 13, 18,
    116
Australian Cricketers' Association
    261
Australian team training 14, 17,
    24–25, 33, 47, 54, 68, 76–77,
    89–90, 106, 169, 171, 174, 189,
    245, 255, 258, 279, 281, 282

B

Bandara, Malinga 140, 154
Benaud, Richie 263
Bernard, Steve 5, 80, 98, 270
Bevan, Michael 138, 190, 263
Bichel, Andy 170, 190
Blackman, John 111–112
Boje, Nicky 106, 120, 211, 223,
    225, 232, 237, 241
Bond, Shane 77
Boon, David 45, 56, 117–118,
    263
Border, Allan 12–13, 53, 57, 69,
    118, 158
Botha, Johan 120, 122, 124–125,
    151
Boucher, Mark 5, 86, 90, 108, 122,
    137, 140, 151, 180, 183, 196,
    197, 218–219, 237, 242, 245,
    264–265; interview in *Wisden
    Cricketer* 172–173, 219; fifth
    ODI at Johannesburg 197,
    201–202; second Test at Durban
    223, 232–233
Bracken, Nathan 8, 19, 20, 26, 27,
    29, 50, 53–57, 60, 68, 78, 89,
    128, 130, 141, 157, 165, 170,
    172, 175, 193, 195–196, 197,
    202, 261, 268, 273
Bradman, Sir Donald 71, 93, 107,
    223, 249
Broad, Chris 98, 181–182, 230
Brown, Bill 55
Brown, Michael 13, 17
Buchanan, John 13, 16, 19, 37, 40,
    52, 95, 169, 173, 200–201, 205,
    210, 270, 282

C

Cairns, Chris 77, 79
Chanderpaul, Shivnarine 48, 55
Channel Nine 27, 107–108, 117
Channel Ten 113

Chappell, Greg 56
Chappell, Ian 17–18, 33, 263
Chappell–Hadlee Trophy series
    2004–05 77
Chappell–Hadlee Trophy series
    2005–06
  Australian squad picked 68
  crowd trouble 80
  first ODI 78–79
  second ODI 79–81
  third ODI 81–82
  timing 76–77
Clark, Stuart 4–5, 8, 26, 30, 50, 68,
    77, 78, 81, 89, 135, 165, 170,
    172, 175, 183, 193, 195, 221,
    237, 240, 241, 254, 267, 268,
    281; Test debut 211–220, 222;
    second Test at Durban 224–226,
    231–233, 235
Clarke, Michael 8, 16, 19, 20, 26,
    30, 37, 41, 50, 55, 58, 62, 68,
    74, 79–80, 134, 136, 140, 157,
    161, 170, 183, 188, 191–192,
    193, 232, 254, 257, 263, 271;
    dropped from Test team
    66–67, 81, 194; cuts head
    272–273
Collymore, Corey 53, 55, 58
Commonwealth Bank Centre of
    Excellence 13, 44
Cooley, Troy 14, 82–83, 134
Cosgrove, Mark 8, 271, 272,
    273–274
Cowdrey, Colin 122
Coyle, Tim 45
Cricket Australia 5, 12–14, 17, 44,
    52, 61, 68, 82, 99, 107, 121,
    125, 139, 144, 148, 156, 169,
    186, 249, 252, 260–261
Crowe, Jeff 268–270
Cullen, Dan 8, 154, 254–255, 261,
    267, 272, 273–274
Cullinan, Daryll 95

D

Daily Star (Dhaka) 249
Davidson, Alan 263
Dawson, David 44
dead rubber syndrome 237–238
Denton, Gerard 51
de Villiers, AB 90, 91, 102, 110, 183, 191, 192, 217, 223, 226, 232
Dilshan, Tillekeratne 136, 140, 161
Dippenaar, Boeta 137, 139, 140, 195
Di Venuto, Michael 44
Doctrove, Billy 92
Dorey, Brett 8, 135, 141, 170, 182, 272
Dravid, Rahul 25, 26, 28, 29, 35, 39, 228
Dwyer, Greg (RP's brother-in-law) 61, 121
Dwyer, Renee (RP's sister) 61, 121

E

Edwards, Fidel 64, 65

F

Fleming, Damien 263
Fleming, Stephen 77, 129, 244
Fletcher, Duncan 14, 46–47
Flintoff, Andrew 19, 20, 32, 37, 39, 40, 89, 174, 192–193, 222, 282–283; ICC Super Series ODIs 25–30; ICC Cricketer of the year 34–35

G

Ganguly, Sourav 86
Gavaskar, Sunil 35
Gayle, Chris 26, 27, 30, 48, 57, 63
Gibbs, Herschelle 21, 102, 108, 140, 151, 179, 181, 183, 213–214, 215, 217, 227, 232, 236, 237; fifth ODI at Johannesburg 197–203

Gilchrist, Adam 8, 19, 20, 21, 26, 27, 28, 30, 35, 37, 53, 57, 58, 67, 89, 90, 95, 97, 100, 110, 122, 137, 151, 152–153, 160, 161, 162, 170, 174, 181, 195, 197, 198, 200, 218, 222, 241, 242, 262, 264, 268, 271, 273; as one-day opener 30–31; batting method 39; batting at No. 7 50–51; break from playing 68, 139–140, 143–147, 166; third VB Series final 157, 160, 164–165; as captain 187–188, 232–233; v Nel at Durban 229; first Test v Bangladesh 255–257; reaction to Gillespie double century 262–263
Gillespie, Jason 8, 18, 20, 100, 170, 172, 253, 254, 256, 257, 268; second Test v Bangladesh 262–267
Gilmour, Gary 265
God Has a Dream 236
Gower, David 35
Greenidge, Gordon 122
Gregory, Jack 265

H

Habibul Bashar 255–256, 262, 267, 271
Haddin, Brad 8, 30, 140
Hadlee, Sir Richard 35
Hair, Darrell 41, 74
Hall, Andrew 137, 140, 154, 179, 181, 195, 202, 211, 214, 219, 223
Harmison, Steve 32, 35, 38, 89, 91, 174, 222, 280
Harper, Daryl 74
Hassett, Lindsay 264
Hayden, Grace 103
Hayden, Kellie 103

Hayden, Matthew 3, 8, 11, 15, 18, 24, 37, 53, 56, 58, 63–65, 69, 91, 97, 102, 104, 109, 123–124, 204, 223, 225, 233, 234, 242, 255, 269, 280; batting method 38–39, 65, 198; catch of Lara 72–73, 165; first Test at Cape Town 212–216; partnership with RP at Durban 228–230; importance to Australian side 283

Healy, Ian 67, 188, 130, 263

Henry, Thierry, 144

Herald–Sun (Melbourne) 100

Hey Hey! it's Saturday 111–112

Hilditch, Andrew 194, 261

Hill, Clem 263

Hills, Dene 13–14, 16, 44, 226–227; on RP's batting method 214–215

Hinds, Wavell 71

Hodge, Brad 8, 18, 19, 20, 37, 50, 68, 74, 77, 81, 89, 96, 100, 105, 136, 147; Test debut 60, 62, 63, 65, 66, 67; double century v South Africa 90, 92, 93–95; dropped from Test squad 193–194; Pura Cup final 261

Hogg, Brad 8, 20, 26, 68, 79, 135, 140, 170, 179, 188, 271, 272, 273; value to Australian team 191–192

Hohns, Trevor 19, 99, 171; stands down as chairman of selectors 261–262

Hookes, David 178

Hopes, James 8, 19, 20, 44, 68, 128, 140, 141, 152, 170, 261, 272

Hopkins, Sir Anthony 249

Howard, Janette 121

Howard, John 121

Hughes, Kim 117, 158

Hughes, Merv 98, 210, 213, 263, 266

Hussey, Michael 6, 8, 20, 26, 28, 32, 50, 57, 74, 81, 88, 90, 93, 100, 122, 136, 137, 151, 170, 176, 183, 189, 191, 197, 200, 223, 224, 233, 244, 254, 272, 280, 281; hits Telstra Dome roof 27, 31; Test debut 52, 54–55; first Test century 63, 64, 66, 67; christened 'Mr Cricket' 64; century in Adelaide 69, 70–71; one-day batting method 82, 138; century in Boxing Day Test 102, 105–106; Border Medal 154–156; birth of son 179–180; third Test at Johannesburg 237, 240, 242–243; second Test v Bangladesh 262–266

Hussey, William Oliver 179

I

ICC (International Cricket Council) 20, 22, 42, 78, 86, 98, 156, 162, 181–182, 249, 270

ICC Cricket Awards 34–35

ICC Super Series 2005–06
Australian squad selected 18–19
criticism of World XI players 33
first ODI 26, 28–29, 40
future of concept 33, 42
second ODI 28, 30–31
Test and ODI status 21
Test match 33–43
third ODI 31–33
use of technology (umpiring) 21–22, 27, 32–33, 41–42

ING Cup 44, 51, 79, 100

Inzamam-ul-Haq 35, 39, 122

J

James, Dr Trefor 51–52, 186

Jaques, Phil 8, 120, 140, 141, 154, 171, 189, 253, 254, 266; Test debut 99–101, 104, 108

Jardine, Douglas 98
Jauncey, Phil 24
Javed Miandad 122
Jayasuriya, Sanath 135, 140–141, 153, 165
Jayawardene, Mahela 134, 136–137, 140, 153, 157; dispute over catch 163–164
Jeter, Derek 144
Johnson, David 91
Johnson, Mitchell 8, 50, 81, 136, 170–171, 172, 184, 253, 255, 261, 268; v Bangladesh 272–274
Jones, Dean 105
Jones, Simon 89, 174, 222

K
Kallis, Jacques 26, 29, 32, 37, 39, 86, 88, 105, 108, 109, 121, 123, 131, 139, 148, 172, 200, 214, 221, 223, 224–225, 226, 232; ICC Cricketer of the Year 34–35; dismissal in Cape Town Test 217–218; South African captain 238–239
Kangaroos (North Melbourne) AFL Club 116; RP No. 1 ticket holder 142–143, 275
Kasprowicz, Michael 8, 18, 20, 44, 50, 170, 172, 193, 194, 204, 211, 214, 224, 232, 235, 253, 268; third Test at Johannesburg 4–6, 240, 243, 244
Katich, Simon 8, 19, 20, 26, 27, 32, 38, 46, 55, 58, 60, 78, 134, 141, 157, 161, 164, 170, 195, 197, 264, 271
Kelleway, Charles 265
Kemp, Justin 90, 94, 95, 96, 104, 137, 139, 152, 183, 189
Kirmani, Syed 265
Koertzen, Rudi 26–27, 41–42

Kountouris, Alex 211, 231, 241
Nuwan Kulasekara 153, 161
Kumble, Anil 35

L
Langer, Justin 8, 11, 20, 24, 38, 56, 64, 66, 69, 90, 93, 99–100, 119, 120, 173, 204, 213, 216, 228, 251, 265, 280; 100th Test 2–7, 238, 241–244, 253–254; injured (first Test v West Indies) 51–52, 54, 57; singing victory song 222, 243–244; value to Australian team 283
Langeveldt, Charl 92, 120, 122
Lara, Brian 26, 29, 32, 35, 39, 48, 52–53, 58, 63, 64; approaching Test run–scoring record 53; breaks record 69–70; caught Hayden 72–73, 165
Lawson, Geoff 170
Laxman VVS 228
Lee, Brett 8, 20, 25, 26, 27, 29, 30, 35, 39, 50, 53, 57, 89, 90, 92–93, 100, 122, 123, 136, 137, 138–39, 140, 151–152, 156, 175, 176, 189, 191, 193, 202, 214, 217, 223, 224, 225, 231, 232, 235, 254, 256, 263, 268, 273; third Test at Johannesburg 4–6, 240–243; bowling at Kallis 31–32, 108, 218; discusses bowling method with RP 58–60, 64, 77; Chappell–Hadlee trophy series 78–81; fined for dissent 124–125; RP rates as best one-day opening bowler 141; workload 211
Lehmann, Darren 11, 31, 263
Lewis, Mick 8, 68, 77, 79–81, 128, 130–131, 136, 170, 175, 179, 195, 202, 254

Lillee, Dennis 7, 10–12, 18, 73, 263, 274

Lindwall, Ray 265

Lorgat, Haroon 147

M

Macartney, Charlie 263

McCullum, Brendon 79–82

McDermott, Craig 100

MacGill, Stuart 8, 18, 20, 35, 37, 40, 49–50, 54, 58, 64, 71, 73, 91, 101, 105–106, 109, 112, 120, 122, 204, 211, 254, 266–267; bowling with Warne 36, 60–61, 104; record at SCG 36; first Test v Bangladesh 255–256

McGrath, Glenn 8, 20, 25, 26, 29–30, 35, 39, 50, 53, 56, 58, 59, 63, 64, 68, 69, 89, 95, 112, 118, 123, 139, 141, 147, 170, 187, 193, 209, 212, 213, 220, 235, 236, 239, 263, 267, 268, 278; leads Australian attack 55, 109–110, 222; as late-order batsman 71, 105–106, 122; making statements 86–87; fined for dissent 124–125; leaves team 151, 171–172; at Lord's in 2005 280–281

McGrath, Jane 151, 236

McIness, Richard 44, 169

McMillan, Craig 79

Madugalle, Ranjan 26

Maher, Jimmy 44

Mandela, Nelson 235, 249

Mann, Tony 263, 265

Marsh, Geoff 263

Marsh, Rod 18, 35, 83, 158, 217, 263

Marshall, Hamish 79

Marshall, James 79

Marylebone Cricket Club 176

Mashrafe Mortaza 257, 271

Martin Chris, 81

Martyn, Damien 8, 11, 20, 24, 26, 27, 30, 32, 50, 61, 62, 68, 93, 128, 130, 134, 136, 151, 161, 170, 216, 223, 225, 235, 263, 266; third Test at Johannesburg 4, 237, 242–244; dropped from Test side 18, 23, 194; back in Test squad 193

Maynard, Matthew 14

Melbourne Cricket Ground pitch 103–104, 120

Miller, Keith 263, 265

Mills, Kyle 80

Mohammad Rafique 255, 262–263

Moody, Tom 134, 137, 153–154

Mowbray Cricket Club 45–46, 61, 82–83, 178

Mubarak, Jehan 140, 153

Muller, Scott 100

Muralitharan, Muttiah 26, 29, 30, 35–36, 38, 40, 136, 149, 153, 157, 163

N

Nasim-ul-Ghani 265

Naved-ul-Hasan 35

Nicknames 8

Nel, Andre 102, 104, 112, 122, 148, 172–173, 183, 214, 216, 229, 230, 232–233, 240, 241, 276

Nielsen, Tim 14

Ntini, Makhaya 3, 4, 6, 26, 31, 32, 86, 90, 91, 105, 111–113, 120, 148, 172, 183, 189, 202, 213, 214, 225, 233, 236, 237, 240, 242

O

O'Connor, Creagh 107

O'Donnell, Simon 158

Oram, James 79

P

Packer, Kerry 107–108

Perera, Ruchira 136

Peterson, Robin 179

Pietersen, Kevin 20, 26, 30, 34, 35, 174, 198, 282

Pollock, Shaun 4–6, 26, 29, 35, 88, 102, 108, 131, 137, 140, 147, 183, 192, 195, 220, 223, 224, 237, 240

Ponting, Graeme (RP's father) 45, 65, 121

Ponting, Lorraine (RP's mother) 61, 65, 121

Ponting, Rianna (RP's wife) 103, 120, 145–146, 275

Ponting, Ricky

  advice to Brett Lee 58–60

  advice to Langer about playing 100th Test 2

  Archbishop Tutu 236–237

  arrives home at end of season 274–276

  attitude to wives and partners on tour 17

  Australian team accused of choking 196–197

  Australian team's scheduling 259–261

  Bangladesh's Test status 249–251

  batting against Warne 36–37

  batting method 15–16, 56, 214–215, 227–228

  break from VB Series 139–140, 143–148, 149, 166

  breaking records 56

  captain of ICC Test team of the year 35

  captaincy style 10, 11, 18, 24–25, 32, 94–95, 242, 267–268, 278–279, 282

  career v South Africa 87–88

  Christmas Day 102–103

Ponting, Ricky *(continued)*

  clash with Graeme Smith 229–230

  condemns racial abuse 98–99, 125, 149

  confrontation with Langer (third Test in Johannesburg) 5–7

  cricket statesman 99

  disputes catch with Jayawardene 162–163

  early years 45–46, 116–117

  fined during 2005 Ashes series 46–47

  fined during second Test v Bangladesh 268–270

  first match against Hussey 54

  food poisoning in Durban 231–234

  golf bug 168, 275–276

  hit on helmet while batting 91–92

  100th Test 2, 116–124

  impressions of Bangladesh 51–253

  informs Clarke he is dropped 66–67

  injures finger 240–241

  injures stomach muscle 183–187

  interview with London *Telegraph* 248–249, 250

  Kangaroos No. 1 ticket–holder 142–143

  Kookaburra bats 176–178

  matches at Port Elizabeth 190

  memories of crowd abuse 98–99

  playing international cricket in Tasmania 61–62, 65, 105, 118

  playing for Tasmania 44–45

  reacts to criticism of captaincy 10–12, 18, 22–23

  reacts to losing fifth ODI in South Africa 202–204

  sailing on ABN AMRO ONE 150–151, 248

Ponting, Ricky *(continued)*
  sledging Lara 70
  views on coaching 13–15
  wins Allan Border Medal
    154–157
  working with selectors 49–50, 51,
    99, 141–142, 194
Power plays 162–163, 182–183
Pratt, Gary 46
Prince, Ashwell 111, 121, 123, 218,
  237, 240, 241
Pura Cup 54, 74, 135, 254; 2005–06
  final 261

R
Rajin Saleh 255, 262
Ramdin, Denesh 63, 72
Reiffel, Paul 263
Rhodes, John 98
Richards, Sir Vivian 56
Robbins, Glenn 111
Rolton, Karen 154
Rudolph, Jacques 90, 92, 94, 95–96,
  140, 212, 219

S
Sanderson, Mike 150–151
Sangakkara, Kumar 26, 27, 30,
  140–141, 153, 154, 157
Sarfraz Nawaz 212
Sarwan, Ramnaresh 48, 57, 69
Sehwag, Virender 26, 29, 30, 35, 38,
  39, 198
Shahadat Hossain 257
Shahid Afridi 26, 30, 32
Shahriar Nafees 255–256, 262, 267
Sheffield Shield 54, 83, 117
Shoaib Akhtar 26, 28, 35
Siddons, Jamie 13–14, 16, 44
Simpson, Bob 13
Simpson, Ian 178
Slater, Michael 130
Smith, Devon 53

Smith, Graeme 34, 35, 39, 68, 86,
  92, 97, 104, 106, 109, 112–113,
  120, 121, 124, 130, 138, 147,
  152, 153, 154, 157, 166, 179,
  182, 188, 209, 213, 216, 223,
  232, 236, 238–239; World XI
  captain 33–34; criticism of
  Australian team 88–89,
  101–102, 196; Sydney Test
  tactics 122–123; batting in
  Twenty20 game 120–121; fifth
  ODI at Johannesburg 197–201;
  confrontation with RP at
  Durban 229–230; lessons
  learned 244–245
South Africa in Australia 2005–06
  Australian squad for first Test 81
  Australian team for second Test 99
  Australia v South Africa recent
    history 87–88
  build-up to series 86–87, 89
  crowds condemned for racial
    abuse 98–99, 125–126
  first Test 90–97
  Lee and McGrath fined 124–125
  over–appealing allegations 111
  second Test 102–113
  South African tactics 98–98
  third Test 116–124
Speed, Malcolm 78
Stewart, Alec 122
Strauss, Andrew 222
Styris, Scott 81
Supersubs 181–182, 183
Sutherland, James 12, 260
Sydney Cricket Ground pitch 120
Symcox, Pat 86–87
Symonds, Andrew 8, 20, 26, 29, 30,
  35, 50, 57, 60, 64, 65, 69, 78,
  96, 101, 102, 128, 130, 134,
  136, 151, 170, 179, 183, 190,
  194, 195, 200, 212–214, 225,
  231, 233, 254, 263, 271, 272,

Symonds, Andrew *(continued)*
273; suspended in England
47–48, 62; positive influence in
Australian dressing-room
71–72, 74; Chappell–Hadlee
Trophy game two 79–80;
second Test at Melbourne
108–109; Border Medal
155–156; second VB Series final
160, 162–163; allrounder in
ODIs 192–193

T

Tait, Shaun 8, 19, 20, 26, 193, 253,
268
Taufel, Simon 26, 34, 74
Taylor, Mark 12, 17, 56, 99, 118,
146
Telegraph (London) 248, 250
Telemachus, Roger 195, 200
Tendulkar, Sachin 21, 69, 93, 198
Tharanga, Upul 153
The Coach's Story 46
Trescothick, Marcus 222, 280
Twenty20 Internationals
v England 2005 32, 128
v New Zealand 2004–05 129
v South Africa 2005–06 128–131,
159, 175–176, 179–181, 184
tactics 129–30, 175
Tufnell, Phil 155
Tutu, Archbishop Desmond
235–237, 244

U

Umpires Panel (ICC) 74, 78
United Cricket Board of South
Africa 149

V

Vaughan, Michael 19, 280
Vettori, Daniel 26, 27, 29, 35, 40,
41, 77, 80, 182

Vaas, Chaminda 35, 153, 157, 161
Vincent, Lou 79, 80
Vandort, Michael 134, 136–137
van der Wath 201–202
VB Series 2005–06
bonus points system 148
crowds condemned for racial
abuse 149
first final (Aust v SL) 157, 159,
160–161
future scheduling 158–160
game one (Aust v SL) 134–137
game two (Aust v SA) 137–139
game three (SA v SL) 140
game four (Aust v SA) 140–141
game five (Aust v SL) 140,
141–142, 143
game six (SA v SL) 140
game seven (Aust v SL) 145
game eight (Aust v SL) 145, 182
game nine (SA v SL) 148
game 10 (Aust v SA) 151–152
game 11 (Aust v SA) 151,
152–153
game 12 (SA v SL) 154, 157, 158
improvement in Sri Lankan team
153–154
second final (Aust v SL) 157, 160,
161–164
third final (Aust v SL) 157, 159,
160, 164–165, 191–192

W

WACA Ground pitch 89–91, 96
Walsh, Courtney 35
Walters, Doug 155
Ware, Tony 101, 104
Warne, Shane 8, 17, 20, 25, 35,
40, 50, 53, 55, 56, 57, 63, 69,
89, 91, 95–96, 103, 107, 118,
120, 123, 152, 181, 192, 204,
211, 217, 219, 221, 241, 244,
254, 256, 257, 263, 266–267,

Warne, Shane *(continued)*
278, 280; potential Australian
captain 10–11; bowling with
MacGill 36, 60–61, 104; record
at SCG 36; bowling to RP
36–37; dismisses Lara 72–73;
making statements 86–87;
v Graeme Smith 101–102,
109–110, 209; accused of
over–appealing 111; Border
Medal 154–155; possible return
to one-day side 209–210; second
Test at Durban 223, 230,
231–234; at Archbishop Tutu
charity dinner 237
Wasim Akram 249
Watson, Shane 8, 18, 19, 20, 26, 27,
29, 31, 37, 38, 50, 54, 57, 60,
61, 68, 170, 175, 191, 193,
194, 261
Waugh, Mark 93, 118, 139,
187, 200, 217, 226, 263,
265, 279
Waugh, Steve 17, 18, 49, 67, 88, 99,
100, 118, 146–147, 160, 161,
187, 259, 263, 264
West Indies Cricket Board 78

West Indies in Australia 2005–06
Australian team for first Test 49–50
Australian team for second Test
57–58, 60
Brett Lee's bowling 58–60
decline of West Indian cricket
48–49
first Test 53–57, 58–60, 63, 71, 95
second Test 60–65
third Test 69–73
umpiring 73–74, 78
v Victoria 60
West Indies' preparation 48
White, Cameron 8, 26, 68, 77, 136
Wide World of Sports Cricket
Yearbook 125, 158
Wikipedia 251
Wisden Cricketer 172
Woods, Tiger 249
World Cup 2006 (football) 64
World Cup 2007 (cricket) 19, 37,
182
World Series Cricket 107

Y
Young, Ian 178
Young, Shaun 178